CLAUDE MONTEFIORE

PARKES-WIENER SERIES ON JEWISH STUDIES

Series Editors: David Cesarani and Tony Kushner

ISSN 1368-5449

The field of Jewish Studies is one of the youngest, but fastest growing and most exciting areas of scholarship in the academic world today. Named after James Parkes and Alfred Wiener and recognising the co-operative relationship between the Parkes Centre at the University of Southampton and the Wiener Library in London, this series aims to publish new research in the field and student materials for use in the seminar room, to disseminate the latest work of established scholars and to re-isssue classic studies which are currently out of print.

The selection of publications reflects the international character and diversity of Jewish Studies; it ranges over Jewish history from Abraham to modern Zionism, and Jewish culture from Moses to post-modernism. The series also reflects the inter-disciplinary approach inherent in Jewish Studies and at the cutting edge of contemporary scholarship, and provides an outlet for innovative work on the interface between Judaism and ethnicity, popular culture, gender, class, space and memory.

Other Books in the Series

CLAUDE MONTEFIORE

His Life and Thought

Daniel R. Langton

VALLENTINE MITCHELL
LONDON • PORTLAND, OR

First published in 2002 in Great Britain by
VALLENTINE MITCHELL
Crown House, 47 Chase Side
Southgate, London N14 5BP

and in the United States of America by
VALLENTINE MITCHELL
c/o ISBS, 5824 N. E. Hassalo Street
Portland, Oregon 97213-3644

Website: www.vmbooks.com

British Library Cataloguing in Publication Data
Langton, Daniel R.
  Claude Montefiore: his life and thought. – (Parkes-Wiener
series on Jewish studies)
  1. Montefiore, Claude Goldsmid, 1858–1938. 2. Jewish scholars
  – Great Britain – Biography. 3. Reform Judaism – Great
Britain
  I. Title
  296.8'341'092

ISBN 0-85303-369-2 (cloth)
ISBN 0-85303-376-5 (paper)
ISSN 1368-5449

A catalog record of this book is available from the Library of Congress

Typeset in Palatino 11/13pt by Cambridge Photosetting Services, Cambridge.
Printed in Great Britain by MPG Books Ltd, Bodmin, Cornwall.

Contents

Acknowledgements

I am very grateful to the University of Southampton for the award of the Lawrence Arthur Burgess scholarship, which made the original PhD thesis possible. Special thanks to my supervisor Prof. Tony Kushner (University of Southampton), my adviser Dr Sarah Pearce (University of Southampton), my external examiner the late Dr David Englander (Open University) and to my unofficial adviser Rev. Canon John Davies (formerly of University of Southampton).

Thanks also to those who have met with me and offered advice. Regarding theology and/or biblical studies, these include: Dr Steven Need (formerly of La Sainte Union), Dr Tom Deidun (Heythrop College), Bishop Hugh Montefiore, Rabbi Louis Jacobs and Rev. Roger Tomes (University of Manchester). Regarding Jewish and/or Anglo-Jewish history, these include: Dr Michael Meyer (Hebrew Union College), Prof. Ellis Rivkin (Hebrew Union College), Rabbi Prof. Dan Cohn-Sherbok (University of Kent), Prof. David Cesarani (University of Southampton) and Bill Williams (University of Manchester).

Thanks also to the staff of the various archives and library collections I have visited over the last six years, including those of the Anglo-Jewish Archive and Parkes Library (University of Southampton), the American Jewish Archives (Cincinnati), the Central Zionist Archives (Jerusalem), the Hebrew University National Library (Jerusalem), the Bodleian Library (Oxford), Balliol College (Oxford), the University of London Library, the John Rylands Library (Manchester), the London Metropolitan Archives, the Liberal Jewish Synagogue Archives (London), Dr Williams's Library (London) and the Study Centre for Jewish–Christian Relations (London).

I am especially grateful to my brothers Michael and Calvin who proof-read the book. And finally, what would I have done without Lizzy and my mother and the rest of the family...?!

Abbreviations

Archives

A.J.A.C. American Jewish Archives, Cincinnati, Ohio, United States
Bodleian Bodleian Library, Oxford
C.Z.A.   Central Zionist Archives, Jerusalem, Israel
D.W.L.   Dr Williams's Library, London
H.U.N.L. Hebrew University National Library, Jerusalem, Israel
L.M.A.   London Metropolitan Archives

Other Abbreviations

A.J.A.   Anglo-Jewish Association
J.B.D.   Jewish Board of Deputies
J.Q.R.   Jewish Quarterly Review
J.R.U.   Jewish Religious Union
L.J.S.   Liberal Jewish Synagogue
L.S.S.R. London Society for the Study of Religion
P.F.J.P. Papers for Jewish People

Note on the System of Reference

Full details of the partial references given in the text can be found in the bibliography, which is divided into Reference Works; Books; Pamphlets, Papers and Sermons; Articles in Journals; and Unpublished Papers and Theses.

Claude Montefiore 1858–1938

Introduction

This book places Claude Montefiore in the context of Jewish thought during the late nineteenth and early twentieth centuries, before considering in what ways he was profoundly influenced by his Christian surroundings. It is primarily an intellectual history of a Jewish religious thinker and as such focuses more upon his thought than upon his life story. In particular, it explores Montefiore's fascination with the relationship between Christianity and Judaism via his approach to the two central figures of Jewish–Christian dialogue, namely Jesus and the apostle Paul.

1

A Sketch of Montefiore's Life

Claude Joseph Goldsmid-Montefiore, the Jewish communal leader, philanthropist, biblical scholar and founder of British Liberal Judaism, was born 6 June 1858, the year when full civil equality was granted to British Jews. The Montefiores were a distinguished Anglo-Jewish family originally of Italian Sephardi stock; the first of Claude's ancestors to make his home in England (London) had been one Moses Vita Montefiore, who had died in 1789.[1] Claude was the great-nephew of Sir Moses Haim Montefiore, the renowned Victorian philanthropist, sheriff of London and the first Jew to be knighted by an English sovereign. He was 27 when Moses died in 1885, 100 years old, and although he had not known his great-uncle very well, he admired him greatly. (This despite the fact that Moses, who was strictly Orthodox, had held very different views to his own. In contrast to the great-nephew, the grand-uncle had been fiercely antagonistic to Reform Judaism and supportive of Zionist enterprises.)[2] Claude, who assumed the additional surname Goldsmid by letters patent in 1883, was the nephew of Sir Francis Henry Goldsmid, the first Jew called to the Bar in England; he was also related to the Rothschilds.[3] As a member of what Chaim Bermant has described as 'the Cousinhood' or the Anglo-Jewish elite, Claude's background was therefore very much one of privilege.[4] His mother, Emma, was the fifth daughter of Sir Isaac Lyon Goldsmid who had been a prominent figure in the struggle for Jewish emancipation, a founder of the non-sectarian University College London, and an early member of the West London Reform Synagogue, Berkeley Street. According to Claude's cousin, Lucy Cohen, his mother was 'hedged round with conventions concerning conduct and proprieties, and what was what'. Montefiore once wrote that he must have cared for his mother very much to have put up with all that he went through on her account. 'But', he added, 'I used to look up at my mother, when she sat in the gallery above me in Synagogue sometimes, and think, "Well, if you *have* prejudices, they must be forgiven, for you are a noble and grand lady".'[5] Emma was the religious force in the family so that Claude was brought up as a Reform Jew and remained a member of the West London Synagogue throughout his life, becoming a warden and a member of its council, and occasionally preaching there.[6] This continued support for and interest in the Reform synagogue certainly raised questions of loyalty for some but never for himself. Three years before his death he mused, 'I would like to be bisected, and half buried by the Head Berkeley St. [Reform Synagogue] man and half by the Head L.J.S. [Liberal Jewish Synagogue] man, but this would not be legal, I suppose!'.[7] Claude's father, Nathaniel Mayer Montefiore (died 1883), was only nominally religious but took his duties as a Montefiore seriously and served as lay head of the Spanish and Portuguese Bevis Marks Synagogue.

Claude grew up comfortably, his parents owning a country estate at Coldeast, near Southampton, and a house in Portland Square, London. Along with his three older siblings, Alice, Leonard and Charlotte, he was taught privately by German tutors and governesses. Poor health, following a severe attack of pneumonia, had made going away to school impossible, and his delicate constitution remained a constant throughout his life. The educationalist Philip Magnus (later Sir), a vehement anti-Zionist and a minister of the West London Reform Synagogue throughout the 1860s, was tutor to the young Montefiore for his general education. His religious education was provided by Rev. David Marks, minister of the West London Synagogue from 1840 to 1900 and Professor of Hebrew at University College London from 1848 to 1898; highly sensitive to Christian criticism Marks undoubtedly influenced Montefiore with his extensive preaching against 'rabbinism' and Jewish particularism.[8] From the age of 17, in preparation for University entrance, Montefiore was taught by Protestant Christian tutors, including Arthur Page, the future Dean of Peterborough, and when Page could not get to Coldeast, by another clergyman, Mr Glazebrook, the future headmaster of Clifton and church dignitary at Ely. Claude's association with these liberal-minded Anglicans certainly influenced his attitude towards Christianity and Christian worship from an early stage. Page later wrote of his former student, 'He and I found nothing inconsistent in worshipping God together, whether in synagogue or in Church, and our religions drew nearer, though they did not coalesce in spirit and in hope.'[9] Reputedly learning Greek in eight weeks, Montefiore matriculated at London University in the top 10 per cent before leaving for Oxford.[10]

In 1878, only seven years after the religious tests for university entry had been abolished, Claude went to Balliol College, Oxford, where he obtained a First Class in Greats (the school of *Literae Humaniores*) in 1881.[11] Due to his delicate health he lived with one of his tutors, Baron Paravicini, a Catholic Italian aristocrat. There is no evidence that he joined any clubs or societies and his days seem to have been spent quietly and studiously. Like other socially conscious and privileged young men of his day, he allocated time to visiting the local workhouse.[12] He also enjoyed memorising and reciting poetry, especially Shakespeare's sonnets; one of his favourite tutors was the Shakespearean scholar A.C. Bradley.[13] Another tutor was the philosopher R.L. Nettleship, whose Idealist thought would have very much suited Montefiore's temperment.[14] In terms of overall influence, however, the most significant tutor for Montefiore was the liberal Anglican scholar Benjamin Jowett, who convinced him that his life's work lay in 'an ideal life … the study of your own people and their literature, and the means of improving and elevating them'.[15] Jowett, who was renowned for his controversial historical-critical contribution to *Essays and Reviews* (1860), also encouraged his student to investigate the relationship of Judaism with other religions.[16]

Following graduation, Montefiore moved to Berlin in 1882 for six months with his widowed mother and sister,[17] his intention apparently being to train as a minister at this renowned centre for German Jewish learning.[18] His exposure to liberal Anglican thought at Oxford and to biblical critical studies in Germany had taken its toll, however, and in the end he decided against the rabbinate, although he did gain a qualification as a lay preacher. While there he studied rabbinics and rabbinical lore under the Romanian Solomon Schechter at the *Hochschule (Lehranstalt) für die Wissenschaft des Judentums* (the Liberal College for Jewish Studies)[19] and brought him back with him upon his return to England as his private tutor. In the preface of his *Hibbert*

Lectures (1893) Montefiore expressed his indebtedness to four other teachers in addition to Schechter, and these included the Protestant scholars B. Stade,[20] J. Wellhausen,[21] A. Kuenen[22] and T.K. Cheyne.[23] Their influence, especially with regard to biblical criticism, will be examined later.

Thus various distinct traditions were woven into Montefiore's make-up, giving him his particular temper, presuppositions and method. Nineteenth-century Christian liberal culture deeply influenced him with its emphasis on classical thought, Hegelian dialectic, progress and the theories of evolution and biblical criticism. Judaism gave him his sense of purpose, a deeply felt obligation to his fellow Jews and the bulk of his subject matter. True to both Jewish rabbinical tradition and Victorian sentiment his general outlook on life was religious rather than philosophical. The attitude behind all his writings and work, which were theological rather than historical in character, was that of one who had a spiritual message to proclaim. The emancipated status of Anglo-Jewry, his association with the West London Synagogue and, to a limited extent, his personal contacts with the Reform Movement in Germany from his time in Berlin[24] all assisted in directing Montefiore's interest towards the great cause in his life, Liberal Judaism.

Claude Montefiore married twice. First, in 1886, to Thérèse Schorstein, whom he had first met at an interview for a position at one of the Jewish schools he supported.[25] Their marriage was short but happy; after three years Thérèse died, giving birth to Montefiore's only child, Leonard, who was nicknamed Robin. In 1902 his mother, Emma Goldsmid, died and he married his second wife Florence Ward the same year (she died in December 1938).[26] Florence, a convert to Judaism, had been vice-principal of Girton College, Cambridge, and a tutor and friend to Thérèse. In deference to his mother's wishes (she took a dim view of his marrying someone who had not been born a Jew) he had promised not to marry Florence during his mother's lifetime and this had entailed a seven-year wait.[27] He ignored the adverse criticism that his marriage attracted at the time, insistent that a true Jew was a religious Jew and that only interfaith marriages threatened the continuity of Judaism. In this he was not regarded as entirely consistent, having supported his sister when she had 'married out' to a Christian in 1884. But Montefiore's support for his sister's decision had been grudging, and he had taken little comfort from a letter Jowett sent him at the time in which his tutor urged upon him the potential of intermarriage as a way to break down 'the wall of distinction between Jew and Christian'.[28] While he was certainly committed to breaking down racial barriers, Montefiore argued against mixed-religion marriages throughout his life. In any case, he regarded Florence as a model Jew and the marriage was ostensibly successful, if less romantic than the first. Her own proclivity for educational and charitable work made her more of an equal for Montefiore, and he was undoubtedly relieved to have found someone who could take over the daily duties of running a large house and bringing up a young son, with whom he was not entirely at his ease during the early years.

Montefiore had an arresting appearance.[29] A close friend of his, the historian and statesman Herbert Fisher, wrote of 'the erect figure, the high dominant brow, the deep-set glowing brown eyes, the clear ringing voice and the upright and down-right ways of speech', which gave Montefiore 'an impression of commanding force'.[30] His cousin, Lucy Cohen, also remarked upon his eyes for their 'strange radiance and soft glow as if lit by some inner fire like a spark of the *shechina* [the indwelling of God]'.[31] He had a pale complexion and wore a short beard. His hair, which was close-cropped, was not a thing to be trifled with. In 1934, the German sculptor Benno Elkan produced the bust of Montefiore that now sits in the Hartley Library of the University of Southampton. Montefiore wrote to Cohen,

> I implored him [Elkan] to come on Monday and get on, so that I can have my hair cut, but I daresay he won't. He presumes on my sacrifice. (1 Feb.). The wretched bust man has gone to Cambridge and left me here very uncomfortable. It is horrid. (4 Feb.). That odious bust man I suppose he laughs – I have warned him that I can't be played with like this, and that he will find the hair off unless he hurries up. (5 Feb.).[32]

From a young age, Montefiore took his privileged position and communal responsibilities seriously. His work, which was entirely voluntary, was frequently disrupted by bouts of ill health; he was nevertheless regarded by those who knew him as singularly dedicated and hardworking.[33] He possessed an intense, religious temperament and, in keeping with other Victorian moralists of his day, he espoused a somewhat narrow moral outlook, although this was muted by a natural tolerance. As a gentleman and a scholar, he frequented Gentlemen's Clubs and a variety of academic societies, but he did not drink or gamble,[34] and he disliked the hunting, artistic pursuits and socialising which other members of the Jewish elite engaged in. He preferred to spend his leisure time reading, writing or walking with old friends or his dogs. Nevertheless, he had an intensely social personality and could write up to 30 or 40 letters a day, especially in his later life when deafness and asthma curtailed his activities.[35] Montefiore hated ostentatiousness. His homes, while large and spacious, were devoid of ornaments or fine paintings and he himself was careless in appearance; London associates remembered him as usually attired in black, often wearing boots and gloves that were too big for him. Throughout his life he demonstrated what one historian has described as an 'obsession' with the moral education of the young,[36] and he spoke and preached frequently on the subject of the improvement of public morals and the importance of the home. His obvious personal religiosity and learning, his wealth and his natural leadership brought him considerable moral authority and prestige within the community. At the same time, his conservative, anti-Zionist politics, certain elitist tendencies and his modernist religious teaching assured that he was very often the focus of controversy in the pages of the *Jewish Chronicle*. His detractors admitted that his character and intentions were irreproachable, but this 'personal regard for Mr Montefiore and his high-minded and zealously-pursued good intentions' only made him more dangerous, as his critics complained.[37]

There was certainly a less attractive side to Montefiore, often overlooked by his biographers. Strongly influenced by a highly class-conscious mother, Montefiore could on occasion be accused of snobbery. He wrote of Israel Zangwill, for example, 'you know I can't bear him. He is a *bête noir* to me and I regard him as a most dangerous man, not only because of his opinions, which I detest, but because of his gross vulgarity and lack of taste and breeding and good manners.'[38] He was also wont to make disparaging remarks about Schechter's manners.[39] Theodore Herzl dismissed Montefiore as a 'stupid ass who affects English correctness' and Lewis Namier called him a 'learned old humbug'.[40] Conservative by nature and Tory by instinct, he was suspicious of socialism and, at times, patronising to those who worked closely with him. In one highly-strung letter to his chief lieutenant at the Liberal Jewish Synagogue, the progressive American Rabbi Israel Mattuck, he wrote of his fear that 'Any identification of *you* or *Liberal Judaism* with Socialism would wreck the movement *utterly* ... The matter is very dangerous and the loose use of the word "socialism" is highly to be deprecated.'[41] Nor was he a natural democrat;[42] he caused considerable resentment over the years among committee members for taking decisions without proper consultation, and for all too often refusing to trust his colleagues and the Jewish Press with information that he believed might cause unnecessary public consternation.[43] Furthermore, despite Montefiore's distaste for nationalism in the context of Jewish identity, he gloried in British superiority and displayed a patriotism for England that bordered upon jingoism.[44] It would be unfair and anachronistic to judge his occasional super-patriotic utterances too harshly; he was certainly less so than were a great many other men of his class and position in the pre-First World War period. Nevertheless, a pamphlet he wrote with Basil Henriques, 'The English Jew and his Religion' (1918), has an almost xenophobic feel to it, and in a disconcerting letter to Israel Mattuck (undated), he was capable of writing, 'Again, for instance, there is a rumour tonight that a German battleship has been sunk. I rejoice ... Even if all have gone down, I rejoice that there is one German battleship less.'[45] Lucy Cohen comments that Montefiore was by no means a pacifist and that 'his eyes would glow over a tale of heroism'.[46]

In the context of Montefiore's cosmopolitan social position and the extent to which he emphasised his Englishness, it is worth briefly considering to what extent he denigrated his Jewishness. Could Montefiore be described as a 'self-hating Jew'? Self-criticism in terms of the surrounding culture has been a hallmark of Jewish life in the modern period, as has the phenomenon of acculturated Jews experiencing the behaviour of other Jews as embarrassing or shameful.[47] If one were prepared to describe those Jews who internalised non-Jewish constructions of Jewishness as 'self-hating', then Montefiore could easily be categorised as such. It is possible to opt for a stricter understanding of the term, however. Endelman recently suggested that the term is most usefully employed when understood as 'a full blown variety [of self-hatred], the kind that Jews who wished to expunge their Jewishness translated in words or actions, rather than the occasional, half-hearted kind that was part and parcel of the ambivalence that most acculturated Jews felt'.[48] Of this, Montefiore was undoubtedly free. He was committed to the development of Judaism and to the well-being of the Jewish people in so far as they represented the means by which Judaism was to be communicated to the wider world. In no sense could he be said to have rejected his Jewish identity, even if the terms by which he defined it were restricted to a religious dimension.

Overwhelmingly, Montefiore is remembered for his cultured sophistication, his modesty, the self-effacing manner that characterised his public speaking, and a quaint, dry sense of humour, which often comes across in his letters and speeches.[49] Cohen noted that he had inherited his father's 'genial simplicity'[50] and he was well regarded for his clarity of understanding and his powers of empathy. Bentwich spoke of 'his wonderful talent for stating the case he opposed fairly and almost convincingly' concerning the Zionist question;[51] and Kessler noted the occasion of a meeting of the Jewish Religious Union (a union of Jewish modernists, which he helped found in 1902) in which Montefiore had excused the behaviour of demonstrators who stormed his platform, stating their views more clearly than they could themselves.[52] Likened to a seventeenth-century Covenanter by one historian for the vigour with which he clung to his views,[53] it would not have been easy to persuade him otherwise once he had made up his mind on an issue. But this certainly did not stop him from tolerating and even encouraging others with differing points of view. His scholarship was well regarded by contemporaries and he received many honours for his contributions to both Jewish and Christian religious studies.[54] Honorary degrees included Doctor of Divinity (D.D.) from the University of Manchester (1921); a degree from the Jewish Institute of Religion, New York (1921); Doctor of Hebrew Law from Hebrew Union College of Cincinnati (1924); a Doctorate of Letters (D.Litt.) from the University of Oxford (1927); and the British Academy Medal for Biblical Studies (1930). Even taking into account the hyperbole used to describe the man in letters, sermons and memoirs, Montefiore comes across as a kindly, humorous gentleman who deeply impressed those around him with his intellectual rigour,

high-mindedness and quiet determination. Rabbi Leo Baeck said
of Montefiore, who died in London, 9 July 1938,

> The most impressive work of art is that which man makes
> of his life – it is granted only to specially favoured men
> to create such a work. When we think of all that Claude
> Montefiore has given to so many of us, the noblest and
> greatest gift is surely his own life, the living personality
> which revealed itself in everything that emanated from it.[55]

MONTEFIORE'S EDUCATIONAL, COMMUNAL AND RELIGIOUS ACTIVITIES

Montefiore inherited a large fortune (£456,000) from his father
Nathaniel and from his mother (£1 million).[56] Other fortunes
came his way from his brother Leonard who died of rheumatic
fever while travelling in America in 1879 (Leonard had himself
inherited a large fortune from their uncle Sir Francis Goldsmid)
and from his father-in-law, Lazar Schorstein, of Reuter's Agency.
Amply endowed with wealth, learning and leisure, Montefiore
used these freely in furthering both Jewish and non-Jewish
charitable and educational ventures, and in promoting the cause
of Liberal Judaism. His devotion to Jewish theology and religious
learning was exceptional for a member of the Anglo-Jewish elite.

Although Montefiore often complained that his responsibilities
kept him from his studies, he was dedicated to his philanthropic
works, performing his duties as a wealthy Jewish patron with
enthusiasm and great attention to detail. Committee work was
very much part of the daily life of a stalwart member of the
Anglo-Jewish elite and the range of committee work with
which Montefiore busied himself was impressive by anyone's
standards.[57] In addition, he made public appeals in aid of strikers,[58]
championed foreign disaster funds,[59] was a familiar figure at
prize-givings and communal celebrations and preached in
numerous synagogues up and down the country. A favoured
cause was the advancement of women and children. He was
associated with the work of Lily Montagu in the West Central
Club for Jewish girls and with Basil Henriques in the St George's
and Bernhard Baron settlement in the East End.[60] He also became
president of the Jewish Association for the Protection of Girls

and Women, an organisation concerned with the welfare of underprivileged and exploited women. He was drawn to this work, at least in part, to salvage the reputation of the Jewish community, which, around the turn of the century, was associated with white slave trafficking. His cousin, Lady Battersea, once asked him to meet with two Jewish girls in the London Docklands 'who were leading immoral lives', so as to 'divert them from their mode of living'. Without knowing precisely what occurred when this distinguished, scholarly gentleman arrived at the docks, it is reported that the effort failed with the result that he decided to leave the more practical aspects of his charitable work to others.[61] His contributions remained mainly on the committee and financial level. Montefiore tended to make his personal gifts anonymously, although the Jewish Press often drew attention to the large donations he made,[62] and Israel Zangwill was inspired to playfully write of him, 'Of men like you / Earth holds but few, / An angel with / A revenue.'[63]

Two aspects of Montefiore's public work deserve closer attention, namely his support of educational projects of all kinds, and his activities as a communal leader, particularly as president of the Anglo-Jewish Association.

As early as 1882 Montefiore had demonstrated his interest in education by helping out at a newly established kindergarten at the Jews Infant School[64] and by joining the board of the Froebel Institute as honorary secretary. He soon became chairman of this progressive educational establishment[65] and Chairman of the Managers of three Jewish Schools in London.[66] Over the years he involved himself in examining a number of religious classes and decrying what he regarded as the over-intensive and backward standards of the traditional Talmud Torah classes.[67] Concerned to raise the standards of Jewish schools in general, Montefiore drew attention to the need for a dedicated college that would cater for the particular requirements of Jews wishing to attend teacher-training courses, as early as 1890.[68] Throughout 1893 he was the 'leading spirit' in a campaign to provide teacher-training specifically for Jewish women, who were not at that time accepted at King's College and University College, London,[69] and was praised by the Press when his efforts finally resulted in the authority's agreement to pay the costs of female Jewish students attending courses at Cambridge and Stockwell.[70] He also became involved in non-Jewish educational work and was elected onto the London School Board in 1888.[71] By 1895 Montefiore was regarded by the *Jewish Chronicle* as 'an authority of the highest rank on educational questions'.[72] This did not protect him from controversy regarding his membership of the Jewish Religious Education Board, however. In December 1905, Sir Samuel Montagu used the occasion of a meeting of the Federation of Synagogues to demand Montefiore's resignation from the Education Board, which he felt had been made necessary by Montefiore's public rejection of the authority of the Mosaic Law.[73] With no evidence having been produced to indicate that his progressive religious views had unduly biased his work, Montefiore declined to resign. He explained in July of the following year that in order to ensure that the religious teachings common to both liberal and orthodox Jews were promoted effectively, he had always been prepared to overlook the inclusion of teachings with which, as a liberal, he disagreed, and to accept the omission of more progressive teachings.[74] His explicit assurance that he would continue to approach his work in this way proved unacceptable. Resisting for several years a sustained campaign led by Montagu to have him removed, Montefiore was finally forced to resign in 1909 following the establishment of the Liberal Jewish Synagogue, when his presence on the Board became in the words of the *Jewish Chronicle* 'a gross anomaly'.[75] Chief Rabbi Hermann Adler accepted Montefiore's resignation despite the fact that he could 'unhesitatingly record' that his colleague had never interfered with the syllabus of instruction.[76]

Montefiore's interest in education also extended to the university level. He helped maintain the Cambridge lectureship (and later readership) in Rabbinic Studies, thereby fostering the works of Schechter, Israel Abrahams and Herbert Loewe.[77] And he had particularly close ties with Hartley University College, Southampton, later the University of Southampton. He was vice-president there in 1908, president from 1913 until 1934,[78] and chairman of the General Purposes Committee, which was set up in 1927 to ensure that proposals put to the Council had been fully investigated.[79] Amongst numerous other gifts and contributions, he presented the university college with an 11-acre sports-ground at South Stoneham during the early days of his presidency, and a large tract of land (between the Common and the Union Building) towards the end. There are several buildings named after him in his honour, and the university college presented him with a volume of essays on his seventieth birthday (*Speculum Religionis*, 1929). As a means by which to disseminate Jewish learning and research specifically, Montefiore became involved in academic journals including the *Transactions of the Jewish Historical Society of England* of which he was the president from 1899 to 1900, and the *Jewish Quarterly Review*, which he and Abrahams founded and co-edited from late 1887 until 1910 when the work-load became too much and the rights were transferred to Dropsie College, Philadelphia.[80] For 15 years he also wrote for and helped to finance the weekly *Jewish Guardian*, which was more liberal and less orthodox than its old rival, the *Jewish Chronicle*.

The second aspect of his public work that brought Montefiore into considerable controversy was his involvement with the Anglo-Jewish Association (A.J.A.). This had been established in 1871 and became an important representative body whose purpose was to contribute towards the educational needs and defend the civil interests of Jews throughout the world. By 1900, it had 22 branches within Britain and 14 others distributed around the British Colonies.[81] The Executive Council of 60 members met monthly in London, and it received over 700 subscriptions from the London area alone.[82] Montefiore was president from 1895 until 1921.[83] He therefore held office during a crucial period in Anglo-Jewish history, covering the growth of antisemitism in Europe, the rise of Zionism, and the Balfour Declaration, which he opposed. Soon after taking over as head of the A.J.A., Montefiore became the president of the Jewish Colonisation Association (I.C.A.), which aided Jewish settlers living abroad, and in 1899 was elected as a representative to the Alliance Israélite Universelle, the French sister organisation to the A.J.A.[84] Both of these positions entailed regular visits to Paris. Montefiore's work with the Conjoint Foreign Committee (a sort of Anglo-Jewish foreign ministry composed of members from the A.J.A. and the Orthodox dominated Board of Deputies) meant that he was integrally involved in representing Anglo-Jewish concerns to British and foreign governments. While he was an important communal figure involved in the work of a number of Anglo-Jewish institutions, it was his leadership of the A.J.A. that proved most influential.

Part of Montefiore's legacy to the A.J.A. was to have increased the participation of the provincial branches. Beginning with Birmingham and Liverpool, he had made a presidential tour of

A.J.A. provincial branches in 1896,[85] and he reinforced this by repeated visitations over the next 25 years. He was always keen to encourage representatives to attend the monthly meetings in London, not least because a considerable proportion of the income from A.J.A. subsidies emanated from these sources. The number of representatives travelling down to London, and the amount of non-metropolitan lobbying, did not increase much until 1905, when Montefiore found it necessary to remind colleagues who were unfamiliar with procedure that A.J.A. funds could not be utilised for English, Scottish or Irish Jewish causes.[86] Encouraged by the increase in numbers, Montefiore pushed through a new constitution in 1906 with the explicit aim of further increasing the involvement of the provincial branches. This doubled the voting power of each branch and allowed for annual meetings of the A.J.A. to be held alternatively in London and the provinces.[87] While he cannot be said to have significantly increased its income, or the number of A.J.A. branches either at home or abroad in his 25 years, Montefiore was responsible for opening the door to participation from outside the world of the London Jewish elite.

The role of the A.J.A. was two-fold. Firstly, it aimed to encourage and support the development of educational opportunities for Jews outside Britain. Without doubt this was the side of the work in which Montefiore was most interested. As a life-long educationalist and philanthropist, he believed passionately that, as an act of humanity, British Jews should help subsidise the education of Jewish children in the Middle East, Africa and Asia. At any one time the A.J.A. made annual grants to around 20 schools and contributed to the teaching of approximately 8,000–10,000 students.[88] In its work, it often collaborated with the Alliance Israélite Universelle, and up until the First World War a large proportion of A.J.A. funds went to shared educational projects in Turkish controlled territories, the largest of which was the Evelina School in Jerusalem, which was the only school for girls in the city.[89] Primarily, this aspect of the work involved Montefiore in fund-raising and administrative activities, and caused him a great deal of anxiety; he approached potential sponsors personally and wrote many appeals himself by hand.[90]

The second function of the A.J.A. was more diplomatic and political in nature, namely, its self-assumed role as the body by which political influence could be brought to bear in defence of

oppressed foreign Jews. Montefiore was less comfortable with
this side of his work and preferred to describe the function of
the A.J.A. as 'a sort of watching brief of the Jews throughout the
world' rather than as an active, overtly political lobby.[91] This was
partly due to his belief, asserted early in his presidency, in the
non-national nature of the Jewish people, which he preferred to
describe as a 'religious brotherhood'.[92] He was constantly on his
guard against those whom he thought wanted to use the A.J.A.
as a means by which to support Jewish nationalism.[93] At his most
hesitant moments, it appeared almost as though he himself
viewed the political work of the A.J.A. as just such a vehicle. By
nature he was a man who followed form and convention, and
he took a cautious, somewhat deferential, approach to defending Jewish interests to governments at home and abroad. His
was the voice of the Anglo-Jewish elite, preferring behind-the-
scenes diplomacy to more radical action. While there were many
who agreed with his general policy of avoiding public demonstrations[94] and limiting governmental lobbying to a minimum,[95]
Montefiore faced considerable pressure from the interventionist
approach of the Zionists within the A.J.A. council. This faction, led
by Dr Moses Gaster and several members from the Manchester
branch, became increasingly active and influential throughout
his presidency, viewing the A.J.A. as a means by which to
demonstrate the strength of Jewish nationalism. Partly as a result
of his natural conservatism, and partly because he feared assist-
ing the nationalist agenda, Montefiore's A.J.A. often appeared
ineffectual. His annual presidential reports tended to come
across as somewhat complacent, his brief reports on troubled
'black-spots' outweighed by his emphasis upon the need for
fund-raising to support positive educational developments and
improving conditions elsewhere.[96] Montefiore's reaction to the
fate of Russian Jewry, which suffered high profile pogroms in
1882, 1891 and 1905, is illustrative of his reticent approach. The
solution to the Russian problem, he believed, could only be
found in Russia and he saw little benefit from organising protests
in Britain. Having emphasised the improving situation in 1901,[97]
for example, the pogroms in 1905 did little to change his opinion,
and he explained the atrocities as the result of the general turmoil
within the country.[98] He argued that the British government
had done all that was necessary and urged that no public
demonstrations be made.[99] In setting up a Relief Fund, he then

infuriated the Zionists by advertising that none of the money collected would be used to repatriate Jews in Palestine and demanded that their own fund-raising be channelled back to the A.J.A. fund.[100] In such ways, Montefiore's presidency did little to convince otherwise those that regarded the A.J.A. as hopelessly bound by tradition, reluctant to take the initiative in protecting Jewish interests abroad, and concerned with consolidating its own power. As the *Jewish Chronicle* editorial put it in July 1921,

> The Anglo-Jewish Association, as an institution, is fairly open to the comment of being ... a communal superfluity; and it is scarcely open to argument that what work the Association has done, as well as the Association itself, must have suffered to some extent by reason of the views which Mr Montefiore holds.[101]

In stark contrast to his conservative approach to communal politics and his progressive but low-key educational work, Montefiore's influence upon institutional Judaism was nothing short of revolutionary. Through his financial and administrative support he was responsible for the development of Liberal Judaism in England. By his spiritual and intellectual leadership the Jewish Religious Union for the Advancement of Liberal Judaism (J.R.U.) was set up in 1902, and he was the first president of the Liberal Jewish Synagogue when it finally declared itself in 1910. When the World Union for Progressive Judaism was founded in 1926, Montefiore was elected as its first president, recognised throughout the world as the leader of Progressive Judaism. In addition, he was involved in early inter-faith dialogue and co-founded (with the Catholic theologian Baron Von Hügel) the London Society for the Study of Religion in 1904, a bi-monthly forum in which the religious issues of the day could be discussed and debated by members of various faiths. The venture, which met at his home at 42 Portman Square from 1922 until 1932 and was referred to in correspondence as 'C.M.'s Night Club' was a source of great pleasure to Montefiore.[102] He worked closely with Rabbi Israel Mattuck, the first minister at the Liberal Jewish Synagogue, who played an important role in the founding of the London Society of Christians and Jews in 1924.[103]

Montefiore was a prolific writer, producing 18 books and over 120 articles and miscellanea.[104] He made his name as the first Jew to give the Hibbert Lectures, which he delivered in 1892 at Oxford on 'The Origin and Growth of Religion as Illustrated by the Religion of the Ancient Hebrews' and published the following year.[105] His most distinctive contributions, however, were in the field of New Testament scholarship. His familiarity with both the rabbinic literature and New Testament biblical criticism, and his apparently non-partisan approach, very much interested Christian scholars. As reflected many times in the Jewish press, which reviewed his books at length, Jewish audiences were caught between admiration for his learning and for his repeated defences of Judaism, and distrust regarding his biblical critical beliefs. *The Synoptic Gospels* (first edition 1909, second edition 1927) was a commentary on the Gospels primarily for Jewish readers, and was followed by the Benjamin Jowett Lectures at Oxford in 1910 on 'Some Elements of the Religious Teaching of Jesus According to the Synoptic Gospels', published the same year. *Judaism and St. Paul* (1914) was a highly original attempt to present the Apostle of the Gentiles sympathetically to Jews. Counter-balancing such studies in Christianity were his writings on Judaism. John Rayner has suggested that 'in his [Montefiore's] religious thought all roads lead to Liberal Judaism' and that to understand his conception of Liberal Judaism was all that was required to understand his religious teaching.[106] Certainly, its theology was the backcloth to all his writings, especially as expressed in *Aspects of Judaism* (1895), a collection of his sermons together with those of Israel Abrahams, *Liberal Judaism* (1903), *Outlines of Liberal Judaism* (1912, 1923), and *Liberal Judaism and Hellenism* (1918). Despite his liberal leanings, his concern to defend the rabbis against Christian criticism was clearly reflected in *Rabbinic Literature and Gospel Teachings* (1930) and *A Rabbinic Anthology* (1938), which is still used as an introduction to rabbinic thought today at Hebrew Union College, Cincinnati.[107] *The Old Testament and After* (1923) encapsulated his essential Liberal Jewish teachings, which remained remarkably consistent throughout his lifetime. His writings were concerned with the problems facing religion generally, and Judaism in particular, in the modern world. While they were intended to bring obscure but significant ideas to the attention of an intelligent lay readership, they were more often of greater interest to scholars, and only his *The Bible for Home Reading*, which went into three editions, was widely appreciated.[108]

NOTES

1. The family tree is reproduced in L. Cohen, *Some Recollections of Claude Goldsmid-Montefiore 1858–1938* (1940), pp. 26, 273.
2. H.W. Montefiore, 'Sir Moses Montefiore and his Great Nephew: A Study in Contrasts', 11th Montefiore Lecture, Southampton (1979), pp. 15, 17.
3. Montefiore was the great-grandson of Mayer Amschel de Rothschild.
4. Chaim Bermant has written a history of the wealthy Jewish minority he called 'the Cousinhood', which he described as 'a compact union of exclusive brethren with blood and money flowing in a small circle'. Their influence lasted from the late eighteenth century until the rise of Zionism in the early twentieth century. C. Bermant, *The Cousinhood: The Anglo-Jewish Gentry* (1971), pp. 1, 3.
5. Letter from C.G. Montefiore to Lucy Cohen (undated). L. Cohen, *Some Recollections of Claude Goldsmid-Montefiore 1858–1938* (1940), p. 50. Emma Montefiore lived from 1819 to 1902.
6. Montefiore first preached at Berkeley Street in June 1893. *Jewish Chronicle*, 16 June 1893, p. 7. His mother contributed substantially towards the cost of the Singer Prayer Book of the West London Synagogue, as did Montefiore himself, who also assisted with the translation of biblical passages. *Jewish Chronicle*, 31 July 1891, p. 14. L. Cohen, *Some Recollections of Claude Goldsmid-Montefiore 1858–1938* (1940), p. 29.
7. Letter from C.G. Montefiore to Lucy Cohen (6 February 1936). Ibid., p. 237.
8. 'For many years he [David Marks] taught my mother, my sister and myself Hebrew, and as I write, the dining room at 36 Hyde Park Gardens, which was our school room, jumps into my mind; I see Mr Marks in the armchair on my right, myself at the table, and our governess, who always, I think, attended our Hebrew lessons, opposite, listening and knitting at the same time … [H]e was strict and yet encouraging. I can hear him now calling out "Paddy" if I made a careless or stupid mistake, and I can see him pinching my cheek – a process which I used half to like and half to fear … He used to tell us also of the conditions of the Jews and Judaism in the 30s, of the establishment of the Reform Synagogue, of our grandfather, Sir Isaac Goldsmid, and of many other members of our family … Some of us talk and feel today about being "English", about Englishmen of the Jewish Persuasion, and all that sort of thing. A great deal of our feelings and ideals in those respects really goes back to Mr Marks and his teaching.' *Jewish Chronicle*, 7 May 1909, p. 20.
9. Cited in L. Cohen, *Some Recollections of Claude Goldsmid-Montefiore 1858–1938* (1940), p. 39.
10. Ibid., p. 38.
11. *Jewish Chronicle*, 9 December 1881, p. 11.
12. L. Cohen, *Some Recollections of Claude Goldsmid-Montefiore 1858–1938* (1940), p. 43.
13. Andrew Cecil Bradley (1851–1935) was a literary critic and pre-eminent Shakespearean scholar of the late nineteenth and early twentieth centuries. Montefiore was fond of poetry throughout his life. Ibid., pp. 39–40.
14. Richard Lewis Nettleship (1846–92) has been described as a disciple of T.H. Green; his thought was Idealist and Hegelian. Montefiore was certainly influenced by the prevailing philosophy of the time, exemplified in the thought of Green, that the nature of ultimate reality was spiritual. Montefiore's friend, Friedrich Von Hügel, was a Catholic theologian with a

similar world-view. J. Barr, 'Judaism – Its Continuity with the Bible', 7th Claude Montefiore Lecture, Southampton (1968), p. 5.

15. Letter from Benjamin Jowett to C.G. Montefiore (1883) in L. Cohen, *Some Recollections of Claude Goldsmid-Montefiore 1858–1938* (1940), p. 47. The classical scholar Benjamin Jowett (1817–93) was considered to be one of the greatest teachers of the nineteenth century. Master of Balliol College, Oxford, he is best known for his translations of Plato and for his historical-critical contribution to *Essays and Reviews* (1860) in which he redefined the interpretation of scripture.

16. Cited in V.G. Simmons, 'Claude Goldsmid Montefiore', *Transactions of the Jewish Historical Society of England*, XIV (1935–39), p. 255.

17. Bentwich gives the move in 1882: 'just graduated from Oxford, [he] came there [to the Hochschule] in 1882'; N. Bentwich, 'Claude Montefiore and his Tutor in Rabbinics: Founders of Liberal and Conservative Judaism', 6th Montefiore Memorial Lecture, Southampton (1966), p. 4. Cohen records that 'After leaving Oxford Claude went to study in Germany' for six months and that 'From 1883 to 1886 he lived at home [in London]'; L. Cohen, *Some Recollections of Claude Goldsmid-Montefiore 1858–1938* (1940), pp. 44–6.

18. 'We understand that Mr Claude Montefiore (second son of Mr Nathaniel Montefiore and a great-nephew of Sir Moses Montefiore) who has just completed his university career at Oxford intends to enter the Jewish ministry.' *Jewish Chronicle*, 30 December 1881, p. 5. Montefiore was still in Berlin in March 1883 and 'has signalled his intention of entering the Jewish ministry for which he is qualifying himself by theological study in Berlin'. *Jewish Chronicle*, 30 March 1883, p. 7.

19. Solomon Schechter (1847–1915) was an outstanding authority on the Talmud and a researcher who, among other things, recovered many priceless documents from the Cairo Geniza. In 1890 he became lecturer in Talmudic studies at Cambridge. From 1902 he was a leader in Conservative Judaism in the US, founding the United Synagogue of America in 1913.

20. Bernhard Stade (1848–1906) was a German Protestant theologian. He became widely known for his critical history of Israel, *Geschichte des Volkes Israel* (1887–88).

21. Julius Wellhausen (1844–1918) was a German biblical scholar best known for his analysis of the structure and dating of the Pentateuch; he argued that they were not written by Moses but were rather a compilation of documents (J, E, D and P) composed at different periods in the history of Israel.

22. Abraham Kuenen (1828–91) was a Dutch Protestant theologian whose works included a historical-critical introduction to the Old Testament, and studies on the religion of Israel and Hebrew prophecy. He gave a course of Hibbert lectures on *National Religions and Universal Religion* (1882).

23. Thomas Kelly Cheyne (1841–1915) was an Anglican theologian and biblical critic who argued for a broad and comprehensive study of the scriptures in the light of literary, historical and scientific considerations. He produced commentaries on the Prophets and the Hagiographa.

24. J. Rayner, 'C.G. Montefiore; his Religious Teaching', *The Synagogue Review*, XXXII (June 1958), p. 256. A close friend of Montefiore suggested that his love of Jewish learning had been greatly encouraged by his friendship with Rabbi Dr F.P. Frankl of Berlin, a friend and associate of Schechter, with whose family Montefiore kept in contact with for many years. V.G. Simmons, 'Claude Goldsmid Montefiore', *Transactions of the Jewish Historical Society of England*, XIV (1935–39), p. 255.

25. L. Cohen, *Some Recollections of Claude Goldsmid-Montefiore 1858–1938* (1940), p. 50.
26. Both marriage ceremonies were performed soberly, without music or flowers, at the Berkeley Street Reform Synagogue. *Jewish Chronicle*, 15 October 1886, p. 11 and 25 July 1902, p. 18.
27. L. Cohen, *Some Recollections of Claude Goldsmid-Montefiore 1858–1938* (1940), pp. 72–3.
28. Letter from Benjamin Jowett to C.G. Montefiore (14 September 1884), ibid., p. 35.
29. There is a portrait of Montefiore by Oswald Birley (1925) in the New Liberal Jewish Synagogue, St John's Wood, London. There is another portrait by William Rothenstein (1928) and a bust by Benno Elkan (1934) in the Hartley Library, University of Southampton.
30. H.A.L. Fisher's Foreword to L. Cohen, *Some Recollections of Claude Goldsmid-Montefiore 1858–1938* (1940), p. 11.
31. Ibid., p. 154.
32. Ibid., p. 210.
33. Rev. David Marks commented of Montefiore that he 'throws himself into public work, fulfilling as he does the axiom of the scriptural moralist, "Whatever thou findest in the power of thy hands to do, do it with all thy might."' *Jewish Chronicle*, 16 July 1897, p. 13. It was two years after taking up its presidency before Montefiore missed one of the monthly meetings of the A.J.A. *Jewish Chronicle*, 31 December 1897, p. 12.
34. The one blemish on his record is the report that he paid a £100 fine for holding two meetings at which liquors were sold, thereby breaking the Municipal Elections Act 1884. The incident was brought up when Montefiore was applying for a place on the London School Board in 1888. *Jewish Chronicle*, 23 November 1888, p. 5.
35. The many brief, hurriedly scrawled notes of his daily correspondence were characteristically sprawled across the page at an angle of 30°. They were filled with references to statistical trivia such as anniversaries, the number of colds he had suffered in a year, the number of visits he had made to particular institutions, etc.
36. According to Black, Montefiore's narrow moral code also led to his 'concern with sexual discipline'. E. Black, *The Social Politics of Anglo-Jewry 1880–1920* (1988), p. 24.
37. The same critic, 'Mentor', rebuked Montefiore's influence upon a certain section of the public, which he described as 'that parsimonious, anaemic, "sappy" section which compromises on everything, is definite on no principle, and which thinks infinitely more of the value of Mr Montefiore's personality than of the damage of his disruptive courses'. *Jewish Chronicle* (28 November 1919), p. 9. Another correspondent, 'Anti-Humbug', wrote: 'It is to be hoped that the personality of Mr Montefiore or his personal qualities will not hide from the Community the mortal danger of allowing the unfettered scope that has hitherto been accorded to his crude inconsistencies on matters vitally affecting Judaism.' *Jewish Chronicle*, 21 June 1918, p. 9.
38. Letter from C.G. Montefiore to Stephen Wise, 17 December 1923. MS 19/27/7, Jewish Institute of Religion Papers, A.J.A.C.
39. 'He's [Schechter's] a dear creature, but we have to remind him sometimes to wash his hands.' Attributed to Montefiore by the daughter of the Dean of Westminster, cited in L. Cohen, *Some Recollections of Claude Goldsmid-Montefiore 1858–1938* (1940), p. 44.

40. Cited in S.A. Cohen, *English Zionists and British Jews: The Communal Politics of Anglo-Jewry, 1895–1920* (c1982), p. 166n.
41. Letter from C.G. Montefiore to Israel Mattuck, 10 November, year uncertain. ACC/3529/4/2, L.M.A.
42. 'The people who will decide a very intricate [political] issue are not … you or I, but my old man [his manservant], and my charwoman and my gardeners. This is the way of democracy and makes me very dubious of its wisdom.' Letter to Lucy Cohen, 16 November 1923. L. Cohen, *Some Recollections of Claude Goldsmid-Montefiore 1858–1938* (1940), p. 113.
43. Montefiore blamed the Press as the reason for his caution. At one meeting of the A.J.A. in 1898, he argued that it was precisely because of 'the powers of misrepresentation in the Press of Europe' that he could not risk the reputation of the A.J.A. by sending delegates to a Zionist Congress. *Jewish Chronicle*, 18 February 1898, p. 17. At another meeting of the A.J.A. in October 1916, and despite the protests of several council members, Montefiore insisted that a discussion of the Conjoint Foreign Committee (a body composed of representatives of both the A.J.A. and Board of Deputies that sought to present a united Anglo-Jewish policy to the public and the government), should be carried out confidentially. The *Jewish Chronicle* published an open letter to Montefiore, complaining, '… we have in our columns constantly raised objection to what we have felt to be the abuse of this prerogative [i.e. ruling a discussion confidential] by either yourself or Mr Alexander as Chairmen at meetings of either the Board of Deputies or the Anglo-Jewish Association Council'. *Jewish Chronicle*, 3 November 1916, p. 16.
44. 'Now Englishmen are certainly more successful than other races in their management of, and relations with, Eastern communities.' *Jewish Chronicle*, 11 December 1908, p. 16.
45. ACC/3529/4/2, L.M.A.
46. L. Cohen, *Some Recollections of Claude Goldsmid-Montefiore 1858–1938* (1940), p. 217. Along with one Lt. Col. Sir M. Nathan, Montefiore wrote to the Jewish Naval and Military Association, offering his services as a patron of the Association. *Jewish Chronicle*, 21 April 1916, p. 9.
47. T. Endelman, 'Jewish Self-Hatred in Britain and Germany', in M. Brenner, R. Liedtke and D. Rechter, *Two Nations: British and German Jews in Comparative Perspective* (1999), pp. 332, 334–5.
48. Ibid., p. 335.
49. A critic, 'Mentor', admitted that Montefiore's 'charming personality, despite his views, has made him one of the most beloved of all his brethren in this country and far beyond it'. *Jewish Chronicle*, 4 November 1921, p. 9.
50. C. Battersea, *Reminiscences* (1922), p. 21.
51. N. Bentwich, 'Claude Montefiore and his Tutor in Rabbinics: Founders of Liberal and Conservative Judaism', 6th Montefiore Memorial Lecture, Southampton (1966), p. 12.
52. E. Kessler, *An English Jew: The Life and Writings of Claude Montefiore* (1989), p. 15.
53. E. Black, *The Social Politics of Anglo-Jewry* (1988), p. 24.
54. For example, Montefiore was asked to contribute to *The Jewish Encyclopædia* by Rabbi Prof. Gotthard Deutsch of Hebrew Union College in 1897. He turned down the opportunity to contribute articles concerning the state of liberal Judaism in England, however, owing to other commitments. MS 123/3/2, Gotthard Deutsch Papers, A.J.A.C.
55. Cited in W.R. Matthews, 'Claude Montefiore: The Man and his Thought', 1st Claude Montefiore Lecture, Southampton (1956), p. 24. Likewise,

Montefiore was very taken with Baeck. 'I have never met a more distinguished minister of religion in any sect, indeed, a more distinguished and
charming man. No wonder that he told me that the fidelity with which
many of his Christian friends had stuck to him since 1933 had amazed
and deeply gratified him. He is altogether an oddity and a sweet oddity.'
Letter from C.G. Montefiore to Lucy Cohen, 26 January 1937. L. Cohen,
Some Recollections of Claude Goldsmid-Montefiore 1858–1938 (1940), p. 245.

56. C. Bermant, *The Cousinhood: The Anglo-Jewish Gentry* (1971), p. 319.

57. A selection of committees with which Montefiore was involved includes:
Russian-Jewish Relief Committee, Jewish Association for the Protection
of Girls and Women, West London Synagogue Association, World Union
of Progressive Judaism, Anglo-Jewish Association, Conjoint Foreign
Committee, Jewish Colonisation Association, Alliance Israélite Universelle,
Jewish Religious Education Board, several school management commit-
tees, London School Board, General Purpose Committee for Southampton
University, London Society for the Study of Religion, Society for the
Diffusion of Religious Knowledge, Jewish Historical Society, Oxford
Theological Society, Society of Biblical Archaeology.

58. Montefiore's appeals for strikers in 1890, for example, were made with the
support of Chief Rabbi Hermann Adler. *Jewish Chronicle*, 4 April 1890, p. 6.

59. One example among many was the relief fund he established for Russian
Jews suffering the pogroms of 1905, which was controversial for his
insistence that none of the money collected would be used to repatriate
Jews in Palestine. *Jewish Chronicle*, 17 November 1905, p. 24.

60. C. Bermant, *The Cousinhood: The Anglo-Jewish Gentry* (1971), p. 320.
Henriques was also involved in plans for a Girls' Club in the East End, to
complement his St George's Boys' Club. *Jewish Chronicle*, 9 July 1915, p. 10.
Another example of Montefiore's interest in children was his proposal
to the West London Synagogue Association that a Jewish children's
magazine should be established to stimulate interest in Judaism in that
same way that he felt general literature did for Christianity. *Jewish Chronicle*, 12 February 1897, p. 20.

61. L. Cohen, *Some Recollections of Claude Goldsmid-Montefiore 1858–1938* (1940),
pp. 147, 69.

62. One surprise among his numerous donations to relief work, and to educational and social organisations such as Jewish Working Lads clubs,
schools, and universities, was his financial support for the Orthodox training college, Jews' College, since at least 1892 when he donated his £100
fee for the Hibbert Lectures. *Jewish Chronicle*, 1 July 1892, p. 8. The Liberal
Jewish Synagogue, as an organisation, explicitly chose not to support it.
Jewish Chronicle, 14 November 1918, p. 14.

63. Cited by Judge Jacob J. Kaplan, 'Claude Montefiore: The Man and his
Works', address delivered during Jewish Book Week (14 May 1939). MS
16/12/4, World Union for Progressive Judaism Records, A.J.A.C.

64. Montefiore assisted Mr Horatio Micholls in giving elocution lessons. The
kindergarten had been introduced by Lady Louisa Goldsmid, a relative of
Montefiore's. *Jewish Chronicle*, 14 July 1882, p. 7.

65. It was largely due to his support that the Institute obtained a permanent
centre at Grove House, Roehampton, at which there is a Montefiore wing.
L. Cohen, *Some Recollections of Claude Goldsmid-Montefiore 1858–1938* (1940),
p. 55.

66. From around the time of the death of his father in 1883, Montefiore contributed considerable money, time and energy to the Westminster Jewish

Free, Hanway Street School, and the Buckle Street and Commercial Street Jewish Infant Schools. Phyllis Abrahams (daughter of Israel Abrahams), 'Claude Goldsmid-Montefiore', *Synagogue Review* (January 1962), p. 135; L. Cohen, *Some Recollections of Claude Goldsmid-Montefiore 1858–1938* (1940), p. 46; *Jewish Chronicle*, 2 November 1894, p. 8. He was vice president of Westminster school from 1884 and was responsible, among other things, for financing their carpentry class for 15 months. *Jewish Chronicle*, 1 February 1884, p. 7 and 3 February 1888, p. 3.

67. Montefiore described two hours of evening study in a Talmud Torah after school as 'positively cruel'. *Jewish Chronicle*, 9 February 1894, p. 7. His own standards were exacting, however, and two-hour examinations were not unheard of. *Jewish Chronicle*, 7 October 1887, p. 11. He regularly travelled as far north as Manchester in his capacity as examiner. *Jewish Chronicle*, 31 March 1893, p. 19.

68. *Jewish Chronicle*, 20 June 1890, p. 6 and 4 July 1890, p. 5.

69. Montefiore even assisted in arranging special provision for their Orthodox dietary requirements. *Jewish Chronicle*, 28 July 1893, p. 6 and 2 November 1894, p. 8.

70. The placements were to be for two years. *Jewish Chronicle*, 29 December 1893, p. 9.

71. *Jewish Chronicle*, 17 February 1888, p. 3. Montefiore was defeated in the 1894 election. *Jewish Chronicle*, 30 November 1894, pp. 9, 11.

72. Attention was drawn to his 'special training in the management of schools'. *Jewish Chronicle*, 8 November 1895, p. 6.

73. Montagu wished to make it clear that although he 'thoroughly appreciated' Montefiore's secular work, he believed that neither Montefiore nor Israel Abrahams should sit on the Jewish Religious Education Board. He passed a motion 'that a letter be sent to [Chief Rabbi] Dr Adler and the Beth Din, signed by Sir Samuel Montagu on behalf of the Federation of Synagogues, to the following effect. To ask "Is anyone who publicly rejects the Mosaic Law and the Ten Commandments a suitable member of the Jewish Religious Education Board?"'. *Jewish Chronicle*, 22 December 1905, p. 22.

74. *Jewish Chronicle*, 27 July 1906, p. 7.

75. *Jewish Chronicle*, 29 October 1909, p. 6.

76. In his resignation letter, Montefiore noted that he had previously offered to resign as soon as either the president of the Educational Board or the Chief Rabbi felt he should do so. The Chief Rabbi explained his acceptance of Montefiore's resignation due to the fact that Montefiore now 'proposes steps to carry out practically opinions antagonistic to our teachings'. *Jewish Chronicle*, 29 October 1909, p. 20.

77. In 1891 Montefiore agreed to upgrade the lectureship to a readership, and to provide a further £250 on top of the £100 p.a. he was already donating, for as long as Schechter held the position. *Jewish Chronicle*, 4 December 1991, p. 6.

78. Montefiore was elected president in March 1913. *Jewish Chronicle*, 21 March 1913, p. 22. 'Montefiore' in *Dictionary of National Biography*, p. 625.

79. W.R. Matthews, 'Claude Montefiore: the Man and his Thought', 1st Claude Montefiore Lecture, Southampton (1956), p. 3.

80. The *Jewish Quarterly Review* was first announced in September 1887. *Jewish Chronicle*, 16 September 1887, p. 13. In November, Montefiore and Abrahams were complaining that there had not been enough subscriptions to begin. *Jewish Chronicle*, 4 November 1887, p. 6.

81. *Encyclopaedia Judaica* (1971), p. 977.

82. The editor of the *Jewish Chronicle* complained, 'One annual meeting of the AJA is necessarily very much like another … less than 50 subscribers attended last Sunday, out of the 700 who reside in the Metropolis.' *Jewish Chronicle*, 5 July 1901, p. 17.

83. Montefiore's nomination, reported in November 1895, followed the retirement of Sir Julian Montefiore, who had been preceded as president by Prof. Jacob Waley and Baron Henry de Worms. *Jewish Chronicle*, 8 November 1895, p. 6. His election in December was met with general support, and a warm welcome by the Chief Rabbi. *Jewish Chronicle*, 6 December 1895, p. 13.

84. Montefiore believed that the A.J.A. and the Alliance Israélite Universelle 'really pursue the same ends and are practically the same body'. *Jewish Chronicle*, 8 May 1896, p. 16. He often seemed to follow the lead of the Alliance Israélite Universelle, for example, in making appeals for the relief of Russian Jews in June 1900. *Jewish Chronicle*, 29 June 1900, p. 8.

85. *Jewish Chronicle*, 27 March 1896, p. 25 and 10 April 1896, p. 25.

86. *Jewish Chronicle*, 3 November 1905, p. 11.

87. According to Montefiore, the new constitution for Anglo-Jewish Association was 'an outcome of the conference with the provincial branches'. Provincial representatives were to have a double vote 'in order to increase the interest of the branches in their work … [They] had complained, and he thought with some reason, that they had nothing to do, but were collecting agencies.' *Jewish Chronicle*, 15 June 1906, p. 22.

88. *Jewish Chronicle*, 16 July 1897, p. 13 and 13 July 1900, p. 22.

89. *Jewish Chronicle*, 16 July 1897, p. 13 and 17 December 1917, p. 16.

90. Montefiore's cousin, Lucy Cohen, recalls him wishing that he had a peerage. 'It would be so good for my begging', he explained. L. Cohen, *Some Recollections of Claude Goldsmid-Montefiore 1858–1938* (1940), p. 151.

91. *Jewish Chronicle*, 5 July 1901, p. 17. Montefiore suggested that 'the Anglo-Jewish Association had been very useful as a sort of intelligence bureau in regard to the Jews of the East'. *Jewish Chronicle*, 6 February 1903, p. 16. Many would have agreed with the *Jewish Chronicle* that 'The Anglo-Jewish Association performs one very useful function in the communal economy. It provides an annual opportunity for a number of distinguished Jews publicly to review the situation and prospects of the Jewish race. Apart from this body, we know of no organisation which offers the same striking opportunity for this important operation.' *Jewish Chronicle*, 5 July 1901, p. 11.

92. Montefiore had accepted the presidency as part of his 'duty to the community and to the religious brotherhood of the Jews as a whole'. *Jewish Chronicle* , 6 December 1895, p. 13.

93. November 1905 was one occasion at which Montefiore argued with the Zionists as to the nature of the A.J.A. '[T]he predominant ideal of the Anglo-Jewish Association has been, and still is, that of each country where communities of Jews exist, our brethren should become its children and its citizens.' *Jewish Chronicle*, 3 November 1905, p. 11.

94. Montefiore explained, '[T]his watching brief is not often translatable into action' due to 'lack of power … It must not be forgotten that public demonstrations when they can do no good are quite likely to do harm. And that is why, though such forms of procedure may relieve the feelings, and give the inward and imaginary consolation that we are "doing something", not merely sitting still in our comfortable English armchairs, with our hands in our pockets, listless, and at ease, calmer and wiser counsellors will prefer to encounter the easy charge of cowardice and indifference, rather

than to do anything which, while not endangering their own welfare, might be harmful to their unfortunate brethren abroad.' *Jewish Chronicle,* 5 July 1901, p. 18.

95. A close and influential friend was Lord Alfred Milner. At one speech at an A.J.A. dinner he criticised 'interfering with the domestic affairs of foreign countries, always a thing which has to be done with the greatest care and circumspection. I am bound to say that as far as I know ... the Association has not transgressed the legitimate bonds which the citizens of one country must always observe in expressing their opinions and bringing their influence to bear on the affairs of another.' *Jewish Chronicle,* 9 May 1913, p. 20.

96. As early as 1896, Montefiore argued, 'putting for the moment Russia and Roumania on one side, persecution and outrage was becoming undoubtedly and satisfactorily less'. This 'amelioration' was due to vigilance and that the English Foreign Office supported and co-operated with the A.J.A. *Jewish Chronicle,* 27 March 1896, p. 25. In 1902, Montefiore took Dr Theodore Herzl to task for having pessimistically and falsely claimed at the Alien Commission that the Argentine colonies were a failure. *Jewish Chronicle,* 18 July 1902, p. 15.

97. Montefiore argued, 'Two factors of hope there are for the Jews of Russia ... there are many sound-healthy elements in the Russian people themselves ... [and in] the Russian Jews. We know that in London, and it has been recognised also in America.' *Jewish Chronicle,* 5 July 1901, p. 9.

98. Montefiore was hopeful that, 'If the good results of the Russian Revolution are permanent, if freedom and citizenship continue to be the lot and the right of all the Jewish inhabitants of Russia, then they must, and they will, work out their own salvation. They will neither need our help nor ask it.' *Jewish Chronicle,* 9 November 1917, p. 13.

99. Montefiore reported that he and David Alexander had decided to approach the English government, but discovered before they arrived that the necessary steps had already been taken: 'So far as the English government is concerned, all has been done that can be done.' Montefiore accepted that the atrocities were worse and on a greater scale than at Kishineff and Homel, but he argued against public demonstrations since the troubles were not due to 'a passive Russia' but to the 'political revolution'. *Jewish Chronicle,* 17 November 1905, p. 16.

100. *Jewish Chronicle,* 17 November 1905, p. 16.

101. *Jewish Chronicle,* 15 July 1921, p. 8. The overall tone of the comments was polite and laudatory.

102. The L.S.S.R. was formed in 1904 mainly through the efforts of Joseph H. Wicksteed and Baron Von Hügel, who had been introduced to each other by Montefiore. L. Barmann, 'Confronting Secularization: Origins of the London Society for the Study of Religion', *Church History,* LXII, no. 1 (March 1993), p. 22; L. Cohen, *Some Recollections of Claude Goldsmid-Montefiore 1858–1938* (1940), p. 83.

103. E. Kessler, 'Claude Montefiore', *Jewish-Christian Relations,* XXI (Winter 1988), p. 7.

104. A full bibliography is provided in E. Kessler, *An English Jew: The Life and Writings of Claude Montefiore* (1989), pp. 198–205.

105. 800 copies were sold within six weeks of its publication. *Jewish Chronicle,* 24 February 1893, p. 6. His older sister, Alice, wrote a poem to celebrate Claude's success. L. Cohen, *Some Recollections of Claude Goldsmid-Montefiore 1858–1938* (1940), p. 58.

Respected reader, you behold/Within this book, my Hibbert lectures./How many copies have been sold/ At present baffles all conjectures./But this I certainly can say,/In fact, I think you ought to know it,/I've given eighty-eight away/And one, of course, to dear B. Jowett.

The Lectures claim your best attention/But ere you study them tonight,/There's just one thing I'd like to mention/In spite of helps and hints no end,/The very list of which would bore you,/I venture to remind my friend,/'Twas I who wrote the book before you.

106. J. Rayner, 'C.G. Montefiore; his Religious Teaching', *The Synagogue Review*, XXXII (June 1958), p. 256.
107. *A Rabbinic Anthology*, published posthumously, was written in collaboration with Herbert Loewe.
108. The second volume of *The Bible for Home Reading* was treated to a lengthy, highly positive review in the *Jewish Chronicle* which ran over three editions, and concluded that it was 'as masterly as it is spiritual, as scholarly as it is attractive'. *Jewish Chronicle*, 30 June 1899, p. 20. The *Jewish Chronicle* noted that the book had been chosen by Dr Berkowitz, rabbi of Synagogue 'Rodef Shalom' in Philadelphia, as his textbook for open study sessions. *Jewish Chronicle*, 6 November 1896, p. 16. It was also observed that it had received a favourable review in *Theologisch Tijdschrift*, 'one of the most important theological reviews on the Continent'. *Jewish Chronicle*, 12 February 1897, p. 14.

2

Historiography

Considering his importance to Anglo-Jewry in terms of his communal leadership and representative responsibilities, his founding role in Liberal Judaism, his eminence as a scholar, and his philanthropic activities, remarkably little has been written about Claude Montefiore. Apart from the eclectic and unrepresentative biographical study by Lucy Cohen, *Some Recollections of Claude Goldsmid-Montefiore* (1940), Maurice Bowler's short treatment of *Claude Montefiore and Christianity* (1988) and Edward Kessler's anthology of Montefiore's writings in *An English Jew* (1989), there have been no books specifically concerned with Montefiore's life or his thought.[109] It is not difficult to find further material, however, since his influence and writings impinged upon many areas of late nineteenth- and early twentieth-century thought. Thus the remainder of the historiography relating to Montefiore is composed of historical studies of Reform Judaism and Anglo-Jewry, together with articles and tributes from works of Jewish thought, Jewish–Christian relations and biblical and New Testament studies.

MAJOR TREATMENTS

Lucy Cohen's *Some Recollections of Claude Goldsmid-Montefiore* (1940), published only two years after his death, was never intended as a true biography or analytical history. Rather, it was an admiring relation's attempt to preserve and record something of the essence of the man. Approached as such, it provides important information about his character, and his familial and social surroundings. In terms of primary source material, it is most useful from 1918, when Montefiore was 60 and Cohen became a more intimate confidante. Cohen herself admitted, 'If only I had known him as intimately before he was sixty as after, in those days when his ideas of religious reform were evolving, and when his hopes were high, the picture would be more vivid.'[110] As a consequence, much of the earlier biographical detail depends upon the reminiscences of mutual friends and associates. The loose, anachronistic composition of the book, whose form is largely dependent upon recurrent themes in the correspondence between Montefiore and Cohen, makes it difficult to contextualise his thought or to understand it. There is a chapter, for example, entitled 'Chassidic Myths' (as a result of the fact that Cohen translated some of Martin Buber's writings on the subject with advice from Montefiore) whose inclusion has encouraged more than one scholar to over-estimate the significance of mysticism to Montefiore.[111] Nor does the fact that Cohen 'did not feel equal to making a more exhaustive selection from his letters to other friends'[112] make the task of tracing the development of his thought any easier. As she observes in the preface, 'a great part of [Montefiore] will remain unrevealed; what mattered most to him was his religion, and with this I am quite inadequate to deal'.[113] Despite her interest in Montefiore's religious activities, Cohen was unfamiliar with the development (both intellectual and institutional) of Liberal Judaism, nor could she have commented critically on the more original aspects of his thought, including his treatment of Jesus and Paul, and what he described as the theology of the rabbis. Considering that *Some Recollections* is the most commonly cited work in writings about Montefiore, these points are worth bearing in mind. As Basil Henriques, a disciple of Montefiore, wrote privately, 'Miss Lucy Cohen's biography is very inadequate, although it gives a good pen picture of his character'.[114] Her memoir certainly gives a sense of what it meant to belong to the Anglo-Jewish elite at that time; it also occasionally hints at his sense of alienation from the Anglo-Jewish community. In addition, it presents a less austere, more whimsical picture of Montefiore than one would otherwise have obtained from his scholarly writings.

The best introduction to Montefiore's thought is Edward Kessler's *An English Jew: The Life and Writings of Claude Montefiore* (1989). While his thematic presentation of selected extracts from Montefiore's writings can only skim the surface, it does provide access for the modern reader who does not have the time to wade through volumes of Montefiore's beautifully written but often heavy prose. Kessler includes a short biographical piece, largely dependent upon Cohen's *Some Recollections*, and introduces each section (on the Hebrew Bible, Christianity and the New Testament, Torah and Rabbinic Judaism, and Modern Judaism) with brief explanatory notes. In his sometimes uneven conclusion, he considers Montefiore as an eclectic scholar, a radical theologian, a defender of Rabbinic Judaism, and a liberal leader, but at no point does he engage with Montefiore's writings in the light of modern thought or scholarship.

Kessler's view of Montefiore is somewhat idealised. The book is, as Louis Jacobs' review reminds us, Kessler's 'account of his hero's life and thought'.[115] Regarding Montefiore's scholarship, for example, Kessler concludes: 'The fact that Christian scholars attacked him for being too Jewish and Jewish scholars for being too Christian is one indication that he approached the neutral position which he sought.'[116] In fact it was Montefiore's determination to demonstrate the superiority of Liberal Judaism over both Christianity and Judaism (in what he regarded as their conventional forms), that put him in this position, since many of his Jewish critics associated his Liberal Judaism with Christianity and his Christian critics often mistakenly believed that he spoke for Judaism. Thus Kessler confuses neutrality with an alternative bias of Montefiore's own making. Similarly, in an earlier article, he argued that Montefiore had been 'the least tendentious' scholar among both his Christian and Jewish contemporaries,[117] which is certainly true if by this he meant that Montefiore was as likely to criticise Judaism as he was Christianity; but Kessler appears at times to overlook the fact that Montefiore certainly had a religious agenda of his own and was concerned to advance it. No one is arguing that Montefiore was a *bad* scholar, but his writings cannot be properly appreciated unless the dialectical relationship between the scholarship that informed his Liberal Judaism, and the Liberal Jewish agenda that lay behind his scholarship, is recognised. His writings *were* designed to advance a cause, and in that sense they were indeed tendentious.

In the context of Jewish–Christian dialogue there is a common view of Montefiore that Kessler endorses when he describes him as 'the interpreter *par excellence* of Judaism to Christians and Christians to Jews'.[118] This view fails to fully comprehend that Montefiore belonged to a rarefied minority of thinkers, mainly comprising liberal Christians, whose views of the two religions would have satisfied very few members of either faith community.

It can (and will) be argued that Montefiore, as an outsider, spoke for neither camp. In making claims associated with Jewish–Christian dialogue, Kessler can be criticised for failing to have adequately stressed Montefiore's religious beliefs as essentially individualist, and for neglecting to have considered in what ways Montefiore had misunderstood or misrepresented both Christianity and Judaism. He makes no attempt, for example, to analyse apparent paradoxes or tensions in Montefiore's loyalties, such as his fierce defence of rabbinic thought (against Christian critique) and his championing of liberation from the Law and authority, tensions that disappear when the nature of Montefiore's allegiance to each camp is properly understood.[119]

A more significant omission, however, is Kessler's failure to attempt to explain precisely what it was about Montefiore that provoked Jewish accusations implying his crypto-Christianity and 'un-Jewishness'. The answer to this complex question is hinted at but never tackled head on, yet it is vital to understanding Montefiore – namely, the influence of Christianity. Both in terms of social influences (such as the environment in which he grew up and his Oxford education) and in terms of intellectual influences (such as contemporary Christian theology and the teachings of Jesus and Paul), Montefiore absorbed and re-cast Christian thought to suit his own needs. In failing to explore the depth of this dependence and the factors responsible for his hero's attraction to non-Jewish sources, Kessler's work leaves many questions unanswered. His anthology outlines Montefiore's thought admirably, but it does not go further and ask: What made it so?

Maurice Bowler's *Claude Montefiore and Christianity* (1988) was published in the Brown Judaic Studies series (edited by Jacob Neusner) a year before Kessler's *An English Jew*. A combination of a M.Phil. thesis and some previously written articles, this short work shows signs of hasty composition and a certain amount of repetition.[120] Its great strength, however, lies in its perception of the importance of Christian influences upon Montefiore and his thought. Bowler highlights the fact that Protestant Christianity was 'the dominant factor' of the time and surroundings,[121] regards Montefiore as very much the product of Christian Victorian England, and finds it significant that 'a vital factor of Jewish life, the close interaction of a tightly knit [Jewish] community, seems to have been missing from his life'.[122]

Moreover, in contrast to Kessler, Bowler attempts to analyse Montefiore's reaction to Christianity, which he describes as 'a Jewish synthesis'. Thus he focuses upon Montefiore's hopes that one day there would be a merging of the best of the two religions.[123] From this point of view, Montefiore's sympathies for and interest in Christianity seemed, to Bowler, entirely explicable:

> A businessman engaged in a desperate struggle for survival against a rival firm might denigrate his rival's products. But if he could foresee a future take-over of the rival firm, it would be in his interests to praise and protect everything in the rival establishment which he intended to incorporate into his own enterprise.[124]

There is no doubt that Montefiore believed that many of the orthodox trappings of Christianity were falling away and that the two religions were coming closer together, theologically. Rather than view them as rivals, he saw Judaism and Christianity as offering complementary teachings, and he felt free to incorporate any Christian teachings that added to and enhanced what he regarded as the basic truths underlying Judaism. Unfortunately, Bowler's work is weakened in two ways. Firstly, in common with the majority of writings on Montefiore in the context of Jewish thought or Jewish–Christian relations, Bowler fails to analyse in any detail how Montefiore felt about specific New Testament passages, why they were of relevance to Liberal Judaism, and how they could actually be used. In a review of Bowler, Joshua Stein remains unclear as to the relation of Liberal Judaism to the life and teaching of the historic Jesus, as well as to the books of the New Testament, and suggests that this is one of the most important matters which has yet to be taken in hand.[125] Secondly, Bowler never really gets to grips with the nature of Liberal Judaism. After reading the study, Richard Libowitz is left wondering how the Holocaust and the creation of the State of Israel would have affected Montefiore's ideas.[126] Such a question reflects poorly on Bowler's presentation of Montefiore's Liberal Judaism and the profoundly anti-nationalist sentiments which lay at the heart of his theology (Montefiore blamed antisemitism at least partially on the Zionists). For Bowler, 'Christianity' and 'Judaism' remain as theological abstracts, and the one attempt made to identify a historical Christian parallel from which Montefiore drew inspiration (Newman's Tractarianism) is quite unsatisfactory.[127] As a result, Bowler's work is a good example of the need for augmentation by historically informed treatments.

HISTORICAL STUDIES OF REFORM JUDAISM AND ANGLO-JEWRY

David Philipson's history, *The Reform Movement in Judaism* (2nd edition 1931), deals fleetingly with Montefiore in a chapter entitled, 'The Latest Developments in Europe'. He describes Montefiore as 'this most distinguished figure in the ranks of liberal Judaism in England, who has fought the fight for religious enlightenment for decades'.[128] Primarily interested in the institutional growth of British Liberal Judaism, from spontaneous attempts to revitalise Jewish religion via the Jewish Religious Union to the Liberal Jewish Synagogue, Philipson is unconcerned with Montefiore's thought. He is portrayed as a pro-active, reform minded Jew (whose role is exaggerated at the expense of Lily Montagu), anxious to retain British Jews who were abandoning Judaism in response to modernity.[129] The image of a reluctant schismatic is very much reinforced by the absence of references to Montefiore's writings. Thus there is no mention of his hostility towards Zionism, his non-nationalist conception of Judaism, or his fascination with Christianity.

An unpublished thesis by Frederick Schwartz, 'Anglo-Jewish Theology at the Turn of the Twentieth Century' (1959), represents the earliest serious attempt to understand elements of Montefiore's thought in a historical context. Specifically, Schwartz points to Benjamin Jowett's teaching and Hellenistic thought as the main influences upon Montefiore's Liberal Judaism and his views on Jesus and Christianity.[130] Jowett's writings are combed for parallels to Montefiore with illuminating results, but Schwartz's analysis of Hellenistic concepts is less satisfactory, mainly due to his failure to take into account the way in which classical thought had been unconsciously modified in the late nineteenth century. Another failing is that, despite his emphasis upon Montefiore's belief in the (Christian) principle of love as an antidote to particular dangers in Judaism,[131] Schwartz continues to treat Christianity as a subject which this particular Jew approached out of personal interest, rather than as part of a symbiotic relationship that ultimately shaped both the content and expression of Montefiore's theology.

Chaim Bermant's history of the Anglo-Jewish gentry, *The Cousinhood* (1971), has a chapter dedicated to Montefiore. As one might have expected, Bermant paints his subject in bright, bold colours and succeeds beautifully in portraying him as an eccentric member of the Anglo-Jewish elite, a turn-of-the-century gentleman-scholar whose quintessential Englishness was as important to him as was his Jewishness. In particular, his anti-nationalist stance against Zionism ('it certainly frightened Montefiore') and his ambivalent attitude towards intermarriage – both issues which divided the Cousinhood – are treated with considerable insight.[132] Montefiore's charitable activities (including his work for the Jewish Association for the Protection of Women and Children), and his educational concerns (including his role in developing Southampton University) are covered in some detail, but his life's work of Liberal Judaism and his scholarship are poorly handled and, in several cases, seriously misrepresented. At one point his Liberal Jewish theology is equated to Unitarianism,[133] and, at another, simplistically explained as differing from Orthodoxy mainly in terms of revelation and authority.[134] No mention whatsoever is made about his writings on Christianity, or its relation to Judaism. Bermant's reliance on Cohen's *Some Recollections* is one of the factors contributing to this superficial treatment (despite being full of human interest) of the man they both described as a Prophet.

After Montefiore the Prophet appears Montefiore the Mystic. Steven Bayme's essay, 'Claude Montefiore, Lily Montagu and the Origins of the Jewish Religious Union' (1982),[135] makes two claims of particular interest. Maintaining that Montefiore's thought did not diverge noticeably from that of Abraham Geiger and other Reform theologians, he argues instead that 'Montefiore's originality lay *in his mysticism* and his approach to Christianity' (italics mine).[136] He also suggests that Montefiore's opposition to religious legalism was limited by the need to endorse 'whatever would bind people together', including Sabbath worship, dietary laws and intermarriage.[137] As has already been mentioned briefly regarding mysticism, Bayme in fact over-emphasises a marginal and often misunderstood aspect of Montefiore's thought. No distinction is made between the sort of mysticism which Montefiore consistently eschewed (as found in Hasidism, for example) and his concern to cultivate a sense of intimate devotion within the individual (largely in emulation of certain Christian circles).[138] Similarly, Bayme underestimates Montefiore's commitment to follow through his principle of freedom from scriptural and 'ecclesiastical' authority. While Montefiore was not fundamentalist in his opposition to religious legalism and certainly made concessions on various issues, the centrality of religious freedom and rationalism to his liberal theology cannot be over-stressed. (In point of fact, while Montefiore did himself observe the dietary laws, he argued against them in principle, was involved in many non-Sabbath worship activities, and even supported a sister to marry a professing Christian.) Bayme's unconventional assessment is not so much the result of mis-reading Montefiore but rather a failure to place Montefiore's comments in context and to weigh them against the rest of his writings. One possible reason for this may be an over-dependence upon material from the *Jewish Chronicle* in which, for obvious reasons, Montefiore tended to tone down his more radical ideas. Another mistake which reflects a superficial familiarity with Montefiore's writings is Bayme's assertion that Israel Abrahams followed and further developed Montefiore's ideas. In fact, Abrahams was never as radical as his friend Montefiore, who readily admitted his intellectual indebtedness to Abrahams with regard to matters rabbinic.[139] On the positive side, the essay provides a needed corrective to the traditional down-playing of Lily Montagu's role in the Jewish Religious Union, while at the same time recognising that 'the movement owed more to the intellectual leadership of a single man than did its counterparts in Europe and America'.[140] In contrast to other American historians, Bayme readily admits that Montefiore 'gave Liberal Judaism in Britain particular forms not found in any other Reform movement' and properly identifies Montefiore's 'serious inspection of Christian teachings' as a main factor in this.[141]

Michael Meyer's seminal work, *Response to Modernity* (1988), was the long awaited replacement of Philipson's history of the world-wide Jewish Reform movement. As far as Montefiore and Anglo-Liberal Judaism are concerned, it is a vast improvement both in terms of institutional and intellectual history.[142] Even so, in a book of almost 500 pages, there is only one short section on 'Liberal Judaism in England and France' with less than eight pages dedicated to Montefiore. One reason for this is Meyer's concentration upon German and American Reform and his assumption that, crudely speaking, Anglo-Reform Judaism is best understood as German Reform Judaism with an English accent. Thus Montefiore's Liberal Judaism 'resembled the German variety which he had discovered [at Oxford]', and its character-istic teachings included ethical monotheism, the Mission of Israel, anti-nationalism, and a view of ritual as inessential.[143] This need not be the case, however. Montefiore's conception of Liberal Judaism was greatly influenced by English liberal Christianity, principally Broad Church (Oxford) Anglicanism. In their respective responses to modernity, German and English Jews had taken different models (the Germans looking to Lutheran Protestantism and Rationalism) and had expressed themselves independently. Having an indigenous alternative that can account for many of the characteristics of Montefiore's Liberal Judaism means that the parallels with German Reform Judaism need not indicate the priority of German influence. Crucially, Meyer also fails to explain adequately the extent of Montefiore's fascination with Christianity and the degree to which he set himself the task of responding to the challenge of Christian theology, despite citing Montefiore's belief that Jowett's religious teaching 'can be translated, and it needs to be trans-lated, into Jewish'.[144] His portrayal of Montefiore does not fully appreciate the man's individual creativity, and although, at times, he seems close to sensing how much Christianity was part of Montefiore's psyche,[145] his assessment is marred by the long shadow cast by German Reform. One might also complain that, in the light of Lucy Cohen's memoirs and the evidence of his cor-respondence, Meyer's Montefiore is too stuffy and humourless.

Finally, it is worth considering briefly the ways in which Montefiore is represented in general Anglo-Jewish histories, and the limitations imposed by adopting an exclusively socio-political approach. Invariably, he is categorised in one of two ways. Those historical studies with a sociological bent are most interested in Montefiore in the context of the Anglo-Jewish elite and in terms of assimilation, while those with a political emphasis concen-trate upon Montefiore's anti-Zionist, pro-English activities. Both types neglect his development of theologically-orientated Judaism and his proto-dialogue with Christians.

Of the first kind, David Englander's article, 'Anglicised but not Anglican' (1988),[146] provides an essential key to understanding Anglo-Jewish psychology, especially that of the Cousinhood, namely, the influence of the British Establishment and the established Church. From a comparative perspective, Englander identifies those characteristics of both Reform and Orthodox Judaism that embarrassed nineteenth- and early twentieth-century middle-class Jews and which led them to emulate English socio-religious norms. In so doing, he provides a useful background for analysing what it was that Montefiore found lacking in conventional Anglo-Jewish religious practice and in what ways he believed his Liberal Judaism could offer an alternative. Touching upon Liberal Judaism itself very briefly, Englander portrays Montefiore and 'the liberal separatists' as somewhat eccentric, and their movement as 'denationalised spiritualism'.[147] Writing from a similar perspective, Todd Endelman's *Radical Assimilation in English Jewish History* (1990) contains two references to Montefiore. In the first case he uses Montefiore's early life as an example of the way in which the Anglo-Jewish elite surrounded themselves with non-Jewish company (quoting Montefiore's claim that 'Our environment was entirely uncosmopolitan and purely English.')[148] The second reference concerns Montefiore's unhappy confirmation that anti-Jewish feeling was on the increase at the time of Morris Joseph's talk to the A.J.A. in 1913 on antisemitic tendencies in England'[149]

Historical studies of the second category include Geoffrey Alderman's *Modern British Jewry* (1992), which focuses upon Montefiore's anti-Zionist agenda in the context of the League of British Jews and the Anglo-Jewish Association.[150] The Liberal Jewish movement is also viewed from this angle and is described as 'a religious refuge for anti-Zionists in the inter-war period'.[151] In *Englishmen and Jews* (1994), David Feldman is only interested in Montefiore's early article 'Is Judaism a Tribal Religion?' (1882), and in setting Montefiore beside Chief Rabbi Hermann Adler as a British proponent of the idea of Judaism as a religious rather than a racial phenomenon. Thus he quotes Montefiore's claim that even Orthodox Judaism was now taught as 'pure religious universalism'[152] and also picks up on Montefiore's belief in the 'Mission of Israel' and the important role a non-tribal Judaism could play in the Progress of Mankind. Montefiore is portrayed as a super-patriot and a representative of a modern, universal faith whose aims were compromised by the influx of the first large wave of eastern immigrants during the 1880s.[153] Stuart

Cohen's *English Zionists and British Jews* (1982) also focuses upon Montefiore's highly developed sense of Englishness and what is viewed as a correspondingly conservative stance with regard to reform within communal institutions.[154] In *The Social Politics of Anglo-Jewry* (1988) Eugene Black's short treatment of Montefiore centres on his sermon 'One God, One Worship' (February 1896), which is used as an early demonstration of the anti-Zionism he would champion as President of the Anglo-Jewish Association; his 'patriotic, even jingoistic' tendencies are also emphasised.[155] Lastly, there is Anne Kershen and Jonathan Romain's *Tradition and Change: A History of Reform Judaism in Britain* (1995), which, as an institutional history, is best approached for the organisational development of Liberal Judaism. In addition to the usual references to Montefiore the Anti-Zionist, he is also referred to in the context of the Jewish Religious Union where he is presented as an ultra-radical, although no reference is made to any radical aspect of his thought, nor do the authors mention his relations with Christianity or its influence upon him.

STUDIES IN JEWISH THOUGHT AND JEWISH–CHRISTIAN
RELATIONS

Very few of the articles, essays and tributes that attempt assessments of Montefiore in the context of 'Jewish thought' or 'Jewish–Christian relations' examine his writings in any depth. This in itself is enough to warrant a more extensive study, but there is also the fact that almost all of them fail to heed Montefiore's own warnings that he looked at religion 'through the spectacles of Liberal Judaism'.[156] Without understanding the nature and roots of his peculiar theology and recognising the centrality of its principles to his thought, most writers are not able to contextualise his writings on Judaism and Christianity, and consequently over-emphasise the significance of one aspect or another. They are either at a loss to explain his sympathy for Christianity, or else they categorise him as an apologist for the traditional enemy. None succeeds in producing a balanced portrait of Montefiore which, without a sense of artificiality, can reconcile his sympathetic approach to Christianity, his criticisms of Orthodox and Reform Judaism, his academic defence of Rabbinic Judaism and the Law, and his own independence of thought and theology.

Crucially, none view Montefiore as a Liberal Jew whose beliefs incorporate, and therefore must defend, elements of Christian thought. The result has been a certain amount of confusion, much of which has never been resolved.

'The Contribution of Claude G. Montefiore to the Advancement of Judaism' (1928) by V.E. Reichert, an American, is one of the earliest assessments of Montefiore, written while its subject was still alive, and therefore provides an interesting perspective.[157] In particular, it is one of the few assessments that highlights the theological nature of Montefiore's conception of Liberal Judaism. Montefiore's hopes for the future of religion, combining complementary aspects of Judaism and Christianity, are viewed as 'condensations of the essentials of the moral law into good precepts'. Reichert contrasts Montefiore's 'extravagant emphasis upon utopian precepts' with the traditional Jewish concern for concrete teaching indispensable for actual conduct in life. In so doing, he accurately captures the spirit of Montefiore's religion:

> From such practical considerations Mr. Montefiore is by temperament removed. *His approach to Judaism is literary and theological.* He moves in a world of ideals. He is content to be a dreamer of prophetic Judaism that shall be wholly spiritual and universal.[158] (My italics)

This highlighting of the theological nature of Montefiore's teaching is significant because it demonstrates how American Reform Jews felt Montefiore's Judaism differed from their own. In fact, Reichert is keen to differentiate between mainstream Anglo-Liberal Jewish teaching and Montefiore's more radical thought; Montefiore's writings are not even to be regarded as 'an official deliverance' although, as Reichert puts it, 'his ties with the Liberal Jewish Synagog [sic] are very close'.[159] Thus from an early stage, Montefiore's Judaism had something about it with which neither German nor American Reform rabbis were quite comfortable. (This is a qualitative difference which Meyer's treatment, among others, fails to detect.)

Arnold Wolf, in his article, 'The Dilemma of Claude Montefiore' (1959), also identifies a distinctive theological angle. In considering Montefiore's interest in Christianity as one of various Jewish responses to 'the problem of Christianity', he suggests:

> [The problem] is not, as Klausner thinks, a national one; nor as Sandmel, a historical one; nor as Asch, mythopoetic. It is an issue, perhaps Montefiore would have said, *the* issue, of Jewish theology.[160]

For Wolf, this realisation that Montefiore's interest in Christianity was theologically driven explains the relative fierceness of Jewish criticism Montefiore received, in comparison with other scholars interested in Christianity, such as Martin Buber. For while Buber was unmistakably Jewish in theology, Montefiore found himself 'impaled on the horns of Liberalism'.[161] The liberal theology which animated his studies, and which placed truth above any creed, was Jewish only because, generally speaking, he found that 'Judaism' coincided with 'truth'. But this only raised the question in Jewish minds: What if it had not? The conclusion can only be that, as regards his theology, Montefiore was first a Liberal, and second a Jew. Wolf's analysis is let down, however, by his dismissal of the importance of Christianity to Montefiore and to his liberal outlook when he comments: 'What seems to be his "acceptance" of Christianity is often no more than the patronising friendliness of the nobleman.'[162] A vital element in the make-up of Montefiore's Liberal Jewish theology is thus overlooked.

Walter Jacob's *Christianity Through Jewish Eyes* (1974) likewise fails to understand the relevance of Christianity for Montefiore's Liberal Jewish thought, although for different reasons. Puzzled by his apparent enthusiasm for the traditional enemy, Jacob describes how Montefiore 'became an apologist for Christianity, seeking to present the best of that religion to his fellow Jews'.[163] While this is not incorrect, Jacob misses an important point by approaching Montefiore's sympathy for Christianity from the wrong perspective. Montefiore was not so much for or against Christianity, as *for Liberal Judaism*. Once the influence of Christian theological expression and certain teachings have been recognised, it becomes clear that Montefiore's alleged defence of Christianity is better understood as a defence of Liberal Judaism, in that Montefiore had absorbed and, in a sense, identified with, Christianity. Unfortunately, Jacob's view is reproduced in the most recent study of Montefiore, Dan Cohn-Sherbok's *Fifty Key Jewish Thinkers* (1997), where Montefiore is again simply compartmentalised as 'an apologist for the Christian faith'.[164]

Approaching Montefiore from a completely different angle is A.T. Hanson's article, 'A Modern Philo' (1977). It begins unpromisingly with a description of Liberal Judaism as 'a back to the Bible movement, comparable to the Karaite movement, but even more radical'.[165] (This is most unhelpful considering that Montefiore spent much time refuting the absolute authority of the Bible and since he regarded the rabbinic literature as a legitimate part of Jewish religious literature.) It goes on, however, to compare Montefiore to the first-century Jew, Philo, since both had incorporated into their Judaism 'the best culture of his day'.[166] This is interesting not least because Montefiore had himself referred to Philo approvingly on many occasions in his writings. While Hanson distinguishes between Philo's use of Hellenistic philosophy and Montefiore's use of modern, scientific thought, in fact, the two men were closer than he imagined. Montefiore consciously sought to enrich Liberal Judaism with Hellenistic thought, although in a modified form, better described as assimilated or Christianised Hellenism. Hanson also suggested that Montefiore's religion was one of 'high principles and idealist philosophy' (echoing Reichert). As a result, Montefiore had, like Philo, 'left one thing out, the God of history, the personal God who addresses men'.[167] Since this is a risk that all liberal theology runs, whether Christian or Jewish, Hanson's treatment amounts to a critique of Montefiore's liberalism (echoing Wolf).

A neat summary of how Montefiore and his liberal movement have generally been regarded within 'Jewish thought' studies is provided in Jacob Agus' article 'Claude Montefiore and Liberal Judaism' (1959):

> While in its basic tenets this group was merely the English branch of the world-wide Reform movement, Claude G. Montefiore was concerned principally with the diminution of the nationalistic elements in Judaism and with the revision of the Jewish attitude towards Jesus and the New Testament.[168]

Agus goes on to deal more controversially with what he describes as Montefiore's 'shocking' central thesis, 'namely, that Liberal Judaism accept the New Testament along with the Hebrew Bible and Talmud in its treasury of sacred literature'.[169] This is a serious accusation and one which, if it were widely accepted, would explain much of the hostility Montefiore has received at the hands of his co-religionists. Reichert recognised this when he insisted, 'But [Montefiore] has been very careful, despite the charge of some critics, to maintain that "at this time of day it is impossible for the Jew to make his Bible include the New Testament."'[170] It is also an accusation at odds with the assessments of other writers, such as Louis Jacobs who maintains, 'Montefiore was opposed to any attempt at placing the New Testament on a par with the Hebrew scriptures or having readings from the New Testament in any act of Jewish worship.'[171] It can (and will) be argued that Montefiore's feelings on the matter were ambiguous and that Agus greatly overstated his case. However much Montefiore might have wished to incorporate parts of the New Testament into the Liberal Jewish repertoire (and there is certainly evidence that he did wish to do so), there is no doubt that he simultaneously recognised the impracticality of the idea for his own time, a fact which Agus neglects to mention.

Agus also complains that Montefiore misunderstood rabbinic Judaism in choosing to contrast it with the Prophets. He suggests, 'Montefiore failed to take account of the prophetic ardour in legalism itself.'[172] But even harsher is the critique of Montefiore's approach to Rabbinic Judaism in Lou Silberman's 'Prolegomenon' to the 1968 edition of Montefiore's *The Synoptic Gospels*. Astounded at what he sees as Montefiore's 'priggish' and 'condescending' attitude, Silberman condemns it as a 'wrong-headed interpretation of the rabbinic attitude towards and understanding of Holy Scriptures'.[173] Yet both men note (with some puzzlement) Montefiore's consistent defence of the rabbis against poor Christian scholarship. Once again scholars are split on how to read Montefiore, for it is this side of his work, this defence of the rabbis, which other Jewish writers choose to emphasise. Walter Jacob, for example, praises him for his 'fine understanding of rabbinic Judaism'.[174] And Frederick Schwartz's 'Claude Montefiore on Law and Tradition' (1964), the most sophisticated treatment of Montefiore's understanding of rabbinics and Torah, fully recognises his positive appreciation of the Law and of Jewish veneration of the Law.[175] Schwartz differs from Silberman in his ability to distinguish between Montefiore's view of modern and pre-modern approaches to Torah. Consequently, Schwartz does not find it patronising (as Silberman did) for Montefiore to have sympathised with and even praised the pre-modern rabbis who had done so much with so little. On the other hand, he recognises that Montefiore rarely spoke positively of Torah in modern times unless it was in the sense of a moral Law.[176] Montefiore's apparently paradoxical approach (both for and against Rabbinic Judaism) is, in fact, quite consistent and comprehensible in the light of his Liberal Jewish theology. Schwartz's subtle analysis goes a long way towards this by avoiding the easy solution (that Montefiore was biased against Rabbinic Judaism), and confronting instead the rationalist assumptions behind his belief that Reason had priority over authoritative texts.[177]

The question of Montefiore's Jewishness is a complex one, and will be treated more fully later. Opinions differ widely among the writers concerned with 'Jewish thought' as to which particular aspects of his teaching could be regarded as Jewish. Almost without exception, however, all have acknowledged the independence and originality of his thought, together with his intellectual honesty. As previously noted, Reichert suggests that Montefiore's teachings should be distanced from official Liberal Jewish teaching, and Herbert Danby puts it even more strongly, warning his readers that Montefiore's views 'must on no account be supposed to be in any sense typically Jewish'.[178] Silberman criticises *The Synoptic Gospels* as 'a party document, that party being a party of one',[179] while Hugh Montefiore praises him for 'the intellectual courage to think out *on his own* his attitude to Christianity'.[180] Jonathan Magonet feels that of the 'eminent figures' of Anglo-Liberal Judaism, Montefiore was 'perhaps the most creative'.[181]

As regards his studies on 'Jewish–Christian relations', opinion is less unanimous. Vivian Simmons, a younger contemporary of Montefiore, marks him out as 'the first man who undertook the great, though perhaps thankless, task of enlightening the English Jew about the religion of Christianity and its relation to Judaism'.[182] Reichert puts this down to a conscious decision to set aside 'the unholy memories of Christian intolerance and persecution',[183] while Wolf praises his determination to face apparent contradictions between Jews and Christians.[184] Walter Jacob goes so far as to suggest that Montefiore 'came closer to a dialogue with Christianity than any other thinker up to his time'.[185] It can (and will) be argued that in terms of inter-faith dialogue, Montefiore's position, both practically and theoretically, was exceptional among Jewish thinkers of his day. Among the ways in which he broke new ground was in his non-polemical, even sympathetic, treatment of the Christian scriptures.

BIBLICAL AND NEW TESTAMENT STUDIES

One of the earliest assessments of Montefiore's contributions to biblical scholarship was F.C. Burkitt's essay in *Speculum Religionis* (1929). It begins by remarking that Montefiore was born the same year as *Essays and Reviews* was published (a collection of controversial essays by leading liberal scholars at Oxford, the theological equivalent to Darwin's *Origin of Species*). For Burkitt, Montefiore's approach to biblical studies is best explained in terms of Jowett and Oxford. As 'a champion of the Rabbinic Religion', Montefiore had succeeded where other Jewish writers had failed largely because of his scholarly credentials and his familiarity with mainstream New Testament scholarship. This had given his challenge an academic legitimacy that was difficult to ignore.[186] His writings on Jesus were, on the other hand, more important for their specialist Jewish knowledge, and Burkitt is impressed by Montefiore's view of Jesus as that of 'a prophet rather than a reformer'.[187] His approach to Paul is described as his 'most original contribution to Biblical study', although it is also criticised for some of the assumptions made.[188] Overall, Burkitt is correct to identify Oxford liberalism as intrinsic to Montefiore's method and conclusions, and to recognise his achievements in denigrating the Protestant view of the Jewish Law. But his assessment of Montefiore's Pauline studies is flawed by ignoring his interest in Paul's relevance for Liberal Judaism.[189] Furthermore, Montefiore's view of Jesus was, contrary to Burkitt, very much one of a reformer.

In large-scale surveys of New Testament scholarship, Montefiore tends to be looked upon with a certain amount of interest for his novelty factor. W.G. Kümmel's *The New Testament: The History of the Investigations of its Problems* (English translation 1973) focuses on Montefiore's significance as a Jewish scholar with rabbinic knowledge capable of accurately comparing and contrasting the New Testament and the rabbinic literature. Quoting only from *The Synoptic Gospels* (1927) and *Rabbinic Literature and Gospel Teachings* (1930), no mention is made of

Montefiore's Pauline studies, nor is there any criticism of any of Montefiore's actual findings. Stephen Neill and Tom Wright's survey, *The Interpretation of the New Testament* (1989), takes a similar view. It acknowledges the contribution of Jewish scholars such as Montefiore and Buber, but adds that 'the Christian feels himself to be in possession of certain keys which are not in their hands'.[190]

Montefiore's views on Jesus are accurately summarised as early as 1931 in Thomas Walker's small book, *Jewish Views of Jesus*. There is no comment or analysis, however, and the choice of Montefiore as representative of the Liberal Jewish position with respect to Jesus is unfortunate since Montefiore's high view of and warm regard for Jesus were very much his own. Samuel Sandmel's *We Jews and Jesus* (1965) is less a survey of Jewish views than it is a presentation of Sandmel's own, in the light of mainstream critical research. Montefiore is held up as the chief Jewish example of objective, well informed New Testament scholarship.[191] The way in which Montefiore dealt with specific passages is ignored, however, and it is left to Donald Hagner in *The Jewish Reclamation of Jesus* (1984) to quote from Montefiore's writings in detail and to set him in the context of both mainstream Jesus scholarship and Jewish approaches to Jesus. In so doing, he also corrects Walter Jacob's 'Claude G. Montefiore's Reappraisal of Christianity' (1970), in which Montefiore is accused of having an amateur approach to New Testament scholarship.[192] What all of these assessments of his writings on Jesus fail to consider in sufficient detail is the practical importance to Montefiore of Jesus' teachings in the support of his own Liberal Jewish agenda. Without an understanding of this, it is impossible to fully appreciate his unique approach to Jesus.

Montefiore is also treated at length in two of the most important post-war Pauline studies, W.D. Davies' *Paul and Rabbinic Judaism* (1955) and E.P. Sanders' *Paul and Palestinian Judaism* (1977). Davies' introduction is, in fact, a comprehensive critique of Montefiore's denial that Paul belonged to mainstream first-century Judaism. That Montefiore is regarded as 'a convenient starting point'[193] reflects how seriously his criticism of Paul was taken. Sanders' introduction also features Montefiore, where he is praised for his challenge of the traditional Protestant understanding of both Paul and the Law. While Sanders agrees with some of Davies' criticism of Montefiore, he goes on to suggest that Pauline scholars have failed to engage with Montefiore's main point: why is it that what is essential to Rabbinic Judaism is missing from Paul and is not taken account of by Paul?[194] Neither Davies nor Sanders considers anything but the bare essentials of Montefiore's thesis, and neither is interested in his hermeneutical treatment of Paul, especially his belief in the relevance of Paul's ethical teachings for Liberal Judaism. Nor are they interested in setting Montefiore in the context of Jewish approaches to Paul, the best example of which has been Donald Hagner's essay, 'Paul in Modern Jewish Thought' (1980)[195]. There are problems with Hagner's treatment, however, including his conclusions regarding the direction in which Jewish scholarship is moving, and his presentation of Montefiore's approach, which is limited to a few lines. No analysis of Montefiore's views on Paul has, to date, quoted him at length or considered his attitude towards specific texts in any detail.

CONCLUSION

One result of the compartmentalisation of his thought into various categories (Reform and Anglo-Jewish history, Jewish thought, Jewish–Christian relations, and biblical studies) has been a frag-mented view of Montefiore. More so than for most thinkers, his thought remained remarkably consistent throughout his life, and can almost always be traced back to a single, consistent set of principles, which he defined under Liberal Judaism.[196] To consider any aspect of his writings apart from his Liberal Jewish agenda is potentially to misunderstand him. Any comprehensive analysis of his thought must begin from a clear understanding of his conception of Liberal Judaism, and what this meant to him historically and theologically.

This book harmonises the findings of previous scholarship so as to clarify areas of contention and to produce a coherent picture of Montefiore's thought. Regarding his Jewishness, it considers the relationship of Liberal Judaism to the concrete, historical expressions of Judaism (especially Reform) around him. It also explores Montefiore's views of an 'essence of Judaism' from a theological perspective. Related to this are questions con-cerning his attitude towards authority, tradition and nationality – and how he might have reacted to the Holocaust and the State of Israel. Regarding Montefiore's approach to Christianity, the aim will be to demonstrate more comprehensively than has so far been achieved the effect of Christian theology upon his own. This depends largely upon understanding his particular conception of Christianity, and analysing the influence of Hellenistic philosophy upon Christian thought around the turn of the century. One of the main objectives will be to ascertain whether or not accusations implying his crypto-Christianity have been justified. This work should also answer the need for a fuller treatment of Montefiore's views on both Jesus and Paul (in particular, the ways in which he utilised them for the cause of Liberal Judaism), and to clarify Montefiore's contribution to the development of Jewish–Christian dialogue.

NOTES

109. A related document is Joshua Stein's *Lieber Freund: The Letters of Claude Goldsmid Montefiore to Solomon Schechter 1885–1902* (1988). This small collection covers the period of their friendship before Schechter left England to play a leading role in Conservative Judaism in America, and before Montefiore established Liberal Judaism. It is best regarded as primary source evidence since Stein does not attempt to analyse the material, other than to comment that the letters contain 'germs of ideas which consistently show up in later life'. The collection is useful in demonstrating Montefiore's intellectual debt to Schechter on rabbinic matters and Schechter's discomfort in receiving Montefiore's financial assistance.

110. L. Cohen, *Some Recollections of Claude Goldsmid-Montefiore 1858–1938* (1940), p. 23.

111. Examples include Steven Bayme and Walter Jacob, who misunderstood what Montefiore meant when he (very occasionally) referred positively to mysticism. See S. Bayme, 'Claude Montefiore, Lily Montagu and the Origins of the Jewish Religious Union', *Transactions of the Jewish Historical Society of England*, XXVII (1982) and W. Jacob, *Christianity Through Jewish Eyes: The Quest for Common Ground* (1974).

112. L. Cohen, *Some Recollections of Claude Goldsmid-Montefiore 1858–1938* (1940), pp. 22–3.

113. Ibid., p. 22.

114. Letter from Basil Henriques to Lily Montagu, 9 May 1939. MS 16/12/4, World Union for Progressive Judaism Records, A.J.A.C.

115. Cited on the cover of E. Kessler, *An English Jew: The Life and Writings of Claude Montefiore* (1989).

116. E. Kessler, *An English Jew: The Life and Writings of Claude Montefiore* (1989), p. 164.

117. E. Kessler, 'Claude Montefiore', *Jewish–Christian Relations*, XXI (Winter 1988), p. 9.

118. Ibid., p. 16.

119. Kessler does recognise the tensions in Montefiore's thought, drawing attention to the fact that on one hand there was Montefiore's own distaste for *halakhah* and the lack of rabbinic emphasis at the West London Synagogue, while on the other there was the influence of Solomon Schechter and his own desire to correct the erroneous understanding of Christian scholars. But he simply concludes: 'As a result of this tension Montefiore struggled throughout his life to offer a comprehensive and consistent view of Torah and Rabbinic Judaism.' E. Kessler, *An English Jew: The Life and Writings of Claude Montefiore* (1989), p. 87. Elsewhere, Kessler concludes that Montefiore was actually a defender of the rabbis, in that, firstly, Montefiore viewed Liberal Judaism as their heir and, secondly, he wished to counteract Christian prejudice. E. Kessler, 'Claude Montefiore: Defender of Rabbinic Judaism?' in *Jewish Historical Studies: Transactions of the Jewish Historical Society of England*, XXXV (1996–98), p. 236.
120. The M.Phil. was completed for the University of London in 1987. Chapter one incorporated 'C.G. Montefiore and his Quest' (1981), which was published in *Judaism*, together with 'Zion – Neither Here nor There?' (1984). Chapter six was based upon 'Montefiore's Three Mentors' (1982), which first appeared in the *Jewish Chronicle*.
121. M.G. Bowler, *Claude Montefiore and Christianity* (1988), p. 1.
122. Ibid., p. 15.
123. Ibid., pp. 84, 85.
124. Ibid., p. 85.
125. J. Stein, *Jewish Quarterly Review*, LXXXII (1992), pp. 569–70.
126. R. Libowitz, *Journal of Ecumenical Studies*, XXVII (1990), pp. 788–9.
127. The Tractarian model and its alternatives will be treated in Chapter 1.
128. The first edition was in 1907. D. Philipson, *The Reform Movement in Judaism* (1931), p. 428.
129. Ibid., p. 407.
130. F.C. Schwartz, 'Anglo-Jewish Theology at the Turn of the Twentieth Century', Doctor of Hebrew Literature dissertation, Hebrew Union College, Cincinnati (1959), p. 44f. In the unpublished thesis, Schwartz also examines the thought of other Anglo-Jewish religious leaders, including Morris Joseph, but has nothing to say about them in the context of Montefiore's thought.
131. Ibid., p. 42.
132. C. Bermant, *The Cousinhood: The Anglo-Jewish Gentry* (1971), pp. 319, 323–4. The matter of intermarriage was not straightforward, even for Montefiore. Bermant points out that Montefiore actually organised his sister's marriage to a professing Christian, but does not draw any conclusions regarding principles. Rather, he suggests that Montefiore 'must have found the whole episode unseemly and painful'.
133. Ibid., p. 318.
134. Ibid., p. 317.
135. Published in *Transactions of the Jewish Historical Society of England*, XXVII (1982). The paper was first delivered to the Society on 4 July 1979.
136. S. Bayme, 'Claude Montefiore, Lily Montagu and the Origins of the Jewish Religious Union', *Transactions of the Jewish Historical Society of England*, XXVII (1982), p. 64.
137. Ibid., p. 65.
138. The application of the label 'mysticism' to Montefiore's Liberal Judaism is examined in detail in Chapter 2. Suffice it to say for now that Bayme's description of Montefiore's faith in terms of 'genuine mysticism', without further qualification, is misleading. Ibid., p. 67.

139. Ibid., p. 65.
140. Ibid., p. 67.
141. Ibid.
142. Meyer bases his treatment upon a selection of Montefiore's own writings together with Cohen's *Some Recollections*, Bermant's *The Cousinhood*, Bayme's 'Claude Montefiore, Lily Montagu and the Origins of the Jewish Religious Union', Reichert's 'The Contribution of Claude G. Montefiore to the Advancement of Judaism' and Montagu's 'Notes on the Life and Work of Claude G. Montefiore'. M.A. Meyer, *Response to Modernity: A History of the Reform Movement in Judaism* (1988), p. 443, n. 94.
143. Ibid., p. 214. Meyer almost certainly over-exaggerates Montefiore's exposure to German Reform whilst at Oxford.
144. Ibid.
145. '[Montefiore's] Liberal Judaism emerged less out of a rejection of tradition than an attraction to broader horizons. Within a regular circle of Christian clergymen, he could frankly discuss the religious issues of the day, feeling fully at home in their midst.' Ibid., p. 217.
146. D. Englander, 'Anglicised but not Anglican', in G. Parsons, ed., *Religion in Victorian Britain*, I (1988).
147. Englander also mistakenly suggests that Liberal Jews incorporated 'trinitarian hymns and other alien practices' into its services.
148. T.M. Endelman, *Radical Assimilation in English Jewish History, 1656–1945* (1990), p. 76.
149. Ibid., p. 102.
150. G. Alderman, *Modern British Jewry* (1992), pp. 245, 254.
151. Ibid., p. 353.
152. C.G. Montefiore, 'Is Judaism a Tribal Religion?', *Contemporary Review* (September 1882), p. 364, cited in D. Feldman, *Englishmen and Jews: Social Relations and Political Culture 1840–1914* (1994), p. 123.
153. D. Feldman, *Englishmen and Jews: Social Relations and Political Culture 1840–1914* (1994), p. 137.
154. Cohen refers to Montefiore regarding: his anti-Zionist letter to *The Times* (18 May 1903); his argument that the discussions of the Conjoint Foreign Committee were 'too confidential' to permit freewheeling inspections of a report which many demanded to see (29 October 1916); and his unhappy response to the Balfour Declaration, 'If H.M. Government is anxious to publish this formula for the sake of *this* country as well as for the Jews, I would, of course, subordinate my Jewish feelings, wishes and interests to the interests of England and the Empire' (12 October 1917). S. Cohen, *English Zionists and British Jews* (1982), pp. 73, 266, 174.
155. *Jewish Chronicle* (14 February 1896), cited in E. Black, *The Social Politics of Anglo-Jewry* (1988), p. 23.
156. This is how he described his point of view in relation to Rabbinic Judaism, but it applied equally to whatever topic he was discussing. C.G. Montefiore, *Rabbinic Literature and Gospel Teachings* (1930), p. xix.
157. It was written on the occasion of Montefiore's seventieth birthday and published in the *American Rabbis Yearbook* of 1928. Reichert relies heavily on Philipson for details of Anglo-Liberal Judaism.
158. V.E. Reichert, 'The Contribution of Claude G. Montefiore to the Advancement of Judaism', *Central Conference of American Rabbis Yearbook*, XXXVIII (1928), p. 511.
159. Ibid., p. 499.

160. A.J. Wolf, 'The Dilemma of Claude Montefiore', *Conservative Judaism*, XIII (Winter 1959), p. 25.
161. Ibid.
162. Ibid., p. 23.
163. W. Jacob, *Christianity Through Jewish Eyes: The Quest for Common Ground* (1974), p. 96.
164. Cohn-Sherbok's study relies very heavily upon Walter Jacob. D. Cohn-Sherbok, *Fifty Key Jewish Thinkers* (1997), p. 95.
165. A.T. Hanson, 'A Modern Philo', *The Modern Churchman*, XX (1977), p. 110.
166. Ibid., p. 111.
167. Ibid., p. 112.
168. J. Agus, 'Claude Montefiore and Liberal Judaism', *Conservative Judaism*, XIII (Winter 1959), p. 1.
169. Ibid.
170. V.E. Reichert, 'The Contribution of Claude G. Montefiore to the Advancement of Judaism', *Central Conference of American Rabbis Yearbook*, XXXVIII (1928), pp. 512–13.
171. L. Jacobs, *The Jewish Religion: A Companion* (1995), p. 353.
172. J. Agus, 'Claude Montefiore and Liberal Judaism', *Conservative Judaism*, XIII (Winter 1959), p. 15.
173. L.H. Silberman, 'Prolegomenon', in the 1968 edition of C.G. Montefiore, *The Synoptic Gospels*, p. 4.
174. W. Jacob, *Christianity Through Jewish Eyes: The Quest for Common Ground* (1974), p. 94.
175. F.C. Schwartz, 'Claude Montefiore on Law and Tradition', *The Jewish Quarterly Review*, LV (1964), p. 26. Schwartz works most closely with Montefiore's *Rabbinic Literature and Gospel Teachings* and, of course, his *Rabbinic Anthology*.
176. Ibid., p. 42.
177. As Schwartz put it, 'In the final analysis, Montefiore wants nothing binding between the Jew and God.' Ibid., p. 52.
178. H. Danby, *The Jew and Christianity: Some Phases, Ancient and Modern, of the Jewish Attitude Towards Christianity* (1927), p. 79.
179. L.H. Silberman, 'Prolegomenon', in the 1968 edition of C.G. Montefiore, *The Synoptic Gospels*, p. 15.
180. H.W. Montefiore, 'Sir Moses Montefiore and his Great Nephew: A Study in Contrasts', 11th Montefiore Lecture, Southampton (1979), p. 14.
181. J. Magonet, 'The Liberal and the Lady: Ester Revisited', *Judaism*, XXIX (Spring 1980), p. 167.
182. V.G. Simmons, 'Claude Goldsmid Montefiore', *Transactions of the Jewish Historical Society of England*, XIV (1935–39), p. 254.
183. V.E. Reichert, 'The Contribution of Claude G. Montefiore to the Advancement of Judaism', *Central Conference of American Rabbis Yearbook*, XXXVIII (1928), p. 510.
184. A.J. Wolf, 'The Dilemma of Claude Montefiore', *Conservative Judaism*, XIII (Winter 1959), p. 23.
185. W. Jacob, 'Claude G. Montefiore's Reappraisal of Christianity', *Judaism*, IXX (Summer 1970), p. 73.
186. F.C. Burkitt, ed., *Speculum Religionis* (1929), pp. 4, 5.
187. Ibid., pp. 7, 8.
188. Namely, Montefiore's mistaken assumption that Judaism from 300–500 CE was much the same as the Judaism from 30–50 CE. Ibid., p. 10.

189. '[Montefiore's book *Judaism and St. Paul*] consists of two essays, of which the second discusses the use that may be made by the Liberal Jew of the Pauline Epistles even today. This does not directly concern us now, but the other essay does.' Ibid., p. 10.
190. S. Neill and T. Wright, *The Interpretation of the New Testament 1861–1986* (1989), p. 94.
191. S. Sandmel, *We Jews and Jesus* (1965), pp. 88–91.
192. W. Jacob, 'Claude G. Montefiore's Reappraisal of Christianity', *Judaism*, IXX (Summer 1970), p. 72. The related criticism, that Montefiore ignored Jewish New Testament scholarship, is more complicated and will be dealt with in Chapters 1 and 2.
193. W.D. Davies, *Paul and Rabbinic Judaism* (1955), p. 1.
194. E.P. Sanders, *Paul and Palestinian Judaism* (1977), p. 10.
195. D. Hagner, 'Paul in Modern Jewish Thought', in Hagner and Harris, eds, *Pauline Studies*.
196. Montefiore produced only one reflective diary, written 1883–86. In it he sketched out an agenda for a reformed Judaism, clearly demonstrating that he 'foresaw while scarcely out of his teens, the need of a reverent and sympathetic approach to biblical criticism, he held for a pruning for ritual and dogma, and he held for a fuller social clarity in Jewry, the need for a fuller social objective'. Letter from Prof. Cock to Lucy Cohen, undated. L. Cohen, *Some Recollections of Claude Goldsmid-Montefiore 1858–1938* (1940), p. 57.

PART ONE

MONTEFIORE IN THE CONTEXT OF JEWISH THOUGHT

Introduction

Claude Montefiore's vision of Liberal Judaism was the product of both Jewish and non-Jewish influences. The focus here will be upon the Jewish context, while the more complex question of how Christianity and Christian society affected Montefiore will be left for later. It should be borne in mind, however, that the very considerable impact of Christian culture and thought upon Western Judaism means that this distinction is somewhat artificial.

This section begins with an overview of British Reform Judaism in the context of related movements in Germany. It then considers the development of Montefiore's movement as a response to the challenges of modern historical criticism and religious apathy, and as an alternative to both British Reform and Orthodox Judaism. After considering the ways in which Liberal Judaism provoked controversy within the Anglo-Jewish community, an attempt is made to establish the limits of influence of German and American Reform Judaism upon it. The section then moves on to outline those aspects of Montefiore's thought which, when compared and contrasted with other Jewish thinkers, can help in an understanding of his unusual conception of Judaism. In particular, it touches on Montefiore's view of Rabbinic Judaism and of the relationship between Judaism and nationalism, and considers the question of exactly what constituted the 'essence of Judaism'. This is followed by an examination of Montefiore's concept of a theological expression of Judaism, highlighting some of the more contentious theological issues. The section ends with a consideration of Montefiore's contributions in terms of Jewish–Christian dialogue, involving a general treatment of the idea of Judaism and Christianity playing complementary roles.

3

Aspects of Anglo-Jewish Reform

EARLY REFORM JUDAISM IN GERMANY AND BRITAIN

A common assumption among historians interested in Montefiore has been that the ideas and practices of the German-Jewish reformers must have featured heavily in his own advanced, non-orthodox theology. Some suggest the direct influence of German Reform thought. For example, Kessler writes, 'It is important to note that Montefiore must not only have been aware of the European Reform position but could even have been influenced by it while living and studying at the *Hochschule* in Berlin.'[1] Other writers imply indirect German influence through his exposure to Anglo-Reform, viewed largely as an extension or echo of German Reform. This view of the West London Reform Synagogue is assumed in world-wide histories of Reform Judaism, in varying degrees, from the time of Philipson's *The Reform Movement in Judaism* (1907) until Michael Meyer's *Response to Modernity* (1988).[2] Montefiore was brought up attending the West London Reform Synagogue, remained a member of its congregation all his life, had a place on its council, and occasionally preached there, often to the disgust of some of its members.[3] While no one would doubt that it left an indelible trace upon his religious thought, the extent to which it can be regarded as a conduit for German influence is debatable. It would be sensible, then, in attempting to assess the relevance of German influence, to begin by examining the growth of the British Reform movement and its relations with the Continent, before considering the degree to which Montefiore and Anglo-Liberal Judaism absorbed German Reform thought directly.

The phenomenon of Reform Judaism first emerged in Germany in the first two decades of the nineteenth century and was followed by similar movements in Britain and France in the 1840s and 1850s. It was primarily a protest movement in which intellectual, middle-class Jews of Europe rebelled against the Orthodox world-view with which they had found themselves increasingly at odds since the time of the Jewish Enlightenment or *Haskalah*. The impetus and pressure came mainly from laymen who pressed for specific socio-religious reforms, although a certain amount of theological rumination soon followed as ministers or rabbis were brought in to justify the need for reform. Typically, a climate of critical opinion was created which affected reforms even among the Orthodox congregations.[4] Chronologically, it appears a straightforward matter that German Reform must have had a considerable influence upon British Reform but, in fact, a comparison of German and British Reform developments reveals important differences and a higher degree of independence than is often supposed.

For example, there were significant distinctions regarding the influence of Government upon the development of Reform Judaism in the two countries. In Germany, the various State authorities had considerable power in regulating religious life and allowed the Jewish communities very little room to manoeuvre. Their common aim was to encourage Jewish conversion and assimilation. Some States achieved this by supporting Jewish attempts to embrace modernity and religious reform (for example, Hamburg)[5] while others prevented reform so as to emphasise and contrast the 'backwardness' of Orthodox Judaism (for example, Prussia).[6] The majority of German Jews in the early nineteenth century came to view conformity to German socio-religious norms as their best hope for political emancipation. As for the influence of the Jewish communal authorities, the establishment of two of the most important Reform centres in Berlin (1815) and Hamburg (1818) was accomplished without 'official' sanction.[7] In Britain, on the other hand, where the Jewish population had already achieved a relatively high degree of autonomy, there was no governmental interference in religious reform. While emancipation politics certainly played a part in the development of British Reform Judaism, it was more a matter of internal dispute among the Jewish community. For Jews such as Moses Montefiore, president of the Orthodox dominated Board of Deputies, who feared assimilation as the inevitable result of total political emancipation, the best policy was to gently attempt to extend already existing privileges. For others, such as Francis

Goldsmid, who were resentful of the Board's procrastination, an alternative power-base was required if true emancipation and full rights were ever to be attained, and the Reform movement seemed to fit the bill. Nevertheless this political dimension of British Reform Judaism had almost nothing to do with State power and was far less significant for its development than had been the case in Germany. What both the early Reform movements did have in common, of course, was finding themselves marginalised by the steadfastly Orthodox community authorities. This opposition was not as effective in Germany, where the Orthodox authorities were de-centralised, dispersed and often without State support. In Britain, the influential Chief Rabbinate (dominated and developed by Hermann and Nathan Adler for a combined total of 66 years) and the centralised Board of Deputies combined to make a powerful, concerted and sustained attack against Reform.[8]

There were also important differences with respect to the character of the religious and intellectual contexts of German and British Reform. In both countries, the context was essentially Christian. Enlightenment Protestantism in Germany did not seem so far from *Haskalah* Judaism, and its forms of expression were often emulated; various Reform synagogue services adopted German Christian socio-religious patterns of decorum, music, clerical dress, and regular, edifying sermons.[9] Some Reform Jews also came to see the biblical critical research of Protestant scholars as a model for approaching their own religious texts. Thus, interwoven with practical, external reforms came historical criticism and an undermining of the literalist approach to scripture, as evidenced in the work of the leading Reform Rabbi Abraham Geiger.[10] These new 'Jewish Science' principles were incorporated institutionally in several German rabbinical colleges that were set up in the second half of the nineteenth century.[11] One consequence was that the Bible was not regarded as any more divine than was the rabbinic literature or, at least, that there was not much of a difference. In England where biblical criticism did not make much of a general impact until the close of the century, the Christian tendency was towards biblical literalism. This had consequences for Anglo-Jewry where Reform thought (in the writings of the first minister of the Reform Synagogue, David Marks) took on these characteristics.[12] In this context, Claude Montefiore appears very much a pioneer, standing alone in publicly and consistently arguing for a critical approach to Jewish religious texts, both rabbinical and biblical, as early as 1891.[13] It comes as no surprise, then, that a rabbinical training college incorporating modern critical scholarship, Leo Baeck College, was not established in Britain until 1956 (and came about largely as a result of the efforts of *German* Jewish refugees).

To what extent was the emergence of British Reform the result of outside (that is, German) influence? Establishing the degree to which native British developments absorbed specifically German Reform practices and theory is by no means easy. The first factor to establish is the degree of exposure to German thought and the manner in which it was generally received. Certain references to the German movement in England in the 1830s might well be viewed as indicative of the growing influence of German Reform. For example, a prominent member of the Orthodox Great Synagogue, Isaac Lyon Goldsmid, wrote a letter to Moses Montefiore in 1831 in which he threatened to establish a new synagogue that would follow the example of the Hamburg Synagogue.[14] And in December 1836, a similar petition was presented to the Sephardi elders at Bevis Marks, the Spanish and Portuguese Synagogue, asking for 'such alterations and modifications as were in the line of changes introduced in the Reform synagogue in Hamburg and other places'.[15] The fact that the Reform Prayer Book, which appeared in 1841 following the establishment of the West London Synagogue in 1840, shared certain ideas with contemporary Continental developments, seems to support the view.[16] In *Response to Modernity* (1988), Meyer offers further evidence which indicates that 'British Reform was not so isolated from its counterparts elsewhere, nor so completely different from them.' He identifies close personal ties between a leading British Reform figure and German ones, notes the admiring way in which 12 German sermons were translated, and cites the regular reports in the *Jewish Chronicle* concerning the progress and anti-ritualism of German Reform synagogues. He points out that bibliocentricism and the abolition of the second day of festivals (both conventionally regarded by historians as peculiarly characteristic of early British Reform) had had their foreshadowing in the proposals of German rabbis. And, despite admitting that the West London Synagogue was 'something other than simply an extension of the German Reform movement', Meyer cannot help but seize upon the

Reform congregation in Manchester, established in 1856, as a clear example of where 'the German influence was more obvious and direct'.[17]

What does such evidence demonstrate? With regard to early references to German reform, nothing concrete developed from either Goldsmid's threat or the petition to Bevis Marks. The Prayer Book actually contained no theological revolutions (for example, it retained the texts calling for the restoration of Israel, the re-establishment of the sacrificial cult, and the coming of a personal messiah, in contrast to the more radical German Reform liturgies).[18] The close personal ties cited are limited to Isaac Lyon's uncle, and the translation of 12 sermons hardly demonstrates a very wide interest. Furthermore, while indicating public awareness, contemporary reports in the *Jewish Chronicle* were almost universal in their condemnation and suspicion of German Reform theology as divisive and irreligious. Following the assembly of rabbis at Frankfurt (1845), the *Jewish Chronicle* ran a series of articles depreciating, *inter alia*, the German reformers' hopes for the vernacular replacing Hebrew and for Sunday services replacing the Sabbath. The line taken was that moderate reform was necessary to pre-empt such radical schisms. As David Cesarani has observed, 'The example of German Reform was always held up [in the *Jewish Chronicle*] to illustrate where the line must be drawn.'[19] The cultural and political character of Anglo-Jewry at the time was not conducive to the Reform movement at least partly because change was associated in the minds of many Englishmen with revolution, and because conformity to an established Anglican Church (or Orthodox Synagogue) was characteristic of those aspiring to Establishment status.[20] Certainly, changes in service ritual were very limited until the arrival of eastern European immigrants in the 1880s. Modifications with regard to decorum and service planning (including the shortening of the services, the formation of a choir, English sermons every Sabbath in 1840 and the introduction of an organ in 1859)[21] can just as easily be explained in terms of the self-consciousness of middle-class London Jewry in the light of Anglican norms of decorum and sensitivity to the relative laxity of their own synagogue services. And the movement's bibliocentricism and reforms concerning the second day of festivals, like many of the external innovations, can be accounted for by other indigenous factors, not least the direct emulation of Anglican services and the impact of the Christian critique of Judaism, as will become clear. In point of fact, while it formed a pivotal subject for discussion, the second day of festivals was never actually abolished.[22] Nor is the example of Manchester of much help in demonstrating the dominance of German influence, since Bill Williams has argued on a socio-political level in *The Making of Manchester Jewry* (1976) for the essentially British roots of reform there in 1856. Such developments are contextualised in Manchester as part of the general Anglo-Jewish experience of 'the development of an anglicised middle-class community, the struggle for social acceptance and political freedom'. The emergence of the Reform movement in Manchester is viewed primarily as a result of assimilationist hopes of 'the most anglicised section of the community', and came about due to 'the evolution by one group of a sense of collective identity as a cultural elite', not as a result of the arrival of German reformers. While he accepts that some of the German immigrant leaders of Reform were undoubtedly inspired by their experiences on the Continent, Williams prefers to explain the phenomenon in terms of the particularly British components of Manchester Reform.[23] Endelman is more emphatic still that German influence was minimal and argues that the Manchester reformers did not look to the Continent for guidance in matters of doctrine and liturgy but rather to the indigenous developments of the London Reform Synagogue.[24]

The extent of the effect of German Reform upon British Reform has undoubtedly been over-estimated. Even if one were to accept a German source of influence, the remarkably un-radical modifications of service decorum and externalities clearly demonstrates the limits. At the time there was no hint of dissatisfaction with the underlying theology behind the Synagogue services in Britain, and this is something that set it apart from the older and more developed Continental Reform movement.[25] In fact, it was not until the 1930s and 1940s that the Continental rabbis who came as refugees to Britain began to have a more direct influence on Anglo-Reform theology.[26]

The whole issue of the place of theology in early British Reform Judaism is a fascinating one. In contrast to its sister movements in Germany and to a lesser degree the United States where 'synods' and 'platforms' respectively attempted doctrinal expressions of Judaism, there were no assemblies of Anglo-Reform rabbis. The long tradition in Britain of subservience to

lay authority meant that the Reform rabbis had no encouragement, nor felt under any pressure, to formulate theological
justifications for the external reforms that were mostly brought
about by the social concerns of upwardly mobile Jewish laymen.
In contrast to what had happened elsewhere, opposition from
the Orthodox in Britain stemmed entirely from the reformers' act
of breaking away from 'ecclesiastical' control in 1840, and had
little or nothing to do with the actual reforms (many of which
were duly adopted by the Orthodox themselves) or a radical
Reform theology (which simply did not materialise). Unlike the
German reformers who, by and large, shared certain theological
premises borne out of a common response to modernity, there
was not a prevailing theological agenda among Anglo-Jewish
reformers. In this sense, the Reform movement in Britain lacked
the power and cohesion of a true religious movement.[27] Those
few attempts at theological writings were certainly less systematic
and more individualist in character.

German Reform theology emphasised from very early on the
idea of Progress. Following the trends in Christian scholarship,
'Jewish Science' postulated that from biblical times until the
contemporary day and on into the future, Judaism and its understanding of God should be regarded as an evolving phenomenon.[28]
In contrast, for David Marks, minister at the West London
Synagogue from 1840 until 1893, Jewish Reform had more to do
with returning to earlier, purer forms of Judaism than it did with
forging new understandings. One obvious consequence was that
while many German reformers regarded the rabbinic literature
as an improvement and development over the more primitive
religion of the Hebrew Bible, Marks (along with many British
Jews) was vehemently anti-talmudic.[29] Marks' position, as traced
out in his *Forms of Prayer* (1841), has been described as one of
'Rational Piety'.[30] He argued that the ethical, behavioural and
attitudinal teachings of Torah were universal in nature and that
therefore Judaism was ultimately rational. On the other hand, he
did not wish to ignore the particularist and dogmatic elements
of Jewish biblical tradition, which he accepted uncritically as an
act of piety, and so urged general observance. As a result, in
explaining the criteria he used in selecting material for his Prayer
Book he simultaneously argued that (i) 'the prayer should be
perfectly intelligible ... the sentiments which it expresses should
be of a pure and elevating character' (i.e. that the selection

should depend on its high moral content), and (ii) 'These sublime portions [of the common ritual] we trust we shall be found to have carefully preserved' (i.e. that he regarded the preservation of tradition as an act of piety).[31] Despite speaking and writing of the 'pure principles' of Judaism, echoing the polemic of the German Reform movement (which in turn echoed the common expression of nineteenth-century Liberal Religion), Marks was uninterested in the theological investigations of 'Jewish Science' and epitomised the English concern for practical and edifying teaching. Here, as elsewhere, his innovations should be understood as an individualist, unsuccessful attempt to reconcile rationalism with pious observance. Marks' writings provide another important key to understanding British Reform at this time, namely the effect of Christian critique of Judaism. Modifications such as increased decorum and sermons in the vernacular reflected Christian practices, as did the bibliocentric basis for arguing for banning the second day of festivals. It is difficult to see direct, clear emulation of German Reform practice in Marks' essentially non-theological reforms.

Morris Joseph succeeded Marks as minister of the Reform Synagogue in 1893. His style of Judaism was based upon rabbinism and was more normative than Marks' anti-Oral Law theology. Best described as 'Conservative Reform', he defined his position in *Judaism as Creed and Life* (1903) as

> midway between Orthodoxy which regards the *Shulchan Aruch*, or at least the Talmud, as the final authority in Judaism and the extreme liberalism which, settling little store by the historic sentiment as a factor in the Jewish consciousness, would lightly cut the religion loose from the bonds of tradition.[32]

Even more so than Marks, Joseph emphasised rationality, arguing, 'Judaism asks us not for credulity, but for true faith – based on reason.'[33] Theological developments were possible, he felt, as long as no attempt was made to negate 'certain recognised principles' which were intrinsic to Judaism. Thus he was able to highlight the continuity of contemporary Judaism with previous historical expressions, especially with regard to the dogmas of God's existence, unity, spiritual nature, providence and selection of Israel.[34] Yet, just as Marks' piety had been tempered by rationality, so Joseph's rationality was tempered by faith and mystery. He admitted,

> There must always be a region into which we cannot penetrate, a mystery we cannot solve. When the intellect has done its uttermost, we must still have recourse to faith. Where we cannot know we must be content to trust.[35]

Explorations into theological realms were, for Joseph, necessarily limited and he preferred to depend upon traditional theories of religious philosophy. This is reflected in the fact that, for a Reform treatise, *Judaism as Creed and Life* was uncharacteristically concerned with the ceremonial and ethical aspects of Judaism. Ultimately then, Joseph, like Marks, did not attempt to justify Reform innovations by any consistent theological or theoretical position in the way that German reformers had tried.

THE PARALYSIS OF REFORM JUDAISM IN BRITAIN

Towards the end of the nineteenth century the German conservative reformers, now known as Liberals (to be distinguished from the more radical *Reformgemeinde* or 'Friends of Reform' in Berlin), included most religiously minded Jews in Germany among their ranks.[36] The neo-Orthodox, despite reassessing their situation and making certain concessions, had nevertheless become entrenched and isolated from much of the surrounding world. Like the *Reformgemeinde*, they were small fringe groups with little or no religious authority and less political clout.[37] In England, on the other hand, it was the reformers who had been sidelined and who survived in the margins, and the neo-Orthodox who retained the dominant position. Institutionally, the reformers' situation had improved considerably from the low point in January 1842, when Chief Rabbi Hirschell pronounced a *herem* on anyone using the Reform Prayer Book. The ban itself was lifted in 1849 and a licence to register marriages in the West London Synagogue was granted in 1856.[38] Yet there was little expansion of the movement in Britain during the nineteenth century. No attempt was made to establish an academic institution to train Reform rabbis or to contribute to Anglo-Jewish scholarship, and new Reform congregations emerged only at

Manchester in 1856 and Bradford in 1873.[39] In practice, many Orthodox customs continued to be observed, including the wearing of phylacteries and prayer shawls.[40] As Philipson observed in 1931, British Reform 'has continued along the lines first laid down, but has not made much further headway in this direction; in fact it has become quite wedded to its traditions as are the orthodox congregations to theirs'.[41]

There are many factors which contributed to this paralysis and which meant that, from a world-wide perspective, Reform did not really become a 'movement' in Britain until much later in the 1930s and 1940s.[42] Contrasting British Reform Judaism in the early stages with the German experience, one can conclude that, firstly, the lack of a rigorous reappraisal of Jewish tradition and the absence of a new, distinct, consensual theological position, were important causes of its failure to gain as popular a following as that enjoyed on the Continent. Secondly, the dearth of vibrant leaders with a radical vision cannot have helped. Thirdly, the Orthodox took much of the wind out of the reformers' sails by replacing their own elderly, out-of-touch leader with Nathan Adler, who had been college-educated and who was prepared to institute regular vernacular sermons and to increase standards of decorum, which were outlined in his reforms in *Laws and Regulations* (1847). Fourthly, the Anglo-reformers failed to offer a viable alternative to Orthodoxy in answering the challenge of modern historical criticism. One result of this was that Reform Judaism was no more successful than Orthodoxy had been in combating religious apathy. Fifthly, in contrast to their German counterparts, the Anglo-Orthodox had followed the example of the Church of England in asking only for a generalised adherence to vague principles. The United Synagogue had been constituted in 1870 by an Act of Parliament, which recognised the headship of the Chief Rabbi. Membership of such a body, boasting establishment status and not requiring strict observance, proved decisive in retaining the support of a conservative Anglo-Jewish elite. This last factor is worth considering in greater detail.

Claude Goldsmid-Montefiore's immediate background was that of the Anglo-Jewish elite or 'the Cousinhood' as Chaim Bermant called it.[43] Both the Montefiore and Goldsmid families had been in England for a number of generations, and by 1858 were well established. While in so many ways Montefiore epitomised the upper-middle class Anglo-Jewish gentleman, in matters of personal religion and theological rigour he can be regarded as atypical. In particular, his distaste for what he regarded as the superficiality of establishment Orthodox worship set him apart.

The Anglo-Jewish elite's attachment to the faith of their fore-fathers is not a straightforward matter to analyse. There were few among them whom the more Orthodox communities on the Continent would consider properly Orthodox, Moses Montefiore being a celebrated exception, although they certainly regarded themselves as Orthodox. The vast majority tended to insist on faithful adherence to halakhic ritual in their synagogues and communal expressions of Judaism, but did not require or practice such conformity in their own private lives.[44] Nevertheless, they were in general respectful of tradition and, in comparison with the Jewish elite of other European countries, the Cousinhood's Jewish self-identity was evident in their observation of the major Jewish festivals and of the Sabbath, and in keeping (loosely) to the dietary laws.[45] Among the wealthy Jewish families who had been settled in England for some time, defection to Christianity had been rare, occurring most often in cases of intermarriage. It has been argued that this was because conversion had ceased to be as *useful* to English Jews as it was to German, Hungarian and Russian Jews who struggled for social acceptance in Christian society.[46] As a result the Anglo-Jewish community felt freer to adhere to tradition if and when it suited them, although tradition was often interpreted in unusual ways, especially among the elite. The Montefiore brothers Leonard and Claude, for example, spent their Sabbaths while at university visiting and entertaining the elderly inhabitants of the local workhouse.[47] Samuel Montagu, father of Lily Montagu (who founded the Jewish Religious Union with Claude Montefiore), allowed his household to play tennis on Sabbath, although he prohibited croquet because chipped mallets constituted 'work'.[48] And Montefiore's disciple, Basil Henriques, was brought up by his mother without synagogue ritual, was taught to kneel in prayer, and understood his Judaism to be based on faith and love of God rather than upon a body of ceremonies, all of which echoed contemporary Evangelical Protestant practices and left him almost entirely unfamiliar with those of Orthodox Judaism.[49] As a result, as Englander explains in 'Anglicised but not Anglican' (1988), the upper-middle classes were content to practise their Judaism with the same sort of inconsistent Victorian religiosity as the British Establishment practised their Christianity.[50]

Despite the fact that rigorous Orthodox practice was uncommon among the Anglo-Jewish elite, very few showed much enthusiasm for the reformation of Judaism. Instead, they tended to adopt a midway position, somewhere between the inconvenience of full observation of Orthodoxy and what they considered the somewhat unseemly, unnecessary disturbances and tensions caused by Reform Judaism (which was quite mild in comparison to the radicalism of American and German Reform Judaism). Endelman explains this in political terms, suggesting that the popularity of Reform within German Jewry was again due to the socio-political pressure on nineteenth-century German Jews to make Judaism 'acceptable' to the Christian majority so as to win emancipation. In contrast, due to the relative tolerance of the English government since the seventeenth century, there was comparatively no pressure upon British Jews to divorce themselves from Jewish 'particularism'.[51] While failing to explain adequately the undeniably *theological* aspects of German and American Reform Judaism, this explanation is useful for understanding the psychology of the Anglo-Jewish elite and their general aversion to Reform. Having adopted Victorian religiosity and patterned themselves on the Anglican upper-middle classes, they felt more secure of their societal position than did their European counterparts, and could afford a greater degree of ideological relaxation. In terms of self-identity, they were more concerned about bonds of ethnicity – failure to concern oneself with the theological tenets of Orthodox Judaism by no means alienated one from the Cousinhood nor prevented one from fully participating within the Anglo-Jewish community. For example, despite his agnosticism, Arthur Cohen played an important role in Jewish affairs, including holding the vice-presidency of the British rabbinic training academy, Jews' College, for 25 years.[52] As a result there developed among the upper-middle classes a conservative interest to preserve the Jewish status quo. Their general lack of interest and even hostility towards reforming tendencies can be understood as opposition to what was regarded as meddling for the sake of meddling.[53] The Reform Synagogue, in its institutional form, was viewed suspiciously by the elite as the harbinger of tension and schism. Montefiore's Liberal Judaism was to face a similar reaction.

NOTES

1. E. Kessler, *An English Jew: The Life and Writings of Claude Montefiore* (1989), p. 87. In passing, it is worth pointing out that Montefiore himself regarded his position as 'Liberal' *before* he studied in Germany. 'I have been an ardent "Liberal" in regard to Judaism ever since I left College.' Letter from C.G. Montefiore to Isadore Singer, 2 February 1910. MS 42/1/4, Isadore Singer Papers, A.J.A.C.

2. As Englander puts it, 'Too often Reform Judaism has been presented as an echo effect of the German Reform Movement rather than an indigenous development that addressed the condition of Anglo-Jewry.' D. Englander, 'Anglicised but not Anglican', in G. Parsons, ed., *Religion in Victorian Britain*, I (1988), p. 257. Interestingly, Meyer's position has softened recently; the comparison of German Reform with British Reform and Liberal Judaism which follows has benefited from a reading of his paper, 'Jewish Religious Reform in Germany and Great Britain' (1997) which was published in M. Brenner, R. Liedtke and D. Rechter, eds, *Two Nations: British and German Jews in Comparative Perspective* (1999).

3. Opposition to Montefiore's occasional preaching at the Reform Synagogue was vocal. 'How long will it be before other communal institutions founded for the maintenance and support of traditional Judaism will rid themselves of his influence ...?' complained one correspondent in 1918. *Jewish Chronicle*, 21 June 1918, p. 9.

4. M. Leigh, 'Reform Judaism in Great Britain', in D. Marmur, ed., *Reform Judaism: Essays on Reform Judaism in Britain* (1973), pp. 12, 15, 31.

5. M.A. Meyer, *Response to Modernity: A History of the Reform Movement in Judaism* (1988), pp. 53–61.

6. Ibid., pp. 52–3.

7. Ibid., pp. 46, 58.

8. Englander explores the degree of centralised power in Britain, observing, 'The traditional rabbinate, which was neither centralised nor hierarchical, was replaced during the Adler years by an ecclesiastical establishment under the supervision of a primate in whose hands all powers were concentrated.' Nathan Adler's *Laws and Regulations for all the Synagogues of the British Empire* (1847) was just one example of how the complete control of 'religious and cognate matters' was claimed for the Chief Rabbinate. D. Englander, 'Anglicised but not Anglican', in G. Parsons, ed., *Religion in Victorian Britain*, I (1988), p. 247.

9. M.A. Meyer, *Response to Modernity: A History of the Reform Movement in Judaism* (1988), pp. 48 (sermons), 61 (dress and decorum), 56, 88 (music).

10. Geiger's writings are characterised by a 'comparative religion' approach (e.g. his doctoral dissertation demonstrated the influence of Jewish tradition upon the Koran) and a sharply historical-critical approach to the development of Judaism (e.g. *Judaism and its History*, originally published in 1865). His lifelong fascination with early Christianity is treated in S. Heschel, *Abraham Geiger and the Jewish Jesus* (1998).

11. 'Jewish Science' or *Jüdische Wissenschaft* heavily influenced the Breslau Rabbinical Seminary (1854) and the Berlin Liberal College for Jewish Studies (1870) in Germany, and Hebrew Union College, Cincinnati (1871) and the Jewish Theological Seminary, New York (1886) in America.

12. Throughout *The Law is Light* (1854) Marks attacked the Chief Rabbi, Nathan Adler, for his defence of the rabbis. Earlier, in a letter to John Simon (29 October 1840), he advised his congregation to 'rest our hopes and form our

observances upon the Laws of God alone'. Cited in M.A. Meyer, *Response to Modernity: A History of the Reform Movement in Judaism* (1988), p. 436, n. 100.

13. C.G. Montefiore, 'Some Notes on the Effects of Biblical Criticism upon the Jewish Religion', *Jewish Quarterly Review*, IV (1891–92).

14. Cited in L. Loewe, *Diaries of Sir Moses & Lady Montefiore* (1890), 1983 edn, vol. I, p. 83.

15. Cited in D. Philipson, *The Reform Movement in Judaism*, 2nd edn (1931), p. 92.

16. Goulston has detected the possible influences of the 1819 Hamburg Prayer Book upon the introduction in *Seder Ha-Tefilot – Forms of Prayer* (published 1841–43 in five volumes), written by the first Reform minister David Marks, in that the criteria given for selecting material was that it should be both rational and aesthetic. M. Goulston, 'The Theology of Reform Judaism in Great Britain', in D. Marmur, ed., *Reform Judaism: Essays on Reform Judaism in Britain* (1973), p. 57.

17. M.A. Meyer, *Response to Modernity: A History of the Reform Movement in Judaism* (1988), p. 177.

18. Sharot remarks that a few original prayers were also added, but that overall 'the changes … were certainly moderate compared with changes … in Germany and America'. S. Sharot, 'Reform and Liberal Judaism in London: 1840–1940', *Jewish Social Studies*, vol. 41 (1979), p. 212. Englander comments, 'Prayer Book reform amounted to little more than abbreviation and omission.' D. Englander, 'Anglicised but not Anglican', in G. Parsons, ed., *Religion in Victorian Britain*, I (1988), p. 256.

19. D. Cesarani, *The Jewish Chronicle and Anglo-Jewry 1841–1991* (1994), pp. 17–18.

20. M. Leigh, 'Reform Judaism in Great Britain', in D. Marmur, ed., *Reform Judaism: Essays on Reform Judaism in Britain* (1973), p. 21. Philipson also held to this explanation, suggesting that 'the doctrine of conformity to an established church which represents the prevailing religious attitude in England reacted and reacts without a doubt upon the Jews, and for that reason it proved so difficult for reform to gain a foothold in Anglo-Judaism'. D. Philipson, *The Reform Movement in Judaism*, 2nd edn (1931), p. 94.

21. S. Sharot, 'Reform and Liberal Judaism in London: 1840–1940', *Jewish Social Studies*, vol. 41 (1979), pp. 212, 213.

22. M. Leigh, 'Reform Judaism in Great Britain', in D. Marmur, ed., *Reform Judaism: Essays on Reform Judaism in Britain* (1973), p. 24.

23. B. Williams, *The Making of Manchester Jewry 1740–1875* (1976), pp. 327, 331, 333.

24. There is some room for interpretation of the evidence compiled by Williams. Endelman suggests that Williams is correct for drawing attention to German influence in terms of inspiring the *idea* of modernising Judaism, but rejects any implication that the influence effected specific reforms. He points out that the idealogue of the Manchester movement, Tobias Theodores, was ignorant of the historical developmental framework of German Reform, and that no attempt was made to denationalise Judaism. T. Endelman, 'Jewish Modernity in England', in J. Katz, ed., *Toward Modernity* (1987), pp. 234–5.

25. M. Leigh, 'Reform Judaism in Great Britain', in D. Marmur, ed., *Reform Judaism: Essays on Reform Judaism in Britain* (1973), pp. 21, 22.

26. Ibid., p. 15.

27. M. Goulston, 'The Theology of Reform Judaism in Great Britain', in D. Marmur, ed., *Reform Judaism: Essays on Reform Judaism in Britain* (1973), p. 55.

28. M.A. Meyer, *Response to Modernity: A History of the Reform Movement in Judaism* (1988), p. 155.
29. Marks regarded the Talmud positively in terms of protecting Jews against proselytism, for maintaining uniformity of custom, for producing certain wise expositions of scripture, and for helping to preserve the integrity of the original Bible texts. D. Marks, *The Law is Light: A Course of Four Lectures on the Sufficiency of the Law of Moses as the Guide of Israel* (1854), pp. 41–4. Crucially, however, only the Torah was divine in Marks' eyes.
30. M. Goulston, 'The Theology of Reform Judaism in Great Britain', in D. Marmur, ed., *Reform Judaism: Essays on Reform Judaism in Britain* (1973), pp. 55, 61.
31. D.W. Marks, *Forms of Prayer for Jewish Worship* (Oxford, 1931) 6th edn, pp. ix ff.
32. Cited in M. Goulston, 'The Theology of Reform Judaism in Great Britain', in D. Marmur, ed., *Reform Judaism: Essays on Reform Judaism in Britain* (1973), p. 62.
33. M. Joseph, *Judaism as Creed and Life*, 2nd edn (1909), pp. 39–40.
34. Ibid., pp. 41–2.
35. Article in *The Listener* (4 May 1967), cited in M. Goulston, 'The Theology of Reform Judaism in Great Britain', in D. Marmur, ed., *Reform Judaism: Essays on Reform Judaism in Britain* (1973), p. 66.
36. Most German Jews, however, were keener supporters of Liberalism than they were of *Liberales Judentum*. M.A. Meyer, *Response to Modernity: A History of the Reform Movement in Judaism* (1988), p. 210.
37. Ibid., p. 183.
38. Blocking Marks' applications to register marriages in the Reform Synagogue was one of the many ways Moses Montefiore used his influence as head of the Board of Deputies to make life difficult for the movement.
39. There were also Reform services held in Hull in the 1850s and in Clapham from 1875 to 1877.
40. D. Englander, 'Anglicised but not Anglican', in G. Parsons, ed., *Religion in Victorian Britain*, I (1988), p. 259.
41. D. Philipson, *The Reform Movement in Judaism*, 2nd edn (1931), p. 106. Israel Zangwill wrote towards the end of the century that it was 'a body which had stood still for fifty years admiring its past self'. Cited in M. Leigh, 'Reform Judaism in Great Britain', in D. Marmur, ed., *Reform Judaism: Essays on Reform Judaism in Britain* (1973), p. 34.
42. Ibid., p. 36.
43. C. Bermant, *The Cousinhood: The Anglo-Jewish Gentry* (1971).
44. S. Singer, 'Jewish Religious Observance in Early Victorian London, 1840–1860', in *Jewish Journal of Sociology*, XXVIII (December 1986), pp. 118, 121, 124, 125, 127. Singer makes the proviso with regard to *mitsvot*, Sabbath observance, festivals and observance of dietary laws that there was always a small minority of traditionalists whose observance compared favourably with the less Westernised continental Jewish communities.
45. Ibid., p. 81.
46. T.M. Endelman, *Radical Assimilation in English Jewish History, 1656–1945* (1990), p. 80.
47. L. Cohen, *Some Recollections of Claude Goldsmid-Montefiore 1858–1938* (1940), p. 43.
48. Monk Gibbon, *Netta* (London: Routledge, 1960), p. 11, cited in T.M. Endelman, *Radical Assimilation in English Jewish History, 1656–1945* (1990), p. 83. Montagu strongly disapproved of Montefiore and Israel Abrahams

being on the Jewish Education Board because they did not accept the authority of the Mosaic Law. *Jewish Chronicle*, 22 December 1905, p. 22.

49. Henriques was a community and youth worker and fellow member of the London Society for the Study of Religion. B.L.Q. Henriques, *The Indiscretions of a Warden* (1937), pp. 11–14.

50. 'Anglo-Jewry nevertheless bore the stamp of its environment. Among the acculturated upper classes the imprint was most apparent. Judaism as practised by the notables was an invertebrate religion – deficient in doctrine, without rigour in ritual and lacking spiritual warmth – that was much influenced by the prevalent pattern of religiosity within the best circles in which they moved.' D. Englander, 'Anglicised but not Anglican', in G. Parsons, ed., *Religion in Victorian Britain*, I (1988), p. 269.

51. T.M. Endelman, *Radical Assimilation in English Jewish History, 1656–1945* (1990), pp. 85–6.

52. Ibid., p. 87.

53. Englander suggests that anglicisation and acceptance rather than separatism and self-sufficiency constituted the dominant concerns of the Anglo-Jewish elite. D. Englander, 'Anglicised but not Anglican', in G. Parsons, ed., *Religion in Victorian Britain*, I (1988), p. 239.

4

The Development of
Anglo-Liberal Judaism

MODERN HISTORICAL CRITICISM AND PROGRESS

The lack of response to biblical criticism is an important factor in understanding the paralysis of Reform Judaism in Britain. The German Reform movement had taken such developments into account from before the 1830s, applying it to their progressive view of Judaism. In England, the historical-critical analysis of religious texts did not become a topical issue until around the time of the publication of *Essays and Reviews* in 1860. The ensuing storm of controversy in the Anglican world was closely followed by the *Jewish Chronicle*, under the editorship of Abraham Benisch. This was the first time that the Anglo-Jewish community had showed any great interest in the question of biblical criticism[54] and by this time, of course, Anglo-Reform had already taken shape. The result was that, while in Germany the reformers could offer a modern, scientifically informed alternative to Orthodoxy, in Britain the reformers were as unprepared and unfit to answer the challenge of evolutionary theory (as applied to the study of the Bible) as were the Orthodox. David Marks' Karaite-like over reliance on the Bible had proved disastrous for Anglo-Reform in the long term.

By the last decade of the nineteenth century, biblical criticism had been well and truly accepted by British universities and by the Christian clergymen they produced. Liberal thought and the idea of Progress were in the ascendant. Amongst the very earliest Anglo-Jewish thinkers to face the inevitable question of whether or not Judaism should follow suit was Claude Montefiore. His article, 'Some Notes on the Effects of Biblical Criticism upon the Jewish Religion' was published in 1891 and laid open the way for a fresh alternative to the Judaism espoused by either the Bevis Marks Synagogue or the West London Synagogue. He argued that should Jews incorporate the findings of historical-critical methodology, the two foundation stones of Judaism would remain unaffected, namely, the belief in a personal, theistic God, and the Moral Law. In line with other Reform thinkers, Montefiore was convinced that it was the 'Mission of Israel' to disperse these fundamental truths throughout the world. Significantly, he recognised the fact that in themselves such beliefs did not differentiate Judaism from other religions, that the practices and rituals peculiar to Jewish tradition were, in themselves, non-essential to the Gentile world.[55]

In that he was more concerned with the nature of God and His relationship to mankind than were Marks or Joseph, Montefiore can be said to have had the most 'theological' approach of the non-Orthodox contributors in the pre-Second World War period.[56] Central to his theology was the idea of a progressive revelation, such that those aspects of rabbinic and biblical teaching that offended Liberal religious philosophy could be rejected as 'early developments' and Judaism proper could emerge as intellectually satisfying and religiously relevant to the modern world. The effect was all the more convincing in being reinforced by his comprehensive scholarship and his fervent nineteenth-century confidence in nineteenth-century rationalism.

Montefiore was the most consistent (and thus radical) of the reform-minded leaders in applying the consequences of this rationalism to Jewish practice.[57] For Morris Joseph, the framework of Jewish life had been provided by religious festivals, the Sabbath, the Decalogue and so on. For Montefiore, these traditional institutions were of interest primarily for their universalist and ethical teachings. Once this dimension of their practice had been comprehended, the actual observance itself was inevitably seen in a different light. Concerning the dietary laws, for example, Montefiore wrote,

> For if I do not believe that they were specially ordered by God, and if I know that they do not belong to the specific teachings of the prophets ... how can I recommend their observance?[58]

In contrast to Marks, he did not advocate observance of the traditional Jewish institutions as an act of piety, nor did he believe them intrinsic and essential elements of Judaism, like

Joseph. Rather, his criteria were based upon his belief that what was intrinsically good, noble and uplifting was inspired by God, and that the rest was of human construction and could be set aside. Acceptable ritual, he felt, while it should not be 'anti-social, nor improperly burdensome, is interesting in itself, is suggestive and useful to children, possesses many valuable symbolic meanings'.[59] Thus Montefiore could, for example, remain committed to preserving the special character of the Sabbath as, ideally, a day of rest.[60] This apparent freedom to select what one wished from the Jewish tradition, at the same time as claiming a historical continuance with it, brought down upon Montefiore a great deal of criticism.[61] He himself recognised the argument that his theology was not an authentic expression of Judaism. His primary answer was that of the 'Mission of Israel' and the idea that Judaism played a special role in convincing the surrounding world that life should have an ethical basis and be orientated towards a God who was immanent in both history and personal experience. The truth of 'ethical monotheism', he claimed, comprised the essential teachings of Judaism.[62] Montefiore explained all this in a private letter to Lily Montagu as early as 1899.

> If the 'old Jews' can say that they are 'bidden to hold together for a religious purpose', this is not essentially different from a proposition which would assert 'the object and justification of our holding together are to effect some religious end and influence'. Here, then, we find a vital principle of 'old Judaism' which extends equally to 'new Judaism' as well. Jews have a religious mission. The 'new Jews' can also say that the 'Unity of God' is the main content of our teaching, though we conceive it less abstractly. It is the close conjunction of God with morality and truth, and of morality with God, which we emphasise at present.[63]

Nevertheless, there was a tension between his emphasis on universalism and his recognition of the unique truth of Judaism ('Judaism' as viewed through the spectacles of Liberal Judaism). There was also a difficulty in his definition of what made a Jew. In *Liberal Judaism and Hellenism* (1918) he called any man who put a 'Torah' of moral principles into action a Jew,[64] that is, he seemed to accept a kind of self-definition, whereby Jewish identity relied upon an individual's personal interpretation of what Judaism required of him. In one of the few works treating Montefiore's theology purely in the context of Reform thought, Goulston concluded,

> It is hard to avoid the conclusion that a good deal of his work on the problem of sin, the relationship of God to man, of 'higher' and 'lower' religion, and of 'religious inwardness' was nothing but Liberal Religion in its nineteenth century form, asserted by people who claimed status as Liberal Jews.[65]

RELIGIOUS APATHY

Religious apathy and secularisation characterised both Christian and Jewish communities throughout nineteenth-century Europe and provided a subject for much heated debate. In contrast to Montefiore, many Jews believed assimilation posed a mortal threat to Judaism and that their future in Western society looked likely to see a slow, lingering death for Jewish culture and religion. In a letter to Montefiore in 1907, Israel Zangwill wrote,

> Nothing has more convinced me than my visit to the provinces of the absolute necessity for a Jewish renaissance, whether territorial or religious. Manchester and Birmingham are object lessons in Jewish disintegration. The communities are in a state of rapid decay, and are honeycombed not only with indifferentialists but with converts. Almost every family of the better class is a house divided against itself ... I see no sign of any inherent strength in the Jewish fabric to resist the environment, and if your Religious Union is to build a dam it will have to go about the work much more strenuously.[66]

In contrast to those who blamed their Christian or secular environment for the crisis, Montefiore felt that the high number of 'nominal' Jews was not merely due to 'indifferentialism, ignorance or sloth'. Although he recognised the contribution of these factors to the deteriorating situation, he did not think that they fully accounted for the facts. What was missing, he insisted, was a Judaism that answered the modern Jew's feelings of

'aloofness or estrangement ... [and] dissatisfaction' with
regard to Orthodoxy.[67] He saw with Zangwill that a rather
more pro-active approach was needed, urging that, unlike his
'traditionalist brother',

> the Liberal Jew has not merely to sit tight and keep still,
> guarding the rampart, maintaining the fort, he has to go
> forward and, in going forward, to grow ... We have to do
> what we can to persuade, to alter, to convert.[68]

Montefiore agreed with contemporary Jewish wisdom that, as
a result of secularisation or 'materialism', things were changing
for British Jews. Where he differed was in failing to view the 'prevailing indifference and growing apostasy' as inevitable unless
Jews closed ranks and fought against the on-coming tide of
assimilation. Rather than fight it, he felt that they should
embrace it, and gloried in his doctrine of 'the Englishman of the
Jewish persuasion'.[69] What was more, in contrast to the Reform
and Orthodox Synagogues, he did not find the idea of a radical
reformulation of Judaism unthinkable. Quite the contrary, he saw
the need for a progressive Judaism, one that would complement
the findings of science and biblical criticism, as essential for
its survival; general Jewish indifference and atrophy simply
illustrated the failure of the Reform and Orthodox to meet the
challenges of modernity. It could hardly be said, he felt, that
'the so-called reform synagogue in London, with its allies in
Manchester and Bradford', had achieved the organised presentation of Judaism necessary for retaining 'modern Jews'.[70]

LIBERAL JUDAISM AS AN ALTERNATIVE TO ORTHODOXY AND REFORM

It should be apparent that, unlike early Anglo-Reform, Liberal
Judaism began with a period of intellectual reflection and
theological musing before taking on an institutional form.
Montefiore's movement away from the Orthodox and Reform
synagogues was by no means abrupt and, in fact, it seems more
accurate to speak of a gradual shift from liberal Jewish thought
within the official camp to Liberal Judaism *outside* it. That is not
to say that he ever regarded himself as Orthodox. In an address

to the Unitarian students of Manchester College, Oxford, in 1896, he felt rather that he was 'speaking as a reformed, liberal or unorthodox Jew, whichever adjective one may choose to adopt'.[71] But in writings as late as 1900, he was defining 'liberal Jews' as those *within* the Orthodox and Reform communities for whom 'the Jewish religion, as it is currently expounded, and as in outward form and embodiment it actually exists, does not seem to appeal'.[72] This somewhat negative self-definition did not yet suggest a permanent split. Rather, Montefiore urged liberal Jews to 'attempt a reform from within [the existing synagogue organisations]'.[73] At this time he was prepared to sacrifice 'theological difference and difficulties' in the interest of religious brotherhood,[74] and was prepared to accept, albeit with dis-satisfaction, that 'liberal Judaism' in England had 'no organised expression or embodiment'.[75]

Thus the founding of the Jewish Religious Union (J.R.U.) in 1902 marks an important stage in Montefiore's development, the point at which he felt that some institutional effort would be more effective in rejuvenating Anglo-Judaism than would continued exhortation or essays. The success of this institutional effort, however, was largely the result of the work of Lily Montagu, as Ellen Umansky demonstrated in *Lily Montagu and the Advancement of Liberal Judaism* (1983). Involved in the Liberal cause from early on, Montagu had written an article in Montefiore's *Jewish Quarterly Review* on 'The Spiritual Possibilities of Judaism Today' (1899), which gave vent to the 'vague thoughts and aspirations which were seething in the minds and hearts of [Montagu's] co-religionists'.[76] In November 1901 she organised a provisional committee and in early 1902 a letter was circulated to around a hundred potential supporters asking for their assistance in establishing a 'Progressive' movement.[77] In so doing, she had persuaded Montefiore, whom she admired enormously and perhaps was even in love with,[78] to make the transition from scholar-thinker to what she described as 'the great protagonist of the Liberal cause'. Dependent upon his theological teaching and spiritual leadership, Montagu focused her energy upon the general administration of the growing movement, and in particular to the promotion of religious education for Jewish women and girls. Montefiore, who highly valued her organisational abilities, appeared content to leave her to set the Liberal agenda (for example, Montagu was responsible for organising the first world conference for Progressive Judaism in 1926).[79] Undoubtedly, her fierce commitment to the cause and revolutionary fervour, made more acute by her father's disapproval, left her frustrated at times with Montefiore's less confrontational, more cautious approach.[80]

At this early stage in the existence of the J.R.U. it is important to bear in mind that the group was conveniently amorphous and vague enough to meet the needs of a wide variety of individuals. The initial private meeting arranged by Montagu in February 1902 had simply set up a provisional committee to organise 'special services supplementary to those now held in the synagogues'.[81] The first circular issued by the governing committee of the new organisation had also been modest in scope. Sent out in June 1902 and published in the *Jewish Chronicle*, it read:

> Object – To provide the means for deepening the religious spirit among those members of the Jewish community who are not in sympathy with the present Synagogue Service, or who are unable to attend them. The Committee ... has decided that Saturday Afternoon Services shall be held weekly ... The services will be held in a suitable hall, and the worshippers will sit together, without distinction of sex ... The services, which will last about an hour, will be mainly in English ... The musical portions (with instrumental accompaniment) will, it is hoped, be led by a voluntary choir.[82]

As a result, the J.R.U. included a number of ministers belonging to the Orthodox United Synagogue, such as Simeon Singer, and to the Reform Synagogue, such as Morris Joseph, in addition to lay preachers like Israel Abrahams and Montefiore himself (who was a warden of the West London Synagogue at the time).[83] There were some difficulties in obtaining a suitable hall; Chief Rabbi Hermann Adler declined to allow the J.R.U. to use any synagogue under his jurisdiction,[84] and the Reform Synagogue set so many stipulations that Montefiore reluctantly advised his colleagues to decline the invitation to use the Berkeley Street Synagogue.[85] Nevertheless, the first public meeting was held in October 1902 and the *Jewish Chronicle*, which followed the progress of the movement closely, reported it was attended by between 300 and 400 people of a variety of backgrounds.[86]

Predictably, Union services were denounced as 'un-Jewish' because the group was perceived to be breaking with tradition.[87] The *Jewish Chronicle*, for example, noted that in the Union's provisional Prayer Book (1902) the prayers for the restoration of the Temple and of the return to Zion had been removed, and no mention had been made of the Sabbath or of the God of Abraham, Isaac and Jacob.[88] The services were characterised by a paucity of Hebrew prayers, no reading from the Scroll,[89] and hymns from altogether too unacceptable a source; the Chief Rabbi complained that 'one of these [hymns] has been composed from so essentially a Trinitarian standpoint that two lines had to be modified'.[90] Two Orthodox ministers left the J.R.U. in response to the Chief Rabbi's criticism,[91] and Montefiore complained of the increasing difficulty in persuading other ministers to preach.[92] Even so, the majority of members would have regarded themselves as remaining under the authority of the Chief Rabbi, especially since the official Prayer Book, published in 1903, was less radical and reinstated a greater portion of the traditional liturgy and particularistic Jewish prayers.[93] At this point in time, the 300 members of the J.R.U. saw their Union 'merely as an elitist intellectual movement which was retaining the interests of Jews who might otherwise have eschewed religion or defected to Christianity'.[94] Within a few years, however, dissonant voices began to be heard, and cracks began to appear, regarding self-definition and Union policy.

In terms of its original remit (namely, rescuing the large numbers of those in the Jewish community who were in danger of falling away from their ancestral faith) the J.R.U. was not a spectacular success. Reports in the *Jewish Chronicle* indicate that the London membership remained around 300 for the first two years.[95] In 1904, Montefiore was making public appeals for larger attendances and admitting that the 'modern' style of service had not attracted the numbers he had originally envisaged.[96] At the annual meeting in 1905 he accepted that the J.R.U. had only brought some 30 or 40 individuals back to Judaism, commenting that 'the problem is more complicated, more deeply rooted, than, perhaps, we had estimated'.[97] By 1907, attendance figures had improved only marginally upon those of four years before.[98] The establishment of an East End branch in 1903 had fared even worse; with audiences of only 60–100 recorded in 1905, it had been closed down altogether by 1911.[99]

In his paper 'The Jewish Religious Union and Its Cause' (1908), Montefiore commented that he had come to see that the original role of the J.R.U. as 'something more than a society, something less than a synagogue' was not enough. If, he reasoned, the J.R.U. had been in complete sympathy with the theory and practice of official Judaism, then its existence could never have been justified. Yet if it really did represent something different to that which Orthodoxy or Reform could offer, then the time had come to move on and develop. The negative definition – the stripping away of what was unnecessary – was no longer satisfactory. As he wrote elsewhere,

> The liberalism which comes to a man from his *reaction* against tradition is *not* the liberalism which is good for him. This [is] not the *positive, warm,* eager inspiring liberalism which I want from him.[100]

Instead, the J.R.U. should be understood as the representative of the 'Cause and the Idea' of progressive, Liberal Judaism (upper case 'Liberal' replacing lower-case 'liberal'). He was at pains to make it clear that this did not mean a fixed or dogmatic creed but rather 'certain progressive principles'; in this way he was able to distance himself from the Orthodox whilst at the same time avoiding committing himself to a position that would immediately divide or offend. He concluded the paper by hinting that a clear break from Orthodox Judaism, although not the original intention, seemed to be the direction in which they were heading.

> It may be true that some of us, when this Union was first founded, did not realise fully what we were doing and whither we were going. It may be true that the real reason for our existence and the Cause to which we pay allegiance, … have to a certain extent been only revealed and realised since our establishment.[101]

In 1909, following a survey of J.R.U. members, the 'storm period of our existence began' with the decision to form a new congregation.[102] It was generally agreed that services would be held on Friday evenings, Saturday mornings and afternoons, and two weekdays a month (one of which was to be a Sunday).[103] In contradiction to the original charter of the J.R.U., which had forbidden the establishment of an independent congregation, a manifesto of the breakaway Liberal group was published in the *Jewish Chronicle* in October of that year denying the divine authority of the Bible and outlining the deficiencies, as Montefiore saw it, of traditional Judaism.[104] In addition to provoking a public outcry,[105] this resulted in the departure of four members of the Committee, including Oswald Simon, and the resignation of many other Orthodox members.[106] With the establishment of a Liberal Jewish synagogue in 1910, Montefiore signalled his own and his fellow Liberal Jews' disassociation from both the Orthodox and the Reform positions.[107] The main weekly service was distinctive in being conducted mainly in English (Hebrew was retained in the form of the *kaddish*, part of the *Shema* and the *Adon Olam*), and included a reading from the Bible and a public address; it also neglected to call up anyone to read Torah.[108] At the same time, Lily Montagu initiated a Liberal Jewish 'Sunday School'.[109]

Montefiore had been working on a theological framework to describe his movement from before the publication of *Liberal Judaism* in 1903.[110] By the time of his 1920 article, 'Is there a Middle Way?', the theological distinctions between Liberal Judaism and Orthodoxy were not only obvious, but formed the main argument. While a certain nebulousness remained – inevitable if the ideas of progression and evolution were to have any meaning for the future – Montefiore could now confidently define Liberal Judaism theologically as:[111]

1. accepting the results of biblical criticism;
2. abandoning the doctrine of verbal inspiration;
3. accepting the human element in the Hebrew Bible;
4. accepting the moral imperfection and growth within the Hebrew Bible;
5. accepting the concept of progressive revelation;
6. regarding 'the past' as authoritative but not binding;
7. separating the 'universal' from the 'particular';
8. emphasising the Mission of Israel to the world.

Such an outline of the central tenets of Liberal Judaism offered a straightforward challenge to 'Historic or Traditional Judaism', Montefiore argued, since a middle ground was impossible: if the traditional Jew could accept elements (1) to (6), then he would be 'really much nearer to Liberal Judaism than to Orthodox Judaism'. Yet if these doctrines were accepted, then the idea of a 'national religion ... as different as possible from its environment and, especially, as different as possible from Christianity' seemed too much 'a sad and narrow conception' to satisfy.[112]

INTER-DENOMINATIONAL CONTROVERSY

Membership of the new Liberal Synagogue rose from 146 in 1912 to 446 in 1915,[113] and other London branches were established.[114] Marriage and burial requirements were met by 1913,[115] and the number of children attending the Liberal Jewish Religious School was recorded as 64 in 1914.[116] In the same year a waiting list was initiated for those wanting to join the synagogue, prompting plans for a larger building.[117] Inevitably, conflict arose between the growing movement and the established orders, and some of it was very bitter indeed. A bizarre example of the enmity of some among the Orthodox was the forgery by parties unknown of a letter from the Liberal Synagogue inviting guests to a Christmas evening celebration.[118] Less dramatic were the sermons and writings of Chief Rabbi Joseph Hertz, which often contained criticisms of Montefiore and which are useful in indicating the areas in which Liberal Jewish teaching was perceived as heretical. Over the years Hertz condemned Montefiore's 'notorious article' on higher criticism for undermining the authority of the Pentateuch,[119] denounced his failure to respect the rabbinical Law in matters of marriage and divorce,[120] and roundly refused Montefiore's request that the qualification 'Orthodox' be added to any future 'Jewish' pronouncements.[121] Similarities with Christian practice made it especially easy to question the authenticity of Montefiore's 'Jewishness'. Thus his experiments with Sunday Synagogue worship were regarded as 'a menace to Judaism calculated to undermine and sap the most sacred institution of our race',[122] and his abrogation of Jewish Law was 'an echo of Paul, as of every Jewish apostate since Paul's day, and is at absolute variance with the truth'.[123] Not unsurprisingly it was Montefiore's conciliatory approach to Christianity which provoked the fiercest recriminations. Hertz, a disciple of Solomon Schechter from his time at the Jewish Theological Seminary, sided with those who felt that 'the London movement' was an 'attempt to start a Jewish Christianity'.[124] In one highly public dispute, he went so far as to imply that Montefiore was trinitarian[125] – Montefiore was infuriated with what he described in the press as 'deftly chosen' quotations from his *The Old Testament and After* (1923), but Hertz responded coolly that 'if he *does* say these things, he must not object if he is told by Jews that the doctrine of Unity is still "an open question" to him'.[126]

Although Todd Endelman and others have demonstrated that nineteenth-century Christian conversionist efforts did not actually have a very great effect upon Anglo-Jewry and that relatively few converted (especially among the Ashkenazim),[127] Jewish religious leaders were deeply suspicious of and generally hostile towards interaction with Christianity, partly for fear of conversion. This attitude found its way into the Jewish media – the *Jewish Chronicle* of the period is full of articles refuting Christian teaching and theology[128] – and into popular Jewish consciousness. Combined with the threat of Christian conversion was the very real threat of the dilution of Jewish culture by the effect of the surrounding Christian culture. Together with the traditional anti-Christian bias, these fears explain the angry opposition Montefiore's attitude towards Christianity met with from many Jews. Montefiore himself reported that fellow Jews often told him, 'You know, Montefiore, I would join your movement if you would only give up your pre-occupation with Jesus and the Gospels.'[129]

Such conflicts emerged in spite of the fact that Montefiore went to great lengths not to antagonise his opponents unnecessarily. Areas in which he was prepared to sacrifice certain liberal principles for the higher sake of continuity and to avoid offence included: retaining a 'traditional' stance on circumcision and the regular Saturday Sabbath; and rejecting the use of the New Testament in synagogue services, something that he was certainly very interested in.[130] In his concern lest Liberal Jews be cut off by themselves from 'the great general mass of Jews with whom we desire to keep in touch',[131] he curtailed many of the progressive reforms to be found in the German and the US liberal movements. This concern to preserve what Jewish unity he could was reflected in correspondence with Lily Montagu before the J.R.U. was formed. 'Clearly we must, especially as regards public worship and the outward embodiment of religion, keep … our relation with other Jews. There must be a certain unity amid variety ... There is something very valuable in historical continuity.'[132] And writing as late as 1935 in an open letter for the Governing Body of the World Union for Progressive Judaism, Montefiore publicly reiterated his 'live and let live' policy with regard to the Orthodox.

> For many generations yet there will be many Jews who will find this [Orthodox] way to God, who will continue to believe in him and love him, through the medium, and on the basis, of Orthodox Judaism. Let them do so. Let us neither disturb them nor fail to do them honour.[133]

The role of Progressive Judaism was, he reiterated, simply to keep within the Jewish fold those for whom 'modern science and philosophy' made the traditional path impossible.

In this context, Montefiore differed from his friends Israel Abrahams and Herbert Loewe. Both men were able to maintain their liberalism within the confines of Orthodoxy in a way that Montefiore could not allow for himself. He did not condemn them for what he would have regarded for himself as 'sitting on the fence', for attempting to combine what could not be combined. Montefiore rationalised Abrahams' position arguing that, in his view, towards the end of his life Abrahams had been more 'extreme' than many members of the Liberal Jewish Synagogue. He preferred to see Abrahams, the co-founder of the J.R.U., as more of a 'defender of Orthodoxy' and a 'Reconciler' than as a *bona fide* Orthodox member, in spite of how others remembered him.[134] And as Loewe put it in the prologue to *A Rabbinic Anthology* (1938), which was itself an example of co-operation and acceptance between Orthodox and Liberal, his own theological differences with Montefiore were very often only a matter of degree.[135] The remaining differences, while causing conflict, were not necessarily to be a cause of concern. He valued Montefiore's liberal contribution as essential to the continued enrichment of Judaism, explaining the apparent 'conflict' as part of God's overall plan.

> In other words, until the Messiah come, the two forces of youth and age, tradition and progress, experience and venture, Orthodoxy and Liberalism, will continue in

equipoise – nay, in apparent conflict. He will reconcile them, for it is only in the end that the truth will become manifest: it needs infinity for two parallel lines to converge. Every conflict that is in the name of heaven is destined to endure, for God's world would be the poorer, would be incomplete, if one of the two forces were spent.[136]

Montefiore's intense sense of intellectual integrity and radicalism meant that he could not fully understand his friends' positions, although his temperament ensured that it did not get in the way of their friendship and academic partnership. He would certainly have approved of Loewe's comment that 'Labels are not religion and must not be mistaken for religion.'[137]

In more general terms, the psychological and social effect upon Anglo-Jewry of Montefiore's Liberal Judaism was not inconsiderable. On the one hand, the concern generated by the setting up of a Liberal Jewish Synagogue focused the minds of both Reform and Orthodox ministers considerably with regard to modernisation; Steven Sharot suggests that while the religious services of the West London Reform Synagogue were closer to those of the Orthodox United Synagogue before about 1920, they gradually became closer in both content and form to the Liberal synagogues from that point on.[138] On the other hand, there was also a direct 'ripple effect' of Montefiore's theology as his own notoriety grew and people were forced to take sides; for example, in 1912 the radical minister of Manchester Reform Synagogue, Harry Lewis, a supporter of the J.R.U., resigned his position after the synagogue's lay leadership refused to sanction sermons by Montefiore and Israel Mattuck.[139]

THE INFLUENCE OF GERMAN JUDAISM ON MONTEFIORE'S LIBERAL JUDAISM

As Michael Meyer points out in his article 'Jewish Religious Reform in Germany and Britain' (1999), Montefiore's Liberal Judaism shared a number of characteristics with the German Reform movement.[140] Together with the earlier Anglo-Reform theology, Anglo-Liberalism emphasised the idea of the 'Mission of Israel', an idea which had first gained currency with Mendelssohn. There was also the conception of the essence of

Judaism as 'ethical monotheism', as popularised by Hermann Cohen. Unlike the early Reform movement in Britain, there was a further parallel between Anglo-Liberal Judaism and the more radical Reform theology in Germany (as practised in Berlin) in that it purported to shift priority towards the 'inward' aspects of religion, such as faith and ethical behaviour, and away from the 'outward' traditional observance of ceremony and almost exclusive use of Hebrew. The Liberal Jewish Prayer Book (1903) was theologically different to that of the Anglo-Reform, and in line with that of the more radical German thought. Negatively, the new liturgy had expunged all petitions for a return of the Jewish people to Palestine, for the restoration of the State of Israel, and for the reinstitution of the sacrificial cult. Positively, it stressed both the election and responsibility of Israel, and emphasised the universalist interpretations of numerous elements of Jewish tradition. Montefiore's biblical critical attitude also echoed that of the German reformers, and Meyer suggests that (in contrast to Anglo-Reform) the Anglo-Liberal movement had 'turned for an answer to the ideology of the German movement'.[141] As the German reformers had done, Montefiore's new emphases were justified as the inevitable consequences of Progress. For Meyer, the similarities are too much to be a coincidence, and he comments, 'it is remarkable how far British Liberal Judaism was dependent upon ideas and practices developed in Germany'.[142]

Parallels do not necessarily indicate emulation, however, and the assumption that Montefiore was directly influenced by German Reform should be carefully examined. Meyer tracked down several articles in which Montefiore referred to German reformers positively, including Montefiore's self-association with Geiger in developing a Judaism which emphasised historical continuity in 'Is Judaism a Tribal Religion?' (1882), and a side reference to S. Formstecher in 'A Justification of Judaism' (1885).[143] In 'Jewish Religious Reform in Germany and Britain' (1999), Meyer emphasises Montefiore's comment in the *Jewish Quarterly Review* (1889) regarding Samuel Holdheim's radical *Reformgemeinde*:

> Without by any means agreeing with all that the Berlin Reformgemeinde has done, it is with this movement ... that I feel the deepest and closest spiritual kinship.[144]

He also finds it significant that the opening essay in the very first issue of Montefiore's *Jewish Quarterly Review* was written by the prominent Jewish historian and professor at the conservative Jewish seminary in Breslau, Heinrich Graetz, whose theology is regarded as almost precisely that of Montefiore.[145] This evidence of Montefiore's exposure to German reform is supported by the fact that Montefiore studied in Berlin and by Meyer's assertion in his earlier *Response to Modernity* (1988) that, 'While still at Oxford, Montefiore steeped himself in the writings of the German Reformers'.[146]

The first point to make is that, despite Meyer's argument, it is remarkable that amongst the many Christian scholars cited throughout his writings, Montefiore only very rarely included references to Jewish writers – Montefiore's apparent silence regarding Jewish scholarship has often been a cause for criticism among later Jewish commentators.[147] Secondly, Montefiore's comments are by no means examples of unqualified praise. In the case of Samuel Holdheim's *Reformgemeinde*, it is clear from the text that Montefiore by no means adopted it uncritically as the model for his own innovations. Likewise, regarding Graetz, Meyer complains elsewhere of Montefiore's apparent inconsistency in deriding the Breslau Reform Seminary.[148] And as Meyer himself recognises but fails to explain, only a few years later in 'Liberal Judaism in England' (1900), a paper dedicated to justifying and describing its development, and recognised at the time as 'one of the most important contributions he has made to the development of Jewish thought',[149] Montefiore made absolutely no reference to Germany. Partly, this can be explained by Montefiore's recognition of the inevitably negative repercussions in England of pointing to German Reform as an example or justification, since the German experience was generally viewed negatively by the Anglo-Jewish public (and certainly by the *Jewish Chronicle*). But it is probably best explained by the fact that by 1900 Montefiore was wrapped up in the peculiar challenges of forwarding a liberal agenda in Britain, rather than in Germany, and that other more useful and relevant religious models were available to him, as will become clear.

Nor is there any real evidence that Montefiore's educational background had saturated him in German Reform thought as Meyer implies. Although Oxford and Cambridge Universities had technically opened their doors to Jewish students, Montefiore would have found himself among a very small number of fellow Jewish undergraduates. Prior to 1914 there would not have been more than 25–30 Jewish undergraduates at Oxford at any one time.[150] Modern communication should not be assumed; cultural and intellectual isolation between Britain and Germany was significant at this time. It will later be argued that Montefiore's education was essentially *Christian* in character. For now it is enough to understand that an Oxford education at that time would certainly not have given Montefiore much exposure to what might be considered Jewish thought or influences.[151] As for his time spent in Berlin, it should be remembered that this only lasted six months and that most of this time was spent studying rabbinics with Schechter. Undoubtedly, Montefiore was well informed about the Reform experience in Germany and had read the writings of its leaders, but it would be going beyond the evidence to suggest that the inspiration for his own reforms originated with the German reformers, or that he had consciously modelled his movement upon what had happened there.

THE INFLUENCE OF AMERICAN JUDAISM ON MONTEFIORE'S LIBERAL JUDAISM

Montefiore's dealings with American Judaism are more straight-forward to analyse. Throughout his life, he kept in frequent contact with the Liberal institutions in the States, and carried out correspondence with, among others, Dr Julian Morgenstein, President of Hebrew Union College,[152] and the Zionist Dr Stephen Wise of the Jewish Institute of Religion in New York.[153] Despite the fact that his books sold badly in America,[154] Montefiore was well received during a tour of Reform and Liberal Synagogues in 1910 according to the accounts given in the *American Hebrew* at the time.[155] Upon his return, Montefiore spoke enthusiastically to the West London Synagogue Association of what he had seen: in contrast to the prevailing customs in England, men and women sat together in the pews; the sermon took a more central part in the service; the services themselves were successfully performed on Friday evenings, Saturdays and Sundays; and interchange between pulpits was common.[156] Despite his generally warm regard for American Jewish practices, however, Montefiore remained cautious of adopting non-British patterns of Synagogue worship. One of the earliest references he made to America was to argue that British Reform would not follow the example of Chicago where a Sunday Sabbath was observed.[157] Even after the establishment of a Liberal Jewish Synagogue, he was keen to play down any hopes of following the American model too closely. As he explained to Isadore Singer in 1910,

> The movement, or rather the new synagogue, which I and others are trying to found is not, and will not be, more radical than the [American] synagogues of Dr. Hirsch and Dr. Wise, but distinctly *less*. We do not, for example, propose to transfer or abolish the Saturday Sabbath. Our *main regular* service is to be on Saturday afternoon, though we also propose to try a monthly service on Sunday afternoon. Moreover, in other respects, the Synagogue … will be less radical than those of Dr. Hirsch and Dr. Wise.[158]

The situation became more 'radical' for Anglo-Liberal Judaism upon the arrival in January 1912 of Rabbi Israel Mattuck, a graduate of Hebrew Union College, who had been hand-picked for the London pulpit by Montefiore after a month-long search of American Reform congregations.[159] Generally speaking, the two men got on well. Mattuck referred to Montefiore as 'our leader' and 'teacher' and was content to work under Montefiore, who continued with the Presidency of the Liberal Synagogue and J.R.U.[160] Mattuck was well received by the members of the Liberal Synagogue, and the increased attendance under his leadership delighted Montefiore who was quite aware of his own limitations in terms of drawing a crowd and holding its attention.[161] By 1915 its members numbered 446 and from the mid-1920s on, its congregation of around 1,500 exceeded that of the West London Reform Synagogue.[162] Mattuck's spirited reforms included giving women permission to preach (1918) and to read prayers from the pulpit (1920), although Lily Montagu was certainly the driving force in forwarding the role of women within the synagogue and indignantly complained at the 'thirteen year delay' before they were able to partake in leading the service.[163] Sunday services took place from 1920 in Mortimer Hall until they became a regular feature of the religious activity of the congregation in 1926.[164] (According to the *Jewish Chronicle*, the numbers attracted to the Sunday service were higher than at the Sabbath morning service.)[165] Thus Mattuck offered the London Liberal congregation a window onto American developments.[166]

Inevitably there was a certain amount of tension between Montefiore and Mattuck, but this was more due to differences in style and attitude than due to specific reforms. As Montefiore once tried to explain,

> My world – the world of the Emancipation and Mr. Marks and Sir Francis Goldsmid and Lord Palmerston – was a good world – and a far better world than some of you think – but it is *so* different from this world in which we live. You must forgive a nearly complete stranger like me finding it very hard to move about in it, and understand the rights and the wrongs of it, its wishes and its ideals. We think in a quite unaccustomed light. Our light was a good light: the new light is doubtless also a good light; but they are oh! such *different* lights![167]

There were two main characteristics of Mattuck's American Liberal Judaism with which Montefiore struggled, as evidenced in their correspondence. (Most of their correspondence had to do with Mattuck's sermons, which Montefiore often wanted clarifying. He once ended a five-page critique by asking, 'Do you like getting these long letters? If not, beware of sermons which provoke them! Or: pray for a deaf day for *me* when I happen to be present.')[168] The first characteristic was Mattuck's dogmatic approach to Judaism which clashed with Montefiore's more aristocratic, individualist views. Montefiore was deeply troubled by what he regarded as his colleague's apparent desire for religious pronouncements on socio-political issues.[169] The second and more interesting characteristic was Mattuck's antagonism towards Christianity, about which Montefiore complained often and at considerable length. In one letter he wrote,

> The something else which I object to, and consider falla-cious, in your sermons is common to you and heaps of other Jews. It is common to most American Rabbis, so far as I know, common to their Teachers, common to the Teachers of their Teachers … It is a constant side reference to, and depreciation of, Christianity. It is a constant attempt to make

up differences between Judaism and Christianity, to the great advantage of Judaism ... I wish, when you revise your sermon, you could blot out from your mind the very existence of Christianity! I wish you could imagine yourself in a purely Buddhist or Confucian majority, or that you could forget all other persons but Jews![170]

In particular, Montefiore objected to the contrast between a very modern Judaism with an illiberal Christianity, that is, a Christianity of isolated texts from the New Testament or evangelical tracts. If one was to confront Christianity on equal terms, he argued, then it had to be Liberal Christianity taken at face value, and he urged his colleague to learn the lesson from the misrepresentations that Judaism had suffered throughout its history.[171] Deep down, however, what Montefiore reacted to was not so much Mattuck's defining of Judaism in terms of Christianity, so much as his aim to demonstrate the superiority of the one over the other. As will become clear, Montefiore was himself engaged in defining Judaism in terms of Christianity, but with a quite different goal; while Mattuck defined Judaism negatively in terms of how Judaism differed from Christianity, Montefiore attempted to define Judaism in terms of those positive elements which the two faiths shared in common. Montefiore's position was very much the unconventional one and, despite great respect for their spiritual leader, Mattuck and those who followed him never fully reconciled themselves to or agreed with Montefiore's sympathetic fascination for Christianity.

NOTES

54. D. Cesarani, *The Jewish Chronicle and Anglo-Jewry 1841–1991* (1994), pp. 45–6.
55. C.G. Montefiore, 'Some Notes on the Effects of Biblical Criticism upon the Jewish Religion', *Jewish Quarterly Review*, IV (1891–92), pp. 297–8.
56. M. Goulston, 'The Theology of Reform Judaism in Great Britain', in D. Marmur, ed., *Reform Judaism: Essays on Reform Judaism in Britain* (1973), p. 69.
57. Goulston suggests that had Morris Joseph been able to close the gap between his theology and practice and followed through the logic of his position more consistently, he would have been almost indistinguishable from Montefiore. Ibid., p. 71.
58. C.G. Montefiore, *Outlines of Liberal Judaism* (1912), p. 255. Elsewhere he wrote, 'They are a practice in self-denial. I would not seek to minimise their importance from this point of view.' C.G. Montefiore, *Liberal Judaism and Hellenism and Other Essays* (1918), pp. 130–1.

59. C.G. Montefiore, *Outlines of Liberal Judaism* (1912), p. 263.

60. With the caveat that 'The mind must be used in these matters, not a mere rule of thumb.' C.G. Montefiore, *Liberal Judaism and Hellenism and Other Essays* (1918), pp. 135–7.

61. A letter by F.S. Spiers to the *Jewish Chronicle* is typical. 'And how, according to Mr Montefiore, are "liberal" Jews thus to identify themselves with the religion of Israel? Not by the study of Israel's history, language and literature ... but by consciously and deliberately cutting themselves off from the community of Israel to form a petty sect, based indeed on an historic Judaism, even as was the primitive Christianity, but sundered forever from it by the substitution of the authority of self for the hallowed authority of the conscience of the Catholic Israel.' *Jewish Chronicle*, 22 October 1909, p. 21.

62. C.G. Montefiore, *The Old Testament and After* (1923), p. 567.

63. Letter from C.G. Montefiore to Lily Montagu, 12 April 1899. Microfilm No. 2718, Correspondence of Lily H. Montagu, A.J.A.C.

64. C.G. Montefiore, *Liberal Judaism and Hellenism and Other Essays* (1918), p. 111.

65. M. Goulston, 'The Theology of Reform Judaism in Great Britain', in D. Marmur, ed., *Reform Judaism: Essays on Reform Judaism in Britain* (1973), p. 71.

66. Letter from Israel Zangwill to C.G. Montefiore, 13 December 1907. MS A36/133, C.Z.A.

67. C.G. Montefiore, 'Liberal Judaism in England: Its Difficulties and Its Duties', *Jewish Quarterly Review*, XII (1899–1900), pp. 626, 631.

68. C.G. Montefiore, 'The Jewish Religious Union and Its Cause', unpublished address at the service of the Union on 20 June 1908.

69. C.G. Montefiore, 'Liberal Judaism in England: Its Difficulties and Its Duties', *Jewish Quarterly Review*, XII (1899–1900), p. 618.

70. Ibid., p. 621.

71. C.G. Montefiore, 'Unitarianism and Judaism in their Relations to Each Other', *Jewish Quarterly Review*, IX (1896), p. 245. Originally an address to Manchester College, Oxford, 20 October 1896.

72. C.G. Montefiore, 'Liberal Judaism in England: Its Difficulties and Its Duties', *Jewish Quarterly Review*, XII (1899–1900), p. 622.

73. Ibid., p. 648.

74. Ibid.

75. Ibid., p. 618.

76. L. Montagu, 'The Jewish Religious Union and Its Beginning', *P.F.J.P.*, XXVII (1927), pp. 1–2.

77. The *Jewish Chronicle* published a report of the development of the J.R.U. *Jewish Chronicle*, 30 October 1903, p. 15.

78. There is some evidence that Montagu's life-long admiration for Montefiore had once been love. Ellen Umansky speculates, 'The semi-autobiographical references in her [Montagu's] novels as well as references in other published works and letters indicate that Lily Montagu at one time may have been in love with Claude Montefiore ... As her secretary Jessie Levy confided, once the man that she loved (presumably Montefiore) married, she directed her love towards God and humanity in general.' E. Umansky, *Lily Montagu and the Advancement of Liberal Judaism* (1983), p. 238.

79. Writing privately in 1926 of her organisation of a world conference for Progressive Judaism, Montefiore enthused, 'It is a *wonderful* achievement; the unaided work of one woman: a remarkable result of faith, enthusiasm,

patience, courage and systemised attention to detail.' Letter from C.G. Montefiore to Lucy Cohen, 20 June 1926. L. Cohen, *Some Recollections of Claude Goldsmid-Montefiore 1858–1938* (1940), p. 155.

80. 'Indeed, he gave the other man's point of view so fully, so fairly, and so attractively, that his own teaching sometimes became a little confused just because he could not be dogmatic.' L. Montagu, 'Claude Montefiore – His Life and Work', address to the Liberal Jewish Synagogue (Sunday 30 January 1944). 'We sometimes thought that his own beliefs were not given the emphasis they deserved, because of the explanation he gave of the opinions of those who thought differently from him.' L. Montagu, 'Claude Montefiore as Man and Prophet', sermon at Liberal Jewish Synagogue (7 June 1958). MS 282/3/7, Lily H. Montagu Papers, Sermons and Addresses, A.J.A.C.

81. *Jewish Chronicle*, 30 October 1903, p. 15.

82. *Jewish Chronicle*, 6 June 1902, p. 11.

83. L. Montagu, 'The Jewish Religious Union and Its Beginning', *P.F.J.P.*, XXVII (1927), p. 20.

84. It was decided that the instrumental music during their services would be abandoned if the Chief Rabbi agreed with their request. With his refusal, the J.R.U. went back to their original plan. *Jewish Chronicle*, 30 October 1903, p. 15.

85. The invitation from the Council of the Reform Synagogue had no doubt been issued as a means by which to control a potential break-away. Service stipulations included: that only Jews could preach, that men and women would be seated separately, that the Ark would be opened and a portion of the Law would be read in Hebrew, that no hymns would be sung that had not been written by Jews, that only previously approved prayers in English could be used, that the *Amidah* would be read, that significant portions of the Hebrew liturgy be retained, and that the general service ritual would have to be approved first. *Jewish Chronicle*, 3 April 1903, p. 13. David Marks himself was more accommodating, although he recommended that 'our own ministers should take no active part in that service'. *Jewish Chronicle*, 3 April 1903, p. 12. Montefiore argued against the option due to its 'restrictive conditions'. *Jewish Chronicle*, 10 April 1903, p. 11.

86. Montefiore gave a talk on 'the validity of different "types" of Jewish services' (which was warmly complimented by the editor of the *Jewish Chronicle*) while Rev. Simeon Singer conducted the service. Caps were kept on. *Jewish Chronicle*, 24 October 1902, p. 9.

87. Sabbath services were held in the 'Wharncliffe Rooms' at the Hotel Great Central from 1902 to 1911, except for a short interruption from June to November 1903 when no services were held, and for a short spell at Steinway Hall when services resumed. *Jewish Chronicle*, 30 October 1903, p. 15 and 13 November 1903, p. 12.

88. *Jewish Chronicle*, 14 November 1902, p. 17.

89. *Jewish Chronicle*, 24 October 1902, p. 9.

90. Sermon reported in *The Jewish Chronicle*, 12 December 1902, p. 8.

91. Members of the United Synagogue included: Albert Jessel (vice-president), Felix Davies (treasurer); Simeon Singer, Aaron Green, J.F. Stern (ministers). Singer, who was also a vice-president for almost a year, left after pressure from his congregation. S. Sharot, 'Reform and Liberal Judaism in London: 1840–1940', *Jewish Social Studies*, Vol. 41 (1979), p. 219.

92. *Jewish Chronicle*, 30 October 1903, p. 16.

93. *Jewish Chronicle*, 16 October 1903, p. 15.

94. A. Kershen and J. Romain, *Tradition and Change: A History of Reform Judaism in Britian 1840–1995* (1995), p. 105. J.R.U. services were held in 'the Hill Street building' in Marylebone from 1911. In 1925, the Liberal Jewish Synagogue was opened in St John's Wood Road. Ibid., pp. 100, 106; also D. Philipson, *The Reform Movement in Judaism*, 2nd edn (1931), pp. 416, 417. A report published in the *Jewish Chronicle* states an attendance of 299. *Jewish Chronicle*, 30 October 1903, p. 15.

95. *Jewish Chronicle*, 30 October 1903, p. 15.

96. *Jewish Chronicle*, 10 June 1904, p. 13.

97. *Jewish Chronicle*, 24 February 1905, p. 26.

98. *Jewish Chronicle*, 17 May 1907, p. 30.

99. *Jewish Chronicle*, 23 October 1903, p. 9, 24 February 1905, p. 27, and 24 March 1911, p. 10. The East End branch was the only one at which there was separate seating for men and women.

100. Letter from C.G. Montefiore, undated. MSS 169 'Claude J.G. Montefiore', H.U.N.L. Montefiore once wrote, 'Mere negation is not necessarily of value. A noble life which observes the dietary laws is not necessarily nobler for giving them up.' Letter from C.G. Montefiore to Lily Montagu, 12 April 1899. Microfilm No. 2718, Correspondence of Lily H. Montagu, A.J.A.C.

101. C.G. Montefiore, 'The Jewish Religious Union and Its Cause', unpublished address (1908), p. 10.

102. L. Montagu, 'The Jewish Religious Union and Its Beginning', *P.F.J.P.*, XXVII (1927), p. 20.

103. *Jewish Chronicle*, 15 October 1909, p. 19.

104. *Jewish Chronicle*, 15 October 1909, pp. 19–22.

105. The *Jewish Chronicle* was highly critical of the 'spirit of revolt' stirred up by the J.R.U., and gave considerable coverage to Montefiore's critics. One edition published four pages of furious letters of complaint. *Jewish Chronicle*, 22 October 1909, pp. 20–3. Another three pages of letters were published the following week, including a number of negative pulpit responses. *Jewish Chronicle*, 29 October 1909, pp. 17–19. The Chief Rabbi's response in the form of a sermon was published the week after that, together with more letters. He was highly critical of what he described as 'the "fluid" principles on which the new synagogue is to be built'. *Jewish Chronicle*, 5 November 1909, pp. 18–19.

106. Oswald Simon, who had worked closely with Montefiore on various reforming experiments since 1881 and who had led the Sunday Movement in 1899, published his letter of resignation to Montefiore in the *Jewish Chronicle*, in explicit protest of the manifesto's denial of the external and divine authority of the Bible. (This, he implied, was the result of Montefiore being too greatly affected by the results of the 'New Criticism'.) He also made it clear that he did not share Montefiore's attitude towards traditional and orthodox Judaism. *Jewish Chronicle*, 29 October 1909, p. 17.

107. For example, Lily Montagu was obliged to resign from her youth work with the Reform Synagogue. *Jewish Chronicle*, 22 October 1909, p. 23.

108. *Jewish Chronicle*, 10 February 1911, p. 19.

109. L. Montagu, 'The Jewish Religious Union and Its Beginning', *P.F.J.P.*, XXVII (1927), p. 24.

110. A review at the time commented, 'The merit of the book consists in this: it is constructive … [I]n no other English book has there been so full, so inspiring a discussion of the fundamentals of the Jewish religion.' *Jewish Chronicle*, 20 February 1903, p. 24.

111. C.G. Montefiore, 'Is There a Middle Way?', *P.F.J.P.*, XXIII (1920), p. 12.
112. Ibid., pp. 13–14.
113. Actual attendance was considerably lower. *J.R.U. Bulletin* (March 1915), cited in S. Sharot, 'Reform and Liberal Judaism in London: 1840–1940', *Jewish Social Studies*, Vol. 41 (1979), p. 221.
114. The West Central and Golders Green & District branches were both created in 1914 and conducted monthly meetings. The first had a membership of 51, and the second of 44. *J.R.U. Bulletin* (November 1914), (March 1915), cited in S. Sharot, 'Reform and Liberal Judaism in London: 1840–1940', *Jewish Social Studies*, Vol. 41 (1979), p. 221. The North London Liberal Jewish congregation was established in 1921 with M. Perlzweig as minister. Between 300 and 400 people attended each of the first four sessions at which Mattuck, Montagu and Montefiore preached. *Jewish Chronicle*, 27 May 1921, pp. 30, 38.
115. In 1913 the Reform Synagogue placed a number of grave spaces at the disposal of the Liberal Synagogue. *Jewish Chronicle*, 24 January 1913, p. 30. In September 1914, Montefiore opened the two-acre Liberal Jewish Synagogue cemetery on Pound Lane, which was designed to hold 1,500 grave spaces, and in which there was erected a chapel and a colunbarium 'for the reception of cremated remains'. *Jewish Chronicle*, 2 October 1914, p. 9. The Liberal Synagogue was granted the right to solemnise civil marriages at the same time as the religious ceremony was performed in 1913. *Jewish Chronicle*, 21 February 1913, p. 20.
116. This number was twice that of the year before. *Jewish Chronicle*, 20 February 1914, p. 19.
117. Thirty households had joined in 1913–14. *Jewish Chronicle*, 20 February 1914, p. 19.
118. In a letter to Lily Montagu, Montefiore fumed, 'What a scandalous shame! I have never heard such a thing in my life. The enemies of the Liberal Movement sent out a forged circular from the Gov. Body of the Liberal [Synagogue?] inviting people to a Xmas evening function and Xmas tree in the Synagogue. I must relate the whole affair to you on Saturday.' Letter from C.G. Montefiore to Lily Montagu, 15 December, year uncertain. Microfilm No. 2718, Correspondence of Lily H. Montagu, A.J.A.C.
119. J.H. Hertz, 'The Five Books of the Torah', *Affirmations of Judaism* (1927), p. 41n. Montefiore complained of the Chief Rabbi, 'I see that our C[hief] R[abbi] has been kicking about again. I don't mind when he vituperates, for vituperation is in a sense neither true nor false, but when he speaks about criticism, and says that Wellhausen is all crumpled up, it makes me sad – that any one should venture to say such awful busters I feel ashamed – for him.' Letter from C.G. Montefiore to Stephen Wise, 28 May 1927. MS 19/27/7, Jewish Institute of Religion Papers, A.J.A.C.
120. J.H. Hertz, 'Marriage, Divorce and the Position of Women in Judaism', *Sermons, Addresses and Studies*, 3 vols (1938), pp. 64–5.
121. The argument had concerned *shechitah* which Hertz had described in *The Times* as 'the Jewish method of slaughter'. Montefiore's request was regarded as divisive and antagonistic. J.H. Hertz, 'The New Paths II', in *Affirmations of Judaism* (1927), p. 187.
122. 'Revolution in Judaism', in *The Express* (1909). ACC/3529/4/9, L.M.A.
123. Address at Conference of Anglo-Jewish Preachers (July 1927) in J.H. Hertz, *Sermons, Addresses and Studies*, II, 3 vols (1938), pp. 156–7.
124. Hertz quoted S. Dubnow in 'The New Paths II', in *Affirmations of Judaism* (1927), p. 170.

125. Hertz suggested that 'Liberals would be prepared to subscribe to the doctrine of the Trinity, if they were permitted to put their own interpretation on it, or that of advanced Christian theologians.' J.H. Hertz, 'The Unity of God', in *Affirmations of Judaism* (1927), pp. 19, 20.

126. Ibid., p. 20n.

127. T.M. Endelman, *Radical Assimilation in English Jewish History, 1656–1945* (1990), p. 97. R. Smith has argued that conversions among Ashkenazim, although rare, were often the result of a religious conviction, in contrast to the many more conversions among the wealthier Sephardic community in the eighteenth and nineteenth centuries, which are explained in terms of social and political disability, the effects of intermarriage and business expediency. R.M. Smith, 'The London Jews' Society and Patterns of Jewish Conversion in England, 1801–1859', in *Jewish Social Studies,* Vol. XLIII (1981).

128. For attacks against Christian conversionists in particular, see D. Cesarani, *The Jewish Chronicle and Anglo-Jewry 1841–1991* (1994), pp. 11, 21, 27–8, 39, 58–9.

129. Cited in L. Edgar, 'Claude Montefiore's Thought and the Present Religious Situation' (1966), p. 21.

130. In an unpublished paper, Montefiore 'went through the N[ew] T[estament] picking out bits which would be suitable for reading out at Sabbath services in Synagogue, if that time *ever* came when such readings would not do more harm than good.' Mrs MacArthur, Montefiore's secretary, cited in L. Cohen, *Some Recollections of Claude Goldsmid-Montefiore 1858–1938* (1940), p. 110.

131. C.G. Montefiore, 'The Jewish Religious Union: Its Principles and Future', *P.F.J.P.,* XXI (1918), p. 11.

132. In the same letter Montefiore wrote, '"New Judaism" should keep Passover, Pentecost, Tabernacles, New Year and Atonement. You can't create new festivals. Our present ones are a bond of union; they can be spiritualised and universalised.' Letter from C.G. Montefiore to Lily Montagu, 12 April 1899, marked 'strictly private and confidential'. Microfilm No. 2718, Correspondence of Lily H. Montagu, A.J.A.C.

133. Letter from C.G. Montefiore to Lily Montagu, 14 July 1935, formally a letter to apologise for missing the meeting of the Governing Body of the World Union in Holland. Microfilm No. 2718, Lily H. Montagu Correspondence, A.J.A.C.

134. C.G. Montefiore, 'IA: 1858–1925', *Transactions of the Jewish Historical Society of England,* XI (1924–27), pp. 245–6.

135. C.G. Montefiore and H. Loewe, eds, *A Rabbinic Anthology* (1938), p. lxxv.

136. Ibid., p. lxxi.

137. Ibid., p. lix.

138. Mixed seating (1923); services altered to meet the 'religious needs of the young' (1928); some traditional prayers were removed and English prayers added; an English hymn was sung and certain prayers read out loud by the congregation (1928). *Jewish Chronicle,* 30 March 1923, p. 12, 24 February 1928, p. 12, 9 March 1928, p. 15.

139. A. Kershen and J. Romain, *Tradition and Change: A History of Reform Judaism in Britian 1840–1995* (1995), p. 108. Lewis, a Zionist Cambridge graduate, left for the States in 1913 to become chaplain and principal of the Jewish Institute of Religion in New York.

140. M.A. Meyer, 'Jewish Religious Reform in Germany and Britain', in M. Brenner, R. Liedtke and D. Rechter, eds, *Two Nations: British and German Jews in Comparative Perspective* (1999), pp. 77–9.

141. Ibid.
142. Ibid.
143. Ibid., p. 444, n97.
144. C.G. Montefiore, 'Dr. Ritter's Text-Book of Reformed Judaism', *Jewish Quarterly Review*, I (1889), p. 278.
145. M.A. Meyer, 'Jewish Religious Reform in Germany and Britain', in M. Brenner, R. Liedtke and D. Rechter, eds, *Two Nations: British and German Jews in Comparative Perspective* (1999), p. 79.
146. M.A. Meyer, *Response to Modernity: A History of the Reform Movement in Judaism* (1988), p. 214.
147. For example, Walter Jacob has taken exception to what he describes as Montefiore's 'insular' studies, which rarely refer to other Jewish writers. W. Jacob, 'Claude G. Montefiore's Reappraisal of Christianity', *Judaism*, IXX (Summer 1970), p. 342. The only other reference that Montefiore makes to German reform is of a collection of sermons by Rabbi Dr Coblenz (of Bielefeld) from which he cites a sermon preached in 1896. The reform sermons are cited for being 'so unusual in a Jewish pulpit' in their assumption of biblical criticism. C.G. Montefiore, 'Should Biblical Criticism be spoken of in Jewish Pulpits?', *Jewish Quarterly Review*, XVIII (1906), p. 306.
148. M.A. Meyer, *Response to Modernity: A History of the Reform Movement in Judaism* (1988), p. 444 n97.
149. The review in the *Jewish Chronicle* was of 'Some Religious Difficulties of Today', based on 'Liberal Judaism in England'. *Jewish Chronicle*, 17 January 1902, p. 17.
150. T.M. Endelman, *Radical Assimilation in English Jewish History, 1656–1945* (1990), pp. 74, 80. The Oxford University Reform Act (1854) and the Cambridge University Reform Act (1856) had abolished the religious test for graduation, and in 1871 Jews were granted the right to take degrees and hold fellowships at Oxbridge colleges.
151. Circumstantial evidence includes Lucy Cohen's claim that Montefiore avoided clubs and societies (of all sorts). L. Cohen, *Some Recollections of Claude Goldsmid-Montefiore 1858–1938* (1940), p. 40.
152. Letters to Morgenstein included advice against asking Dr Abelson, an Anglo-Jewish rabbi, to teach Jewish philosophy at H.U.C. (advice which corresponded with that of I. Abrahams' and which was followed), and fears that 'your younger Rabbis are getting very radical!' with regard to Zionism and 'ethical culture'. Letters from C.G. Montefiore to J. Morgenstein, 23 March 1925, 14 January 1935. MS 5 A-19/12, Hebrew Union College Papers, A.J.A.C.
153. Despite Wise's Zionism, Montefiore greatly admired him, and his letters included such sensitive material as attacks on Israel Zangwill and the Chief Rabbi. Letters from C.G. Montefiore to Stephen Wise, 17 December 1923, 28 May 1928. MS 19/27/7, Jewish Institute of Religion Papers, A.J.A.C.
154. In one letter to an American Rabbi, Montefiore bemoaned the lack of sales. 'This is going to be THE MOST CONCEITED letter you ever read. I often wonder why it is that practically no copies of my books sell in America. I venture to think that you have no book … Of course nobody pushes them. Macmillan has no interest in doing so, practically. Do you think that there is anything which can be done?' Letter from C.G. Montefiore to Louis Wolsey, 27 September c1924. MS 15/3/5, Wolsey Papers, A.J.A.C.

155. Highly effusive reports of Montefiore are given in the Conservative Reform journal, *American Hebrew*, 10 June and 8 July 1910.

156. As reported in *American Hebrew*, 24 February 1911.

157. Defending Oswald Simon's Sunday Movement in 1899, Montefiore argued that the fear of a Sunday Sabbath could be shown to be baseless when one considered America where only one such example (Chicago) existed (in addition to many examples of strong Saturday Sabbaths). He added, 'It is very unlikely, I think, that Hampstead would follow Chicago; it is far more likely to follow New York or Philadelphia.' *Jewish Chronicle*, 30 June 1899, pp. 8–9.

158. Letter from C.G. Montefiore to Dr Isadore Singer, 2 February 1910. MS 42/1/4, Isadore Singer Papers, A.J.A.C.

159. Montefiore had considered many possibilities for a suitable rabbi. In a letter dated 22 May 1910, Israel Zangwill wrote, 'I am posting you an American paper with a portrait of Rabbi Charles Fleischer because I have read somewhere that he is one of those in your mind for your movement. He certainly impressed me favourably when I met him in Boston.' MS A36/133, C.Z.A. Montefiore settled on Mattuck after he had spent over a month in America. He attended the Conference of American Reform Rabbis, and visited Reform Temples in New York, Chicago, Pittsburgh, Philadelphia and Cincinnati. C. Bermant, *The Cousinhood: The Anglo-Jewish Gentry* (1971), p. 318.

160. I. Mattuck, 'Our Debt to Claude G. Montefiore', sermon (1938).

161. 'Very large congregation today. They *do* like M[attuck].' Letter from C.G. Montefiore to Lucy Cohen, 30 March 1928. L. Cohen, *Some Recollections of Claude Goldsmid-Montefiore 1858–1938* (1940), p. 173. 'I fear that I am not a sensitive person enough in some directions. E.g. Mattuck says he can always feel if his audience is bored or interested, sympathetic or antagonistic. I feel nothing, one way or the other.' Letter from C.G. Montefiore to Lucy Cohen, 9 September 1931. Ibid., p. 205.

162. Liberal Jewish Synagogue, St John's Wood: 784 (1921), 1,491 (1928), 1,622 (1939). West London Reform Synagogue: 1,197 (1924), 1,266 (1930), 1,386 (1936). S. Sharot, 'Reform and Liberal Judaism in London: 1840–1940', *Jewish Social Studies*, Vol. 41 (1979), pp. 221–2.

163. L. Montagu, 'The Jewish Religious Union and Its Beginning', *P.F.J.P.*, XXVII (1927), p. 27. Montefiore had made public his support in principle for women ministers in 1920. *Jewish Chronicle*, 19 March 1920, p. 21.

164. D. Philipson, *The Reform Movement in Judaism*, 2nd edn (1931), p. 417.

165. *Jewish Chronicle*, 30 October 1925, p. 13, 23 March 1928, p. 20, 29 March 1935, p. 38.

166. Later, the Liberal congregation in Liverpool also enjoyed an American influence in the shape of Rabbi Morris Goldstein. D. Philipson, *The Reform Movement in Judaism* (1931), p. 418. Goldstein had graduated from Hebrew Union College in 1927 and had a deep interest in Christianity. His *Jesus Within the Jewish Tradition* was published in 1950.

167. Letter from C.G. Montefiore to Israel Mattuck, date uncertain. MS 165/1/12, Sheldon and Amy Blank Papers, A.J.A.C.

168. Letter from C.G. Montefiore to Israel Mattuck, 6 January 1935. ACC/3529/4/2, L.M.A.

169. Montefiore once wrote, 'I am inclined to think that you do *hanker* after a collective, definite Jewish attitude, – a categorical pronouncement – towards social, political and international questions. Here I find great

difficulties.' Letter from C.G. Montefiore to Israel Mattuck, 5 January 1935. ACC/3529/4/2, L.M.A.

170. Letter from C.G. Montefiore to Israel Mattuck, undated. MS 165/1/12, Sheldon and Amy Blank Papers, A.J.A.C.

171. Montefiore warned, 'For us Liberals to say, "If you think thus and thus, you are not a Christian" or "such an opinion in you is not Christian" is a very dangerous argument. Surely we have suffered from, and indignantly reject, such an argument ourselves.' Letter from C.G. Montefiore to Israel Mattuck, undated. MS 165/1/12, Sheldon and Amy Blank Papers, A.J.A.C.

5

Influences upon Montefiore's View of Rabbinic Judaism

Bowler has suggested that a vital factor in Jewish life, namely, the close interaction of a tightly knit community, was missing in Montefiore's early life.[172] But although his parents encouraged non-Jewish friendships and associations,[173] this was not in itself unusual for a wealthy Anglo-Jewish family of the period. If anything, Montefiore's upbringing was more Jewish (certainly in a religious sense) than it was for many of the contemporary Anglo-Jewish elite. Nevertheless, it is significant that in a study of one of the most important English religious Jews in recent times, the list that can be drawn-up of Jewish and rabbinic influences upon Montefiore seems relatively short in comparison with the list of non-Jewish influences, and its impact less profound.

During their childhood, Montefiore and his siblings attended the Berkeley Street Reform Synagogue with their mother.[174] Receiving his early religious instruction and tutoring in Hebrew from its first minister, David Wolf Marks, meant that Montefiore grew up under the auspices of the father of Anglo-Jewish Reform (Marks was minister of the West London Synagogue from 1840 to 1900, and Professor of Hebrew at U.C.L. from 1848 to 1898). The importance of this lies in the fact that Marks wrote and preached extensively against 'rabbinism' and Jewish particularism, arguing that Reform was necessary to preserve Judaism from external attack, that is, Christian criticism.[175] He was keen to be seen to be as respectable and spiritually minded as he perceived contemporary Christians to be; David Feldman has even offered evidence that in formulating his reforms for the West London Synagogue, Marks consulted one of the most anti-rabbinical Christian conversionists of the time, Alexander McCaul.[176] This anxiety to imitate and react to Christian critique reflects a high regard for contemporary Christian practice and intellectualism. Montefiore undoubtedly absorbed a great deal from Marks – he was fond of referring to his influence in his letters[177] – and it is tempting to locate the source of Montefiore's positive view of Christianity and correspondingly relatively low opinion of the rabbinic writings in Marks' assumed value-judgements. Montefiore, whose Liberal Jewish views were a good deal more radical than those of Marks, himself wrote,

> I have no doubt that the roots of my belief *are* through Mr. Marks … A man often and often rebels against his tradition and is *really* deeply influenced by it all the same. Don't you think so?[178]

A second powerful influence on the young Montefiore, but one from a very different point of view, was the Romanian Solomon Schechter (1847–1915) who taught Montefiore rabbinics and rabbinical lore at the Liberal College for Jewish Studies in Berlin for six months after Montefiore had finished at Oxford. Describing him later as 'one of the greatest Rabbinical scholars of the world',[179] Montefiore was impressed enough to bring Schechter back with him upon his return to England as his private tutor. Schechter went on to become lecturer in Talmudic studies at Cambridge from 1890 until 1902.[180] To Schechter, Montefiore felt he owed his 'whole conception of the Law and its place in the Jewish religion and life … most of the rabbinical material on which that conception rests was put to my notice and explained to me by him'.[181] That this is no exaggeration can be seen from their extensive correspondence at this time. Subjects that turn up repeatedly in their letters included the joy of the Law, dogmas of Judaism, and queries regarding the Talmud and the Hasidic mystics of Schechter's home environment.[182] Schechter contributed to Montefiore's *Jewish Quarterly Review* and even wrote an appendix for his *Hibbert Lectures* (1893). In return, Montefiore helped him in composing and publishing his articles, and in the provision of financial support for years after Schechter arrived in England. Schechter's struggle to keep afloat financially and hints of his growing resentment on his dependence upon Montefiore are reflected in their correspondence.[183] For a long time Schechter felt compelled to down-play any differences between himself and Montefiore's views, and Montefiore came to regard him as a fellow reformer. As he explained, 'There is no orthodoxy which would receive you. You would be too original for any creed ... You can call yourself what you please, but to me you are a liberal all round.'[184]

Yet the differences were in fact significant. While Montefiore accepted Schechter's teachings regarding rabbinic thought, the two men differed significantly on their interpretation and understanding of modern Judaism and also with regard to Zionism. As Norman Bentwich commented,[185] Schechter was from a 'low synagogue', ghetto background; he retained a love of mystic saints and mystic yearning, and composed no systematic theology but worked intuitively, like the rabbis. He emphasised tradition and the continuity of past and present Judaism; he vehemently opposed schism. Montefiore, on the other hand, had been educated in Jowett's Oxford, home of Liberal Christianity. His approach to Judaism was coloured by his view of Progress, rather than continuity; he rejected tradition as binding and eventually broke away to form a liberal branch of Judaism. He imbibed much of the Christian doctrine and attempted to produce a positive Jewish attitude towards it, in contrast to Schechter who was traditionally negative and very sensitive to Christian antisemitism. (Montefiore once commented that Schechter seemed to suffer from some sort of 'anti-anti-semitic fever'.)[186] Eventually, much to Montefiore's regret, the tension that developed between them ended their friendship. Schechter wrote to Norman Bentwich in 1902 that he had made his name in England without needing either Montefiore or Chief Rabbi Adler 'and largely against them'.[187] He left for America to found Conservative Judaism in the same year (1902) that Montefiore initiated the Jewish Religious Union for the Advancement of Liberal Judaism.

Until 1902 Montefiore had depended heavily upon Schechter for his rabbinic expertise and intellectual support. Schechter's place at Cambridge was filled by Israel Abrahams (1858–1925). Montefiore and Abrahams had worked together as joint-editors of the *Jewish Quarterly Review* (1888–1908) and had jointly published *Aspects of Judaism* (1895), a collection of sermons. It was, however, for his support in the founding of the J.R.U. that Montefiore was most grateful to Abrahams, especially during the early, most difficult stages from 1902 to 1912.[188] As with Schechter, Montefiore claimed Abrahams as 'an enthusiastic Liberal Jew',[189] his admiration and affection making it possible for him to breeze over their theological differences. But Herbert Loewe was probably more accurate when he observed,

> Abrahams was more a man of the Jewish Religious Union than of the Liberal Jewish Synagogue ... The Liberal Jewish Synagogue had his warm support but he played a much greater part in the Jewish Religious Union ... Criticism appealed to him but he was essentially conservative ... Generally [he] was Orthodox.[190]

Certainly, the Law was of central importance to Abrahams' understanding of Judaism, and he criticised the early reformers including David Marks, for having rejected its authority and ignored its permanent value.[191] This was a mistake, Abrahams felt, which had kept them blind to an important truth. Just as people were coming to accept that man had played a part in the production of the Bible, through the findings of biblical criticism, so it was the case that God had played a part in the Tradition. 'If the Bible is not all of God', he asked, 'is the Talmud all of man?' The idea of the evolution of religion allowed a modern Jew to rediscover a value in the recently denigrated texts of his religion. This was, he asserted, 'the great discovery of our time, and it is the Talmud that has helped us to the discovery'. For the Talmud presented the processes as well as the results of religious thought, and in it could be seen 'religious evolution in action ... The Talmud comes into line with modern theories of the evolution of religion.'[192]

Personifying Montefiore's ideal of 'an Englishman of the Jewish persuasion' and as anti-Zionist as Montefiore, Abrahams was an important friend, collaborator and supporter. Both were among the literary mainstays of the anti-Zionist *Jewish Guardian* from its founding in 1919. And both were concerned with correcting the erroneous views of the Law in mainstream biblical scholarship and worked hard to increase the respectability of Judaism in academic circles. Thus Abrahams eloquently supported Montefiore's criticism of Schürer's misportrayal of Torah-centric Judaism in his article, 'Prof. Schürer on Life under the Law' (1899).[193] Using an argument which Montefiore would later adopt as his own, Abrahams claimed: 'I have enough sympathy with the Law to do it justice, and not enough sympathy to do it the injustice of unqualified flattery.'[194] While there were obvious differences of opinion between Montefiore and Abrahams, the latter certainly did not take the pains to articulate them. For example, Abrahams had originally intended to contribute a third volume to Montefiore's *Synoptic Gospels*, but it was never written, probably for the very reason that he did not feel comfortable contributing to a work whose value-judgement of first-century Judaism was so foreign to his own. Specifically, Abrahams differed too greatly from Montefiore with regard to the rabbis and he eventually decided it was best to publish his material separately in *Studies in Pharisaism and the Gospels* (2 vols, 1917–24).

Abrahams' successor at Cambridge was Herbert Loewe (1882–1940), remembered for his tolerant and informed Orthodoxy. Like Abrahams, Loewe was regarded within English academic circles as the chief representative of Anglo-Jewish scholarship. Just as his grandfather, Louis Loewe, had been the confidant and adviser of Moses Montefiore, so Herbert became a close friend to Claude. Together, they produced the renowned *A Rabbinic Anthology* (1938) in which both the Liberal and the Orthodox points of view were set down next to each other. Loewe's 50-page prologue was concerned to contrast their positions and yet, significantly, he finished by describing his co-author as 'My master, my guide and my intimate friend'.[195] He held Montefiore's grasp of the rabbinic literature in high regard.[196] In spite of, or perhaps because of, their great respect for one another, each was comfortable enough to disagree openly without compromise. This had not been possible with Schechter, whose eventual burst of condemnation regarding his former pupil's anti-Zionism in the *Jewish Chronicle* came as a shock and a great hurt to the latter. Nor had it really been possible with Montefiore's exact contemporary, Abrahams, whose position as co-member of the fragile J.R.U. had left him little room to manoeuvre. Thus Loewe and Montefiore were able to use each other as foils in order to better clarify his own position within the Jewish tradition.

Despite his defence of the rabbinic veneration of Torah, Montefiore ultimately rejected rabbinic authority. Down through the years, this has provoked two main responses from Jewish scholars. On the one hand, there are those who concentrate upon his attempt to champion Jewish teachings to Christians. Examples include Walter Jacob, for whom Montefiore's correction of erroneous views of the Law (*à la* Paul) reflected his 'fine understanding of rabbinic Judaism',[197] and Edward Kessler, who focuses upon Montefiore's infrequent claims that Liberal Judaism was the heir of Rabbinic Judaism, and emphasises his role as its defender against Christian prejudice.[198] On the other hand, there are others who detect a certain superficiality. In his lecture, 'Montefiore and Loewe on the Rabbis' (1962), Louis Jacobs found Montefiore's observation that 'these old gentlemen' could have benefited from a course in Greek philosophy 'rather condescending'.[199] He also criticised the attempt to portray rabbinic thought almost exclusively from *aggadah* (often described as the story-like, non-legal material in the rabbinic literature) rather than *halakhah* (matters of law), and regarded Montefiore's justification for doing so (namely, that the halakhic material was in modern times regarded as 'distant and obsolete ... a waste of mental energy and time') as quite unsatisfactory.[200] Montefiore is simply wrong, according to Jacobs, to accept charges of 'legalism' against Judaism, since Judaism displays not a love of law but is rather a law of love.[201] Similarly, in a lecture on 'Legalism' (1979), Bernard Jackson observed, 'It must be counted a weakness in his work that he [Montefiore] assumed the identity of the distinction between *halakhah* and *aggadah* with our distinction (itself a secularisation of Protestant theology) between law and morality.'[202] For Jackson, Montefiore's view of the Law resulted from his attempt to justify Judaism in Christian, not Jewish, terms.[203] Like Jacobs, Lou Silberman was astounded at what he described as Montefiore's 'priggish' and 'condescending' attitude towards the rabbinic approach. In his 'Prolegomenon' to the 1968 edition of Montefiore's *The Synoptic Gospels*, Silberman condemned Montefiore's treatment as a 'wrong-headed interpretation of the rabbinic attitude towards and understanding of Holy Scriptures'.[204] Jacobs and Silberman cannot accept that Montefiore could, on occasion, speak approvingly of the rabbinic approach to *halakhah*, and while Jackson at least recognises that Montefiore's views were 'complex' and seemed to mellow with time,[205] he emphasises what he sees as Montefiore's view of the Law as something to be distinguished from morality/ethics and thus rejected.

The most comprehensive analysis of Montefiore's understanding of rabbinics and Torah, Frederick Schwartz's essay 'Claude Montefiore on Law and Tradition' (1964), manages to reconcile Montefiore's frequently negative comments about the Law with his underlying positive appreciation of it, and thus with his defence of the Jewish veneration of the Law.[206] He does this by distinguishing between Montefiore's view of modern and pre-modern approaches to Torah, rather than distinguishing between Montefiore's use of *aggadah* and *halakhah*. Thus Schwartz does not find it patronising, as Silberman and Jacobs did, for Montefiore to have sympathised with and even praised the pre-modern rabbis who had achieved so much given the limitations of human knowledge at the time. Furthermore, he recognises that Montefiore, who usually spoke positively of the Law in modern times only in the sense of a moral Law,[207] did not by this only mean *aggadah*. Montefiore was always respectful of *halakhah* and ritual observance and regarded them as entirely legitimate religious phenomena (after all, he had enormous respect for Schechter, Loewe and others). He saw no role for Liberal Judaism with regard to those who accepted the literal inspiration of Torah, and repeatedly denied that the Liberal Jewish cause sought to poach observant Jews.[208] Montefiore's apparently paradoxical approach (both for and against Rabbinic Judaism, viewing *halakhah* at times as 'legalistic' and redundant, while at other times a source of inspiration and morally wholesome) is, in fact, quite consistent and comprehensible in the light of his Liberal Jewish theology. In his eyes, what was once useful – and could still be useful for many – in bridging the gap between man and God (in terms of outlining a path for personal morality/sanctification and for collective justice) had all too often in too many individual cases become a barrier in modern times. While there was nothing wrong with the Law in itself, Montefiore was nevertheless wary of the dangers, as he saw it, of a tendency of some Orthodox towards externalism and casuistry, and it was in this context he spoke polemically against it. As Schwartz put it, in the final analysis Montefiore wanted nothing binding between the Jew and God, one way or the other.[209] Ultimately, it was his firm faith in Progress and the rationalist assumption that Reason has priority over authoritative texts – rather than a belief that the texts could not be ethical, or an arrogant disregard of rabbinic thought-processes – that accounts for Montefiore's often negative treatment of halakhic material. Such confidence and belief in man's ability to discover the Truth could be found, to a lesser extent, in the writings of his tutors in rabbinics. But Montefiore's radicalism, the degree to which he was prepared to sacrifice the rabbinic roots of his Jewish faith, marks him out more as the disciple of Jowett than of Schechter, Abrahams or Loewe.

NOTES

172. M.G. Bowler, *Claude Montefiore and Christianity* (1988), p. 15.
173. L. Cohen, *Some Recollections of Claude Goldsmid-Montefiore 1858–1938* (1940), p. 31.
174. Ibid., p. 29.
175. Englander makes the point that 'the progressives, drawn from the most acculturated elements of the elite, moved in the best circles and were not unmindful of the antagonism provoked by Rabbinic Judaism [among Christians]'. Montefiore was not entirely above such peer pressure. D. Englander, 'Anglicised but not Anglican', in G. Parsons, ed., *Religion in Victorian Britain*, I (1988), p. 260.
176. D. Feldman, *Englishmen and Jews: Social Relations and Political Culture 1840–1914* (1994), p. 58. McCaul taught Hebrew at King's College, London from 1841 and was an influential pamphletist.
177. At least, he often referred to Marks' influence in letters to Lucy Cohen. L. Cohen, *Some Recollections of Claude Goldsmid-Montefiore 1858–1938* (1940), p. 37.
178. Letter from C.G. Montefiore to Lucy Cohen, 6 January 1932. Ibid., p. 208.
179. C.G. Montefiore, 'Jewish Scholarship and Christian Silence', *Hibbert Journal*, I (1903), p. 338.
180. Solomon Schechter (1847–1915) was an outstanding authority on the Talmud. His *Some Aspects of Rabbinic Theology* (1909) led to a sympathetic reappraisal of the teachings of the Pharisees. After having discovered many important documents in the Cairo Synagogue *genizah* in 1896–97, he published *Documents of Jewish Sectaries* (1910). In 1902 Schechter left for the US to serve as President of the Jewish Theological Seminary in New York, which he developed as a major centre for the training of rabbis in Conservative Judaism. In 1913 he founded the United Synagogues of America which grew from 23 to 800 Conservative congregations. He considered this organisation to be his greatest legacy, believing deeply in a strong congregational base for Conservative Judaism.
181. From the preface to his *Hibbert Lectures* (1893).
182. See J.B. Stein, *Lieber Freund: The Letters of Claude Goldsmid Montefiore to Solomon Schechter 1885–1902* (1988).
183. Ibid., pp. 1–2, 13, 23, 36.
184. Letter from C.G. Montefiore to Solomon Schechter, undated. Ibid., p. 52.
185. N. Bentwich, 'Claude Montefiore and his Tutor in Rabbinics: Founders of Liberal and Conservative Judaism', 6th Montefiore Memorial Lecture, Southampton (1966), p. 11.
186. 'You seem to me to have a sort of anti-anti-Semitic fever. I don't see these horrors in England but we shall probably neither convince the other!' Letter from C.G. Montefiore to Solomon Schechter, 9 December 1898. J.B. Stein, *Lieber Freund: The Letters of Claude Goldsmid Montefiore to Solomon Schechter 1885–1902* (1988), p. 42.
187. Cited in S.A. Cohen, *English Zionists and British Jews: The Communal Politics of Anglo-Jewry, 1895–1920* (c.1982), p. 164n.
188. C.G. Montefiore, *Studies in Memory of Israel Abrahams* (1927), p. lxiv.
189. Ibid., p. lxii.
190. H. Loewe, *Israel Abrahams* (1944), pp. 68–9.
191. 'In his first sermon, the late Prof. Marks proclaimed this rejection, and declared with thorough-going emphasis, that the Bible and the Bible alone

is the authoritative and inspired guide to Jewish life.' I. Abrahams, *Some Permanent Values in Judaism: Four Lectures* (1924), p. 77.

192. Ibid., pp. 78, 81.
193. One of Abrahams' main complaints was that Schürer had failed to take into account the criticisms of Montefiore (regarding, for example, ritual uncleanliness) in the new edition of his book. He asked rhetorically, 'Why is it that a man like Mr. Montefiore has been moved to such unwonted heat when dealing with Schürer's charges against the Law?' I. Abrahams, 'Prof. Schürer on Life Under Jewish Law', *Jewish Quarterly Review*, XI (1899), p. 641.
194. Ibid., p. 626.
195. Prologue to C.G. Montefiore and H. Loewe, eds, *A Rabbinic Anthology* (1938), p. civ.
196. He [Montefiore] had an uncanny genius for distinguishing the real from the apparent ... he would wander through the mazes of commentaries without a guide, whether the passage was in Hebrew or Aramaic ... His memory was uncanny.' Letter from Herbert Loewe to Lucy Cohen, undated. L. Cohen, *Some Recollections of Claude Goldsmid-Montefiore 1858–1938* (1940), p. 202.
197. W. Jacob, *Christianity Through Jewish Eyes: The Quest for Common Ground* (1974), p. 94.
198. Montefiore's occasional suggestion that Liberal Judaism was heir to the rabbis referred to a particular aspect of their approach. 'It is rather anachronistic to regard the Rabbis as a sort of early example of Progressive and Liberal Jews, but, nevertheless, they did a great work for Judaism. They saved us from becoming a book religion in the sense that every word of the book must be accepted in its most literal sense, as perfect and unimprovable. Their "readings in", their developments, their additions, maintained a certain flow, a certain unrigidity. They prevented the slaughter of the spirit by the letter ... In a pre-critical age the Rabbinic interpretations and developments were, in a sense, the pre-cursor ... of Modernist freedom. The old Rabbinic development paved the way for the new liberal developments.' C.G. Montefiore, 'The Old Testament and Judaism', in W. Robinson, ed., *Record and Revelation* (1938), pp. 428–9. Even so, Kessler accepts that Montefiore actually viewed rabbinic Judaism as 'primarily a legalistic religion'. E. Kessler, 'Claude Montefiore: Defender of Rabbinic Judaism?', *Jewish Historical Studies: Transactions of the Jewish Historical Society of England*, XXXV (1996–98), pp. 234, 236.
199. L. Jacobs, 'Montefiore and Loewe on the Rabbis', The Liberal Jewish Synagogue, Claude Montefiore Lecture (1962), pp. 4, 9.
200. Ibid., pp. 19–24.
201. Ibid., pp. 18f.
202. B. Jackson, 'Legalism', *Journal of Jewish Studies*, III (1979), p. 14.
203. Ibid., p. 2.
204. L.H. Silberman, 'Prolegomenon', in the 1968 edition of C.G. Montefiore, *The Synoptic Gospels*, p. 4.
205. Jackson noted, 'Montefiore's attitude to the *halakhah* ... was complex, and not without internal development over the years' and 'Thus the strident tone of some passages in the Hibbert Lectures (as at p. 496) is hardly found in Montefiore's later writings.' B. Jackson, 'Legalism', *Journal of Jewish Studies*, III (1979), p. 1 and p. 1, n2.
206. F.C. Schwartz, 'Claude Montefiore on Law and Tradition', *The Jewish Quarterly Review*, LV (1964), p. 26. Schwartz works most closely with

Montefiore's *Rabbinic Literature and Gospel Teachings* and, of course, his *Rabbinic Anthology*.

207. F.C. Schwartz, 'Claude Montefiore on Law and Tradition', *The Jewish Quarterly Review*, LV (1964), p. 42.

208. '[L]et me repeat for the hundreth time that we [the J.R.U.] do not want to take away a single soul from those who now attend, and are satisfied with, the existing synagogue services.' *Jewish Chronicle*, 29 October 1909, p. 18.

209. F.C. Schwartz, 'Claude Montefiore on Law and Tradition', *The Jewish Quarterly Review*, LV (1964), p. 52.

6

Judaism and Nationalism

The modern dichotomy between Jewish religion and/or Jewish nation originated with the Enlightenment and Moses Mendelssohn (1729–86). As both a cultured German philosopher and a religious Jew he made credible to Europe the existence of rational Judaism and the possibility of what Arthur Cohen calls 'the de-Judaised Jew' who maintains that 'Judaism is not revealed religion, but revealed legislation'.[210] In his influential view, only their ceremonial laws were peculiar to the people of Israel and were unchangeable; doctrines and historical truths were not the product of Divine revelation and were therefore available to the rest of mankind. What was important, he believed, was that which was designed to preserve the Jewish ethnic group. Mendelssohn is therefore generally credited with the innovation of severing the interconnection of the Jewish faith and people. The ultimate influence of Mendelssohn's conception of a rational Jewish religion, to be distinguished from Jewish culture, is traceable in Montefiore's position, although his definition of Jewish religion differed enormously from Mendelssohn's. Mendelssohn's view that *halakhah* was the sectarian expression that differentiated the Jew from the non-Jew infuriated Montefiore, *halakhah* being precisely that aspect of Orthodoxy in which he had least interest.[211]

Montefiore regarded himself, along with the majority of the Anglo-Jewish elite, as a patriotic Englishman who happened to be Jewish by religion. Jewish culture, so far as it existed, was best discarded and replaced by the customs and manners of one's host nation. As an influential communal leader he was keen to encourage good citizenship, and often urged young Jews to join the armed forces (so as to help steer them away from the kinds of employment upon which they were over-dependent and to help improve their 'present inadequate Jewish physique'). It was essential, he felt, that foreigners should anglicise themselves as rapidly as possible.[212] Moreover, he believed that where conflict existed between loyalty to one's country and loyalty to one's fellow Jews, the first automatically overrode the second.[213] While he himself dismissed the idea of Jewish traits such as ostentatiousness, he was highly sensitive to the prejudices of non-Jews, and often preached that it was up to the Jews to disprove such slurs and to go on to demonstrate their high-mindedness and usefulness to England.[214]

In sharp contrast to his English patriotism, Montefiore was resolutely opposed to the Jewish nationalism and particularism of many of his contemporaries, whether it was integrated into a religious outlook, as it was for many Orthodox Jews, or took on a purely political form as Zionism. This was partly to do with his early upbringing and, specifically, to the influence of Philip Magnus, a vehement anti-Zionist who became the second minister at the West London Reform Synagogue in 1866.[215] Magnus made a name for himself as an educationalist and had been selected as one of Montefiore's private tutors, responsible for his general education. He continued to guide and work alongside Montefiore for the rest of his life. Along with his former pupil, Magnus was among the group of 'representative Jews' approached by the government in 1917 for their opinion on the proposed Balfour Declaration, and, like Montefiore, he opposed the recognition of Palestine as '*the* national home for the Jewish people'. He was also a founder of the League of British Jews formed just prior to the Declaration.

Certainly, Montefiore was highly antagonistic to Zionism. Lucy Cohen recalls that it was 'the *one* point to which his tolerance did not stretch'.[216] He described the plans for a mass return to Israel as 'the fashionable Zionist Baal'[217] and 'the disease of Jewish nationalisation'.[218] His opposition was, however, consistent and carefully thought out. In a widely reported sermon he gave in 1896, he maintained that

> The bond of religion is not merely wider than the bond of race, it is of a different kind. Their union in any monotheistic religion is arbitrary and galling … In Judaism the needed and logical separation of religion and race, the triumph of one and the disappearance of the other, still awaits accomplishment.[219]

He believed that Zionism was dangerous because it ultimately provoked greater antisemitism: the desire for their own homeland seemed to give the lie to the generations of Jews who had protested their sole allegiance to their adopted countries. He felt that the Jews would no longer be able to participate in the social, cultural and political life of their host countries, a possibility that frightened this cultured and well-integrated Oxford graduate who saw his own experience as the model for Jewish progress.[220] He also cautioned that antisemites in the Jews' adopted countries would see the establishment of Israel as an excuse for ridding their country of them.[221] Most of all, Montefiore opposed Zionism for its negative effect upon the growth of a future universalist Judaism. He was convinced that 'Zion and Jerusalem for us are terms of purely spiritual significance. Whether Jews prosper and multiply in Israel has nothing to do with the future of Judaism.'[222]

In a paper delivered at the London Society for the Study of Religion, 'A Die-Hard's Confession' (1935), Montefiore recounted a meeting with Theodore Herzl in which the Austrian Zionist leader attempted to win him over to the cause and persuade him to become 'his English Zionist Lieutenant'. (Herzl later dismissed Montefiore as a 'stupid ass who affects English correctness'.)[223] With rather muddled imagery, Herzl had compared the Jews in the world to water in a sponge, arguing that when too much water was added, or too many Jews, antisemitism trickled out.[224] Montefiore was almost convinced at the time, but rejected the sponge theory upon reflection:

> Not so: at least the percentage must vary greatly in different countries, and, then, is *nothing* to be allowed for any progress in toleration, in understanding, in appreciation, in good will? Must these hatreds continue forever?[225]

The activities of Herzl's successor, Chaim Weizmann, were likewise disapproved of, although the man himself, likewise admired. He regarded Weizmann as head and shoulders above other Zionist proponents, and as a masterly orator.[226] Weizmann's leadership was undoubtedly inspirational, but this only made him all the more dangerous to Montefiore, who believed that many contemporary woes facing European Jewry could be attributed to the trouble that the Zionist leader stirred up. Writing in 1937, Montefiore commented privately,

> Weizmann is abler than all the other Jews in the world lumped together ... He is a Jewish Parnell, but even abler, and alas respectably married ... But Hitlerism is, at least partly, *Weizmann's creation*.[227]

Against the collective forces of 'Zionism, and Nationalism and anti-Semitism',[228] Montefiore forwarded his 'counter-theory of "an Englishman of the Jewish persuasion"', the idea that one could be an Englishman by nationality and a Jew by religion.[229] He believed that by ridding Judaism of its nationalistic overtones, he could do away with the Jewish problem.[230] 'One thing is certain', he told the Jewish cabinet minister Herbert Samuel[231] in 1915,

> namely, that the Jewish position in England, our emancipation etc, etc, were achieved by the works of men who held my views and not the views of the Zionists. Had Zionism then existed, the Jews would never have won their victory. The debates and pamphlets of the time make this clear.[232]

In one of his most vehemently argued pamphlets, 'The Dangers of Zionism' (1918), Montefiore defended the case for outright cultural assimilation, blaming the Zionists for having 'spoilt it all, and made the Christians once more believe that the word "Jew" means a man of a particular race'.[233] He wanted the word to be understood in the sense of 'His Majesty's subjects professing the Jewish religion', and refused to accept a national definition, or as he put it, to 'accept the advice to commit suicide. For we want our religion to continue.'[234] For Montefiore, granting legitimacy to the idea of Jewish nationality would severely damage if not destroy the legitimacy of Judaism as a religion. With this understanding he went far beyond the boundaries of the traditional Jewish position, for although no-one but the ultra-Zionists would have supported a purely nationalistic view of Judaism, it seemed that Montefiore belonged to a very small minority when he denounced *completely* all nationalistic Jewish sentiments.

Tension between the purely national or racial definition and the religious definition had been evident in popular Anglo-Jewish thought for some time. In 1876, the *Jewish Chronicle* had claimed that 'Benjamin Disraeli belongs to the Jewish people, despite his baptismal certificate. His talents, his virtues and short-comings alike, are purely of the Jewish cast.'[235] Yet, when the historian Goldwin Smith then extrapolated upon this theme, suggesting that a Jew could not then be 'an Englishman or Frenchman holding particular theological tenets', it fiercely condemned him.[236] As Feldman has argued, many British Jews were prepared to use the notion of 'race' until it brought them trouble, when they would switch to the 'religious brotherhood' concept.[237] It was this dichotomy which, Montefiore and other like-minded Jews felt, led to a confusion of the issues and resulted in the Judaeophobia of the late nineteenth century.[238]

Many Jewish leaders and the Anglo-Jewish press worked hard at developing ways to convey a sense of their collective identity as Jews that did not contradict their obligations as English nationals. As president of the Anglo-Jewish Association from 1895 until 1921, Montefiore had been heavily involved in one such institutional effort. As one of the most influential of the Anglo-Jewish representative organisations, it attempted to reconcile the defence of Jewish interests around the world with the demands and duties of English citizenship and patriotism. In a letter to Lucien Wolf, another anti-Zionist campaigner and a leading member of the A.J.A., Montefiore admitted that he had trouble reconciling what he described as 'my own rather extreme views' with his official duties. In fact, he was quite prepared to use his position as a communal leader to oppose the Zionists. Among other things, he argued without consultation against the Jewish Colonisation Association accepting responsibility for seven Palestinian colonies previously established by Baron de Rothschild;[239] he refused Moses Gaster's demand that the A.J.A. send representatives to Zionist conferences;[240] he defeated Norman Bentwich's attempt to divert A.J.A. funds to refugee work in Palestine;[241] and, on at least one occasion, he demanded that the Zionists channel their relief funds back to the A.J.A., having previous stated that the A.J.A. fund would not be used for settling refugees in Palestine.[242] He even accused the *Jewish Chronicle* with being concerned for Jewish refugees in Palestine at the expense of those throughout the rest of the world, much to the editor's chagrin.[243] Montefiore was well aware that his A.J.A. colleagues would view any overtly partisan behaviour as inappropriate for the president of such a body, and tended to avoid public pronouncements on the subject of Zionism outside his religious writings.[244] His anti-Zionist activities were maintained with a somewhat guilty conscience, evidenced, for example, by a request to Wolf to destroy a copy of a fiercely anti-Zionist letter he had written to Herbert Samuel.[245]

Montefiore eventually overcame his inhibitions and publicly and officially expressed his anti-Zionist concerns. In June 1917, his open support of the anti-Zionist manifesto published in *The Times* attracted great criticism[246] and led to the break-up of the Conjoint Foreign Committee (which liaised between the A.J.A. and the Board of Deputies).[247] In addition, only a few weeks before the Balfour Declaration (2 November 1917), Montefiore was involved in the establishment of a League of British Jews, which openly opposed the Zionist belief that 'the Jew was an alien in the land of his birth' and was determined to 'uphold the status of British Jews professing the Jewish religion'.[248] As for the Balfour Declaration itself, Montefiore was responsible (as a member of a select group of Jewish leaders asked by the cabinet for their assistance) to modify the clause which described Palestine as '*the* national home for the Jewish people' to the final draft of '*a* national home for the Jewish people'.[249] As he wrote in a letter to Herbert Samuel, 'The Zionists are exceedingly active and those who, like myself, regard their policy and aims as most dangerous and false, can no longer afford to go to sleep ...'[250] Essentially then, Montefiore was against Zionism because he understood it as a form of nationalism and because his conception of Judaism had no room for nationalist sentiments. The issue was not quite as clear-cut for others, for whom Montefiore appeared to be over-simplifying the problem.[251] To understand this contemporary criticism, it is worth considering the positions of two of his most well-known critics, Ahad Ha-Am and Solomon Schechter.

For Ahad Ha-Am or Asher Ginzberg (1856–1927), one of the most eloquent protagonists of Zionism, disunity was the inevitable product of Montefiore's concept of Judaism and the essential factor that made it impractical. Ukrainian born and brought up in a hassidic household, Ahad Ha-Am embraced the *Haskalah* or Jewish Enlightenment and became a renowned political writer and thinker, living in London from 1908 until 1922. In a powerful essay in 1891, he argued that if people 'of the Jewish Persuasion' had agreed for the sake of Emancipation to deny the existence of the Jews as a people, preferring to regard Judaism simply as a religion, then their hopes for future Jewish unity

rested entirely upon *religious* unity. However, because emancipation had demanded certain practical changes in religious
matters, and because not everyone had accepted this, schisms
had resulted and the *religious* unity of what he called 'the
Jewish Church' now depended wholly upon 'its theoretical side
– that is to say, certain abstract beliefs which are held by all Jews'.
With the scientific developments that had shaken the foundations of every faith, Ahad Ha-Am reasoned, it was becoming
increasingly impractical to hope to ensure Jewish unity on
religious terms.[252]

In an essay in 1898, Ahad Ha-Am outlined his Zionist vision
of Palestine as 'the *spiritual* centre' for Jewish art, thought and
activity. Emancipation, he argued, would only lead to a dead end
if its supporters understood themselves exclusively in religious
terms. In another sense, it had come about as the only means for
cultural self-expression. Ahad Ha-Am was passionate in his belief
in Judaism's superiority over Christianity and the importance of
its contributions to world culture. Yet he admitted, 'now that we
have left the ghetto and begun to participate in European
culture, we cannot help seeing that our superiority is only
potential'. The Jewish genius had not been allowed to shine free
of non-Jewish influences and Zionism was the consequence,
resulting from 'the sense of this contrast between what is and
what might be'. It offered the possibility to 'order our life in our
own way'.[253]

Ahad Ha-Am has been criticised for his emphasis on a vision
of Israel that left the Jews of the Diaspora somewhat out in the cold,
too dependent upon Israel for their inspiration.[254] Montefiore's
Liberal Judaism, of course, was very much a product of the
Diaspora communities of the West, and he could never have
regarded Ahad Ha-Am's argument as anything but critically
flawed. For Montefiore, the essential thing was not, as Ahad
Ha-Am maintained, the preservation and encouragement of
Jewish culture, but rather the preservation and encouragement
of Jewish religious truth. Essentially, Montefiore valued only the
religious contribution of Jewish culture, and had no interest in
Jews remaining 'picturesque orientals'.[255] What is more, he
believed it could be improved upon by continued synthesis with
Western (Hellenistic and Christian) philosophy. In contrast, Ahad
Ha-Am did not believe it was possible to extract the religion from
the culture, and saw its preservation and natural development

as possible only by keeping it safe from non-Jewish influences in a wholly Jewish cultural environment. He furiously condemned Montefiore for his interest in the New Testament. The diametrical opposition of the methods by which their objectives were to be achieved came about as a direct result of their respective prioritisation of what each recognised as of permanent value within Judaism.

Solomon Schechter's attacks on Montefiore's conception of a purely religious definition of Judaism were, if anything, even fiercer than those of Ahad Ha-Am. In his 'Four Epistles to the Jews of England', published in the *Jewish Chronicle* in late 1900 and early 1901, just prior to his departure to the US, Schechter contested the idea, revived by the Boer War, that Jews could be merely Englishman of a different faith. He concluded,

> The doctrine professed by those who are not carried away by the new fanatical 'yellow' [sc. cowardly] theology is, there is no Judaism without Jews and no Jews without Judaism. We can thus be only Jews of the Jewish persuasion.[256]

Montefiore was not being over-sensitive when he construed the articles as being targeted against his own teachings. Schechter's harsh criticism cut him to the quick and he appealed to his former tutor privately:

> Considering all things, when and since you know that the doctrine 'Englishmen of the Jewish Persuasion' is my heart's blood doctrine, for which I labour and give my life, *you* might be more courteous than to call it a 'sickly platitude'.[257]

He believed that Judaism should be universalised and Westernised since it was intrinsically a religion of and for the West. But Schechter was unmoved. He felt that, wrapped up in his hopes for his Universalist Jewish theology, Montefiore suffered from tunnel vision. For Schechter, it was not only impossible but also self-destructive to separate the cultural and national elements of Judaism. Montefiore's concentration upon Western Liberal Judaism at the expense of Eastern Orthodox Judaism was, Schechter wrote, actually postponing the universalisation of Judaism.

The religious energies of all our brethren of the West and East in closest communion will be required. We in the West have the money, and a good deal of system too; but they have the simple faith, they have the knowledge of Jewish lore, and they have the strength, inured as they are by suffering, to live and die for their conception of Judaism. They permit no free love in religion. Universality means to them what it meant to the prophets and their Jewish successors, that the whole world should become Jewish. We have the method, they have the madness; only if we combine can victory be ours.[258]

While Schechter would have been as unhappy about a purely nationalistic definition of Judaism as Montefiore, his conception of 'Catholic Israel' and his appreciation of what the different traditions could contribute meant that, like Ahad Ha-Am, he recognised the validity of a cultural or racial aspect to Judaism.

Thus for many Jewish thinkers, including both Ahad Ha-Am and Schechter, Judaism was a garment in which the two strands of nationalism and religion were closely interwoven. Israel Zangwill, among others, put it forcibly in a letter to Montefiore: 'Our [Jewish] past has undoubtedly been nationalistic as well as religious, and it was a mis-statement of the facts ever to have denied it.'[259] Montefiore, however, opted for a wholly religious definition in the best Reform tradition. To put it another way, the two strands were, for him, separable and represented quite different things. As he remarked in a letter to Lucy Cohen,

There should really be *two* words. (1) say 'Jew' = man of Jewish race or Jewish 'nationality' just as he himself preferred to call himself; (2) say 'Israélite', man who believes in and practices the (hitherto called) 'Jewish religion'.

(1) Could be 'Israélite' or not. He could also be a Christian or an Atheist; (2) Could be either a 'Jew' or not ... e.g. Florence [Montefiore's proselyte wife] is an ardent Israélite, but not a Jew.

This would prevent (a) all confusion; (b) my temperature going up.[260]

His characteristic ability to see the validity of another's point of view allowed him to effectively subdivide Jewry into two groups. In this way he could insist on distinguishing between the two aspects whilst at the same time acknowledging both religion and nationalism as part of the Jewish experience. This solution also afforded him an opportunity to have another dig at what he saw as the self-contradictory position of the Zionists. He argued that the national position was valid only when it did not confuse itself with the religious concept, which was exactly what he accused the Zionists of doing.

> The absurd thing is that your Zionist has no objection whatever to the Combination Jew + Atheist but he does consider the Combination Jew + Christian absurd. Yet! It is *he* who is absurd. If 'Jew' = a man of a particular nation, then, just as an Englishman can be a Christian, an Israelite or an Atheist, so a 'Jew' must be able to be an Israelite, a Christian, or an Atheist. My logic is impeccable.[261]

Towards the end of his life, Montefiore seemed to recognise the ultimate failure of his doctrine of 'the Englishman of the Jewish faith' and the victory of the Zionists. He was well aware that Zionism was gaining ground and complained in his letters that the nationalists seemed to be the only motivated party among European Jewry,[262] and that he was often tempted to give up the struggle. Behind the scenes he was clearly tired and disillusioned. He confided in one letter,

> I cannot tell you the anxiety the Zionists cause me. Sometimes I get so sick of their intrigues and mischief, that I feel tempted to chuck all Jewish work ... How the disease is growing in USA of all places grieves me *most*. Its triumph means the ruin of Judaism and (as I believe *too*) of the Jews. I mind the latter much less for they will have brought it upon themselves. I feel often sick at heart about it.[263]

He also became more sensitive to antisemitism. Whereas in 1898 he had criticised Schechter for his 'anti-anti-Semitic fever', maintaining that he did not recognise such horrors in England,[264] by 1913 he was gloomily seconding Morris Joseph's claim that there had been an increase in anti-Jewish feeling. In response to a talk Joseph had given to the annual meeting of the Anglo-Jewish

Association on the theme 'Anti-Semitic Tendencies in Britain', Montefiore admitted to his own confidence having been shaken. Using a characteristically elitist benchmark, he pointed out that it was now more difficult for a Jew to join certain gentlemen's clubs than it had been six or seven years previously.[265] And in a paper given to the L.S.S.R., 'A Die-Hard's Confession' (1935), he spoke of himself as 'a disillusioned, sad and embittered old man'. Some have wondered if he might have changed his position had he lived a few years longer and witnessed the destruction of European Jewry.[266] But they have underestimated the centrality of the non-nationalist, anti-Zionist stance to his theology. In a sense, Montefiore did not need to witness the Shoah. Certainly, he did not believe that pogroms and antisemitism had ended; in 1929 he lamented the fate 'of the [Jewish] race whose secular martyrdom is even yet by no means over'.[267] In all probability, he would have maintained his ideals, as his did his son Leonard who continued to work with the anti-Zionist League of British Jews after the Second World War. To Montefiore, Zionism represented both the cause of antisemitism and the greatest obstacle to his dream of a universalist Judaism. The tone of 'A Die-Hard's Confession' was bitterly defiant and he spoke of his refusal 'to succumb to Jewish nationalism, on the one hand, or to gentile antisemitism on the other' believing, as he did, that the one stimulated the other. His disagreement with the Zionists boiled down to the question of Jewish identity, and the abandonment of the religious definition of Judaism would have meant the abandonment of his Liberal Judaism. In Montefiore's eyes, the nationalist view of Judaism amounted to a betrayal of the very essence of Judaism.

NOTES

210. A. Cohen, *The Natural and the Supernatural Jew: An Historical and Theological Introduction* (1962), pp. 28–9.
211. I. Epstein, *Judaism: A Historical Presentation* (1968), p. 288; also H.J. Schoeps, *The Jewish–Christian Argument* (1963), p. 104.
212. *Jewish Chronicle*, 1 July 1897, p. 15.
213. 'It seems to be forgotten that if we are Jews, we are also Englishmen, and that in all matters wherein the interests of England may possibly conflict with the interests of Jews, it is our bounden duty, if we claim the rights and privileges of Englishmen, to place the former above the latter, and to act accordingly.' *Jewish Chronicle*, 10 December 1886, p. 6.

214. '"Plain living and high thinking" must be our reply as a community to the attacks of prejudice … Our lives ought not only to be less showy, they ought also to be more useful.' *Jewish Chronicle*, 21 July 1899, p. 16. Montefiore accepted the reality of antisemitism in, among other places, Morocco, Arabia, Persia, Russia, Romania, Austria and France, but felt that this was often the fault of the Jews themselves. 'We shall ill-serve the cause of Judaism and of the Jews throughout the world if we always attempt to assert, or without assertion to assume, that in every country where anti-Semitism, in one of its many forms, exists, the fault is wholly and solely on the side of the persecutors and not in the smallest degree our own.' He stressed the need to 'cultivate the virtues of integrity and simplicity'. *Jewish Chronicle*, 8 July 1898, p. 13.

215. Chaim Bermant suggests that Magnus's anti-Zionism might have been responsible for Montefiore's similar view. C. Bermant, *The Cousinhood: The Anglo-Jewish Gentry* (1971), p. 279.

216. L. Cohen, *Some Recollections of Claude Goldsmid-Montefiore 1858–1938* (1940), p. 265.

217. C.G. Montefiore, 'A Die-Hard's Confession', paper read at London Society for the Study of Religion (1935).

218. Letter from C.G. Montefiore to Lucy Cohen, undated. L. Cohen, *Some Recollections of Claude Goldsmid-Montefiore 1858–1938* (1940), p. 138.

219. 'One God, One Worship' was preached at the West London Synagogue on 1 February 1896. *Jewish Chronicle*, 14 February 1896, p. 11.

220. Integration was central to Montefiore's thinking and was fiercely defended at all times. For example, in response to a pro-Zionist interview that Norman Bentwich gave to the *Jewish Chronicle*, 26 March 1909, Montefiore mobilised support for an open letter which read, 'We deeply deplore the statement that Jews are not and can never be "entirely English in thought".' The 24 signatories included Arthur Cohen, Laurie Magnus, R. Waley-Cohen, Philip Magnus, Leopold de Rothschild, I. Gollancz, Isadore Harris, Oswald Simon. *Jewish Chronicle*, 9 April 1909, p. 6.

221. C.G. Montefiore, 'The Dangers of Zionism', *P.F.J.P.*, XX (1918), pp. 5–6. Elsewhere, Montefiore explained, 'If, as I have said before, and as I once more repeat – if Palestine can become a happy home for a million or half-a-million of our brethren, without injuring the status, the prosperity, and the freedom of the twelve or thirteen millions of Jews who must continue to live outside its borders, who will be so churlish as not warmly to congratulate all those who have co-operated in, or contributed to, that result?' *Jewish Chronicle*, 16 December 1921, p. 29.

222. C.G. Montefiore, cited in N. Bentwich, 'Claude Montefiore and his Tutor in Rabbinics: Founders of Liberal and Conservative Judaism', 6th Montefiore Memorial Lecture, Southampton (1966), p. 8.

223. Cited in S.A. Cohen, *English Zionists and British Jews: The Communal Politics of Anglo-Jewry, 1895–1920* (c1982), p. 166n.

224. Montefiore recalled in 1895 that Herzl had argued, 'If you lived in a city and a country where the most unquestioned desire on the part of the Jews to be citizens and patriots has been met by the fury and passion of anti-Semitism, you would understand better the genesis and the justification of the Zionist movement.' *Jewish Chronicle*, 8 June 1898, p. 13.

225. C.G. Montefiore 'A Die-Hard's Confession', paper read at the London Society for the Study of Religion (1935), cited in L. Cohen, *Some Recollections of Claude Goldsmid-Montefiore 1858–1938* (1940), pp. 225–7.

226. Montefiore wrote on one occasion, 'Weizmann made a stately, eloquent speech of *masterly* ability, and most unfair, party, and sophistical. He stands head and shoulders above everybody in consummate ability.' Letter from C.G. Montefiore to Israel Mattuck, 24 May, year uncertain. ACC/3529/4/2, L.M.A.

227. Letter from C.G. Montefiore to Lucy Cohen, 13 July 1937. L. Cohen, *Some Recollections of Claude Goldsmid-Montefiore 1858–1938* (1940), p. 253.

228. Letter from C.G. Montefiore to Lucy Cohen, date uncertain. L. Cohen, *Some Recollections of Claude Goldsmid-Montefiore 1858–1938* (1940), p. 138.

229. C.G. Montefiore, 'Liberal Judaism in England: Its Difficulties and Its Duties', *Jewish Quarterly Review*, XII (1899–1900), pp. 642, 643.

230. Letter from C.G. Montefiore to Lucy Cohen, 16 June 1934. L. Cohen, *Some Recollections of Claude Goldsmid-Montefiore 1858–1938* (1940), p. 212.

231. Herbert Samuel was the first Jew to sit in the Cabinet. He became a friend of Weizmann and is regarded by Bermant as largely responsible for the Balfour Declaration. He was also the first High Commissioner of Palestine. C. Bermant, *The Cousinhood: The Anglo-Jewish Gentry* (1971), pp. 342, 344.

232. Letter from C.G. Montefiore to Herbert Samuel, 3 March 1915. MS A77/3/13, C.Z.A.

233. C.G. Montefiore, 'The Dangers of Zionism' (1918), p. 3.

234. Ibid.

235. *The Jewish Chronicle*, 18 August 1876, p. 312.

236. G. Smith, 'Can Jews be Patriots?', *Nineteenth Century*, III (May 1878), p. 876, cited in D. Feldman, *Englishmen and Jews: Social Relations and Political Culture 1840–1914* (1994), p. 90.

237. Ibid., p. 126.

238. An example of political antisemitism was the proto-fascist British Brothers League which marched the streets of the East End of London at the turn of the century. D. Englander, 'Anglicised but not Anglican', in G. Parsons, ed., *Religion in Victorian Britain*, I (1988), p. 266.

239. In January 1900, Montefiore reported to the A.J.A. that Jewish Colonisation Association had been asked by Baron Edmond de Rothschild to take over the administration of his seven colonies (470 Jewish families). At the Council of J.C.A. the three English representatives (including Montefiore) had voted against the idea. Montefiore argued that, previously, the J.C.A. had contributed grants to colonies on condition that it was not helping to found new ones. *Jewish Chronicle*, 12 January 1900, p. 17.

240. Gaster failed to persuade the A.J.A. to send delegates to the Basle Conference in 1898. Montefiore argued that the A.J.A. could not afford to prejudice its work with foreign governments by being seen as supportive of Zionist activities, even if this appearance was only due to 'the powers of misrepresentation of the Press in Europe'. *Jewish Chronicle*, 18 February 1898, p. 17.

241. *Jewish Chronicle*, 27 August 1915, p. 13.

242. Moses Gaster argued that Zionists should not be required to put their money into the General Fund for the relief of Russian Jews if they were unhappy about the money being handed over to the British Consuls rather than to Jewish hands. Montefiore's Relief Fund appeal also stated that the money was not to be used for the purpose of helping the people to emigrate. Gaster commented, 'This statement in the appeal has grieved me more than the massacres in Russia, and I am amazed that representative Jews in English [*sic*] should justify the Aliens Act and play down to

anti-Semitic prejudice throughout the length and breadth of the country.' *Jewish Chronicle*, 17 November 1905, p. 16.

243. An editorial written as Montefiore was retiring from the A.J.A. criticises him severely for a recent attack on the paper: 'an altogether reprehensible spirit, when out of the bitter narrowness with which he views Zionism, he suggests that the only Jews outside England for whom we [the *Jewish Chronicle*] care are the Jews in Palestine.' *Jewish Chronicle*, 6 December 1921, p. 10.

244. Writing in 1915, Montefiore admitted that 'at the present anxious time, it would not be well for me as President of the Anglo-Jewish Association and Joint Chairman of the Conjoint Foreign Committee, to say anything that might cause irritation to any party in Judaism, however opposed to that party I may be. Where I can easily hold my tongue, I will.' Letter from C.G. Montefiore to Henry Hurwitz of *The Menorah Journal*, 20 January 1915. MS 2/36/1, Henry Hurwitz/Menorah Association Memorial Collection, A.J.A.C.

245. Letter from C.G. Montefiore to Lucien Wolf, 3 March 1915, including a copy of a letter from C.G. Montefiore to Herbert Samuel, 3 March 1915. MS A77/3/13, C.Z.A.

246. Montefiore's manifesto, published 28 May 1917, caused one council member of the A.J.A. (E.N. Adler) to tender his resignation, and provoked Moses Gaster to attempt to pass a motion which read, 'that this council [A.J.A.] expresses its regret at the publication of this anti-Zionist manifesto by the representatives of the Conjoint [Foreign] Committee without previous consultation and approval'. Another member of the council believed that 'publication of the manifesto was imprudent and premature ... [although] he did not entirely disagree with its contents'. In the event, Gaster withdrew his motion, and Alder withdrew his resignation. *Jewish Chronicle*, 8 June 1917, pp. 14, 17–19.

247. At first, Montefiore argued that responsibility for collapse of Conjoint Foreign Committee 'rested upon shoulders other those of the Anglo-Jewish Association', maintaining that the Board of Deputies had 'desired the termination of the present arrangement'. *Jewish Chronicle*, 14 September 1917, p. 16. By November, he admitted that the dissolving of the Committee had been due to 'a statement issued by the old Conjoint Committee on the subject of Palestine'. *Jewish Chronicle*, 9 November 1917, p. 12.

248. *Jewish Chronicle*, 16 November 1917, p. 6.

249. Montefiore supported an A.J.A. motion of thanks to the British government in response to the Balfour Declaration unhappily. He is recorded as dismissing one delegate's enthusiastic praise of the Declaration as 'the greatest event in Jewish history since the Dispensation', replying that the greatest event had been when the Jews had obtained emancipation. *Jewish Chronicle*, 7 December 1917, p. 8.

250. Letter from C.G. Montefiore to Herbert Samuel, 3 March 1915. MS A77/3/13, C.Z.A.

251. Some even attributed a more ominous motivation to Montefiore. His argument regarding the divided loyalties that would face Jews in many lands once a national homeland had been founded was described as 'a calumny in genuine anti-Semitic style'. B. Drachman, 'An Answer to Mr. Claude G. Montefiore', *American Hebrew Journal*, LXII, no. 24 (8 April 1898), p. 679.

252. Ahad Ha-Am, *Slavery in Freedom* (1891), in L. Simon, ed., *Selected Essays of Ahad Ha-Am* (1962), pp. 182–3.

253. Ahad Ha-Am, *Transvaluation of Values* (1898), reproduced in S. Noveck, ed., *Contemporary Jewish Thought* (1964), p. 19.

254. For example, Simon Dubnow (1860–1941) argued that Ahad Ha-Am's formulation made the Diaspora communities nothing but automated appendages. Cited in A. Cohen, *The Natural and the Supernatural Jew: An Historical and Theological Introduction* (1962), p. 64.

255. Cited from Montefiore's lecture 'The Place of Judaism Among the Religions of the World', *Jewish Chronicle*, 31 May 1918, p. 9.

256. The article is reproduced in S. Schechter, *Studies in Judaism*, 2nd series, p. 183.

257. Letter from C.G. Montefiore to Solomon Schechter, 12 December 1900. J.B. Stein, *Lieber Freund: The Letters of Claude Goldsmid Montefiore to Solomon Schechter 1885–1902* (1988), pp. 45–6.

258. S. Schechter, *Studies in Judaism*, 2nd series, cited in N. Bentwich, 'Claude Montefiore and his Tutor in Rabbinics: Founders of Liberal and Conservative Judaism', 6th Montefiore Memorial Lecture, Southampton (1966), p. 12.

259. Letter from Israel Zangwill to C.G. Montefiore, 3 February 1909. MS A120/454, C.Z.A.

260. Letter from C.G. Montefiore to Lucy Cohen, 27 September 1930. L. Cohen, *Some Recollections of Claude Goldsmid-Montefiore 1858–1938* (1940), pp. 201–2.

261. Ibid.

262. Letter to Lucy Cohen, 19 March 1934. Ibid.

263. Letter from C.G. Montefiore to Dr [Morris] J[oseph]? 15 April, year uncertain. MS 165/1/12, Sheldon and Amy Blank Papers, A.J.A.C.

264. Letter from C.G. Montefiore to Solomon Schechter, 9 December 1898. J.B. Stein, *Lieber Freund: The Letters of Claude Goldsmid Montefiore to Solomon Schechter 1885–1902* (1988), p. 42.

265. *Jewish Chronicle*, 4 July 1913, p. 19.

266. For example, see Richard Libowitz's review of M. Bowler, *Claude Montefiore and Christianity* in *Journal of Ecumenical Studies*, XXVII (1990), pp. 788–9.

267. C.G. Montefiore, 'The Originality of Jesus', *Hibbert Journal*, XXVIII (1929), p. 100.

7

The Essence of Judaism

As Yosef Yerushalmi has argued in *Zakhor* (1989), the recent phenomenon of Jewish historiography has led to an approach to Judaism as something to be qualified temporally and spatially rather than as something to be viewed as an eternal 'Idea'.[268] Modern scholarship has thus tended away from the idea of an 'essence of Judaism'. It has become impossible to speak of 'Judaism' without constant reference to its development through history, or to think of it in generalised terms rather than in its concrete manifestations in time. Even the concept of a normative Judaism, the essentials of which constitute a common denominator of differing Judaisms, has been largely discredited.[269]

Towards the end of the nineteenth century and even into the early decades of the twentieth, however, the idea of an 'essence of Judaism' was very much in vogue. It took centre stage in internal disputes and theological wranglings among Jewish intellectuals, and gave a sharper edge to inter-faith relations. This philosophical or theological approach made inevitable Leo Baeck's *The Essence of Judaism* (1905) as a Jewish response to Harnack's *The Essence of Christianity* (1901).[270] Since then, an increasingly historical outlook has blurred the lines of what exactly makes a Judaism or a Christianity. Chilton and Neusner's *Judaism in the New Testament* (1995) is a good example of an attempt to treat early New Testament Christianity as a legitimate Judaism instead of looking for what is 'Jewish' in a 'Christian' or non-Jewish collection of writings. And Michael Hilton's *The Christian Effect on Jewish Life* (1994) highlights the numerous ways in which Christian practice down through the centuries has influenced Jewish practice and thought, both directly and indirectly. Such works reflect the modern historical trend to question the meaning and usefulness of the traditional definitions of 'Jewish' and 'Christian'. What is it that makes something 'Jewish' or 'Christian'? Before examining some of the theological attempts of nineteenth- and early twentieth-century Jewish thinkers to answer this question and comparing them with Montefiore's own distinct view, it would be useful to outline Montefiore's thought with regard to Liberal Judaism, since this embodied the very essence of Judaism for him.

One of the aims of the Liberal Jewish exercise, as far as Montefiore was concerned, had been to clear away the debris of tradition, particularism and ignorance that had built up around the essential doctrines and teachings of the Jewish religion over the centuries. It included those aspects of Judaism that could be salvaged from the Orthodox and Reform traditions, traditions which nonetheless he had regretfully felt obliged to disassociate with. But it was more than this. Montefiore believed that Judaism was very much an evolving phenomenon. Man's understanding of it had developed and would continue to develop, for it had not yet arrived at its final form. For Montefiore, then, the essence of Judaism was not completely fixed, and so Liberal Judaism was characterised by a certain nebulousness or flexibility. A second point to keep in mind is that, to an extent unparalleled in other Jewish Reform movements, Liberal Judaism was an attempt to describe the essence of Judaism from a purely theological point of view, as will become clear.

Montefiore's Liberal Judaism has been described as monotheism with special reference to the Hebrew prophets as great revealers of the monotheistic faith; a sort of ethical theism.[271] He committed himself to a prophecy-orientated position in contrast to the Law-orientated position maintained by the Jewish Orthodoxy, arguing 'The great prophets (Amos, Hosea, Isaiah, Jeremiah) are primary: the Law is secondary; secondary in both importance and date.'[272] Although Montefiore certainly did not abrogate the Law, just as his critics did not reject prophecy, the relative importance of the Prophets' teaching in his thought can be gauged from his one-time suggestion that, in the future, it would be proper when building a synagogue to house the Prophets' writings in the ark, the most sacred place, rather than the Pentateuch.[273] Unsurprisingly, such provocative comments had the effect of polarising the Liberal and traditional positions.

Lucy Cohen has commented that the difference between Montefiore's faith and that of the Prophets was that he regarded his belief in God as 'a venture', a theological search, while to them the existence of God was the greatest certainty in their lives. His belief was founded, he had told her many times, on the perception of the good in mankind and in the order of the universe, which made it easier for him to believe in a supreme personality characterised by 'Wisdom and Love' than in chance or 'toss up'.[274] He described his faith as a 'childish religion', and admitted that there was no authority for it, except in the soul of man. This 'difficult belief' was, he felt, the surest foundation for faith. It also led to independence of thought and of action, and Montefiore clung fiercely to the concept of free will.[275]

To Montefiore, the essence of the Liberal Jewish movement was freedom. It was freedom firstly from the trappings of Orthodoxy and the rabbinical 'hedge around the Law', that is, freedom from human authority. Traditional religious rites and institutions came second to an emphasis upon universal doctrine that emphasised the prophetic element and minimised the priestly and legal elements. Secondly, it offered intellectual freedom, and specifically freedom from the fear of the consequences of biblical criticism; as a theological Judaism, it possessed validity regardless of the date or authorship of the biblical writings. Hence Liberal Judaism offered, through the use of Reason, 'A happy and serene freedom, ready to pick and choose, to accept and reject, to adapt and adopt, to purify or universalise'.[276]

This seemingly arbitrary method was not a purely *ad hoc* religious exercise. A man's conscience was for Montefiore to be an *instructed* conscience, that is, one which had learned from the mistakes and achievements of past religious thought; it was thus rational and not, in fact, arbitrary. As he wrote in a paper on 'Authority',

> But what is he [the Liberal Jew], and what is his reason? What is his moral judgement? What is his religious judgement? They have all been formed by the Bible; formed before his birth, on the Bible they largely depend ... He is their child.[277]

The Jewish scriptures, as a record of man's past spiritual experiences, were not to be viewed so much as an infallible authority but as a source of guidance whose advice could be qualified or augmented in the light of modern thought and personal enlightenment. In a sense, the religious texts illustrated for him his own preconceived opinion of what was right or wrong. Of course, his 'preconceived opinion' had been very much shaped by these very religious texts, in addition to Classical philosophy and modern thought. One consequence of this 'free' position with regard to scripture was that Montefiore was more concerned with the religious value of the teaching than the 'legitimacy' of its source. As a result of his firm belief that 'All the light has not shone through Jewish windows',[278] he was even prepared to argue for adopting New Testament ethical teachings when he thought they appeared superior, even when they differed from the traditional Jewish ones, as will become clear.

Montefiore's apparent arbitrary approach to scripture in fact characterises liberal thought and method in general. His high estimation of, and dependence upon, rationality had led to his abandonment of scriptural or hierarchical authority. As he rather dramatically put it,

> No creed, no tradition, can Canute-like, prevent the on-set of criticism and historical enquiry … If all the creeds in the world were to tell me that Moses wrote the Pentateuch, and the accredited specialists, with entirely negligible exceptions tell me that he did not, the creeds weigh nothing in my reason's scales.[279]

Any fear he had concerning the weakness of his position, that is, of the fallibility and limitation of the human mind, was counterbalanced by his trust that God was guiding the evolution of understanding, a commonly held belief in the late nineteenth century. Montefiore's high estimation of Reason by no means placed him outside the pale of traditional Jewish thought, as he himself argued. On several occasions he referred to no less an authority than the philosopher Maimonides (1135–1204) who had maintained that Judaism was *essentially* reasonable, in contrast to other faiths.[280] And as Moses Mendelssohn had argued, it was this very reasonableness of Judaism which commended it to all men and that once Christians had abandoned their irrational beliefs, a common faith might one day be possible (a view which was not so very different from Montefiore's own). Thus few Jewish thinkers would have suggested that Montefiore's emphasis upon rationality was, in itself, wrong. What offended both the Orthodox and the Reform, however, and what many have criticised him for since, was his determination to value Reason above tradition at all costs, and his energy and consistency in following through the logic of this position.

Montefiore and the Liberal community believed that Orthodoxy was becoming less and less relevant. This was because of what they regarded as the out-of-touch nature of its worship, which was uninspiring and little understood by the everyday Jew, and its out-of-touch doctrines, which flew in the face of modern, enlightened thought and civilisation. According to Montefiore's early analysis in 'Some Notes on the Effects of Biblical Criticism upon Jewish Religion' (1891),[281] the present state of affairs was due to the fact that in recent times Jews had defined their Jewishness in terms of what set them apart. Overly influenced by Mendelssohn, they had laid too great an emphasis upon rites that distinguished them from other theists. The ancient theological doctrines regarding God's nature and unity, his moral order, immortality, and so on, were reckoned to be too similar – 'and thus the essence of Judaism [was] altogether removed from the sphere of religious belief'.[282] Montefiore was not unsuccessful in persuading people of his position. In 1897, the *Jewish Chronicle* supported him in a public dispute with Israel Zangwill over a letter that Montefiore had written to the non-Jewish *Daily Chronicle*. In this letter, he had defended Jews against the paper's charge of separatism, arguing that the majority of ideas emanating from Judaism had been absorbed already into Gentile thought at one stage or another. In an open letter of protest, Zangwill implied that Montefiore should follow commonsense and simply assimilate if, as he maintained, everything distinctively Jewish had already been adopted. The *Jewish Chronicle*, and many among its readers, chose to side with Montefiore on this occasion.[283]

Mendelssohn was not the only Jewish authority who was to blame for Jewish atrophy in the face of modernity. In 'Some Notes on the Effects of Biblical Criticism', Montefiore argued that Orthodox Jews clung to particularistic beliefs which were based upon several of Maimonides' Principles, including belief in the words of the prophets (6), that Moses was the greatest of the prophets (7), in the revelation at Sinai (8), in the immutability of the Revealed Law (9), and in the coming messiah (12).[284] Such doctrines did not represent the essential teachings of Judaism for Montefiore, and only impeded the understanding of the core of Jewish theology.

The answer to the dilemma, he felt, was to be found not in external modifications of religious ceremonies, such as he saw advocated by the Reform community, but in self-examination and re-interpretation at a more profound level: a theological reappraisal of the essence of Judaism. According to Montefiore, only Liberal Judaism offered a system that concentrated more on meaning and significance than on historical tradition, scholarship or culture; it alone freed itself from the chains of both history and academic criticism.[285] In 1912, he produced a treatise of 23 chapters, *Outlines of Liberal Judaism*, that was intended as a theology of Liberal Judaism.[286] Montefiore, who was keen to stress that it failed as a systematic treatise on Judaism or even Liberal Judaism, and who called for someone with a more philosophic mind to produce the required textbook, nevertheless regarded it as a pioneering work.[287] He covered a range of theological topics, progressing from 'First notions about God and why we believe in Him' to consider, *inter alia*, the nature of God's unity and goodness, the problem of evil, human free will, the nature of God's action in the world, immortality, the relationship of God to man, the mission of Israel, and the roles of inspiration and personal conscience. He also included chapters outlining how Liberal Jewish thought distinguished itself from other forms of Jewish thought with regard to the Laws of the Pentateuch, dietary laws and festivals, nation and race, its attitude to Christianity and to the New Testament, and its relationship to Conservative and Prophetic forms of Judaism. His conclusion makes the aim of the work crystal clear:

> enough has been said to make good my case that Liberal Judaism is a religion well furnished and stocked with conceptions and doctrines. It is not a residuum ... It could, if it pleased, set forth Articles of Faith as numerous as, or more numerous than, the Articles of Maimonides.[288]

The underlying assumption behind this attempt to outline a systematic Jewish theology was that Liberal Judaism could absorb what was useful and reject what was not, in accordance with what he regarded as its ethical-theistic fundamentals (and in this way it remained a historical religion that honoured its roots).[289] Central to his approach was the concept of Progress and the capacity of Judaism for development. Rather than offering a dry, irrelevant religion, he felt that Liberal Judaism offered the alternative of a vibrant faith that was theologically and intellectually robust, having stripped away the superfluous to leave belief in God at its centre. Perhaps most significantly of all, it attempted to realise the capacity of Judaism to become universal, that is, to universalise its monotheistic and ethical message.[290] These essentially ethical-religious goals led away from what he saw as the destructive nationalism and particularism of Orthodoxy.

As he would have been the first to admit, little of Montefiore's early reforming agenda was original in terms of a world-wide perspective. His fierce condemnation of the lack of theological vigour among Jewish thinkers and his intense interest in intellectually encapsulating Judaism in doctrinal terms, while certainly unfamiliar in a British context, were echoed elsewhere in Europe and America. As his confidence and support developed, however, his vision of Liberal Judaism as expressed in the idea of the 'essence of Judaism' did begin to stand out from those of other Jewish thinkers more generally. There would not have been many among even Continental Reformers who would have been as disinterested in the particular source or origin of good ethical teachings as he was, or who were as determined to follow through liberal principles and reject previous means of distancing Judaism from surrounding religious thought, thereby risking its purity. Certainly, his stress upon the idea of a developing Judaism would have set him at odds with those who believed in an eternal Judaism, no matter how 'reformed' that definition might be. Montefiore was simply more radical in terms of applying liberal thought and values over and above Jewish tradition and law, and was prepared to go further than others in his attempt to make visible and viable his understanding of the essence of Judaism to the modern world. This should become clearer after a comparison with some other Jewish thinkers' views regarding the 'essence of Judaism'.

For a great many Jews, the whole question of what constituted the 'essence of Judaism' could be boiled down to the question of one's regard for the *halakhah*, the legal/ritual teachings. Any notion of *halakhah* as non-essential to Judaism, as Montefiore and liberally minded Jews maintained, met with stiff opposition and hostility from the Orthodox. A series of Montefiore's letters in 1926 reveals the clash between his own ideology and that championed by the Chief Rabbi Joseph Hertz. Referring to a radio sermon in which Hertz had spoken about the importance of Law, Montefiore commented,

> The fixed separation between the Laws of God and Laws of man (a side hit at Liberal Judaism) will not work in the last resort; even the ethical laws of the Ten Commandments are man made. But it does not follow that they are not divine as well. The matter is unfortunately very difficult to explain ... but it is certain that there are no Laws of *God* in the C[hief] R[abbi]'s sense at all.[291]

Liberally minded thinkers, such as the American Kaufmann Kohler (1843–1926), were of course closer to Montefiore in this respect. For Kohler, who was probably the most influential American Reform theologian in the early twentieth century, the essence of Judaism lay plainly in its ethics and theology; like Montefiore, he emphasised its universalist teachings over its *halakhah*. As he put it, 'The Torah, as the expression of Judaism was never limited to a mere system of Law', and by setting its teachings (*Lehre*) over its Law (*Gesetz*), he effectively de-legalised the Torah.[292] In contrast to Montefiore, however, Kohler was unwilling to relegate the traditional scriptures to a position below modern thought when conflict between the two occurred. In line with most other liberal Jews, he could not imagine Judaism without the Hebrew Bible, albeit with certain qualifications, taking a central position.

This was also true of Hermann Cohen (1842–1918).[293] As a West European liberal academic, Cohen's world-view was closer to Montefiore's than was that of many other Jewish thinkers, especially with regard to his anti-Zionism and interest in the *religious* consciousness of the Jew. (He wrote on Jewish unity but only in terms of a religious community; he was not a nationalist.) Cohen believed that Jewish religious community had to adapt to the challenges of modernity; the ensuing controversy was therefore to be expected and even welcomed as a sign of true religious development. He wrote,

> Ultimately the controversies which are agitating our communal life today must be interpreted rather as significant symptoms of the inner life of our religion. A modern religion can never regard itself anywhere as firmly fixed and

anchored. Rather must it create anew, by independent effort, the bases and the warranties of its faith. In this process error and deviations are inevitable, as are also fictions and attacks. It does no good at all to register complaints on this score or to make lamentations over it for such is the course of human affairs. There is no life without struggle and no religion without evolution.[294]

Significantly, Cohen returned to the past and to the ancient literature to find the answers to the problems of the early twentieth century; he insisted that Judaism had to speak from its own sources. For Cohen, it had become increasingly clear that the essence of Judaism, the direction in which it had been evolving, could be defined as 'ethical monotheism'. And so he argued that the Sabbath was 'the quintessence of the monotheistic ethic', the laws of the Day of Atonement meant that 'atonement with God becomes at the same time a summons to atonement with man', and the prophets were described as 'founders of social religion' who did not 'concentrate upon God alone [mysticism] ... but rather set him into relationship, connection and interaction with men'.[295] Such institutions represented clear examples of the essentially ethical concerns of Judaism. Although never referred to by Montefiore, Cohen's influence in these areas upon Jewish liberal thought is ever apparent in Montefiore's own writings, and a similar question mark hangs over both men. As Arnold J. Wolf put it in 'The Dilemma of Claude Montefiore' (1959), both had compared other ethical and religious views with Judaism and had decided, generally speaking, that Judaism came out best. But what if they had not? Such an open, apparently uncommitted approach appeared threatening to non-liberals and provoked accusations of superficial, intellectualised Judaism.[296]

For many, such a philosophical view of Judaism did not capture the essence of Judaism satisfactorily. One example was Leo Baeck (1873–1956) who, like Montefiore, had been strongly influenced by Hermann Cohen's interpretation of Judaism as 'ethical monotheism' and was also 'liberal' in the sense of emphasising the ethical aspect of Jewish practice over the *halakhah*. Baeck, Montefiore's successor as world leader of Progressive Judaism, appears to have held his English counterpart in high esteem; and he dedicated the English translation of *The Essence of Judaism* (1936) to Montefiore 'in sincere friendship and deep regard'.

Montefiore reciprocated his friendship warmly, writing privately that he had never met a more distinguished minister of religion of any sect and describing him admiringly as 'altogether an oddity and a sweet oddity'.[297] Baeck's 'oddity' for Montefiore seems to have stemmed from their differing views of the essential nature of Judaism. This can probably be accounted for by the fact that Baeck had been influenced by mysticism to a far greater extent than had Montefiore.

According to Baeck, the essence of Judaism lay in the dialectical polarity between 'mystery' and 'commandment'. 'Mysticism' meant for Baeck a sense or awareness of God's reality. 'Commandment' referred to more than the *halakhah*, which imposed a required and fixed way of life; it referred to the inward awareness of what was required for ethical living, instructions that seemed to emanate from the divine 'mystery'. According to Baeck, it was only when one aspect had been over-emphasised to the exclusion of the other that the religion had ceased to be Judaism, for 'in Judaism, all ethics has its mysticism and all mysticism its ethics'. This relationship had existed and defined the Jewish faith down through the centuries. He wrote,

> The history of Judaism from ancient times to the present could be written as a history of mysticism; the history of Judaism from its origins until now could also be written as a history of 'the Law' – and it would be the same history. And for the most part it would be the history of the very same men.[298]

For Montefiore, history told a quite different story. The mystical element was, for him, merely one of many fascinating strands of thought that had woven themselves into the fabric of Judaism. Despite the fact that he translated an early essay on Hasidism by Solomon Schechter,[299] assisted in the translation of similar writings by Martin Buber,[300] and even once offered a prize in the *Jewish Quarterly Review* for the best study on mysticism,[301] he nevertheless confessed privately, 'I am no good at mysticism, only respectful.'[302] In addition, he was repelled by the superstition which he felt was often associated with mystical teachings and dismissed its writings as unnecessarily 'obscure'.[303] There were certainly occasions when he did speak positively of mysticism, generally in the context of Pauline or Johannine mysticism, and this has led Walter Jacobs to over-emphasise his interest in the matter[304] and Steven Bayme to suggest that 'Montefiore's originality lay *in his mysticism* and his approach to Christianity'.[305] By such references, however, Montefiore meant a sort of individual faith and spirituality, achievable in both Christianity and Judaism, which could only be labelled as 'mysticism' in a limited sense. Ultimately, he felt that Judaism 'did not readily produce that mystic temper or soul which seems to find itself afresh by losing itself in God'.[306] Along with the *halakhah* and verbal inspiration, such mysticism merely detracted from what was of greater concern, that is, the continued development of ethical monotheism towards his liberal, theologically determined Judaism.

Even towards the end of his life, Montefiore remained certain that the essence of Judaism could be expressed theologically and that the future Jewish religion was essentially encapsulated within his own Liberal Judaism. Baeck was more uncertain, preferring to see Judaism as a whole only in its unfolding historical past, and not as some sort of philosophical development. The 'essence of Judaism' was for Baeck concerned with man's response to God expressed in his attitude towards the world. It had nothing to do with precision of understanding and could not be defined by doctrine. Montefiore recognised the validity of both religious experience and a theological/doctrinal dimension, explaining,

> In one aspect it is a religious system, a harmony of ideas; in another aspect it is a certain attitude or condition of mind and soul.[307]

In practice, however, he emphasised the theology. For Baeck, God functioned as the reality that sanctified and supported mankind's involvement in the work of creation and redemption.[308] For Montefiore, God was more the goal of a theological search.

Another Jewish thinker who emphasised the mystical aspect of the essence of Judaism was Martin Buber (1878–1965). On and off through 1930 and 1931 and in spite of his general lack of affinity with mysticism, Montefiore assisted his cousin Lucy Cohen in her translations of Buber's hasidic writings. In several ways, the two men were quite similar since each was attempting to communicate what they regarded as the essential teachings of

Judaism to a European (Protestant) public, and each similarly utilised the norms of that thought. Both emphasised certain aspects of the Jewish tradition while neglecting others; Buber stressed the vital religiosity of Hasidism and, like Montefiore, ignored the halakhic tradition of Rabbinic Judaism. Again like Montefiore, Buber concentrated most of his efforts upon the Pentateuch, the Prophets, and the Psalms, primarily interested in their moral-ethical teachings. And, again, each man's particular understanding of Judaism left him sympathetic towards Protestant Christianity, since both were anti-legalistic and emphasised faith and belief combined with ethical living. Buber's neglect of *halakhah* was, however, for quite different reasons than Montefiore's. Montefiore saw the Law as something from which Judaism should be freed, not because it was necessarily bad but simply because it was a tradition and therefore an impediment to free development. Buber's reasons were more complex.

Whereas Baeck had started with man's attitude to the world, Buber began with man's dialogue with the world. In *Ich und Du* (1923)[309] he outlined the two types of relation man can have with the world around him: I–It (monologue) in which the two participants are not equals but in which one is attempting to use the other; and I–Thou (true dialogue), which is characterised by mutuality, openness, directness and presentness. Individually, one's relationship with God could thus be understood as a dialogue with the Eternal Thou. Collectively, the dialogue of God with Israel had been expressed in his Covenant with them, the basis of their faith. For Buber, no group had invested so much in this concept of God and man as had the Jews. The essence of Judaism was not then, as Christians (and Montefiore) tended towards, affirmation of religious beliefs, but dialogue with the Eternal Thou through the hallowing of everyday life. His attitude to *halakhah* was derived from this view.

Buber distinguished between the two terms *halakhah* and *mitzvah*, or law (*Gesetz*) and commandment (*Gebot*), as mutually exclusive. Commandment/*mitzvah* belonged in the realm of the I–Thou relationship while law/*halakhah* worked only in the context of I–It relationships. Both could exist, but not at the same time. A commandment/*mitzvah* was defined as revelation from the divine Thou to the human I; it could not become law/ *halakhah*, defined as a (generalised) prescription to a collective entity or people whose duration was determined by tradition.[310]

Almost exclusively concerned as he was with dialogue between the individual and God (I–Thou relationship), Buber thus turned his back on *halakhah*, the human response to revelation. In this sense of approaching religion essentially in terms of the individual rather than the collective, both Buber and Montefiore parted company with the mainstream Jewish tradition. Neither used *halakhah* to bond the religious community; Montefiore replaced it with a (liberal) theology, and Buber with a Covenant that had to be realised individually.

A close friend and associate of Buber, Franz Rosenzweig (1886–1929), also agreed that the Law could no longer be used to define the essence of Judaism. Worse than that, it threatened to destroy what bonds remained among Jewry. As he observed, 'Today the Law brings out more conspicuously the difference between Jew and Jew than between Jew and Gentile.'[311] But while Orthodoxy had failed, Liberalism had fared no better – 'the nimble air squadron of ideas' had achieved nothing 'except dilute the spirit of Judaism (or what passed for it)'.[312] For Rosenzweig, then, the search for the essence of Judaism, the religion, had become a search for the essence of Jewishness, the state of being. It could not be reduced to 'what the century of Emancipation with its cultural mania wanted to reduce it to', namely, a religion. Rather,

> The point is simply that it is no entity, ... no one sphere of life among other spheres of life. It is something inside the individual that makes him a Jew ... The Jewishness I mean is no 'literature'. It can be grasped neither through the writing nor reading of books ... It is only lived – and perhaps not even that. One is it.[313]

There are certainly similarities between Rosenzweig's essence of Jewishness as a state of being, and Montefiore's understanding of the essence of (Liberal) Judaism as an attitude. Both men, for example, sought with their Judaism to pro-actively embrace the surrounding non-Jewish world rather than retreat from it; both wanted to adopt the best of non-Jewish culture and hoped, ultimately, to make it their own. As Rosenzweig put it,

> All of us to whom Judaism, to whom being a Jew, has again become the pivot of our lives ... we all know that in being

> Jews we must not give up anything, not renounce anything, but lead everything back to Judaism. From the periphery back to the centre.[314]

Montefiore's eclectic method of liberalising Judaism so as to make it relevant is not far from the duty, as Rosenzweig saw it, to enrich the Jewish experience. But Rosenzweig's existentialism gave his concept of Jewishness a degree of subjectivity and individuality that distinguished it from Montefiore's strictly religious approach. The result was a redefinition of the essence of Judaism in terms of personal life-experience, rather than from the point of view of religious–historical experience. Rosenzweig explained,

> It is not a matter of pointing out relations between what is Jewish and what is non-Jewish. There has been enough of that. It is not a matter of apologetics, but rather of finding the way back into the heart of our life. And of being confident that this heart is a Jewish heart. For we are Jews.[315]

While Rosenzweig might have viewed 'Jewishness' in this way, as little more than recognition (without explanation) of the phenomenon of Jews in the world, he explained how he regarded Judaism as an Idea, to be contrasted with the Idea of Christianity, in *The Star of Redemption* (1921). This philosophical approach, something like a parallel covenant theory, was vague and indistinct with regard to details, however. It did not offer a definition of Judaism so much as an explanation of its role as the means by which Jews had already entered God's eternal kingdom and so existed outside the stream of history,[316] in contrast to Christianity which was the vehicle for non-Jews to reach God at the end of time, when God would be 'all in all'.[317] In any case, the essence of Judaism was as natural and obvious for Rosenzweig as it was difficult to define.

Although several Jewish thinkers, including Buber and Rosenzweig, have been criticised for stressing what some have regarded as un-Jewish elements, or for expressing in un-Jewish ways their understanding of Judaism, Montefiore appears to have been singled out especially for criticism, both by his contemporaries and by later critics. The Jewish press in his own day was ambiguous, at best, with regard to his writings. The *Jewish Chronicle* slammed him repeatedly for 'constantly bringing

Judaism into comparison with Christianity'[318] and in a typical response to one of his public lectures, the *Jewish World* commented, 'We really believe that to this declaration Mr Montefiore could rally every Christian Jew, as the perverts call themselves … Mr Montefiore has provided us with an awful example of what so-called "liberal" Judaism may descend to.'[319] Rumours were rife among the Orthodox that Montefiore incorporated Christian practices into J.R.U. and Liberal services,[320] and members of the Reform Synagogue accused him of adopting the methods of Christian conversionists.[321] A number of rabbis and scholars aired their suspicions publicly. Rev. Gerald Friedlander described Montefiore's treatment of Jesus in *The Synoptic Gospels* (1909) as 'an estimate of Jesus which one might expect from a missionary whose task it is to convert the Jews and lead them to appreciate his saviour's "striking character and personality"'.[322] Michael Friedländer, head of the Orthodox rabbinical training school, Jews' College, maintained that Montefiore's writings revealed an 'anti-Jewish tendency'.[323] Schechter suggested that Montefiore's movement was not so much liberal Judaism as liberal Christianity.[324] Ahad Ha-Am felt that Montefiore had imbibed too much Christian thought and that his *Synoptic Gospels*, in particular, reflected a Jewish mind tarnished by Christian influence rather than a genuinely Jewish treatment of the subject.[325] Israel Zangwill bestowed a backhanded compliment that Montefiore's originality lay in his 'queer mixture, half Jew, half Christian'.[326] As far away as America Montefiore was attacked as preaching Jesus and denigrating Jewish views.[327] More recently, Walter Jacob cites as 'incredible' the way in which 'the long and terrible history of the charge of deicide' was 'brushed aside' by Montefiore.[328] And Dan Cohn-Sherbok has described him simply as 'an apologist for the Christian faith'.[329] The list of those who questioned the authenticity of his Jewishness goes on and on, and cannot be fully explained without reference to his particular concept of Judaism and his controversial attitudes towards Zionism and Christianity, which stemmed from it.

In the period before 1909, when the Jewish Religious Union still represented a loose collective of liberally minded Jews, Montefiore had been regarded as something of a meddler, even a reformer, by the Orthodox leadership. After 1909 and his launch of a movement for the cause of Liberal Judaism, however, he came to be seen as a much greater threat and soon brought down upon himself the wrath of Chief Rabbi Hermann Adler, who threatened excommunication and roundly denounced 'the "fluid" principles on which the new synagogue is to be established'.[330] That Montefiore's version of Judaism came to be recognised as a sect or denomination by British Jewry was something that distinguished his Judaism from that of other less 'political' Jewish thinkers. It put him into the line of fire. His claim that Liberal Judaism could rejuvenate, or even replace Orthodox and Reform Judaism in the future, angered his opponents whilst at the same time, ironically, it often failed to satisfy his supporters because the practical expression of his Judaism was too intellectualised. While he claimed that Liberal Judaism was not essentially an 'externality' but rather a certain attitude or condition of the mind and soul, some have suggested that its form was too ephemeral.[331] As Bentwich puts it,

> It was surely that to him, to Lily Montagu, and to a few faithful pioneers; but it was hardly that to the bulk of his followers. They gave up most of the Jewish tradition and the idea of religious law affecting daily life and put little in its place.[332]

Opposition to the traditional Jewish institutions combined with the failure to provide something people could recognise as a replacement, goes a long way in explaining why the Jewishness of Montefiore's movement was so often called into question.

Similarly, his emphasis upon religious individualism was regarded by some as suspicious. Writing to Lucy Cohen in 1924 he admitted: 'I don't think I like or approve of *that* religion or philosophy *at all* which "tries to inculcate not too much of the individual". What religion is that? I don't believe in Humanity at all. It does not, in the last resort, exist. There are only Toms and Claras.'[333] This stress upon individual religious consciousness over and above a religious, or worse, a nationalist, brotherhood was not something particular to his movement. Many other Jewish thinkers, not least his beloved Emancipationists, shared his concern that the essence of Judaism be described in terms of individual religious faith. However, Montefiore's timing seemed unfortunate and his vehement, active anti-Zionism set him at odds with the prevailing current of popular European Jewish opinion early in the twentieth century and led him into dispute with those like Schechter who emphasised the collectivity and peoplehood of Judaism. Buber and Rosenzweig were closer to Montefiore's individualist position, but theirs was a more philosophical argument, and they did not threaten the Orthodox in the radical way Montefiore did, who claimed to offer a denominational alternative. To some of his Orthodox and Reform critics, both then and now, Montefiore's religious world-view appeared somewhat obsessed with the individual, carrying overtones of Protestantism, and demonstrated that he had leaned too far towards Christianity (and certainly further than Buber or Rosenzweig had ever done). Montefiore's paper 'Do Liberal Jews Teach Christianity?' (1924) was addressed to all those who accused him of threatening the continuity of Judaism by teaching in such a way as to promote Jewish conversions to Christianity. These accusations will be examined more fully later. For now it is enough to see that for Montefiore to speak favourably about the traditional enemy, which he did often, was disconcerting and threatening for many of his fellow Jews.

Another related factor that might explain the charges of un-Jewishness brought against Montefiore is how he was perceived to relate to Jewish tradition. As previously noted, Montefiore cut himself adrift from traditional beliefs and authorities to a greater degree than most other Jewish thinkers who had remained religiously orientated; he was often condemned for what were regarded as his attacks upon the Jewish heritage.[334] But these were differences of degree rather than of kind; other Jews else-where were attempting similar things. Where the difference was more telling was in his vision of a future Judaism. For however far others had strayed from Orthodoxy, very few had ever suggested that as Judaism developed it would one day abandon its traditional position so far as to meld or identify with a future, developed Christianity, as Montefiore did.[335] Whatever the practicality of his vision, it was vastly more ambitious. This put him in a unique position and, significantly, gave him a sense of distance from Judaism. Bowler has commented that, despite his defence of the rabbis, Pharisees and the Law, it would be difficult to describe Montefiore as their heir.[336] And in a letter to Schechter, Montefiore wrote revealingly, 'I have often defended *your* Rabbis …' (italics mine),[337] as if to distinguish between Schechter's forebears and his own. Consequently, a sense of alienation from his fellow Jews permeates Montefiore's works and letters, a feeling of 'us and them'. Others were quick to sense the difference in quality, and to put it down to foreign, that is, Christian influence. Rightly or wrongly, Montefiore's ideas regarding the essence of Judaism were criticised as un-Jewish, at least partly, because he failed to take up a clearly defined position on the side of Jewish tradition against Jesus and Christianity.

One final factor was Montefiore's determination to achieve a greater systematisation of Judaism than had been achieved before. Throughout the years of their friendship, he badgered Schechter to produce a systematic Jewish theology. And towards the end of his life, he was still criticising the rabbinic writings for being so 'inconvenient' because 'it will not readily fit into a nice system; you cannot classify it comfortably'.[338] As has been argued, his Liberal Judaism was itself essentially a theological approach to Judaism as a religious system. While he was by no means alone in this endeavour, many of the brightest and best Jewish minds of the period could not quite accept such a presentation of Judaism (Schechter, for example, never satisfied Montefiore's demand for a rigorously theological alternative to Weber's work).[339] Later Jewish thinking, too, would challenge Montefiore's hope; few religious teachers today would seek to represent Judaism in terms of a systematic theology.[340] Thus, with regard to his tangential emphasis on theology, Montefiore could today be criticised for having mistaken the medium by which the essence of Judaism could be treated – although it should be borne in mind that such an anti-theological understanding was rarely, if ever, articulated during his lifetime. A closer look at this idea of a theologically expressed Judaism now follows.

NOTES

268. Y. H. Yerushalmi, *Zakhor: Jewish History and Jewish Memory* (1989), p. 92.
269. One good example of this is first-century Judaism. Jacob Neusner has attacked the view, held by E.P. Sanders among others, that there is a normative or general Judaism that provides the background theology to the various Judaisms of the different first-century Jewish communities. B. Chilton and J. Neusner, *Judaism in the New Testament: Practices and Beliefs* (1995), pp. 22–4.
270. L. Baeck, *Wesen des Judentums* (1905, English translation 1936).
271. W.R. Matthews, 'Claude Montefiore: The Man and his Thought', 1st Claude Montefiore Lecture, Southampton (1956), pp. 19–20.

272. C.G. Montefiore, 'The Justification of Liberal Judaism', *P.F.J.P.*, XXII (1919), pp. 19–20.
273. C.G. Montefiore, *Liberal Judaism and Hellenism and Other Essays* (1918), p. 125.
274. Letter from C.G. Montefiore to Lucy Cohen, 21 July 1923. L. Cohen, *Some Recollections of Claude Goldsmid-Montefiore 1858–1938* (1940), p. 109.
275. One of his favourite verses, Cohen recalls, was 'See I have put before you life and good and death and evil, choose life'. Ibid., pp. 264–5.
276. C.G. Montefiore, *The Old Testament and After* (1923), p. 550.
277. C.G. Montefiore, 'Authority' (c.1932), p. 12, paper presented to the Commission on Present Thought and Practice in Progressive Judaism (Authority Committee). MS 16/2/13, World Union for Progressive Judaism Papers, A.J.A.C.
278. C.G. Montefiore cited in N. Bentwich, 'Claude Montefiore and his Tutor in Rabbinics: Founders of Liberal and Conservative Judaism', 6th Montefiore Memorial Lecture, Southampton (1966), p. 15.
279. C.G. Montefiore, 'Authority' (c.1932), p. 9, paper presented to the Commission on Present Thought and Practice in Progressive Judaism (Authority Committee). MS 16/2/13, World Union for Progressive Judaism Papers, A.J.A.C.
280. Maimonides had argued that Jewish Law was the best means by which an unreasoning mankind could hope to attain a lifestyle pleasing to God, and while Montefiore agreed with emphasis upon reason, Maimonides' solution of dependence upon the Law was, of course, entirely unacceptable.
281. C.G. Montefiore, 'Some Notes on the Effects of Biblical Criticism upon the Jewish Religion', *Jewish Quarterly Review*, IV (1891–92).
282. Ibid., pp. 297–8.
283. Montefiore wrote: 'For there are no Jewish idées mères in those matters which have not been absorbed by one phase or another of Aryan thought.' Zangwill understood this to mean that Judaism was therefore redundant, that 'Judaism as a spiritual force has survived its function'. The *Jewish Chronicle* condemned both Zangwill and the *Daily Chronicle* for attacking Montefiore's position. *Jewish Chronicle*, 29 October 1897, p. 12.
284. C.G. Montefiore, 'Some Notes on the Effects of Biblical Criticism upon the Jewish Religion', *Jewish Quarterly Review*, IV (1891–92), p. 298.
285. C.G. Montefiore, *The Old Testament and After* (1923), pp. 558–9.
286. A good illustration of how little Montefiore's views changed over time, an almost identical second edition was published in 1923.
287. C.G. Montefiore, *Outlines of Liberal Judaism* (1912), pp. 9, 11.
288. Ibid., p. 366.
289. C.G. Montefiore, *The Old Testament and After* (1923), p. 557.
290. Ibid., p. 558.
291. Letter from C.G. Montefiore to Lucy Cohen, 18 May 1926. L. Cohen, *Some Recollections of Claude Goldsmid-Montefiore 1858–1938* (1940), p. 145.
292. K. Kohler, *Jewish Theology: Systematically and Historically Considered* (1918), p. 45.
293. Cohen has been described as 'the most important Jewish philosopher since Maimonides ... the philosophical spokesman for liberal Judaism'. S. Noveck, ed., *Contemporary Jewish Thought: A Reader* (1964), p. 129.
294. H. Cohen, 'The Importance of Jewish Unity', reproduced in ibid., p. 167.
295. H. Cohen, 'The Sabbath', 'The Atonement', 'The Nature of Hebrew Prophecy', in H. Cohen, *Jewish Writings* (1924) reproduced in ibid., pp. 144, 151, 154.

296. A.J. Wolf, 'The Dilemma of Claude Montefiore', *Conservative Judaism*, XIII (Winter 1959), p. 25.
297. Letter from C.G. Montefiore to Lucy Cohen, 26 January 1937. L. Cohen, *Some Recollections of Claude Goldsmid-Montefiore 1858–1938* (1940), p. 245.
298. L. Baeck, *Judaism and Christianity* (1958), pp. 171–84.
299. Reprinted in S. Schechter, *Studies in Judaism*, 3 vols (1896–1924), pp. 150–189.
300. Montefiore assisted Lucy Cohen's work. L. Cohen, *Some Recollections of Claude Goldsmid-Montefiore 1858–1938* (1940), p. 186.
301. An advertisement in the *Jewish Quarterly Review*, XVIII, reflects Montefiore's interest in the matter: 'A prize of £200 is offered by Mr. C.G. Montefiore for the best book on "Jewish Mysticism".'
302. Letter from C.G. Montefiore to Lucy Cohen, 18 December 1923. L. Cohen, *Some Recollections of Claude Goldsmid-Montefiore 1858–1938* (1940), p. 113.
303. Regarding one of Buber's hasidic stories, he commented, 'I found that story all too hard. It is like vaulting ambition, etc. Be *too* mystical and you become obscure.' Ibid., p. 188.
304. W. Jacob, *Christianity Through Jewish Eyes: The Quest for Common Ground* (1974), p. 98.
305. S. Bayme, 'Claude Montefiore, Lily Montagu and the Origins of the Jewish Religious Union', *Transactions of the Jewish Historical Society of England*, XXVII (1982), p. 64.
306. C.G. Montefiore, *Judaism and St. Paul: Two Essays* (1914), pp. 50–1.
307. C.G. Montefiore, *The Old Testament and After* (1923), p. 551.
308. A. Cohen, *The Natural and the Supernatural Jew: An Historical and Theological Introduction* (1962), p. 109.
309. The first English translation *I and Thou* was published in 1937.
310. M. Buber, *I and Thou*, trans. by W. Kaufmann (1970), pp. 156ff.
311. F. Rosenzweig, 'On Being a Jewish Person' (1920), reproduced in S. Noveck, ed., *Contemporary Jewish Thought: A Reader* (1964), p. 219. Later, however, he did accept that *halakhah* was a potentially authentic means by which to relate to God. F. Rosenzweig, 'The Builders' (1924), ibid., pp. 229–33.
312. F. Rosenzweig, 'On Jewish Learning' (1920), ibid., p. 223.
313. F. Rosenzweig, 'On Being a Jewish Person' (1920), ibid., p. 218.
314. F. Rosenzweig, 'On Jewish Learning' (1920), ibid., p. 224.
315. Ibid.
316. Rosenzweig's concept of Judaism was in its essence meta-historical since Israel, at Sinai, had reached the goal of all human existence and thus history (that is, change, growth and decline) had ended. F. Rosenzweig, *The Star of Redemption* (1985), pp. 328, 346, 335.
317. Ibid., p. 412.
318. From an otherwise positive review of Montefiore's *Liberal Judaism* (1903) in the *Jewish Chronicle*, 20 February 1903, p. 24.
319. This was a reaction to his lecture, 'The Place of Judaism Among the Religions of the World' (1918). Cited in the *Jewish Chronicle*, 7 June 1918, p. 7.
320. Englander suggests that 'trinitarian hymns and other alien practices incorporated into its liturgy made liberal Judaism abhorrent' to British Jews. D. Englander, 'Anglicised but not Anglican', G. Parsons, *Religion in Victorian Britain*, 4 vols (1988), I, p. 262. The *perception* that such practices occurred certainly explained the Jewish Orthodox suspicion of the 'de-nationalised spiritualism' of Montefiore and the 'liberal separatists'. In reality, the Jewish Religious Union did not even incorporate into the

service readings from the New Testament (which Montefiore regarded as Jewish and useful), let alone (un-modified) Christian devotional hymns. Despite a philosophical interest in trinitarianism, which he distinguished from tritheism, Montefiore was undoubtedly unitarian (see his sympathetic treatment of God as Trinity in *The Old Testament and After*, p. 561).

321. For example, Montefiore was criticised by one member of the Berkeley Street Synagogue for arriving to preach unannounced, thereby ensuring a captive audience. 'This is characteristic of "Liberal" methods which they seem to have assimilated from the other missionaries who seek to beguile Jews away from the faith.' *Jewish Chronicle*, 25 February 1921, p. 14.

322. *Jewish Chronicle*, 21 March 1919, p. 11.

323. M. Friedländer, 'Notes in Reply to My Critic', *Jewish Quarterly Review*, III (1892), p. 437.

324. 'What the whole thing means, is not Liberal Judaism, but Liberal Christianity.' Cited in R. Apple, *The Hampstead Synagogue* (1967), p. 38.

325. Ahad Ha-Am, 'Judaism and the Gospels', reprinted in *American Hebrew Journal*, LXXXVII, no. 21 (23 September 1910), p. 513.

326. Cited by Montefiore in a letter to Lucy Cohen, 5 August 1931. L. Cohen, *Some Recollections of Claude Goldsmid-Montefiore 1858–1938* (1940), p. 189.

327. The American Rabbi Joseph Jacobs was highly critical of what he saw as Montefiore's determination to contrast 'Jewish views of life' with those of Jesus in an unfavourable light so as to recommend Jesus' teachings to Liberal Jews. J. Jacobs, 'The Gospel According to Claude Montefiore', *American Hebrew*, LXXXVII (17 June 1910), p. 157.

328. W. Jacob, *Christianity through Jewish Eyes* (1974), p. 103.

329. D. Cohn-Sherbok, *Fifty Key Jewish Thinkers* (1997), p. 95.

330. 'We have learnt by bitter experience the unwisdom of ex-communication. Why will you cut yourselves off from communion with your brethren by seeking to form a new sect or section, why will ye forsake places of worship that must have established a profound claim upon your filial piety and reverence?' *Jewish Chronicle*, 5 November 1909, pp. 18–19.

331. In a letter to the *Jewish Chronicle*, one correspondent argued that Montefiore's use of the word 'faith' lost all meaning upon close inspection. *Jewish Chronicle*, 22 October 1909, pp. 20–1.

332. N. Bentwich, 'Claude Montefiore and his Tutor in Rabbinics: Founders of Liberal and Conservative Judaism', 6th Montefiore Memorial Lecture, Southampton (1966), p. 19.

333. Letter from C.G. Montefiore to Lucy Cohen, 1923. L. Cohen, *Some Recollections of Claude Goldsmid-Montefiore 1858–1938* (1940), p. 132.

334. For example, 'Mentor' accuses Montefiore of an 'un-Jewish attitude towards what we have always taught to believe – and some of us do believe – is the precious, unquestionable heritage of the Jews [the Torah] … Only because Mr Montefiore is weak in his love for what is Jewish was he impelled to make the damning "defence" of the Old Testament [published in *Nineteenth Century* (November 1921)].' *Jewish Chronicle*, 9 December 1921, p. 11.

335. 'There are thousands of persons to-day who would call themselves Christians … [T]hese men are nearer to Liberal Judaism as it is, and as it will be, than to *that* Christianity which Judaism was bound to offer its protest for so many generations in the past. And their descendants will, as we believe, be nearer still. We do not mind about the name.' C.G. Montefiore, *The Old Testament and After* (1923), p. 568. 'We do believe that the doctrines of Liberal Judaism, purified and developed, will win their

way more and more to a larger and larger acceptance. They may do that without even assuming a Jewish name.' Ibid., p. 590. 'It is not for me to explain or defend the separate identity and the justified separate consciousness of those who hold the essence of the Jewish faith, but not the Jewish name.' C.G. Montefiore, 'Enlarge the Place of Thy Tent' (1906), p. 15.

336. M.G. Bowler, *Claude Montefiore and Christianity* (1988), p. 73.
337. Letter from C.G. Montefiore to Solomon Schechter, 12 December 1900. J.B. Stein, *Lieber Freund: The Letters of Claude Goldsmid Montefiore to Solomon Schechter 1885–1902* (1988), p. 45.
338. C.G. Montefiore and H. Loewe, eds, *A Rabbinic Anthology* (1938), p. liii.
339. Ferdinand Weber, *System of Palestinian Theology in the Early Synagogues* (1880). Second edition entitled *Jewish Theology Exhibited on the Basis of the Talmud and Allied Writings* (1897).
340. Chief Rabbi Jonathan Sacks writes approvingly, 'Judaism, it has often been noted, does not attach the same significance to creed as it does to deed. Few of the Talmud's thousands of pages are devoted to doctrine.' J. Sacks, *One People: Tradition, Modernity, and Jewish Unity* (1993), p. 117. The present reader of Hebrew and Jewish Studies at Cambridge, Nicholas de Lange, prefers to speak of 'a collection of stories' than of a rabbinic theology. N. de Lange, 'Covenant' (C.C.J. conference, 24 June 1996).

8

Jewish 'Theology'

THEOLOGICAL EXPRESSION

It has become unfashionable in modern times to speak in terms of Jewish 'doctrine'. Even in Montefiore's day no knowledgeable Jew would have attempted to *define* his Judaism in terms of an authoritative creed in the Christian manner (Mendelssohn, of course, had gloried in the idea that Judaism was not dependent upon dogma). But the disputes regarding various Jewish 'beliefs' among Western Jewry at that time often seem to reflect a doctrinal approach to religion, an approach which might loosely be described as Christian. As is evident in Michael Hilton's *The Christian Effect on Jewish Life*, certain subjects (which he calls ' special themes') such as Messianism and Missionism came to take on an almost doctrinal sense in Jewish thought.[341] For example, the importance of the messiah and details concerning him and the messianic age came to occupy a significant, if not central, position in Jewish thought as a 'bounce-back' response to the traditional messiah-centric focus of Christianity. This was not a natural Jewish development but, instead, illustrates Hilton's main thesis that Christianity has, on numerous occasions down through the centuries, significantly shaped Jewish thought.[342] The process seemed to have found its personification in Montefiore, who stressed the need for a doctrinally informed Judaism that could be compared favourably with a doctrinally informed Christianity (or any other religion, for that matter).

Many of Montefiore's contemporaries disagreed with his theological or doctrinal agenda, of course. Solomon Schechter described traditional Jewish theology as tending 'against the certain' and thus avoided systematic or dogmatic approaches,[343] and Leo Baeck, Montefiore's friend and fellow Liberal Jew, argued vehemently against the idea of a theologically defined Judaism.[344] One of the earliest assessments of Montefiore to concentrate upon this particular characteristic was by the American V.E.

Reichert. Reichert complained at Montefiore's 'extravagant emphasis upon utopian precepts' and that his approach 'is literary and theological. He moves in a world of ideals. He is content to be a dreamer of prophetic Judaism that shall be wholly spiritual and universal.'[345] But unlike those for whom a theological approach seemed too similar to Christian practice for comfort, Montefiore was unabashed. It appeared a straightforward matter to him and he grew increasingly frustrated at the failure of Jews to express their religious world-view in clear-cut doctrinal terms.

In an article for the *Jewish Quarterly Review* in 1891, Montefiore argued that he had heard enough of the 'duties' of Orthodoxy and now wanted to hear about its 'creed'.[346] Dr M. Friedländer, head of Jews' College, had written *The Jewish Religion*, and in a review of the book Montefiore had treated it as a window into the hearts and minds of 'modern Jewish Orthodoxy ... [and] the Judaism of the Jews' College'.[347] What he read had disconcerted him, for, while he was assured that Judaism was destined to become 'in its simplest principles the universal religion', he had been unable to determine what these principles were. Similarly, he had failed to discover the Orthodox position with regard to other creeds (especially Unitarianism and Theism), could make out little of what was meant by 'the Mission of Israel', and remained in the dark concerning the Orthodox Jewish doctrine on 'Sin, Reconciliation, Atonement and Divine Grace'.[348] He was impressed by the emphasis Friedländer gave to faith but concluded that the doctrinal weakness of Orthodoxy, which was the result of its narrow-minded, sheltered existence and which had prevented it from adopting a (Hellenistic) logical, structured approach, boded ill for the future of Judaism within what he called 'the wide stream of general civilisation'.[349]

Almost 30 years on, and Montefiore was still complaining that doctrine was, for a variety of reasons, 'driven into the shade'.[350] One of these reasons was the unnecessary Jewish reaction to Christian emphasis upon belief. He felt that, since the time of Mendelssohn, Judaism had lost its sense of balance and had emphasised action while neglecting doctrine. For Montefiore, it was entirely unsatisfactory to define Judaism in terms of its particular practices – in that case, he argued, food laws could be viewed as more distinctly Jewish than the belief in the Unity of God.[351] The result of this observance-orientated self-definition, he complained, was that it was unclear exactly what the traditionalists did believe in.[352] Surely, he reasoned, ever conscious of Christian observers, a theological dimension was essential for a healthy Judaism.

> We [Liberal Jews], too, believe that life is more than a creed, that conduct is more important than dogma, and the love of God more urgent than elaborate beliefs about his nature. But neither Christians nor Jews need, therefore, hold ... that either individuals or communities can get on *without* beliefs, even though those beliefs need not be very intricate or exceedingly numerous.[353]

In Montefiore's opinion, what the traditionalists had failed to achieve was a combination of belief and practice. They had not understood that 'the Practice was ever sustained and nourished by the Belief'.[354]

THEOLOGICAL ISSUES

As a Liberal Jew, Montefiore not only differed from other Jewish thinkers in his insistence that Judaism should emphasise its essential doctrines but also with regard to the content of such beliefs. Again and again, these differences, and the doctrinal form in which he expressed them, can be traced back to the influence of his prolonged exposure to Western European Christian ethical and theological thought.

Montefiore had looked with interest in Friedländer's book for an Orthodox theology of God. As far has he was concerned, however, it had failed to provide any clear indication regarding the immanence or the transcendence of God; although 'painfully silent upon this momentous question', the overall impression tended towards one of a highly transcendental deity. 'Let us therefore for the present hope', he concluded, 'that Dr. Friedländer's conception is by no means Orthodoxy's last word'.[355] Montefiore himself believed that it was possible to defend a doctrinally held position that God could be both things at once, depending upon one's point of view; elsewhere he referred to the Jewish scriptural images of the *ruach ha'kodesh* (i.e. God in nature) and God the Creator (i.e. God the source of nature) which supported this dual model, and argued 'There is no reason why Judaism should not teach both aspects of the Divine Unity'.[356] This was not very different from Leo Baeck's view. For Baeck it was the bi-polar nature of Judaism, the co-existence of both mystery and commandment, which allowed the apparently mutually exclusive concepts to be reconciled. As he put it,

> Judaism lacks any foundation for the conflict between tran-
> scendence and immanence. Jewish piety lives in the paradox,
> in the polarity with all its tension and compactness.[357]

What is interesting here is that Montefiore differed from Baeck, Friedländer and other Jewish thinkers on this subject in his emphasis upon clear doctrinal expression, a form of expression which could easily be viewed as characteristically Christian or Hellenistic (or, at least, not typically Jewish). In other words, his heavily Christianised background and the corresponding influence of rationalist, Aristotelian thinking coloured the way in which he understood and the way in which he described his faith.

Montefiore was also disappointed to discover that Friedländer's book had ignored what he described as 'the virtue of self-sacrifice ... of suffering voluntarily for the sake of others'.[358] He complained that although the Orthodox spoke a great deal about 'duty', there was little about 'love', a doctrine central to Montefiore's understanding of Judaism. He was care-ful to differentiate between 'vicarious suffering' which was voluntary, moral and, moreover, an ideal Judaism shared with Christianity, and 'vicarious punishment' which was a judicial act, immoral, and, as expressed in Christ's atoning death, a teaching Judaism could never accept.[359] Yet, while Christianity had moved too far in this direction in his opinion, Montefiore argued that 'the doctrine of sacrifice, of suffering voluntarily undergone for the sake of others' was taught in Isaiah 53 and could be found in the rabbinic literature and was thus essentially a Jewish doctrine. This was by no means a point of view shared by other Jewish thinkers. His arch-critic, Ahad Ha-Am, had attacked Montefiore for this very claim in a review of his *Synoptic Gospels*.[360] Arguing that absolute justice rather than self-sacrificing love characterised Judaism, Ahad Ha-Am had likewise quoted from the rabbinic sources at length, managing to produce an entirely opposite effect to Montefiore's positive assessment of the doctrine of Love. Ahad Ha-Am was adamant that love or altruism, which were for him interchangeable terms, almost always detracted from justice. As he put it,

> Judaism cannot accept the altruistic principle; it cannot put the 'other' in the centre of the circle, because that place belongs to justice, which knows no distinction between 'self' and 'other'.[361]

Ahad Ha-Am also pointed out that an altruistic standpoint could not be maintained at an international level – 'a nation can never believe that its moral duty lies in self-abasement or in the renunciation of its rights for the benefits of other nations'[362] – and this proved for him the ultimately illogical nature of Christian belief in the supremacy of love. It is clear, however, that an essential factor in Ahad Ha-Am's opposition to Montefiore in this matter lay in the latter's perceived adoption of Christian value-judgements and ideas. Ahad Ha-Am's attack on love as a non-Jewish doctrine seems to have stemmed from his concern to cleanse Judaism from what he saw as unwelcome Christian influences. Interestingly, Ahad Ha-Am, even as a cultural Zionist, tacitly accepted the idea that Judaism could be described in doctrinal, theological terms (that is, Ahad Ha-Am defined Judaism doctrinally in terms of 'justice' rather than in terms of 'love' in opposition to Montefiore) even though it was just this Christian- or Hellenistic-influenced form of expression which differentiated Liberal Jewish teaching from Orthodox Jewish teaching in general and the writings of others like Baeck in particular.

As has already been noted, the (Reform) doctrine of the Mission of Israel was an important one for Montefiore. When others attacked him for holding theological views which better suited Theism or Unitarianism rather than Judaism, Montefiore defended his position as a Jew primarily through his identification with the Religion whose duty it had been from time immemorial to propagate morality and ethical belief throughout the rest of the world. As he put it in a letter in 1934,

> The Jews, please God, will never be absorbed. God has chosen them for a religious purpose in the History of the World, and till the earth is filled with the knowledge of the

One God – the God of Israel – the Jews will be his witnesses.
I should collapse morally and *spiritually* if I did not believe
that.[363]

Thus it was Montefiore's duty, as he saw it, to further the Mission
of Israel from within the camp of Israel, that is, as a Jew. Although
the phrase was current in Orthodox circles, Montefiore complained
that Friedländer's vagueness in defining the 'Mission of Israel'
was typical.[364] Not all Jewish thinkers were as vague, however.
Ahad Ha-Am uncompromisingly decried the idea of a Mission
of Israel (in any sense other than a fulfilment of duties) as
'entirely without foundation in fact'.[365] In response to Reform
claims that the Prophets had envisaged the positive influence of
Judaism upon the morality of the surrounding world, Ahad
Ha-Am argued that this result would have followed automatically
from the existence of the superior morality Judaism offered. The
furthest he was prepared to go was to accept the idea of the
Chosenness of Israel, in the sense of its moral development. But
this, he felt, had nothing to do with the idea of Judaism converting
the rest of humanity. As he put it: 'There was no thought of ... the
rest of mankind; the sole object was the existence of the superior
type.'[366] This was a position entirely at odds with Montefiore's
Liberal Judaism for two reasons. Firstly, in *Liberal Judaism and
Hellenism* (1918) Montefiore had called for a world-wide mission
if the 'new and purified Judaism' was to fulfil its destiny as a
universal religion. 'The object of Israel's election', he wrote, 'is to
disseminate throughout the world the knowledge of God.'[367] The
fact that he was content to see Liberal Jewish doctrine victorious
'without even assuming a Jewish name', and even confused by
many as Christianity,[368] would not have endeared him to Ahad
Ha-Am. It was another example of the excessive lengths Montefiore
was, in theory, prepared to go to in order to further his doctrinal
form of Judaism. Secondly, Montefiore was quite against the idea
of a Chosen people in the sense of 'privilege' and was adamant in
defining the doctrine in terms of 'service'.[369] His position on this
matter was not atypical for a Jew – the doctrine of the Chosen
People, in the sense of service, had been foreshadowed in
Continental and American Reform theology – but his emphasis
of this role was regarded suspiciously by his opponents. After
all, Christianity had traditionally emphasised the role of the
'Suffering Servant' with regard to the messiah. It was, perhaps,

too much of a Christian emphasis and seemed to reinforce the image of Montefiore as a sort of crypto-Christian.

The concept of universalism greatly appealed to Montefiore. It was one of the aspects of the apostle Paul's theology upon which he was prepared to comment positively; he admired Paul for having preached a universalist message and for having solved the 'puzzle of the universal God and the national cult',[370] although needless to say he disagreed about the exact form it took. Montefiore was by no means alone, however; there were many others who believed that, eventually, Judaism would take its rightful place as the world religion. Of course, almost all of them were talking about their own version of Judaism. Montefiore condemned Friedländer for the vagueness of his claim that Judaism 'in its simplest principles' would triumph.[371] Solomon Schechter recognised no geographical limit for Judaism nor was he against the idea of proselytising, but he disagreed with Montefiore regarding the form of Judaism that would ultimately prove to be universally acceptable. Concerned to preserve the traditions of both Western and Eastern Jewish communities, Schechter was doubtful that Montefiore's Anglicised Liberal Judaism could ever meet the needs of world Jewry. Indeed, he argued fiercely that Liberal Judaism would only bring about further disunity.

In contrast, Montefiore viewed Liberal Judaism as a unifying force and a means by which the East–West split could be bridged. In accomplishing this universalist task, he was prepared to make compromises. Thus, in spite of his abhorrence for particularism in religion, Montefiore rejected many pro-universalist options in the interests of continuity and to avoid offending the wider Jewish community (including substituting Sunday services for Saturday ones, renouncing circumcision or traditional festivals, and using New Testament texts in worship). Long before the J.R.U. or the Liberal Jewish movement were established, Montefiore had suggested that any tensions would disappear as a result of the western education of Eastern Jews. In his essay 'A Justification of Judaism' (1885), referring to Western Christian literature, he wrote,

> To all these influences the Jews are necessarily subjected. Indeed, they are needful influences to the required trans-formation of Judaism from an Eastern into a Western faith.[372]

What he appears to have meant by 'Western faith' in contrast to 'Eastern [faith]' was a systematic, rationalistic form of Jewish truth of the Hellenistic or Christian kind. What Montefiore wanted to see adopted by this Judaism was a doctrinally worked out, clear-cut, belief-based expression of itself. This would provide a common ground for Jews from the East and the West and, more importantly, would appeal to and include the Gentile world. At best, Montefiore's hope that a given set of doctrinal beliefs would, in historical fact, unify peoples of different cultures and religious thought patterns can be described as naïvely optimistic. As Israel Zangwill pointed out in 1919, Montefiore's doctrinally universalist movement actually made very little difference. 'No more than the old Synagogue has it [Liberal Judaism] been of any universalist value in the spiritual eclipse whose shadow still rests heavily upon Europe.'[373] Nevertheless, Montefiore remained firmly convinced throughout his life that eventually, some day, the essential (Liberal) Jewish doctrines would triumph universally.

NOTES

341. M. Hilton, *The Christian Effect on Jewish Life* (1994), pp. 63–85, 87–9.
342. Hilton writes, 'I am fully aware that this is a highly controversial area. It is indeed painful to discover that someone you have always thought of as your parent is in fact not parent but brother or sister.' Ibid., p. 4.
343. N. Bentwich, 'Claude Montefiore and his Tutor in Rabbinics: Founders of Liberal and Conservative Judaism', 6th Montefiore Memorial Lecture, Southampton (1966), p. 11.
344. Rather, Judaism was to be defined in terms of 'man's attitude towards the world' for Baeck. A. Cohen, *The Natural and the Supernatural Jew: An Historical and Theological Introduction* (1962), p. 108.
345. V.E. Reichert, 'The Contribution of Claude G. Montefiore to the Advancement of Judaism', *Central Conference of American Rabbis Yearbook*, XXXVIII (1928), pp. 510–11.
346. C.G. Montefiore, 'Dr. Friedländer on the Jewish Religion', *Jewish Quarterly Review*, IV (1891), p. 234.
347. Jews' College was, after all, the rabbinical training school 'in which nearly every Jewish minister for the last 25 years has been taught'. Ibid., p. 205.
348. Ibid., pp. 231–2.
349. Ibid., p. 244.
350. C.G. Montefiore, 'Is There a Middle Way?', *P.F.J.P.*, XXIII (1920), p. 2.
351. Ibid., p. 3.
352. Ibid., p. 2.
353. Ibid., p. 10.
354. Ibid., p. 7.

355. C.G. Montefiore, 'Dr. Friedländer on the Jewish Religion', *Jewish Quarterly Review*, IV (1891), pp. 212–15.
356. C.G. Montefiore, 'A Justification of Judaism', *Unitarian Review* (1885), pp. 8–9.
357. L. Baeck, 'Mystery and Commandment' (1922), reproduced in S. Noveck, ed., *Contemporary Jewish Thought: A Reader* (1964), p. 197.
358. C.G. Montefiore, 'Dr. Friedländer on the Jewish Religion', *Jewish Quarterly Review*, IV (1891), p. 223.
359. Ibid.
360. Ahad Ha-Am, 'Judaism and the Gospels', *The Jewish Review*, I (3 September 1910).
361. L. Simon, ed., *Ahad Ha-Am; Essays, Letters, Memoirs* (1946), p. 135.
362. Ibid., p. 137.
363. Letter from C.G. Montefiore to Lucy Cohen, 5 January 1934. L. Cohen, *Some Recollections of Claude Goldsmid-Montefiore 1858–1938* (1940), pp. 217–18.
364. C.G. Montefiore, 'Dr. Friedländer on the Jewish Religion', *Jewish Quarterly Review*, IV (1891), p. 231.
365. L. Simon, ed., *Ahad Ha-Am: Essays, Letters, Memoirs* (1946), p. 81.
366. Ibid., p. 80.
367. C.G. Montefiore, *Liberal Judaism and Hellenism and Other Essays* (1918), p. 45.
368. C.G. Montefiore, *The Old Testament and After* (1923), p. 568.
369. Ibid., p. 569.
370. C.G. Montefiore, *Liberal Judaism and Hellenism and Other Essays* (1918), p. 119.
371. C.G. Montefiore, 'Dr. Friedländer on the Jewish Religion', *Jewish Quarterly Review*, IV (1891), p. 231.
372. C.G. Montefiore, 'A Justification of Judaism', *Unitarian Review* (1885), p. 23.
373. Letter from Israel Zangwill to C.G. Montefiore, 21 February 1919. MS A120/454, C.Z.A.

9

Judaism and Christianity

In 1895, as honorary president of the Theological Society of the University of Glasgow,[374] Montefiore read a paper entitled 'Some Misconceptions of Judaism and Christianity by Each Other'. The paper is interesting for the concern it showed in preparing the ground for what today might be described as dialogue. Non-polemical in character, it suggested that important benefits could be gained from genuine attempts to understand the other faith. Montefiore suggested that,

> The way by which one pilgrim travels seems strange and rugged to another, and yet, perhaps it is well for him to learn something of his fellow pilgrim's road. At least let him realise that the many pathways may all lead Godward, and that the world is richer for that the paths are not a few.[375]

The respect with which Montefiore treats the traditional foe was remarkable but more remarkable still was his apparent acceptance of the other's self-definition. It was this which most of all set him apart from the vast majority of other Jewish thinkers and gives credence to the claim made here that, with the exception of Franz Rosenzweig, Montefiore was closer to true dialogue than any other pre-Holocaust Jew.

In 'Some Misconceptions of Judaism and Christianity by Each Other', Montefiore drew up two shortlists of contributions which he believed each of the faiths had made to religion. On the Jewish side, he included the concepts of:

- a Deity who was just and loving and was a Unity;
- morality as central to religion;
- social justice;
- social unity and love;
- dogmatic simplicity and comprehensive unity of belief;
- an ideal of religion as the stuff of everyday life.

On the Christian side, the contributions included:

- a high and spiritual estimate of suffering;
- sacrifice and self-sacrifice as ideal;
- a loving attitude towards one's enemies;
- universalism, i.e. God's acceptance of all men;
- non-racial religion;
- subordinated ritual; a lack of confusion of outward and inward piety.

That there was a great common ground between Judaism and Christianity was illustrated for Montefiore by the fact that in modern times each camp had adopted 'as its own children and property' all these 12 concepts (and others). Significantly, Montefiore was prepared to acknowledge, as a Jew, that Christianity had produced truths that Judaism had done well to absorb (and vice versa). The high regard in which he viewed Christianity, and his public expression of it, set him apart from his contemporary co-religionists. He was prepared to give credit where he believed credit was due, even if this meant giving it to the traditional foe. It goes without saying that such a sympathetic, non-antagonistic attitude is one prerequisite for inter-faith dialogue.

Another prerequisite is the mutual recognition of each faith as valid expressions of the knowledge of God. Montefiore, like Rosenzweig, went even further in this with his belief that Christianity and Judaism actually complemented each other. For Rosenzweig, as noted earlier, Judaism was the star and Christianity the rays radiating from its centre; the two were intertwined. In *The Star of Redemption*, Rosenzweig wrote that each group was dependent upon the other within the context of world history. For both, this responsibility brought suffering – for the Jew, due to his 'negation of the world' and for the Christian, due to his 'affirmation of the world'.[376] What Rosenzweig meant by 'negation' was the idea of an election, or a setting apart, of a people who would witness to the rest of the world; their suffering had resulted from their separation. By 'affirmation', he referred to the position of the Church in attempting to missionise the pagan world; likewise, different temptations and sufferings had come about from its 'being in the world'.

> Before God, the two – the Jew and the Christian, are thus
> labourers in the same task. He can dispense with neither.
> Between the two He has set an eternal hostility, and yet He
> has intertwined them with one another most intimately.[377]

Thus both religions played essential and complementary roles
within world history; both were necessary and related (although
he undoubtedly regarded being Jewish as preferable to being
Christian).[378] For this reason, Rosenzweig's thinking has been
described as dialogical rather than dialectical.[379]

Montefiore, too, supported the idea that Judaism needed
Christianity. Towards the end of his life, he observed that the
'moderns of today' could benefit from an understanding of the
intimate relationship that exists between Rabbinic Judaism and
Christianity.

> The one is often (in a good sense) the complement or
> supplement of the other ... Of the two brothers [Judaism
> and Christianity] one has remained more at home; the other
> has gone out into the world ... The character of each is a
> fresh creation, and the excellences of each, though kindred,
> are yet distinct. As society is the richer for both brothers, so
> it is, I think, with the teachings of both Rabbinic Judaism
> and of Christianity.[380]

But while Rosenzweig's 'doctrine of the two covenants' viewed
Christianity and Judaism as partial truths which would be
superseded by the absolute truth in 'the end of days', Montefiore
hoped and believed that the synthesis would occur before the end
of time. This difference can be partly explained by the differing
images of Christianity each held. The paramount factor, and the
most obvious one in determining a Jewish thinker's place within
Jewish–Christian relations, is that of his personal comprehension
of Christianity. Determining his actual position is, however, a
complex issue because of two obvious yet often overlooked
complications. Firstly, just as there is no consensus on what
exactly defines Judaism, so there is no consensus regarding
the precise nature of Christianity. The fact that different people
experience different expressions of 'Christianity' means one
person's views on its 'essence' may in fact be referring to quite
a different thing than another's. It thus becomes essential to

determine what experience of 'Christianity' each Jewish thinker has undergone before attempting to compare and contrast his or her apparently differing views. Secondly, it is quite possible, and even likely, that a Jewish thinker's position might well change over his lifetime as his personal comprehension and appreciation of 'Christianity' develops.

As has already been mentioned, Rosenzweig's view of Christianity was highly philosophical and shaped by his conversations with intellectual Christian relatives and friends (such as Hans Ehrenburg and Eugene Rosenstock). Static and ahistorical (emphasising, for example, the divinity of Christ), his image accurately mirrored the contemporary Protestant theology as influenced by German Idealism. Montefiore, on the other hand, held a far more complicated view of Christianity. His humanitarian and philanthropic activities in London and elsewhere had placed him in constant contact with Evangelical Christian charities, while a close friend of his, Baron Von Hügel, was Catholic with mystical leanings. He had a special interest in the Unitarian theological training school, Manchester College, and regarded the Unitarian minister, Joseph Estlin Carpenter, as a friend. With regard to biblical studies, his own position was close to the German rationalistic writings. Overall, however, it was the British modernists and liberals to whom he had been most exposed and was most familiar. From his days at Oxford he had become intimately aware of what it meant to be an Anglican liberal. Generally speaking, this de-mystified, ethical, liberal Anglican theology came to represent for him Christianity *per se*. Unlike Rosenzweig, then, Montefiore's treatment of Christianity in this context was based less upon a philosophical idea of Christianity and more upon Christianity as it was practised and believed by Christians themselves (especially Jowett). He was very aware that liberal attacks on the verbal inspiration of Scripture, for example, had brought about a shaking of the foundations of Western Christianity. The vacuum left by this weakened Christianity and by a stagnant Orthodox Judaism would best be filled, he argued, with 'a developed and purified Judaism' composed of the best aspects of each religion.[381] While it might not reach its fullest form for some time, Montefiore was convinced that his own Liberal Judaism had already managed to articulate the universalist principles and rationalist attitude of this future faith.

Leo Baeck, who played an important role in the history of Jewish–Christian relations, did not accept for a long time the partnership of Judaism and Christianity, which both Rosenzweig and Montefiore recognised in their different ways. Baeck's *The Essence of Judaism* (1905), a polemical response to Harnack's *The Essence of Christianity* (1900), was written in total disregard of Montefiore's sentiments articulated as early as 1896 against 'the habit we all have of using another religion as a foil to our own'.[382] Elsewhere, Baeck contrasted the equal mix of 'mystery' and 'commandment' in Judaism, with the lopsided emphasis of 'mystery' in Christianity. 'Paul left Judaism', Baeck argued, 'when he preached *sola fide* (by faith alone) ... Mystery became everything for him.'[383] In his famous essay *Romantic Religion* (1922) Baeck contrasted Christianity (that is, the contemporary German Protestantism) which was a 'Romantic' religion, with Judaism, which was essentially 'Classical'. Baeck used Schleiermacher's definition of religion as 'the feeling of absolute dependence'[384] as evidence for his claim that the Romantic aspect 'fixes the direction' in Christianity.[385]

Baeck's polemicism, however, became more subdued towards the end of his life. Spending time in America had shown him another face of Christianity, a more open Christianity, and one which was less threatening than the often hostile, overly intellectual Church of the Old World. Was this the same face which Montefiore and Rosenzweig had caught a glimpse of in turn-of-the-century Europe? Certainly, Baeck's later writing regarding Jewish–Christian relations sounds similar. Like Rosenzweig and Montefiore, the older Baeck was able to see complementary roles by which Judaism and Christianity could co-exist and prosper. In 1954 he wrote,

> Inner voices will be heard. To each other Judaism and Christianity will be admonitions and warnings: Christianity becoming Judaism's conscience and Judaism Christianity's. That common ground, that common outlook, that common problem which they come to be aware of will call them to make a joint venture.[386]

Even then, however, Baeck was more comfortable with the idea of sharing 'a common ground' than he was with the idea that the two faiths actually needed each other if the future of their essential teachings were to be assured (Montefiore's position), or that the partial truth of each one would meet in one absolute truth at the end of time (Rosenzweig's position). Baeck's position was more conservative and closer to that of Kaufmann Kohler who had spoken of 'Jewish ethics' expressed 'through Synagogue and Church alike'.[387] For Baeck, as for Kohler, the fact that the two faiths shared a common aim of holiness was, ultimately, simply a result of the influence of Judaism. As Kohler put it, '[striving for Holiness] is the ethical principle and the moral idea of the Jew, and through him also of the Christian'.[388] For Jewish thinkers like Kohler and the older Baeck, Christianity no longer represented the arch-enemy but neither was it in the same league as Judaism; for them there was no absolute need for Christianity as such, as there had been for both Montefiore and Rosenzweig. In contrast to most other Jews, their idea of Christianity was one with which they could identify and thus sympathise; although they were quite capable of defining the differences between the 'essence of Judaism' and the 'essence of Christianity', they generally did so in a manner far less antagonistic than, for example, the young Leo Baeck. This seems to boil down to a difference in value judgement rather than a difference of intellectual or spiritual ideals.

No doubt their differing value judgements were largely due to the fact that both Montefiore and Rosenzweig had grown up in environments which had instilled in them a high regard for Christian culture, and also the fact that both had enjoyed the companionship and friendship of Christians whom they deeply respected. But they were by no means the only Jews in this position. Likewise, while their interest in Christianity set them apart from the majority of Jews, there were others who were also actively engaged in attempting to come to terms with Christianity. What made Rosenzweig and Montefiore different from Baeck and others was the way in which they had *felt* about Christianity from their youth onwards. This appears to have been the decisive factor in determining the tone of their Jewish–Christian writings.

It has been well documented that the number of Jews who have been converted to Christianity throughout history has been few.[389] Around the turn of the twentieth century, however, relatively large numbers of European Jews did abandon the faith of their forefathers. In Germany they did so for mainly social and financial considerations.[390] In England, where the granting of emancipation had made baptism unnecessary for Jews to 'get along', the majority of the Anglo-Jewish elite remained within the Jewish fold or at least indifferent to Christianity. In both cases, it was an extremely small minority who did apostasise for the sake of the spiritual teachings or ethical values of Christianity. Nevertheless, there were a few for whom, from their often nominally Jewish point of view, Christianity appeared culturally and religiously light years ahead of Judaism. Certainly, both Rosenzweig and Montefiore were acutely conscious of the fact that the Western European culture in which they immersed themselves and with which they found themselves so much a part, included Christianity as a major component. It seems fair to place the young Rosenzweig within this tiny minority since, at one stage in his youth, he did decide to become Christian for these reasons.[391] Similarly, it also seems right to place Montefiore here, for although he apparently never contemplated conversion, he too regarded the best of the contemporary Christianity as superior to much of what Judaism generally stood for at the time. While both eventually became intensely concerned to forward the cause of Judaism, neither could quite leave behind the admiration and appreciation they had developed for Christianity. Thus they represent a minute fraction of the afore-mentioned minority of usually nominal Jews whose high regard for Christianity might have tempted them to convert but who, instead, were able to reconcile their regard for Christianity with their loyalty to their Jewish roots. The next logical step would be for them to construct a coherent (Jewish) world-view that could incorporate Christianity in a positive way. And this is exactly what both Montefiore and Rosenzweig did.

Reference has been made to the characteristics of 'dialogue' and the conditions under which it can take place. For our pur-poses, 'dialogue' refers to the face-to-face interaction between equal partners who aim to develop themselves and learn from the encounter. While several of the necessary preconditions are to be found espoused in the writings of Baeck, Montefiore and especially Rosenzweig, true dialogue in its modern sense had to wait for Martin Buber. Montefiore and Rosenzweig were close to the spirit of dialogue in their high estimation of the value of Christianity – especially significant were Montefiore's readiness to learn from Christianity and Rosenzweig's recognition of its equally legitimate yet unique role as a pathway to God for pagans. But before Buber, no one had fully accepted the self-definition of the Other, that is to say, Jews had failed to actually take on trust what Christians had to say about their own faith from the depth of their own private, inner knowledge. Both Montefiore and Rosenzweig had come to hold a very definite and particular view of Christianity. For Montefiore, even the very best Christian thinkers were, ultimately, mistaken if they held to traditional Christology.[392] For Rosenzweig, while Christianity had much to say to the surrounding (pagan) world, ultimately, it had little to say to the Jew. Their writings regarding Jewish–Christian relations, while eloquent and generous, failed to accept the paradox of dialogue (that the experience of the Other is as real and true as it is for oneself) and would have been assessed by Buber as I–It monologues.

The acceptance of the Other's self-definition was something that Buber was prepared to attempt in spite of the inherent difficulties. Writing in 1936 he argued,

> We can acknowledge as a mystery that which someone else confesses as the reality of his faith, though it opposes our own existence and is contrary to the knowledge of our own being. We are not capable of judging its meaning, because we do not know it from within.[393]

Buber was prepared to acknowledge that there was more to Christianity than he, as an outsider, could understand; Rosenzweig and Montefiore both believed that they understood what it meant to be Christian and could describe its essence – and thus failed to recognise the mystery and 'unknowableness' that is intrinsic to the partner in dialogue, an awareness of the Other as 'absolutely not oneself'.[394] In a sense, defining the precise nature of a Jewish thinker's idea of Christianity becomes a moot point in the context of dialogue. Whatever the depth of his understanding, it is essential for dialogue that there be recognition of the limitation of his actual knowledge, since the source of knowledge is external.

In what sense can Montefiore be said to have engaged in inter-faith dialogue? In addition to his lively personal correspondence with Christian thinkers, his non-polemical studies of the New Testament, and his belief in the eventual merging of the best of Christian and Jewish teaching, Montefiore was also intimately involved in one of the earliest institutional attempts to utilise dialogue as a vehicle for religious self-understanding. The London Society for the Study of Religion was set up in 1904 by the Roman Catholic Baron von Hügel and the Unitarian missionary Joseph Wicksteed (who were introduced to each other by Montefiore). A small group was formed, Montefiore being the only Jew, with the aim 'to include devout men of every school, and to welcome all new thought that seeks to restore and re-state for our own time and in the language of today those revelations and apprehensions of the Eternal which have in different ages given greatness to the past'.[395] Papers which Montefiore himself delivered to the Society included 'The Synoptic Gospels and the Jewish Consciousness', 'Apocalyptic and Rabbinic', 'Has Judaism any Future?', 'The Originality of Jesus', 'Some Reflections about the Jews' and 'A Die-Hard's Confession'. One of the most important aspects of this forum for dialogue was that, for all practical purposes, each participant spoke for himself first, and his denomination second; little or no emphasis was placed upon 'the official' position and no minutes were published, so as to protect the reputations of those involved. Such an arrangement suited all those who recognised the reality of another individual's faith and experience even if they disagreed with the teachings of the tradition to which they belonged. It certainly suited Montefiore's personal disposition, reflected in his comment to a Christian friend and fellow member of the Society, 'Is there such a thing as Judaism and Christianity apart from the men who hold it?'[396] Thus, while the L.S.S.R. did not represent dialogue between the respective institutional traditions, it did encourage increased mutual understanding among individuals.[397]

Like other liberal thinkers involved in proto-dialogue, Montefiore was well aware of the Orthodox argument that without authority in some form or another, whether scriptural, traditional or individual, there would be nothing to hold Judaism together. Liberalism was vilified, then as now, as the work of man rather than of God, with the traditionalists fearing that a dialogical approach would lead men away from the revealed truth. Certainly, Montefiore placed great emphasis upon Reason and its ability to reach ultimate religious truth. Liberal Judaism was, for him, the supreme example of a religion that utilised man's conscience as the pivotal point about which to assess this truth. But, equally, he stressed the importance of an *instructed* conscience, that is, one which had learned from the mistakes and achievements of the past, one shaped by the very traditions from which it could later largely free itself.[398] The instruction was to be gained from what can only be described as a dialogical relationship with the traditional scriptures. While they were not to dictate to an individual, they were, apparently, useful in shaping and forming him. He wrote of the Hebrew Bible, for example,

> However great and significant the changes in Liberal Judaism from ... the prevailing doctrines of the Old Testament may be, still more remarkable, perhaps, is the fact that Liberal Judaism still finds in the Old Testament both its spiritual ancestry and its nourishment.[399]

Montefiore's own life illustrates his ideal: a life of study and instruction within the Jewish tradition (with reference to other wisdom literatures). But in articulating the essence of Liberal Judaism, Montefiore also made it clear that once the authentic Jewish 'spirit' had been developed in the Jew through the 'religious system', he should realise that he 'stands above' it. It was of paramount importance to Montefiore that the tradition did not inhibit development: 'We possess a large measure of freedom, and this freedom is of the essence of our religion.'[400] This is not far, perhaps, from Buber's dialogical Judaism in the sense of a developing, individualised, and internalised Judaism, which is guided and inspired by tradition but not dictated to by it.

NOTES

374. Montefiore was the first Jew to hold this position.
375. C.G. Montefiore, 'Some Misconceptions of Judaism and Christianity by Each Other', *Jewish Quarterly Review*, VIII (1896), p. 216.
376. F. Rosenzweig, *The Star of Redemption* (1985), pp. 343, 397, 405–7.
377. Ibid., p. 415.
378. Schwartzchild has argued that Rosenzweig does not in fact accept the equal validity of Judaism and Christianity; rather, he 'grants to Christianity a legitimate place in God's economy of history ... [and] as he himself pointed out, this accords with the classic position which Judaism has taken towards it [Christianity] as a daughter-religion which prepares the way for the Messiah'. S. Schwartzchild, 'Franz Rosenzweig (1886–1929): Guide of Reversioners', pp. 33–4.
379. By Bernard Casper in F.A. Rothschild, ed., *Jewish Perspectives on Christianity* (1990), p. 167.

380. C.G. Montefiore and H. Loewe, eds, *A Rabbinic Anthology* (1938), p. xxi.
381. C.G. Montefiore, *The Synoptic Gospels* (1927), p. 163.
382. C.G. Montefiore, 'Some Misconceptions of Judaism and Christianity by Each Other', *Jewish Quarterly Review*, VIII (1896), p. 196. Although his negative intent is clear, Baeck's work was very much an oblique attack, however. Apart from the title and the polemical tone, he rarely mentions Christianity.
383. L. Baeck, 'Mystery and Commandment' (1922), reproduced in S. Noveck, ed., *Contemporary Jewish Thought: A Reader* (1964), p. 199.
384. Schleiermacher (1768–1834) is usually regarded as the founder of modern Protestant theology; he had been much involved in German Romanticism.
385. L. Baeck, 'Romantic Religion' (1922), reproduced in S. Noveck, ed., *Contemporary Jewish Thought: A Reader* (1964), p. 209.
386. L. Baeck, 'Some Questions to the Christian Church from the Jewish Point of View', cited in L. Klenicki, ed., *Towards a Theological Encounter: Jewish Understandings of Christianity* (1991), p. 71.
387. K. Kohler in *The Reform Advocate* (6 May 1911).
388. Ibid.
389. See, for example, T.M. Endelman, ed., *Jewish Apostasy in the Modern World* (1987).
390. Ibid., pp. 83–4.
391. Rosenzweig contemplated baptism from as early as 1906. In July 1913 after a long discussion with his Christian friend Rosenstock, he decided to convert (although, famously, he felt he should do so only after he had familiarised himself with his Jewish origins).
392. This is the position implicit throughout his writings, although he once mused rather doubtfully, '... perhaps it was Roman Catholicism (though I personally hate Rome with an ancestral hate) which made v. Hügel the saint and wonderful creature that *he* was? Perhaps different natures need different religions, and different stages of society need different religions.' Letter from C.G. Montefiore to W.R. Matthews, November 1930. ACC/3529/4/7, L.M.A.
393. M. Buber, *Die Stunde und die Erkenntnis* (Berlin, 1936), p. 152, cited in L. Klenicki, ed., *Towards a Theological Encounter: Jewish Understandings of Christianity* (1991), p. 75.
394. M. Buber, *I–Thou*, 2nd edn (1958), p. 11.
395. From the Founder's Statement, D.W.L.; see also L. Barmann, 'Confronting Secularization: Origins of the London Society for the Study of Religion' (1993).
396. Letter from C.G. Montefiore to W.R. Matthews, November 1930. ACC/3529/4/7, L.M.A.
397. Buber himself rejected the idea of a dialogical relationship between groups. He argued, for example, that a Christian could not have a dialogical relationship with a triune God (that is, three persons related to each other) since it was not possible to relate to a whole 'class' at a one-to-one level. M. Buber, *I and Thou*, trans. by W. Kaufmann (1970), pp. 62–3.
398. J. Rayner, 'C.G. Montefiore: His Religious Teaching', *The Synagogue Review*, XXXII (June 1958), p. 258.
399. C.G. Montefiore, *The Old Testament and After* (1923), p. 587.
400. Ibid., p. 552.

Conclusion

This section has attempted to demonstrate that although parallels to much of Montefiore's teaching can be found in the various forms of Judaism in his day, there were also important differences that suggest independent development. Both Reform and Liberal Judaism in Britain had been shaped by indigenous circumstances and by the peculiar psychology of Anglo-Jewry, and therefore foreign influence, whether German or American Reform, need not be overstated. One striking difference, the lack of a theological and intellectual justification for Anglo-Reform, was a factor leading to its stagnation and religious apathy. Montefiore's solution was to re-evaluate Reform Judaism and, by incorporating historical criticism, to re-package it with a more progressive theology. His liberal movement began with the negative self-definition of the Jewish Religious Union, which continued from where the paralysed Reform movement had left off in stripping away what were perceived to be outdated Jewish traditions. It went on to develop the more positive hopes of the Liberal Jewish Synagogue, which championed a universalist, non-nationalistic, ethical monotheism. Controversial aspects of his teaching included his anti-Zionist stance, his view of rabbinic tradition, and especially his sympathetic attitude towards Christianity.

In propounding the idea of an evolving 'essence of Judaism', Montefiore emphasised the individual's freedom from authority, the need for an instructed conscience, and a continuous theological reappraisal of the tenets of Judaism. This formulation set him apart not only from the Orthodox, but also from other reform minded thinkers such as Rosenzweig, Buber and Baeck. The very attempt to express Judaism in doctrinal terms, so as to meet the intellectual and theological challenge of liberal Christianity, made other Jewish thinkers uncomfortable. And his belief that the teachings of Christianity and Judaism complemented one another, and that the future of religion lay in the amalgamation of the best of each, won little support even among his followers.

For these reasons and for others, many have doubted the authenticity of Montefiore's Jewishness and have tried to identify non-Jewish influences upon his thought. It is the extent of the influence of Christianity upon his Liberal Judaism, both in substance and form, which will now be explored more fully.

PART TWO

CHRISTIAN INFLUENCES UPON MONTEFIORE

Introduction

By the late nineteenth century, the often vicious antagonism that had characterised two millennia of Jewish–Christian relations had for some time been challenged by individuals of both faiths. Neither mainstream Christians nor mainstream Jews were remotely near accepting the self-definition of the other, since the imprint of the traditional teachings was too deeply embedded. But certain individual scholars had begun to approach the writings of their opposite counterparts with a degree less hostility, and there was a new determination among a small number of Jewish thinkers to counter Christian misconceptions of Judaism with solid scholarly argument. This became possible after the emergence of *Jüdische Wissenschaft* (Jewish Science), the early nineteenth-century German-Jewish movement for the historical study of Judaism. Continental Jewish scholars who wrote extensively on Christianity included Abraham Geiger,[1] Heinrich Graetz[2] and later Leo Baeck.[3] In England, Solomon Schechter in particular spent a considerable amount of time and energy attempting to wean Christian scholars away from their perception of the Law as a burden. His academic activities at Cambridge had given him a special insight into Christian cultural life and he produced a number of academic studies on Judaism, convinced as he was that the study of rabbinic literature would give Christians a better understanding of Jesus' historical context and a more positive appreciation of Judaism.[4] Generally speaking, such nineteenth-century and early twentieth-century Jewish approaches were focused upon disproving the negative portrayal of Pharisees and Rabbinic Judaism in the New Testament and New Testament scholarship. All were characterised by a concern to demonstrate the superiority of Judaism over Christianity.[5]

Montefiore had a different agenda. It was not that he failed to understand what lay behind the traditional antagonistic stance. Considering what Judaism had suffered in the past at the hands of the Christians, he was not surprised that Jewish

writers had restricted themselves to looking for parallels or for
defects in Christian scriptures. But while he, too, ultimately rejected
Christianity as a religious alternative to Judaism, Montefiore
saw elements of beauty and truth within Christian teaching and
practice which he felt that the Jewish tradition could and should
profit from. These he regarded mostly as developments of, or
extrapolations from, Judaism; in his opinion the books of the
New Testament, and especially the Synoptic Gospels, were part
of the Liberal Jewish heritage. Consequently, he saw no reason
why a sympathetic examination of them could not lead to an
enrichment of the Jewish religion. As he put it in 1899,

> There is much in the New Testament which is great and
> noble, much which is sublime and tender, much which is
> good and true. Of this 'much', the greater part consists in a
> fresh presentment of some of the best and highest teaching
> in the Old Testament, in a vivid reformulation of it, in an
> admirable picking and choosing, an excellent bringing
> together. Not a [small] part consists in a further develop-
> ment, or in a clearer and more emphatic expression of certain
> truths which previously were only implicit or not fully
> drawn out.[6]

For most Jews, the New Testament added nothing of any
value to the Hebrew Bible. Montefiore disagreed and, at the risk
of being misunderstood as a Christian apologist, attempted to
present what he regarded as the best of that religion to his fellow
Jews. He felt little or no need to defend Judaism, emphasise the
defects of Christianity, or write apologetically. He hoped that, in
contrast to those Jews who conversed with Christians only in
order to demonstrate the superiority of Judaism over Christianity,
his work would illustrate the ways in which teachings from each
tradition could be used to augment those of the other, and he
argued for further study and greater tolerance of Christianity.[7]
In this way he introduced into Jewish–Christian relations what
Jacob Agus has described as an original policy of 'Mutual
Supplementation and Acceptation'.[8]

In this context, Montefiore strikes a rather lonely figure in
nineteenth- and early twentieth-century Anglo-Jewry. For while
a number of his Jewish contemporaries, such as those belonging
to the Jewish Religious Union, accepted his liberal biblical

interpretations and teachings, few of them shared his intense interest in Christianity or Christian texts. The degree of tolerance and even admiration with which Montefiore approached Christianity marked him out as a highly unusual Jew of his time, even on an international level. It is this uniquely positive understanding of, and relationship with, the Christianity of his day that makes him of such interest in the study of Jewish–Christian relations. It was also the cause of the mistrust with which many of his Jewish contemporaries viewed him. The question, of course, is what made Montefiore take up his non-traditional and unpopular position regarding Christianity? What made him different in this way from other Jewish thinkers? What gave him his unique perspective? Montefiore himself commented,

> I feel that by odd chance I am the only English Jew who can approach the Gospels fairly impartially, and who also has the time and the inclination to write about them.[9]

It is perhaps possible to explain the 'odd chance' in terms of a combination of non-Jewish influences, influences that might loosely be described as Christian.

(For Notes 1–9 see page 211.)

10

The Surrounding Victorian Christian Culture

ASSIMILATION

Montefiore once commented with regard to English and American Jews that 'five-sixths of their conception of life are Christian'.[10] He believed that many English Jews felt spiritually akin to their Christian environment, remarking that he found 'in middle-class Jews, when not corrupted by Zionism, curious resemblances and odd likenesses to middle-class Christians'.[11] He did not find this surprising since they lived within a society that had been shaped by the forces of Christianity. It was only a matter of time, he felt, before a complete identification with the Gentile population in all matters except that of religious persuasion would be possible. It was even in their own interest for the Jews to come to terms with Christianity and to embrace and assimilate Christian culture, he argued, since this was the best way to deal with anti-Jewish feeling: 'My slogan, "Englishmen of the Jewish faith" is the solution of anti-Semitism and the answer to it.'[12] In contrast to the majority of English Jews, Montefiore was prepared both to identify wholly with the surrounding cultural environment and to label it as 'Christian'. In an essay on 'Liberal Judaism and the New Testament' (1918) he wrote,

> [For] the Jews of Europe and America who live in a Christian environment and amid a civilisation which has been partially created by the New Testament, our right relation towards it must surely be of grave and peculiar importance. For this civilisation is also ours. The literature, which is soaked through and through with New Testament influences, is also our literature. The thought, which has been partially produced by the New Testament, is the thought amid which we are reared, which we absorb, to which we react ... The

very air we breathe, the moral, literary, artistic influences which we suck up from our childhood, are to a large extent, the same as those which surround and affect our Christian fellow citizens.[13]

He frequently denounced what he saw as a characteristic trait of the traditional Jewish community that it was always thinking about Christianity with a view to locating and excluding any trace of its influence.[14] Occasionally, and privately, he claimed to identify more closely with the non-Jewish community than with the Jewish.[15] This is best explained by his own recollection that although his upbringing was Jewish in teaching, observance and atmosphere, very few Jews except their relations ever came to the house; the family friends were mainly Gentile: 'Our [childhood] environment was entirely uncosmopolitan and purely English.'[16] Several of his tutors had been Christian clerics and he regarded their influence positively throughout his life; in a letter to Hastings Rashdall he explained,

> I don't feel so far apart. You see, I have lived with and loved, Christians all my life. My dearest friends have been and are passionate Roman Catholics, Anglicans (of all sorts) and so on ... I can see with their eyes and feel with their feelings. It is a curious position which can only happen to those who belong to a wee minority and mix (thank God) very intimately with a big majority.[17]

Both consciously and subconsciously he adopted many of their presuppositions and attitudes as his own.

Montefiore was by no means alone in recognising the effect of assimilation or acculturalisation and the adoption of the values and practices of the dominant Christian culture. From the mid-century onwards this 'Anglicisation' (as Abraham Benisch, editor of the *Jewish Chronicle*, called it) was viewed very negatively within Anglo-Jewry and often equated with 'de-judaisation'.[18] A great deal of time and energy was spent deciding where the line should be drawn. On one hand Anglo-Jewry remained a clearly defined sub-culture, since both the new arrivals and those long-established took the threat of conversion and intermarriage very seriously indeed. Both groups tended to adhere to traditional forms of Judaism that set certain limits on the influence of the host society; the majority of the Jewish immigrants in particular stubbornly retained much of their native background and culture.[19] On the other hand, the level of socio-cultural assimilation or acculturalisation among the upper- and middle-classes was high in comparison with European Jewry. As Cesarani has put it, the Jews' sense of their social and political acceptance as to some extent conditional, contributed greatly to reshaping the nature of Jewishness and Judaism, and they minimised that which, aside from their creed, set them apart.[20] Endelman has shown how during the nineteenth century among middle-class Jews there was increased interest in public school and university education, and greater success in winning social acceptance among the non-Jewish population.[21] A great deal of zealous work was done by the elite in attempting to anglicise and to teach British ways to the rest of the community through their dominance of the schools, the creation of youth clubs and their influence through the communal institutions.[22] It became increasingly acceptable, even desirable, to adopt the manners, speech, dress, habits of thought and taste of the English.[23] Their readiness to adopt so much of the surrounding Victorian culture meant that, increasingly, British Jews absorbed and emulated much of the Christian world-view (without admitting it as such). Among some members of the community, the pressures of Anglicisation led to a more profound reshaping of Anglo-Jewish religious culture and to a heightened sensitivity to Christian critique. Jewish reaction to Christian criticism can be argued to have played an important part in the emergence of the Reform movement and the reforming tendencies within Orthodox Judaism. Together with Jewish emulation of Church practices, it can also be seen to account for later developments including Montefiore's Jewish Religious Union and Liberal Jewish Synagogue.

THE NATURE OF THE JEWISH REFORM MOVEMENT

Before looking more closely at the influence of Christianity on Anglo-Reform and on Montefiore himself, it may be useful to look briefly at the ways in which the emergence of the Reform has been explained in the past without reference to Christian influence *per se*. These explanations include a natural response to 'modernity' (mediated through the Jewish Enlightenment), the influence of the German Reform movement, and as the result of political manoeuvring by the patriotic Anglo-Jewish elite. The first theory, that a reforming tendency came about as part of the Jewish response to 'modernity', can be dispensed with quickly. The eighteenth-century Jewish Enlightenment, or *Haskalah*, emphasised the universalist teachings and doctrines of Judaism and regulated the significance of particularistic rituals. While it is tempting to find the inspiration for the reformers' more universalist tendencies here, there are several studies that demonstrate that the German *Haskalah* had, in fact, very little effect on England.[24] The engagement of English religious Jews with 'modernity' was patchy and no obvious path of influence exists from the eighteenth-century individual contributions to the founding of the Reform Synagogue in 1840.

Some historians, including David Philipson,[25] Eugene Black[26] and Michael Meyer[27] have viewed Anglo-Jewish Reform as an echo effect of the German Reform movement, itself a product of the Jewish Enlightenment. Although well reported in the Anglo-Jewish press, however, it seems as though the results of German 'Jewish Science' and the emergent Reform movement had little or no tangible influence in Britain. Orthodox and would-be reformers alike viewed the German model as a recipe for dissolution. Unlike the later migrations from countries in Eastern Europe,[28] the emergence of Reform had a well publicised but relatively minor effect upon communal Anglo-Jewry, reflected by the interests of the small sub-section of the elite who joined. In contrast to their more iconoclastic German counterparts, the English reformers' modifications basically amounted to abbreviations and omissions within the Prayer Book; ideas such as moving the Sabbath to Sunday were regarded as 'inroads' of assimilation rather than reforms. On the other hand, the militant anti-rabbinism and decrying of rabbinic tradition which was characteristic of English Jewish Reform had no parallel in Germany or the United States. The driving forces behind the British movement appear to have emerged largely independent of German developments.

Jonathan Romain has suggested that the foundation of the West London Synagogue was a pronouncement of British nationality and citizenship, in that the founders chose the denomination 'British', specified that the sermons be in English, adopted the term 'synagogue' rather than the continental 'temple', and ignored the Hamburg Prayer Book. He also suggests that it was initiated as a means to overcome the Sephardi-Ashkenazi divide, in that the new synagogue was the result of the combined efforts of 24 founder members, largely made up from the Mocattas (Sephardim) and the Goldsmids (Ashkenazim).[29] A related view is to see the Anglo-Reform movement as a vehicle for certain members of the social elite to flex their political muscles. The trend towards assimilation or acculturalisation of British Jewry as a whole, especially around the mid-nineteenth century, has been explained in terms of the wider political scene by Michael Leigh[30] and Robert Liberles.[31] From early in the century there had been demographic pressures upon the growing population of wealthy Jews living in the West End of London to provide for themselves a synagogue which the East Enders refused to provide (these, in turn, were fearful of financial loss and damage to their own membership and status). When the West London Synagogue was finally established in 1840, the founder members were dominated by members of the Anglo-Jewish elite. There can be little doubt that these families intended to use the new Reform synagogue as a base from which to challenge the temporal, as well as spiritual, authorities. Isaac Lyon Goldsmid, the grandfather of Claude Montefiore, was a bullion broker and leading campaigner for political emancipation. Along with other dissidents within the Anglo-Jewish elite, he felt frustrated by the moderate stance of the Jewish Board of Deputies (J.B.D.) and found the West London Synagogue a useful political tool in challenging the J.B.D.'s claim to represent the Jewish community to the government.

A socio-political interpretation goes some way in explaining the timing of the emergence of the new movement, in that certain highly anglicised individuals concerned with the campaign for Jewish emancipation and the struggle for communal authority took the opportunity afforded them. It also allows for the conservative nature of its liturgical reforms since those members of the Anglo-Jewish elite who were involved were not primarily interested in theological innovation: if all they wanted was an alternative political structure to the J.B.D., they would not have wished to antagonise the Orthodox with theological controversy any more than was absolutely necessary. But the socio-political argument is not entirely satisfactory. As Feldman has pointed out, programmes for synagogue reform had existed from the

1820s and thus preceded the emergence of Jewish emancipation as a political consideration.[32] And as Englander hints,[33] it also ultimately fails to account for the particular emphasis of the reforms introduced, which were initially characterised by external modifications (including the shortening of the services, the formation of a choir, English sermons every Sabbath),[34] that increased the solemnity and intelligibility of the public service, and by a discriminatory approach to the Oral Law, a kind of neo-Karaism.[35] While many of the reformers had political goals, greater significance surely lies in the fact that they were the members of the community most interested in emulating the surrounding culture, and most sensitive to Christian criticism.

CHRISTIAN CRITIQUE AND REFORM JUDAISM

Montefiore was very much a product of the Reform Synagogue. By looking at Reform Judaism in the context of English society in general and the Christian critique of Judaism in particular, it is possible to identify various indirect influences of Christianity upon Montefiore himself. The fermentation provoked by the constitutional reforms of 1829 and 1832,[36] and the battling forces of Evangelicalism, tractarianism, liberal Anglicanism and non-conformity meant that, as with Jewish Reform, religion and politics intermeshed in early Victorian public life. That it was now possible for Jews to become more fully involved in British society and politics made the situation very different to earlier Christian critiques on Judaism; the criticism was now far more effective as David Feldman has argued in *Englishmen and Jews* (1994).[37]

Some indication of how Judaism was regarded by Christians in the mid-nineteenth century is suggested by popular writings on the subject by acknowledged authorities. Rev. Prof. Alexander McCaul was professor of Hebrew and Rabbinical Literature at King's College, London, and one of the leaders of the London Society for Promoting Christianity amongst the Jews.[38] He was regarded as an expert on the subject of Talmudic Judaism and on the methods by which conversion might be achieved, and was the best-selling author of *The Old Paths* (1837) and *Sketches of Judaism and the Jews* (1838). Rev. Alfred Myers was also an active member of the London Society; he was a 'Hebrew Christian clergyman', having converted to Christianity as a boy. His book,

The Jew (1840), ran to six editions over a period of 34 years. Both men were undoubtedly influential in shaping contemporary views of Rabbinic Judaism.

McCaul's analysis óf Judaism led him to view it as a petrified, unbiblical ritualism.[39] He contrasted what he described as 'the religion of Moses and the Prophets' with Talmudic Judaism which he argued was 'a new and totally different system … [that] has for its authors wicked men, unworthy of credit'.[40] Myers also wrote of his wonder that 'opinions so much at variance with the scriptures could have gained ascendancy among a studious people such as the Jews'.[41] Both encouraged a Christian view of Judaism as a faith corrupted by the rabbis and their Oral Law. In the sense that Rabbinic Judaism was viewed as an elaborate ritual sustained by a tradition that had no biblical support, the Christian critique was a very bibliocentric, Protestant Evangelical one. It also drew upon other traditional antagonisms. Comparison with Catholicism provided terms within which Judaism could be understood – Christians saw in 'rabbinism' the same flaws as they found in 'popery'. Myers suggested that Jewish devotion to Talmudic doctrine 'can only be equalled, but not surpassed, by the most zealous devotee in the Church of Rome'.[42] And McCaul wrote,

> If asked to give a concise yet adequate idea of this system, I should say it is Jewish Popery: just as Popery may be defined to [sic] by Gentile Rabbinism. Its distinguishing feature is that it asserts the transmission of an oral or tradi- tional law of equal authority with the written law of God, at the same time, that, like Popery, it resolves tradition into the present opinions of the existing Church.[43]

This is significant, for although antisemitism in Victorian Britain was well entrenched, it was not comparable in its intensity with anti-Catholicism. During the nineteenth century, traditional English hostility towards the Church of Rome pervaded all levels of society. To liken Judaism to Catholicism was to bring into the argument a whole range of negative connotations and to associate it with the arbitrary exercise of power and other allegedly un-English traits.[44] It was a line of attack that many Jews felt called into question their Englishness, and which many felt duty-bound to refute.

Similarly, Christian writings maintained and reinforced the view of the Jew as existing in a kind of theological limbo. McCaul claimed that the oral law 'has made the intellectual and moral state of all those who receive it almost stationary' and that 'the Judaism of this country and age is just the same as the Judaism of Poland and Morocco, or of the tenth century'.[45] Myers wrote that 'the Hebrew olive is by this time paralyzed and dried up to the roots', and that Judaism currently existed in 'a state of suspension'.[46] While Roman Catholicism was regarded as a perversion of Christianity, Judaism was viewed as frozen in a primitive state. This charge of religious petrifaction would have been all the more odious in the context of Victorian England's fixation on Progress. Almost a generation later, even the liberal Christian thinker (and Montefiore's tutor), Benjamin Jowett, felt that much more could be done to 'raise the manners and ways of their [Jews'] teachers and educators'[47] and he urged Montefiore to dedicate his life to 'improving and elevating them'.[48]

In passing, it should be noted that the view of Christian experts such as McCaul and Myers was by no means entirely negative with regard to the Jewish people. Judaism was viewed as the precursor of Christianity, and the success of the Jews in having maintained their covenant religion down through the centuries was greatly admired. This attachment was understood to explain the survival of the Hebrew religion during 1,800 years of exile, and was wound up with prophecies and expectations for the Second Coming of Christ.[49] In addition, some Christians recognised the pro-educational influence of rabbinism, and spoke highly of the great (if somewhat narrow) learning of Talmudists. But these positive achievements only made such Christians more determined to rescue the Jew and bring him to a fuller knowledge.

The charge of rabbinism was answered in different ways by the Orthodox and by the reformers. The Orthodox Jewish response to Christian claims of rabbinism and petrification was itself varied. Some saw no reason to apologise for their position. Chief Rabbi Nathan Adler argued that Judaism was in fact a living religion, not least because, in contrast to Christianity, 'there is no necessity to force our reason to the adoption of theories against which it revolts', and he stressed that without the Talmud and rabbinic learning, 'every doctrine, every ordinance, and every law [in the Hebrew Bible] would be a sealed book, a riddle without solution'.[50] Other argued that Christians were simply misinformed and ignorant. According to Moses Angel, Orthodox headmaster of the Jews' Free School and an important figure in nineteenth-century Jewish religious and secular education,

> Judaism has come to be entirely misunderstood. It has been universally described as a thing of obsolete forms and customs – as incompatible with progress – as the associate of a low standard of morality – as the obstacle preventing the approach to heaven rather than the ladder reaching thither – that the world has grown to believe what few have taken the trouble to contradict.[51]

However, not all the Orthodox were so unmoved by the Christian criticism that they did not feel the need to internally reassess the situation. Angel himself revealed a reforming tendency in his admission that in times of peace many of the traditional Jewish institutions became 'frequently unnecessary, sometimes objectionable'. And when the Jews' College was finally established in 1855, Hebrew was taught only to elementary level while classics and general literature were also introduced; Adler's plans for a more traditional Beth Hamidrash had been ignored. Such happenings were, at least partly, attempts to convince the surrounding Christian world of Jewish development and compatibility with Reason.

The reformers proper, on the other hand, accepted the charge of rabbinism and petrification as a valid attack upon Orthodoxy and even adopted it as a weapon themselves. For example, the first minister of the West London Synagogue, David Marks, denounced 'a large class of our Jewish brethren, who receive unconditionally, the rabbinical system as a whole'. In his anti-rabbinic *The Law is Light* (1854) he attacked Nathan Adler's defence of the necessity of rabbinical authority. Significantly, he did so by drawing upon (familiar) Evangelical anti-Catholic feeling.

> A doctrine like this, which is so boldly asserted in the sermon of the Reverend Rabbi, may well startle us and induce us to question whether instead of listening to the voice of Judaism, we are not having rehearsed to us the substance, though in a different phraseology, of the theology of Rome.[52]

Marks, of course, was later personally responsible for the religious instruction of the young Montefiore.

However, the reformers refuted accusations of rabbinism when applied to Judaism in the abstract. Taking the lead from their Evangelical critics, they fell back upon the Bible and attempted to cleanse their new synagogue of anything that could be used against them to suggest a lack of piety and proper devotion. In his sermon at the consecration of the West London Synagogue in 1845, David Marks argued that contemporary Orthodox services lacked devotion, failed to improve the mind or deliver a sense of nearness to God, inculcated indifference, neglected the spiritual development of women, and preserved irrelevant liturgical and ritualistic customs. It was, he maintained, 'to remedy these glaring evils that this [Reform] synagogue has been formed, and the improvements we have introduced therein will, I trust in God, prove most effectual in restoring the house of worship to a state so pure, that the presence of God may abide there'.[53]

Many Orthodox Jews favoured religious change along similar lines and, in fact, reforms which emulated Christian custom had begun to make their way into Jewish practice since the inauguration of the first Chief Rabbi, Solomon Hirschell, in 1802, including the clerical dress of rabbis. Much of the Victorian-Christian decorum desired by the reformers was explicitly advocated by Chief Rabbi Nathan Adler in his *Laws and Regulations* (1847) and 'new' practices including the introduction of a choir, of English sermons and of greater service decorum were adopted during the 1850s.[54] All this had the effect of taking much of the ground away from under the reformers' feet and partly explains why the Reform Synagogue venture never really caught the imagination of Anglo-Jewry as a whole.[55]

As has already been argued, it appears likely that these reforms came about as a result of Christian criticism, and especially Evangelical criticism, since the conversionists were very vocal in their critique.[56] This does not, however, adequately explain why the actual pattern or style of service adopted by the Reform Synagogue was so obviously influenced by the Church of England's majestic form of worship. Endelman has argued that this emphasis on decorum was a reflection of the desire of certain members of the Anglo-Jewish elite to conform to Anglican or Victorian norms of conduct. While this may seem simplistic and inadequate at a causal level (surely it was not simply a matter of manners?), it probably goes a long way in describing the determining factors upon the form in which the Reform movement shaped itself; after all, the Church of England was the church of the Establishment. In this sense, the Anglican Church supplied the major influence upon the minority religion.[57]

Another way to view the reform of decorum is to view it as an external expression of the search for an inner religion. The reformers agreed with Christian critics that ritual and rabbinism did not encourage the (somewhat fashionable) development of a personal piety. The Orthodox service was regarded as antiquated and unsuited to inspire a devotional frame of mind. The new emphasis upon service style reflected the congregation's desire to conform to what in Victorian Christian circles would have been regarded as the decorum appropriate for a more spiritual worship. In summary, then, the increased decorum in both Reform and Orthodox Synagogue services was caused by the desire for a religion of the heart (mirroring the Evangelical emphasis), and was shaped by the Victorian-Christian service ethos (particularly that of the Church of England).

Many reforms made by the West London Synagogue represented a conscious breaking away from the Orthodox position. One was the rejection of the traditional celebration of a festival over two days. They argued that in modern times and with accurate calendars, it was no longer necessary to do so. More significantly, they felt that such a practice was not ordained in scripture. The Reform minister David Marks, for whom Montefiore retained a warm admiration throughout his life, protested that they could not 'recognise as sacred, days which are evidently not ordained as such in scripture' and rejected prayers and references made to angels and demons that had no biblical basis.[58] He thus challenged the claim of traditional rabbinic authority to determine religious practice. In *The Christian Effect on Jewish Life* (1994), Hilton implies that this 'fundamentalist veneration of scripture' can be understood simply in terms of a Jewish emulation of the Evangelical rejection of Church authorities, effected as if by osmosis.[59] In fact, it was provoked by Evangelical criticism, as Marks himself made clear when he explicitly advised his congregation to 'rest our hopes and form our observances upon the laws of God alone'[60] in answer to Christian attacks on rabbinism. This neo-Karaism is therefore evidence of the impact of Evangelical criticism, since it was the conversionists who kept

up the attack and who alone were bibliocentric. The differences
between Reform and Orthodox were likewise clear-cut on the issue
of universalism versus nationalism. Again, Christian attacks on
what was viewed as a particularistic, primitive religion were
largely responsible. Rabbinic, Orthodox Judaism emphasised
election, exile, expiation and restoration within a nationalistic
framework, while Reform Judaism rejected the notion of a
Chosen People and saw its role as the bearer rather than the
sole beneficiary of God's grace. The Orthodox messiah was
transformed into the reformers' messianic age, which would be
initiated by the priesthood of the whole people of Israel, not by
an individual of the House of David. A universalist tendency
meant that Judaism was reinterpreted in terms of a religious
community and not in terms of a nation. Ironically, while the
Evangelicals approved of the Reformers' rejection of ritual, they
were less keen on some of the other changes, especially those
that had reinforced their romantic conceptions of God's People.
McCaul himself lamented,

> Reform has unjudaized all its disciples ... Old Jewish
> manners have passed away ... Jewish education has well
> nigh vanished ... Their national language has been
> desposed from its place ... They have renounced the land
> of their forefathers.[61]

CHRISTIAN CRITIQUE AND LIBERAL JUDAISM

In *Response to Modernity* (1988), Michael Meyer observed that the
Protestant environment had proved more conducive to the
Reform Judaism than had the Catholic, on a world-wide level. It
had provided a greater impetus in terms of the theological
model, the rejection of an old hierarchy, the vernacular liturgy,
the central importance of the sermon in services and the lessen-
ing of the importance of ritual.[62] It is possible to further identify
the specific 'contributions' of those groups within the Protestant
fold. In England, for example, many Jews came to feel that the
West London Synagogue had not gone far enough in its reforms.
In 1881, Montefiore and Oswald Simon introduced a synagogue
'Sunday School'.[63] More radical developments followed in the
shape of special 'supplementary services', which allowed greater

freedom for sermons and music. Around 1885, the two men were involved in organising Saturday morning services at the Hanway Street School, which attracted between 120 and 200 congregants.[64] Saturday afternoon services were held at West Hampstead Town Hall from 1890; the progression from a school to a hall, and from an audience of children to adults, made this service more un-settling to many observers and Simon was forced to publicly defend charges that people were paid to attend.[65] By the time Simon initiated the Sunday Movement in 1899 with the public support of Montefiore,[66] the idea of supplementary services had become a good deal more controversial, and negative com-parisons to Christian practice had become common.[67] In 1896 Montefiore pressed for various modifications to the Reform service ritual, involving further readings in the vernacular and psalms sung in English, together with certain prayer book omissions, but after lengthy consideration these were rejected by the council of the West London Synagogue in 1896,[68] and again in 1898.[69] Most significant, however, was the founding of Montefiore's Jewish Religious Union (J.R.U.) in 1902, from which eventually emerged the Liberal Judaism movement. This, too, was profoundly influenced by Christian critique, although now from a more liberal Anglican angle.

The J.R.U. hoped primarily to combat Jewish 'indifferentism' more effectively than the Reform movement had done and to con-tinue from where they had left off with regard to developing a religion of the heart. Lily Montagu's article, 'Spiritual Possibilities of Judaism Today' (1899), focused upon the need to correct the deficiencies of both 'West End Jews' whose Reform Judaism was disinterested and materialistic in character, and 'East End Jews' whose more vigorous observance was lacking appreciation of the 'God within'.[70] Many of those who joined the new movement had grown up in Reform synagogues in West London, Manchester and Bradford[71] (Montefiore himself was a warden of the West London synagogue and a council member) and were heavily influenced by a reforming ethos. They were therefore also keen to put up a strong defence against the perceived Christian critique, and were prepared to express their own dissatisfaction with current Reform theology. Development in this direction was possible due to their relative freedom from political inter-ference; for the Anglo-Jewish elite, the J.R.U. served no useful political purpose (as the West London Reform Synagogue had done before) and the criteria for change no longer depended upon the non-theological concerns of its wealthiest supporters. This independence allowed the J.R.U. greater scope and gave it its particular character, concerned as it was with rescuing Jews, incorporating biblical criticism, developing individual piety, and expanding its horizon as a truly universalist religion.

Not surprisingly, their new concerns also reflected changes going on within Christianity at this time. If the majority of the reforms of the West London Synagogue are to be explained in terms of Evangelical bibliocentricity, then the critically informed liberal Jewish movement should be understood in terms of Anglican liberalism and the biblical criticism which had been gaining ground from Evangelical literalism from as early as the 1850s. The decline in Evangelicalism was linked to a decline in the religious authority of the Hebrew Bible brought about by the results of biblical criticism (which will be examined in greater detail later). It left the Anglican liberals in the forefront. In terms of the Christian critique of Judaism there was a corresponding shift of emphasis from Evangelical to Anglican liberal concerns: Jewish ritualism and rabbinism were no longer attacked or emphasised as much. From this time on, the perceived deficiencies focused upon inferior, out-of-date Old Testament principles and Jewish particularistic teachings. In 'Liberal Judaism in England' (1899), for example, Montefiore wrote that 'a sort of critical shiver' ran through him when the sacred scroll was elevated during the synagogue service, and he cited the idea of a perfect law given to Moses and passed on as the Pentateuch to Israel as the first of a number of biblical critical stumbling blocks facing the educated Western Jew.[72]

The Evangelical view of the Jews had been conditioned to a great degree by their veneration of the Hebrew Bible. They had had sympathy for the Jews as the Chosen People and for the part they were destined to play in future times, in accordance to the Word of God. The Jews had exemplified the fallen nature of mankind and the inevitability of divine punishment; rabbinism had been understood as the cause of Jewish stagnation. In contrast, the Anglican liberal view of the Bible as non-verbally inspired meant that Judaism was stripped of its special role. While they agreed with the Evangelicals that the development of Judaism had been arrested, the liberals did not see this to be the outcome of rabbinism but as a matter of essentials; Judaism had been intrinsically flawed from Old Testament times onwards. Implicit in the celebrated *Essays and Reviews* (1860), for example, was the idea that Israel's spiritual understanding had developed through time.[73] This idea meant that Judaism was regarded as an early stage in God's progressive revelation to mankind. The perception that it had failed to develop meant it was now regarded something of an anachronism.

The contemporary Christian view of Judaism was of a highly particularistic, nationalistic religion. While the essays of the Liberal Oxford historian Goldwin Smith are, perhaps, more extreme than most, they are useful in giving us an idea of what was being written at the time. In the same year that Montefiore went to Oxford, Goldwin Smith wrote an antisemitic article 'Can Jews be Patriots?' (1878) in which he vehemently attacked Jewish 'tribal' characteristics including the refusal to proselytise, 'the primeval rite' of circumcision and the common view of intermarriage as a form of apostasy.[74] While Judaism represented the best that tribal religion could offer it was pathetically inadequate in the light of Christianity and the 'advent of humanity'. Goldwin Smith interwove developmental interpretations of the Hebrew Bible with racial doctrine to conclude that a 'genuine' Jew

> is not an Englishman or Frenchman holding particular theological tenets: he is a Jew, with a special Deity for his own race. The rest of mankind are to him not merely people holding a different creed, but aliens in blood.[75]

The Jewish response (both Orthodox and Reform) to Christian condemnation for the nationalism and tribalism of traditional Judaism was to stress the universalist tendencies of their religion. Chief Rabbi Hermann Adler replied to Goldwin Smith's essay with two public articles of his own.[76] In them he attempted to express the claims of his religion in ways acceptable to an increasingly liberal, British culture. He defended circumcision as a divine command not to be questioned and argued that the practice of endogamy was primarily designed to preserve religion, not race. Jews were reluctant to convert Gentiles because they believed God would also accept righteous Gentiles; it was further evidence of the universalism of Judaism. He urged Christians to remember that

the sublime religious and moral principles which the book
[Hebrew Bible] enunciates are applicable to the whole of
mankind and have beyond a doubt become, by their having
formed the foundation of Christianity and Islam, the great
dynamic agent of modern civilisation.[77]

And the Reform minister Morris Joseph published an article in
the following year on 'The God of Israel' (1879) which further
negated the idea of a tribal Israel by emphasising the influences
of Egypt, Phoenicia, Assyria and Persia, Hellenism, Rome,
Islam, Sufism, the Renaissance and modern democracy upon the
development of Judaism.[78]

In 1882 Montefiore, still a Reform Jew, wrote an essay entitled,
'Is Judaism a Tribal Religion?' in which he argued along similar
lines to Adler that 'the great bond which unites Israel is not one
of race but the common bond of religion'.[79] He, too, felt that
Judaism could be understood as a 'pure religious universalism'
but he was prepared to take this further. In sharp contrast to
Adler, Montefiore and other liberally minded Jews accepted the
German Protestant inspired developmental and critically
informed approach to the biblical teachings. He made it clear
in the essay that he was no longer willing to publicly defend
that view of Judaism which the Christian critics regarded as a
particularist religion of prohibition and punishment (in contrast
to Christianity as a universalist religion of love and moral liberty)
and his defence of Judaism became a defence of an abstract
Judaism, a Judaism free from traditionalist trappings. The
response of liberal Jews came to echo that of the earlier Reform
Jews when confronted by Christian criticism: they accepted the
Christian accusations of particularism as true with respect to
Orthodoxy but denied it when applied to what they saw as true
Judaism, that is, their own modernist Judaism. In this sense,
then, they were able to conform to the changing emphases of
Christian criticism and adopt it as their own. As the *Jewish
Chronicle* commented on Montefiore's 1882 essay, 'Does not
Reformed Judaism as interpreted by Mr Claude Montefiore bear
the mere stamp of nineteenth-century religious opinion?'[80]

Recoil from Evangelical doctrines in mid-Victorian England
meant that there was a growing emphasis of the humanity of
Christ at the expense of the doctrine of Atonement in much
Christian teaching.[81] One result was that many Christians

(initially Anglicans but later non-conformists) began to think of Jesus more as a noble exemplar than as a saviour, a trend which reflected Victorian society's concern for ethics and high morality. The period 1860–80 has been described as something of a hey-day for 'Incarnational thought' and saw Anglicanism come to the forefront.[82] Their exemplarist theology was at odds with what they regarded as the legalism implicit in Talmudism. Predictably, while Jewish Orthodox and Reform apologists attempted to justify their loyalty to traditional authorities, the liberals sided with the Anglicans on this matter. In one of his later *Papers for Jewish People*, Montefiore was keen to contrast the position taken by the J.R.U. with that of the traditionalists.

> We recognise no binding outside authority between us and God, whether in man or in a book, whether in a church or in God, whether in a tradition or in a ritual. Most, if not all, of our differences from the traditionalists spring from this rejection of an authority which they unhesitatingly accept ... To free ourselves from the heavy bondage of the Rabbinic law and of the Shulchan Aruch ... is desirable and necessary.[83]

The Liberals' sensitivity to Christian criticism of Judaism as a limited, particularist religion is not only reflected in the emphasis they placed on the universal nature of Liberal Judaism, but also in the need they felt to explain such apparent discrepancies as the absence of Jewish missionaries. In October 1932, Mattuck wrote an article, 'Why the Jews have no Missionaries',[84] as a response to Christian critics who interpreted the phenomenon as evidence of its national, tribal or racial nature (his argument contained numerous explanations as to how the situation of Christianity differed to that of Judaism). While he accepted the criticism as to some extent valid as directed towards Orthodox Judaism,[85] his main argument was that Judaism's historical lack of missionaries had nothing to do with its alleged particularism. In a pamphlet they published together a year later, Montefiore went further and argued that Christians and Unitarians had strengthened themselves by their missionary endeavours and that Jews too often dwelt on the Christian missionary failures and ignored their successes. His own position was that once the practical barriers to missionary work among heathen were overcome, much would be gained if their example was followed by Jews.[86] Thus Montefiore came to champion an active missionary stance at least partly as a response to the Christian criticism of Judaism as a particularist religion, so as to demonstrate Liberal Jewish confidence in their own universalist Judaism.

In this context it is interesting to note that in spite of the increased influence of the Church of England in general, and in spite of his Broad Church contacts (through his Oxford mentors) and his friendships with leading Anglican intellectuals such as Hastings Rashdall, Montefiore's comments on Christianity often seem to presuppose Evangelical Christianity. That is, when Montefiore spoke about Christianity, he often seemed to have in mind the sort of Protestant who emphasised salvation by faith through the atoning death of Christ. This could be explained by a lifelong exposure to the London scene where the Evangelical conversionists tended to concentrate their efforts and where, through his own extensive philanthropic interests, he would have been very aware of their high profile social work. Heasman in *Evangelicals in Action* (1962) has suggested that 'as many as three-quarters of the total number of voluntary charitable organisations in the second half of the nineteenth century can be regarded as Evangelical in character'.[87] According to Englander, Jewish philanthropic organisations consciously 'mirrored the theory, practice and discourse of the Evangelical movement'.[88] Certainly, Evangelical models can be found for societies such as Montefiore's own 'Jewish Association for the Protection of Women and Children'.[89] He was also closely associated with the social work of Basil Henriques, whom he described as 'that engaging young saint', whose St George's and Bernhard Baron Settlement in the East End of London had been inspired by Canon Barnett's Christian project, the Toynbee Hall settlement.[90] So while Montefiore generally thought in terms of Liberal Christianity (especially when in an academic, theological context) he also understood Christianity in its Evangelical form. And while he might have deplored its conversionist policy,[91] he also recognised certain benefits to missionary endeavour. The seeking out of the lost and fallen was, he felt, an element of Christ's teaching which was not emphasised enough in Judaism and which he felt his fellow Jews would do well to imitate.

TRACTARIANISM

The example of Victorian Christianity and the criticism of its
Evangelical and liberal Anglican sects profoundly affected the
development of reforming movements within nineteenth- and
early twentieth-century Judaism. Rather than understanding
this as a complex, multilevel reaction to the changing currents
of Christian thought and a progressive world-view, there is a
temptation to define what is, after all, an essentially Jewish
phenomenon in wholly Christian terms. Maurice Bowler's
Claude Montefiore and Christianity (1988) is just such an attempt.
In it the author has identified a specific Christian model, the
early nineteenth-century Oxford Movement, and has tentatively
put forward the argument that the many interesting parallels
between the two movements suggest the emulation of
Tractarianism by the Jewish Religious Union.

Bowler sees the leaders of the two movements as reforming
prophets, arguing that both Montefiore and John Henry Newman
worked against the religious teachings of institutional monolithic
communities.[92] He pointed out that both groups did so largely
through the medium of pamphlets, Newman publishing *Tracts
for the Times* and Montefiore *Papers for Jewish People*. In addition,
both movements were precipitated by provocative outbursts: John
Keble's sermon 'On National Apostasy' (1833) and Lily Montagu's
Jewish Quarterly Review article, 'The Spiritual Possibilities of
Judaism Today' (1899). These similarities, however, offer very
little in the way of arguing the development of the J.R.U. upon
the Tractarian pattern other than highlighting characteristics
common to many nineteenth-century reforming movements.
More significant are the differences (to which Bowler himself
refers). One example is the fact that their respective motivations
and philosophies were diametrically opposed – Montefiore was
moving towards liberalism and Newman away from it. Another
is that while Newman's was essentially a clerical movement,
supported by professional colleagues, Montefiore's J.R.U. was
driven by lay forces and enjoyed a mainly non-professional
membership.

Bowler sees another similarity between Newman and
Montefiore in their unorthodox attitude to their traditional
enemies; Newman was viewed as too sympathetic to the Roman
Catholics and Montefiore too tolerant of Christianity. Both were

accused by their co-religionists as being, at heart, too close to the object of their respective community's hostility. And it is not difficult to understand why this might be. It was not uncommon for Montefiore to threaten Jewish identity with comments like, 'In the biggest and deepest things of all, you are not severed from your Christian neighbour, but at one with him.'[93] In this context, Bowler's comparison of Newman's celebrated *Tract XC* (which reinterpreted the Anglican Thirty-nine Articles from a more Catholic point of view), with Montefiore's 1906 address 'Enlarge the Place of my Tent' (which treated Maimonides' 13 Principles of Faith), seems at first glance to be a more profitable use of the Tractarian model.[94] After all, both men were under pressure from their respective communities to prove their true colours, and in his treatment of foundational documents Montefiore might conceivably have been influenced by Newman's example. But while many Anglicans responded to Newman's *Tract XC* suspiciously, interpreting his efforts as a covert re-introduction of Roman Catholic doctrine, Newman's actual aim had been to argue the legitimacy of the Tractarians' support of certain Catholic teachings within the Church of England. In contrast, Montefiore had at no point been concerned to show that he was committed to the 13 Principles of Faith. His analysis was, unlike Newman's subtle diplomacy, critical and unapologetic; he used the Principles as a foil to show the superiority of the J.R.U.'s non-traditionalist position.

Bowler also seems to imply that some insight can be gained by looking at Montefiore's occasional anti-Christian polemic in the light of Newman's fierce anti-Catholic writings. He argues that both men felt obliged to use polemic occasionally to defend themselves against the accusations of their co-religionist opponents.[95] For this he cites some examples from Montefiore's writings. These include the suggestion that the cruelties of the Inquisitors could be derived from the New Testament,[96] the description of Matthew 23 as 'doctrine from which we [Liberal Jews] turn in horror ... odious ... an awful aberration'[97] and an assessment of much of Paul's teaching as 'so crude, so remote, so false, so unworthy of God, so valueless for ourselves'.[98] Bowler feels that such language is very strong for the normally tactful Montefiore. In fact, these criticisms of Christian teaching are quite in keeping with his character. It did not matter what the subject under consideration was, whether first-century

Christianity, medieval Jewish philosophy,[99] or nineteenth-century Zionism,[100] Montefiore's approach was always the same: he would attempt to adopt what he saw as good and true for the Liberal Jewish cause and reject the rest, giving his reasons clearly and uncompromisingly. While he was extremely generous in his praise of what he saw as the positive aspects of Christianity, he was equally forthright in his denunciation of much of its teaching. Thus his language in this context was no more extreme than elsewhere. While he was certainly aware of his vulnerability to accusations of being unduly influenced by liberal Christianity,[101] it is unlikely that this would have concerned him as much as similar accusations had concerned Newman.

Finally, Bowler presents two examples in which Montefiore appears to be consciously aware of following in the footsteps of Newman. The first is a letter to Lucy Cohen in 1904, two years after the establishment of the J.R.U., in which, describing his state of mind, he comments 'I do not ask to see the distant shore'.[102] This, Bowler suggests, is certainly an allusion to Newman's hymn 'I do not ask to see the distant scene, one step enough for me.'[103] But it is difficult to see how this literary (mis)quotation illustrates anything more than Montefiore's acquaintance with Victorian Church hymns. Considering that from his childhood onwards Montefiore had felt as much at home in a Christian environment as in a Jewish one, there is surely nothing remarkable in this. And in fact, this is not the only possible source for the quotation.[104]

The second instance is more interesting. Newman has long been remembered for his strategy of the *via media*; in 1839 he looked forward to 'a system [which] will be rising up, superior to the age, yet harmonising with, and carrying out its higher points'.[105] Bowler finds it highly significant that in 1920 Montefiore published a pamphlet actually entitled, 'Is There a Middle Way?'[106] in which he discusses the alternatives facing the Liberal Jewish movement. And, indeed, one might have expected Montefiore to have propounded a view which reflected his lifelong experience of the Anglo-Jewish *via media* of the Reform Synagogue. But unlike Newman who initially argued for a gradualist approach, Montefiore rejected the middle path, and regarded a separate movement as 'the Only Way'.[107] Thus, if indeed Montefiore was aware of an echo of Newman's *via media*, it was very much in the background of his thought.

The essay was a direct appeal to those liberally minded Jews who, in Montefiore's eyes, were too inclined to compromise their spirituality.

In any case, it is too simplistic to see Newman as pro-Roman Catholic from the beginning and to see his anti-Catholic tracts as defensive half-truths, as Bowler suggests. At the time, he had hoped that his *via media* would allow him to remain Anglican and that his diatribes would convince his opponents of his loyalty. In contrast, Montefiore never changed from his original attitude towards Christianity, and was comfortable from the start with his relationship with 'the enemy'; his negative comments did not originate as defences of his controversial pro-Christian stance. The driving force behind the Oxford Movement was a desire to encourage greater respect for the Church Fathers and the traditional authorities in the face of growing liberalism within the Anglican Church. While Montefiore held ancient sources of knowledge in high respect, it would have been impossible for him to have expressed his concerns in anything other than liberal, non-traditionalist terms. Essentially, then, while Newman wanted to re-emphasise the place of tradition within the Church gradually (the *via media*), Montefiore sought to radically purify the existing tradition (the 'Only Way') and transform it into something quite different. The similarities that Bowler finds between the two movements are mistaken. If any Christian model is to be used to account for the Liberal Jewish movement in Christian terms, it must be the liberal Anglican movement, as suggested earlier.

ASSIMILATED HELLENISM

Condemnation by Montefiore's contemporary Jewish critics for what they saw as his excessive Christian sympathies has led many to identify the primary non-Jewish influence upon his theology as Christian. But it is not as simple as that. Victorian society was characterised by its religiosity, Hellenistic thought and the idea of Progress, and all three contributed to Montefiore's thought. In considering Montefiore's familiarity with Greek learning, it is possible to argue that what in the past has been attributed to the influence of Christianity can, perhaps, be more accurately described as Christianised or assimilated Hellenism.

The classics thoroughly permeated nineteenth-century contemporary Christian thought. From early on, Greek philosophy
proved highly influential upon theologians and clergymen
educated at Oxford and Cambridge. By the 1830s the patristic
revival, championed by the Tractarians, had stimulated interest
in the relationship between Greek and Christian thought and
had fostered new approaches to the study of Plato. In the 1860s
the Idealist works of Benjamin Jowett had encouraged a greater
appreciation of Platonic thought and had increased the sense of
its relevance. Thus throughout the nineteenth century, Anglican
clerics and an essentially Anglican Oxford caused classical
literature, in the forms of philosophy, mythology and history, to
become fully integrated into the fundamental areas of Victorian
thought, theology, education and political theory.

A great many of those who shaped the tone of the Victorian
age were schooled from their youth in Hellenistic thought.
Montefiore's childhood tutors, for example, were educated
Churchmen, familiar with the classics. His tutor in religious
instruction, 'the admirable Jewish minister whose excellent
pulpit addresses I used to listen to Saturday after Saturday all my
boyhood and youth', Rabbi David Marks, also referred to ancient
Greece positively in his sermons.[108] But far more significant in
this context was the role of Oxford in developing in Montefiore
a profound appreciation for Hellenistic culture and philosophy.

The Oxford School of *Literae Humaniores* or Greats, which
Montefiore read for his degree, reinforced the use of Greece
(and Rome) as points of cultural and intellectual self-reference.
It involved detailed translation and criticism of a set list of
texts: Five terms were spent on Greek and Latin literature,
examined as 'Moderations', followed by seven terms of history,
ethics, metaphysics and political philosophy, examined as
'Schools'.[109] The degree was structured so as to make the classics
relevant to modern thought and concerns.[110] John Stuart Mill,
commenting upon the benefits of studying classical history,
wrote that

> we are taught ... to appreciate ... intrinsic greatness amidst
> opinions, habits and institutions most remote from ours;
> and are thus trained to that large and catholic toleration,
> which is founded on understanding, not on indifference.[111]

This certainly seemed to be true of Montefiore whose attitude towards Christianity exemplified the idea of toleration founded upon understanding. In an appreciation of Montefiore in *Speculum Religionis* (1929), F.C. Burkitt commented upon the debt which Montefiore owed to Oxford, and singled out 'the Oxford point of view' as a major determining influence and that which sent him in a liberal direction.[112] Burkitt also recognised the effect of Oxford classicism upon Montefiore. His work showed

> the influence of ... 'Baylioll Colledge'. It is the voice of Shem who has dwelt in the tents of Japhet, [who] has indeed more or less been brought up there. There is an ease, a discarding of what is unnecessary, an inclusion and recognition of essential features, an accurate idealisation of the type, which is by ultimate derivation neither Jewish nor English but Greek, the product of the study of the humane literature and philosophy which Montefiore learned from Benjamin Jowett.[113]

The ancient Greeks were regarded as having played an important role in preparing the world for Christianity, their (collective) thought representing several stages in the development towards divine revelation. As one of Montefiore's own tutors, T.K. Cheyne, would later put it, 'A persuasive presentation of true religion only became possible in the Hellenistic age.'[114] Furthermore, many considered the Greeks to have displayed the highest moral character that human nature could assume without the light of the Gospel. The Bishop of Durham, B.F. Westcott, had been able to write, 'the work of Greece ... lives for the simplest Christian in the New Testament'.[115] And as late as 1916, William Temples' lectures on 'Plato and Christianity' reflected the firm belief of an eminent Churchman in the enduring beauty and moral force of Greek thought.[116] The result was that it had become common to view Hellenistic thought as complementary rather than antagonistic to the dominant Christian religion of the day. Montefiore, very much a product of his age, adopted these value-judgements and held the ancient Greeks in equally high esteem.

For those in nineteenth-century England who held to a Hegelian concept of history, Greek thought and culture was of special relevance since Christianity, the dominant religion, was understood to be a synthesis of Hebraic and Hellenistic thought. One proponent of this theory was the celebrated Victorian Hellenist, Matthew Arnold, who had attempted to define the two forces in *Culture and Anarchy* (1869). In this work, Hellenism was represented by intellectual freedom and spontaneity, and Hebraism by conduct and obedience. Arnold argued that Western history had oscillated between the two and that the New Testament had eventually perfected what each had been lacking by combining them. Interest in Hellenism was further encouraged by the popular belief, especially among Anglican liberals, that certain ages of Greek history (usually the fifth century BCE) were seen to be analogous to certain periods of modern history, and that it was therefore possible to draw parallels from their own time to the Classical period. Jowett, for example, wrote,

> Although we cannot maintain that ancient and modern philosophy are one and continuous … for they are separated by an interval thousand years, yet they seem to recur in a sort of cycle, and we are surprised to find that the new is ever old and that the teaching of the past has still a meaning for us.[117]

For Montefiore, this 'meaning' was very real. It was important for him, as it had been for Arnold, to show that Hellenistic thought was compatible with that of his own theology. He, too, argued that an amalgamation of the best of both Greece and Israel was possible (although in Liberal Judaism rather than in Christianity). But while Arnold concentrated upon civilisation, Montefiore was concerned with religious truth. As he explained in *Liberal Judaism and Hellenism* (1918),

> I am not thinking primarily of any reconciliation of Hellenism with Judaism in the sense that Judaism is to stand for religion and morality, and Hellenism for art and culture. Nor am I even primarily thinking of Judaism and Hellenism in the sense that Matthew Arnold was wont to contrast Hellenism and Hebraism with each other, and to discuss the right amalgamation of the two. I am thinking primarily of religion on both sides: of Hellenistic religion – religion produced … by men nurtured on Greek philosophy.[118]

In other words, Montefiore saw the value of Hellenism in essentially religious terms; as he put it, 'Hellenism is less a matter of birth than of mind. It is a spiritual, not a physical, quality.'[119] It is not surprising, then, that Montefiore also differed from Arnold on his appreciation of what was best in Greek thought.

> When I say 'best', I mean only 'best' from our particular [Liberal Jewish] point of view, for while, for instance, Aristotle is a greater genius and a greater philosopher than Epictetus, it may well be that religiously we can learn more from Epictetus than from Aristotle.[120]

Montefiore felt that Judaism and this spiritual Hellenism shared a great deal in common. Many aspects of Greek thought contained teaching complementary to the best doctrine of the Bible. That is why it was useful for the Jew to learn the teachings of the Greeks: he could always find connections for it in his own writings.[121] There was much to be gained by fortifying Hebraic thought with Hellenistic thought. Montefiore disagreed with those who argued that philosophy was antagonistic to Judaism and to the Jewish spirit. He felt that there was a kinship between 'Hellas' and 'Judaea' and that it was possible to fuse the two together. He argued that liberal Jews would feel this kinship more acutely than their Orthodox brethren would because they had come to see that, 'like the Greeks, we were a mere petty race, a petty nation, and we became something better, larger, higher. We were a petty nation; we became a spirit.'[122]

Montefiore felt that he could point to modern day instances where Judaism had already merged with Hellenism. For example, he felt that the influence of Hellenism could be traced to the decorum of the Synagogue, where the congregation had sought to imbue their worship with order, proportion, limit and to make their services 'reverent and beautiful, in other words to unite Hellenism and Hebraism'.[123] Like Arnold, he was not always consistent in distinguishing between the cultural, aesthetic concepts and the philosophical teachings of Hellenism.

Montefiore also attributed the religious universalism that his liberal Judaism espoused to Hellenistic influences.[124] He later identified these as the teaching of St Paul (whose background he identified as Hellenistic Judaism) and Stoicism, although he qualified this by adding that neither Paul nor the

Stoics could have achieved what they had for Europe without the monotheism of the Jews.[125]

Montefiore justified his attempt to amalgamate Hellenistic teachings with Jewish thought by drawing attention to several important precedents. Twice before in its history had Judaism sought to come to terms with, and to 'assimilate', Greek thought and philosophy. The first occasion had been the advent of Christianity, which, he suggested, had made use of the Jewish pioneers' work for its own purposes. Contemporary writings such as the Wisdom of Solomon and the works of Philo remained as striking, if transitional, monuments of what was then accomplished in the attempt to bring together into a higher unity the products of Hellas and of Judaea. The second occasion was in the time of Maimonides, and Montefiore felt that the influence of this attempt at 'amalgamation' had been enormous and had lasted until his own day.[126] If Liberal Judaism now wished to take its place as a genuine religion of the Western world, he reasoned, then the time had come once again to think out and determine its relation to Hellenism.[127]

It is important to remember that, in this context, Montefiore was not seeking to produce a consistent system. He felt that it was neither necessary nor possible to have an absolutely harmonious system of thought. He was not interested in an intellectual exercise, but in any teaching which would encourage personal religious growth. Consistency was not as important as devotional effect. As he put it,

> We may be rightly stirred to different bits of well-doing now by Epictetus and now by Hosea, even though Epictetus's view of the world could not have harmonised altogether with the view of Hosea.[128]

In common with many other nineteenth-century thinkers, it was the collective effect of the best of Greek (religious) thought and teachings that interested Montefiore the most. This was consistent with his approach to religions in general; he often argued that a few out-of-context verses were not enough to justify a particular point of view, whether it be from the rabbinic literature, the Hebrew Bible or the New Testament. He firmly believed in judging a work in its entirety. This did not, however, mean that he was unaware of distinctive strains within Greek thought. He understood and appreciated the individual contributions. But while he used the epic poetry of Homer occasionally,[129] more often than not he kept to Stoic and Platonic thought.

Throughout *Liberal Judaism and Hellenism* (1918), Montefiore made constant reference to the first-century Greek Stoic, Epictetus, who had taught a gospel of inner freedom through self-abnegation, submission to Providence and the love of one's enemies. Stoicism obviously had great appeal for the very Victorian Montefiore who felt that, while their teachings had been unable to conquer the world, he could see no reason why Liberal Jews could not 'add to our quiver an arrow from the Stoic armoury [since] it is a fine and fair arrow, even if not the finest and fairest'.[130] He admired the way in which Stoics expected no outward reward from God whether in this life or the next and he quoted Jowett who had written, 'to feel habitually that he is part of the order of the universe is one of the highest ethical motives of which man is capable'.[131] Likewise, the Stoics' attitude to suffering taught him the 'unimportance in relation to the whole of the individual's outward fortunes or sufferings', and also the idea that 'the only true good is inward: virtue and the mind. The only true evil is sin and the mind's corruption'.[132] With regard to Jewish eudaemonism, which he defined as 'the coarse doctrine of reward and punishment', there was, he felt, a need to supplement and correct Old Testament teaching in these respects with the idealism of Platonic philosophy and the Stoics.[133]

Montefiore's appreciation of Plato had been formed by his studies at Oxford under his tutor, Benjamin Jowett. In this, Montefiore was by no means unique. Due to Jowett's reputation as a Greek scholar and his position as Master of Balliol, his interpretation of Plato (primarily as a religious thinker and political reformer) became *the* Plato for several generations of Oxford educated men. He was to be understood as a philosopher whose thought could sustain traditional moral values and inculcate a new sense of secular duty in a time when this was dying in society. Jowett's great crusade was to propagate a moral stance born of liberal Christianity and supported by the wisdom of Plato. He did not go so far as to make Plato a Christian, but his translations brought out what he saw as undogmatic Christian ethical values and spiritual truths. The influence of Jowett and of his treatment of Plato can clearly be seen reflected in the writings of Montefiore. Both men regarded ethical idealism as ennobling to human endeavour and essential to the preservation of the essence of religion, which was composed of 'self-sacrifice, self-denial, a death unto life, having for its own rule an absolute morality, a law of God and nature'.[134]

Richard Nettleship was another Balliol classical scholar who left his mark upon Montefiore. He had characterised Plato as a philosopher who had been 'intensely anxious to reform and revolutionise' human life.[135] His lectures on Plato's *Republic* had been influenced by the Idealist T.H. Green who had argued that the educated classes bore special responsibility for moral reform and the improvement of society. In the light of his future philanthropic and educational achievements, the influence of this interpretation of Platonic thought on the young Montefiore appears considerable.

As should be clear by now, Montefiore valued 'Hellenism' very highly. He believed Stoic and Platonic thought comple-mented and completed traditional Jewish teachings (and vice versa). He wrote, 'God our refuge, God the object of our love – that is mainly Jewish. The dignity of man and of the human mind – that is mainly Greek.'[136] In this Montefiore went further than many of his fellow Jews. Certainly, few of them viewed the ancient Greek philosophy as a kind of devotional aid, as he did. Care should be taken, however, in taking the term 'Hellenism' too literally. Since Montefiore gained his (religious) appreciation of Hellenism from his exposure to Anglican liberal teaching, both prior to and at Oxford, it seems sensible to take into account some Christian influence. His idea of Hellenism is therefore probably better thought of as assimilated, Christianised Hellenism.

For many in the nineteenth century, the best of Greek thought had been perfected in Christianity. In Montefiore's mind also, the two overlapped considerably. It made good sense to him that 'Christianity conquered the world partly because it underwent a considerable infiltration from Hellenism.'[137] To a great extent Montefiore grew up with a culturally formed, positive image of Christianity; it was this intellectual, classically augmented religion of Milton's *Paradise Lost* which he found at Oxford, not New Testament or creedal Christianity. Having learned to appreciate Hellenistic thought through Christian channels, Montefiore recog-nised its influence in the liberal Anglicanism that surrounded him and had come to represent for him Christianity *per se*. It is therefore not surprising that he could find in Christianity so much to identify with, in contrast to the majority of his fellow Jews.

The liberal Anglicans had been infusing their system with Greek thought throughout the century, and in claiming aspects of Hellenistic thought for use by liberal Jews, Montefiore was, in fact, following in their footsteps. Most of the non-Jewish additions to synagogue worship and theology could be understood as following Christianity in a similar manner since they were effected by the influence of assimilated or Christianised Hellenism. It could, for example, be argued that increased service decorum was the result of Jewish emulation of Christian assimilation of Hellenistic culture. In other cases, however, the influence was more directly Hellenistic in origin, such as Montefiore's sympathy with the Stoic position which denied all evil 'except moral evil, for which man himself is responsible, and from which of his own efforts and discipline he can set himself free'.[138] This certainly differed from the traditional Christian doctrine of Original Sin.

Of course, liberals of both faiths regarded much Greek thought as unsatisfactory. Amongst other weaknesses, Montefiore cited the 'faint and inadequate ... Greek teaching regarding immortality' and 'the sad resignation in much of their literature'.[139] He also saw it as significant that they had never imagined 'the doctrine of the progress of Mankind and of the messianic age' (which he merged together). This idea of Progress is an important element in his thinking.

RELIGIOUS PROGRESS

The European fixation upon Progress in the nineteenth century had a very great effect upon the approach to the study of religion. Amongst Jews and Christians, one of the more controversial developments was a new interpretation of the inspiration of the scriptures. While earlier in the century English biblical scholars had been content to accept the general reliability of the Hebrew scriptures, the Germans had not. Their philosophical approach to religion and source-critical techniques had produced many radical reconstructions of the Israelite history, and had thus eroded confidence in scriptural reliability. By the mid-century, German liberalism was influencing the British intelligentsia, and liberal Anglican scholars such as Jowett effectively rejected the doctrine of verbal inspiration of scripture. Inspiration came to take on a whole new meaning. As Jowett put it,

> In the higher part [of inspiration] we include the truer and more spiritual conceptions of God, the more perfect morality, the holy life. In the lower part we may place the historical facts, whether true or invented, the passions of a war-like and semi-barbarous race, imprecations against enemies and the like. I think it worthy of remark that in precept, though not always in practice, the Old and the New Testament everywhere rise above the animal passions and also above the deceits and falsehoods of mankind. These remarks seem to me to apply more or less to all the religions of the world; they are all more or less inspired, more or less human and also divine.[140]

In rejecting the doctrine of verbal or literal inspiration, the liberals substituted a doctrine that allowed for human error and inadequacy. Divine inspiration came to be thought of more as an editorial seal of approval upon a collection of ancient man-made documents. Jowett and other liberals felt that these could, and should, be critically examined, arguing in *Essays and Reviews* (1860) that it was quite possible to interpret the scripture like any other book. Elsewhere he had written that the documented facts of a religious history, whilst 'amongst the most important of all facts ... are frequently uncertain'. The proper approach to all such documents was therefore to 'place ourselves above them'.[141] Montefiore took this advice very much to heart; the passage is reproduced at the front of his *Hibbert Lectures* (1893). By removing any suggestion of intrinsic divine authority for the New Testament, the liberals also made it easier for non-Christians such as Montefiore to approach the New Testament without incurring a charge of compromise. With the new concept of inspiration, however, came the trauma of the effects of biblical criticism. Inevitably, liberal scholars began to question the reliability of scripture, and one of the first casualties was the idea of revelation as a once-and-for-all phenomenon.

The nineteenth-century fascination with the ancient Greek world had provided a source of information on the secular history of mankind. It confirmed, supplemented and offered alternatives to the traditional Judaeo-Christian historical account. In doing so it had prepared the ground for a non-biblical view of spiritual development. The liberal re-interpretation of biblical inspiration and the consequent rejection of the doctrine of literal or verbal revelation reinforced this independence from scripture and made it possible for European progressive ideas of religion to take root. German ideas regarding the developmental nature of religious thought had been filtering into England for a long time. They finally surfaced with Frederick Temple's contribution to *Essays and Reviews* (1860), 'The Education of the Human Race'. This viewed the Hebrew Bible as analogous to the childhood of mankind, when the Mosaic religion had taught law rather than freedom of conscience. Liberal claims and progressive models were soon supported by the discoveries of geologists and biologists which seemed to refute the literal understanding of the Genesis account(s) of creation, and even the idea of a purposeful creation (fossils revealed the existence of extinct species). It has been argued that the bitter controversies surrounding biblical criticism from this time were not so much due to the novelty of liberalism as to its gaining ground.[142]

Jewish responses to Christian biblical criticism through the 1860s and 1870s were mixed. The majority rejected anything that undermined the authority and authenticity of the Hebrew Bible. Some felt able to accept the developmental and historically informed interpretation of biblical teachings. The scholar Emanuel Deutsch (1829–73), for example, argued that the Talmud and the rabbinical religion could be viewed as a step forward from the Old Testament religion in the moral education of mankind.[143] None, however, could accept the relegation of Judaism below Christianity in the scheme of progressive revelation. As Abraham Benisch, editor of the *Jewish Chronicle* at the time saw it,

> It is morally certain that the gross heathen mind is incapable of at once grasping the sublime Jewish verities. A state of transition is absolutely necessary for it. The abyss yawning between spiritual Judaism and material pragmatism has to be bridged over. Christianity is that bridge ... It is for this purpose that providence allowed Christianity to come into existence, inserting it between paganism and Mosaism.[144]

His confident tone was partly due to a belief shared by many Jews (including Montefiore) that, reeling from the blow of biblical criticism, Christianity was on the defensive. He felt that scientific criticism would surely result in the abandonment of the 'irrational foundations' of Christianity, and took it for granted that Judaism was completely compatible with Reason.

While Montefiore would have agreed with Benisch's assessment that Christianity was moving, theologically, in the direction of Judaism, he did not overlook the consequences of biblical criticism with regard to Judaism itself. In this, he was ahead of his time. As he observed in his article, 'Some Notes on the Effects of Biblical Criticism' (1891), most Jewish religious leaders were reluctant to rely too heavily upon the findings of biblical criticism, since these could be applied just as destructively to Judaism. He believed that Judaism could no longer afford to ignore the results of biblical criticism, the most important of which he identified as 'the disintegration of the Pentateuch'.[145] The general tendency of biblical criticism had been to emphasise the originality and importance of the Prophets and to place the Law in a new relation to them. The traditional, biblical account of Sinai and the priority of the Law had to give way to a progressive vision of the ethical monotheism of the Prophets leading to an eventual codification. Montefiore argued that a historically-critically informed Jew could no longer hold to Maimonides' eighth principle of faith ('I believe with perfect faith that the whole law, now in our possession, is the same that was given to Moses, our teacher'). All this begged the question: was it possible to reconcile modern scholarship with a faith in Orthodox Judaism? After considering the traditional position, he concluded that it was not. According to Montefiore's analysis, this was because in recent times Jews had defined their Jewishness in terms of what set them apart. Overly influenced by Mendelssohn,[146] they had laid too great an emphasis upon rites that distinguished them from other theists. The ancient doctrines regarding God's nature and unity, his moral order, immortality and so on, were reckoned to be too similar – 'and thus the essence of Judaism [was] altogether removed from the sphere of religious belief'.[147] Orthodox Jews clung to particularistic rites which were based upon several of Maimonides' Principles, including belief in: the words of the prophets (6), that Moses was the greatest of the prophets (7), in the revelation at Sinai (8), in the immutability of the Revealed Law (9), in the coming messiah (12). For such Jews, biblical criticism rang the death-knell.

But this did not need to be the case, continued Montefiore. For Jews who understood themselves in terms of their religious doctrines (even if those doctrines were paralleled in other faiths), biblical criticism could do little harm – theology alone dealt with matters as lofty as the nature of God. As a consequence, he went on to spend his life propounding a form of Judaism that explicitly addressed itself to questions of theological inquiry and divorced itself from beliefs that he felt had originated at a particular time in history and no longer served any useful purpose. Montefiore was convinced that such a flexible, critically informed Judaism was quite practicable and represented the only tenable position for an educated Jew. What was more, it was essential for the survival of Judaism.

> There can exist a phase of Judaism ... capable of accepting and assimilating the results of criticism ... For the teaching of no one age and the teaching of no one man constitute the Jewish religion. Because Judaism changes, it abides.[148]

In this sense, then, Liberal Judaism can be understood to have come about as a result of the failure of both Orthodox and Reform Judaism to accommodate the findings of biblical criticism. It is important to remember, however, that while proficient in historical-critical techniques and familiar with the latest academic findings, Montefiore did not see his most important work to be in this area. He was primarily concerned with the practical religious thought of Liberal Judaism. Jowett once wrote,

> I hope that the age of biblical criticism is passing away ... I do not see that we have gained from it except negatively, and there of course we have gained a great deal by clearing away so much, but positively we have gained little or nothing. Even if we knew the manner of composition of the Old and New Testaments ... we should be no nearer the true form of religion.[149]

While Montefiore would certainly have sympathised with Jowett's greater concern for the condition of the human soul, he knew only too well that the 'age of biblical criticism' was here to stay.

Increasingly, the traditional history of Israel came under fire. It became more acceptable to talk in terms of Israel itself receiving a progressive education. This was a central thesis in Montefiore's own Hibbert Lectures, 'On the Origin and Growth of Religion as illustrated by the Religion of the Ancient Hebrews', given in 1892. It allowed Montefiore to explain away any unpalatable teachings of the Hebrew Bible in a way which Orthodox literalists simply could not. After clearing away these more primitive beliefs, a 'purified Judaism' was revealed which looked suspiciously like contemporary Christianity as it had evolved in the hands of liberals like Jowett.

One important lesson that Montefiore had learned from his religious tutor David Marks, and had had reinforced from his time spent with the Master of Balliol, was the ability to recognise the validity of another's faith.[150] This was an essential require-ment for true dialogue between the faiths to take place, and was characteristic of Jowett's attitude as recalled by Montefiore in an article for the *Jewish Quarterly Review* entitled 'The Religious Teachings of Jowett' (1899). Montefiore greatly admired his tutor's religious broadness and toleration. This he put down to Jowett's insistence on the simplicity of religion as well as 'his penetrating capacity to recognise agreement in essentials under the widest apparent differences of form and of belief'.[151] While Jowett's Christian theism was 'simple', Montefiore went on,

> It was simplicity with a difference. It was simplicity which, so to speak, lies on the other side of complexity. It was the result of thought ... It was the unessential which (to his mind) had been eliminated; the essential remained. This essential was large and living.[152]

The same could have been said of Montefiore himself who was increasingly persuaded that true Religion, in its essentials, was a relatively simple affair. They approached their religion in a similar manner and both would (ultimately) have held to a non-creedal concept of religious faith. At times, this emphasis upon an 'inner faith' allowed them to appear as Christian and Jewish sides of the same coin. Montefiore wrote,

> The main tenor of [Jowett's] teaching was in harmony and agreement with a progressive and enlightened Judaism. It

can be translated, and it needs to be translated, into Jewish. Very imperfectly and stumblingly I have sought to do this from time to time.[153]

He felt very much at home with Jowett's liberalism and described his tutor's thinking as belonging 'to a sphere where the purer Judaism and the purer Christianity fade into each other' and where 'differences merge into a higher and more Catholic unity'. In fact, Montefiore found himself in closer theological agreement to Jowett regarding the essentials of religion, than he did to many of his contemporary co-religionists. In a confidential letter to Lily Montagu in 1899, Montefiore wrote,

> ... I admit that my 'new Judaism' is Jowett pur et simple. Idea for idea I seem to accept his teachings ... Perhaps I am more a disciple of Jowett (to whom I owe more religiously than to any other man or book, except the Bible, in the world) than I am a Jew.[154]

The important thing for both tutor and student was the idea of an over-arching ethical system of values. Its label was insignificant, and 'Christian' or 'Jewish' were terms that could easily include those outside the traditional fold. In a sermon published in 1906, Montefiore explained that the J.R.U. was a Union united with whoever accepted the Hebrew prophets' conception that 'religion and morality are inseparably welded and wedded together', including Unitarians and Theists.[155] In this wider and more generous view of religion, Montefiore was directly influenced by Jowett. As a liberal Anglican, Jowett had written, 'As there are nominal Christians in the world who say that they are [Christian] and are not, so there are unconscious Christians in the world who say they are not and yet are.'[156] Similarly, as a liberal Jew who could include in his Judaism all that was 'best and most permanent in the teaching of Jesus', Montefiore wrote about the 'unconscious Jew'.[157] Both men tended towards universalism, and rejected the exclusive dogma of their traditional faiths. As Burkitt put it,

> It is not that [Montefiore] wants all men to dress alike, but that he recognises under the Christian garment and the Jewish gabardine very much the same sort of human being,

and as he has learned to see the meaning and the profundity that often underlies the Jewish gesture, he is quite ready to believe that there may be a worthy meaning in some of our Christian prejudices and peculiarities.[158]

Both men were convinced that any future religion would have to be fundamentally universal. In this and in other ways, Montefiore's grand vision of where Progress and biblical criticism were taking religion was very much influenced by his tutor.

Jowett also believed that revelation was an ongoing phenomenon, writing that 'There is no real resting place ... all true knowledge is a revelation of the will of God ... It is a duty of religious men to submit to the progress of knowledge.'[159] Montefiore, too, recognised the inevitability and significance of scientific development. He was well aware of the confusion and distress that developments such as biblical criticism had brought, and accepted that religion would be profoundly affected by biblical criticism. He cautioned,

> That gulf must be bridged over so that men may pass gradually and not be lost in the blackness of the abyss beneath. Each step of the bridge will seem the final resting place to him who makes it, and yet each step will but lead to another.[160]

Like Jowett, however, Montefiore had no doubt that progress was necessary for religion. He thought that the religion of the future would be a purified Judaism, although not the actual Judaism of his own day or of his own Liberal Judaism, and not even the Judaism that his son would practice. Characteristically, he also thought that it would contain Christian elements, for it would be

> absurd and ridiculous to suppose that the great drama of Christianity would pass away, if it ever does pass away, without leaving traces and influences upon the religion of the distant future.[161]

Christianity had certainly become a more plastic, flexible entity in the hands of liberals like Jowett who had himself regarded a future 'Christianity, whether under that or some other name' as essentially concerned with 'the simple love of truth and of God, and the desire to do good to man'.[162] Viewing progress in distinctly Hegelian terms[163] and recognising that 'Christianity was once the great antithesis ... [but] is not so today',[164] Montefiore envisaged a future universal system which would incorporate the best of both faiths while replacing them, as their traditional forms withered away.

NOTES

1. The Reform rabbi Geiger sought to reconstruct Christian history by demonstrating that Jesus was a Pharisee who taught Rabbinic Judaism, and that the Pharisees had been the liberal democratisers of their day in *Das Judentum und seine Geschichte* (1910) in particular. Susannah Heschel has described Geiger as the great pioneer in reversing the theological gaze. S. Heschel, *Abraham Geiger and the Jewish Jesus* (1998), pp. 2, 7.

2. In Graetz's great work, *The History of Judaism*, of which the first volume of the German original was published in 1846, the historian and biblical scholar pointed to what he regarded as the failure of Christianity as a religion and treated the Gospels and the Epistles of Paul to radical historical criticism; Jesus' teaching was presented as well within the confines of first-century Judaism.

3. The Liberal rabbi's *Romantische Religion* (1922) was a powerful polemic that contrasted the weak elements of the 'Romantic' eastern beliefs found in Christianity with those of 'Classic' Judaism.

4. Two of the most important collections of his essays were *Studies in Judaism* (3 vols, 1896–1924), and *Some Aspects of Rabbinic Theology* (1909).

5. As much as Geiger railed against Christian anti-Judaism, his own anti-Christian attitudes remained equally tenacious. S. Heschel, *Abraham Geiger and the Jewish Jesus* (1998), p. 22. Schechter refused to enter theological discussion of Christianity and denounced Jews who aped Christian religiosity. N. Bentwich, *Solomon Schechter: A Biography* (1938), pp. 290–1. Leo Baeck's *The Essence of Judaism* (1905) was a powerful polemical response to Harnack's *The Essence of Christianity* (1900).

6. C.G. Montefiore, *The Bible for Home Reading* (1899), II, p. 779.

7. As early as 1893 Montefiore was writing of the need for a book that would assist in 'accustoming [Jewish] people to an intelligent appreciation of the N[ew] T[estament] and of the Greeks, without which we cannot in the long run get on'. Letter from Montefiore to Lucy Cohen, 26 January 1893. L. Cohen, *Some Recollections of Claude Goldsmid-Montefiore 1858–1938* (1940), p. 64.

8. Agus contrasted previous stages in Jewish–Christian relations (those of *Mutual Negation* and *Mutual Derogation*) with Montefiore's new approach, of which he commented, 'At times, [Montefiore] speaks only of ... the two faiths learning from each other, but on occasion he pleads that the leaders of Judaism supplement rabbinic teaching by passages, parables and principles of the New Testament, accepting these teachings as part of the sacred tradition of Judaism.' J. Agus, 'Claude Montefiore and Liberal Judaism', *Conservative Judaism*, XIII (Winter 1959), p. 7.

9. Letter from C.G. Montefiore to Lucy Cohen, August 1906. L. Cohen, *Some Recollections of Claude Goldsmid-Montefiore 1858–1938* (1940), p. 77.
10. C.G. Montefiore, 'Judaism and Democracy', *P.F.J.P.*, XVI (1917), p. 22.
11. Letter from C.G. Montefiore to Lucy Cohen, uncertain date. L. Cohen, *Some Recollections of Claude Goldsmid-Montefiore 1858–1938* (1940), p. 105.
12. C.G. Montefiore, 'Anti-Semitism in England', *The Hibbert Journal*, IXX (1921), p. 16. In a letter from C.G. Montefiore to Schechter (12 December 1900) Montefiore wrote, '… you know that the doctrine "Englishmen of the Jewish Persuasion" is my heart's blood doctrine, for which I labour and give my life'. J.B. Stein, ed., *Lieber Freund: The Letters of Claude Goldsmid Montefiore to Solomon Schechter 1885–1902* (1988), p. 45.
13. C.G. Montefiore, *Liberal Judaism and Hellenism and Other Essays* (1918), pp. 78–9.
14. L. Cohen, *Some Recollections of Claude Goldsmid-Montefiore 1858–1938* (1940), pp. 171–2.
15. He sometimes described the Jewish community as 'Rutlandshire'. Ibid., p. 46. He once wrote, '… I feel tempted to chuck all Jewish work and retire to Coldeast and live exclusively as an ordinary Englishman among my English neighbours – my own people, as I call them, unlike the J[ewish] C[ommunity]: I feel inclined to live and work and die there among them.' Letter from C.G. Montefiore to Dr [Morris] J[oseph]? 15 April, year uncertain. MS 165/1/12, Sheldon and Amy Blank Papers, A.J.A.C.
16. Letters from Montefiore to Lucy Cohen, undated. L. Cohen, *Some Recollections of Claude Goldsmid-Montefiore 1858–1938* (1940), pp. 31, 230.
17. Letter from C.G. Montefiore to Hastings Rashdall, 7 November, year uncertain. MS Eng. Lett. 351, fol. 97, Bodleian.
18. Abraham Benisch was editor of the *Jewish Chronicle* from 1855 to 1868. D. Cesarani, *The Jewish Chronicle and Anglo-Jewry 1841–1991* (1994), pp. 47–8.
19. T. Endelman, *Radical Assimilation in English Jewish History* (1990), pp. 114–44.
20. D. Cesarani, *The Jewish Chronicle and Anglo-Jewry 1841–1991* (1994), p. 47.
21. T. Endelman, *Radical Assimilation in English Jewish History* (1990), pp. 74–9.
22. E. Black, *The Social Politics of Anglo-Jewry: 1880–1920* (1988), chapters 3–6. Also R. Livshin, 'Acculturation of Immigrant Jewish Children, 1890–1930', in D. Cesarani, ed., *The Making of Modern Anglo-Jewry* (1990), pp. 79–96.
23. T. Endelman, *Radical Assimilation in English Jewish History* (1990), pp. 73–114.
24. Ruderman has argued that although it is difficult to speak of an English *Haskalah*, what intellectual life there was 'emerged uniquely in England and had little to do with, and in some cases pre-dated, the intellectual developments of German *Haskalah*'. D. Ruderman, 'Was there an English Parallel to the German Haskalah?' and in M. Brenner, R. Liedtke and D. Rechter, eds, *Two Nations: British and German Jews in Comparative Perspective* (1999), p. 17. Endelman argues that consideration of the impact of the German *Haskalah* upon Anglo-Reform Judaism is not productive since 'it obscures the impress of native currents and structures'. T. Endelman, 'Jewish Modernity in England', in J. Katz, ed., *Toward Modernity* (1987), pp. 242–3.
25. Philipson's treatment contains numerous references to the German experience and emphasised the influence of German reform. D. Philipson, *The Reform Movement in Judaism*, 2nd edn (1931), p. 92.
26. E. Black, *The Social Politics of Anglo-Jewry: 1880–1920* (1988), p. 67.
27. M.A. Meyer, *Response to Modernity: A History of the Reform Movement in Judaism* (1988); also M.A. Meyer, 'Jewish Religious Reform in Germany and

Britain', in M. Brenner, R. Liedtke and D. Rechter, eds, *Two Nations: British and German Jews in Comparative Perspective* (1999), pp. 67–85.

28. Between 1881 and 1914, over 100,000 poor and mostly unskilled Russian, Polish, Galacian and Romanian Jews arrived in Britain. A. Kershen and J. Romain, *Tradition and Change: A History of Reform Judaism in Britain 1840–1995* (1995), p. 92; also D. Cesarani, *The Jewish Chronicle and Anglo-Jewry 1841–1991* (1994), p. 70.

29. A. Kershen and J. Romain, *Tradition and Change: A History of Reform Judaism in Britain 1840–1995* (1995), p. 26.

30. M. Leigh, 'Reform Judaism in Britain 1840–1970', in D. Marmur, *Reform Judaism* (1973), pp. 3–50. Leigh discounts Continental influence (p. 21).

31. R. Liberles, 'The Origins of the Jewish Reform Movement in England', *AJS Review*, I (1976), pp. 121–50. Liberles did not find any significant German influence.

32. D. Feldman, *Englishmen and Jews: Social Relations and Political Culture 1840–1914* (1994), p. 51.

33. Englander focuses primarily upon the *differences* of Anglo-Reform with reforming movements elsewhere. 'Political considerations, though doubtlessly important, do not, however, supply an adequate explanation for the curious combination of liturgical conservatism and militant anti-rabbinism that was without parallel in either Germany or the United States. It is the singularity of Anglo-Jewry that invites attention.' D. Englander, 'Anglicised but not Anglican', in G. Parsons, ed., *Religion in Victorian Britain*, 4 vols (1988), I, pp. 257–8.

34. S. Sharot, 'Reform and Liberal Judaism in London: 1840–1940', *Jewish Social Studies*, vol. 41 (1979), p. 212.

35. The Karaites were a heretical Jewish sect, originated in eighth-century Persia, flourished later in Palestine and Egypt, and still exist in the Crimea and in Israel. They rejected the rabbinic traditions and based their tenets upon a literal interpretation of the Bible.

36. The Catholic Emancipation Act (1829) allowed Catholics to sit in Parliament; the Reform Act (1832) reorganised the British political scene, widening the voting franchise.

37. Much of the material in this section is drawn from D. Feldman, *Englishmen and Jews: Social Relations and Political Culture 1840–1914* (1994), chap. 2, 'Rabbinism, Popery and Reform'.

38. The London Society, which developed from the Missionary Society, was established in 1809 and was dominated by Evangelical Anglicans by mid-century. It was well funded and focused its pamphleteering activities upon the Ashkenazim, despite the fact that statistically the Sephardic community provided many more converts to Christianity in the eighteenth and nineteenth centuries. R.M. Smith, 'The London Jews' Society and Patterns of Jewish Conversion in England, 1801–1859', *Jewish Social Studies*, vol. XLIII (1981), pp. 276, 285.

39. Originally a series of 60 weekly pamphlets, *The Old Paths: or A Comparison of the Principles and Doctrines of Modern Judaism with the Religion of Moses and the Prophets* (1837) sold more than 10,000 copies in its first year and was translated into nine languages; a second edition was published in 1846. W.T. Gidney, *History of the London Society for Promoting Christianity amongst the Jews* (1908), pp. 159–60; W.T. Gidney, *Missions to the Jews* (1912), p. 68. *Sketches of Judaism and the Jews* (1838) was a collection of articles originally published in the *British Magazine* between 1834 and 1838.

40. A. McCaul, *The Old Paths* (1846), pp. 645, 649.

41. A. Myers, *The Jew* (1874, 6th edition), p. 82.
42. Ibid., p. 83.
43. A. McCaul, *Sketches of Judaism and the Jews* (1838), p. 2.
44. T. Endelman, 'Jewish Modernity in England', in J. Katz, ed., *Toward Modernity* (1987), p. 238.
45. A. McCaul, *Sketches of Judaism and the Jews* (1838), pp. 2, 169.
46. A. Myers, *The Jew* (1874, 6th edition), pp. 28, 26.
47. Letter from Benjamin Jowett to C.G. Montefiore, 1883. L. Cohen, *Some Recollections of Claude Goldsmid-Montefiore 1858–1938* (1940), p. 47.
48. Letter from Benjamin Jowett to C.G. Montefiore, 1893. Ibid., p. 59.
49. R.M. Smith, 'The London Jews' Society and Patterns of Jewish Conversion in England, 1801–1859', *Jewish Social Studies*, vol. XLIII (1981), pp. 279–81, 284.
50. N. Adler, 'Solomon's Judgement: A Picture of Israel' (1854), pp. 8–9.
51. M. Angel, *The Law of Sinai and Its Appointed Times* (London: 1858), cited in D. Feldman, *Englishmen and Jews: Social Relations and Political Culture 1840–1914* (1994), p. 60. Born in the same year as Angel wrote these words, Montefiore was later to write in a similar vein. In the context of biblical scholarship, Montefiore's article 'Jewish Scholarship and Christian Silence' (1903) asked how it was that Christian New Testament scholars could continue to ignore the Jewish evidence that contradicted their presuppositions of Judaism.
52. David Marks, *The Law is Light: A Course of Four Lectures on the Sufficiency of the Law of Moses as the Guide of Israel* (1854), p. 8.
53. D. Marks, 'Introductory Discourse', in *Sermons Preached on Various Occasions* (1851), pp. 17–20.
54. These and other innovations are detailed in M. Hilton, *The Christian Effect on Jewish Life* (1994), pp. 141–60. Minor innovations had been introduced since the 1820s amongst London congregations, including limiting the number of *misheberachs*, requiring *hazzanim* to chant in a straightforward rather than florid manner, prohibiting children from interrupting the reading of Esther on Purim, and some slight modifications of the singing of Psalms on the Sabbath. Endelman suggests that all such modifications were 'cosmetic' and not radical in nature. T. Endelman, 'Jewish Modernity in England', in J. Katz, ed., *Toward Modernity* (1987), pp. 231–2.
55. The creation of two branch synagogues as in the West End of London under the jurisdiction of the Great Synagogue and Bevis Marks in 1853 and 1855 meant that there were geographical alternatives.
56. Systematic and regular missionary efforts in London were inaugurated in 1829 by Rev. J.C. Reichardt. The next major boost to missionary endeavours was provided by the first edition of *Old Paths* (1837) by Alexander McCaul, who became a leading light in the Society for Promoting Christianity amongst the Jews. 'The twenty years ending in 1850 may be considered the palmy days in the entire history of the London mission, which then reached its highest level. The work of these years has never been surpassed.' W.T. Gidney, *History of the London Society for Promoting Christianity amongst the Jews* (1908), pp. 158–9, 216–17.
57. D. Englander, 'Anglicised but not Anglican', in G. Parsons, ed., *Religion in Victorian Britain*, 4 vols (1988), I, p. 237.
58. Letter from David Marks to the elders at the Orthodox Bevis Marks Synagogue, August 1841, cited in D. Feldman, *Englishmen and Jews: Social Relations and Political Culture 1840–1914* (1994), p. 50.
59. M. Hilton, *The Christian Effect on Jewish Life* (1994), pp. 130, 145–6.

60. Letter from David Marks to the elders at the Orthodox Bevis Marks Synagogue, August 1841, cited in D. Feldman, *Englishmen and Jews: Social Relations and Political Culture 1840–1914* (1994), p. 50.
61. A. McCaul, *The Old Paths* (1846), pp. 66–7. He observed: 'Reform,
wherever it has prevailed, has robbed the Jews of their holy nationality,
and sunk them to the level of a common-place religious sect.' Ibid., p. 68.
62. M.A. Meyer, *Response to Modernity: A History of the Reform Movement in
Judaism* (1988), p. 143.
63. These religious classes for the young, which met on Sunday mornings and
followed a brief synagogue service, were non-congregational in character
and were taught by voluntary lay teachers. The minister, David Marks,
commented on 'his deep interest in it', while the *Jewish Chronicle* wished
the movement every success. *Jewish Chronicle*, 2 December 1881, p. 7.
64. Oswald Simon wrote to the *Jewish Chronicle* in 1891 claiming to have
supported with Montefiore the Saturday morning services for six years.
Those attending were mostly women and children 'and a few men and
boys'. It was 'a simple service with proper singing on the part of the girls'.
Jewish Chronicle, 23 January 1891, p. 8.
65. *Jewish Chronicle*, 13 February 1891, p. 7. About 200 people attended the
first one-hour service in 1890, which included modifications to the ritual,
instrumental accompaniment and a mixed choir. *Jewish Chronicle*, 28
February 1890, p. 11.
66. Montefiore and Oswald Simon were both associated with plans for a
regular Sunday morning service to be held at the Hampstead Reform
Synagogue in June 1899. An open letter explained 'that whilst being
determined to safeguard the observance of the seventh day Sabbath, it is
an *indispensable* feature of this new movement that the daily morning
service shall be so adapted as to enable many persons with children to avail
themselves of public worship on Sunday mornings'. *Jewish Chronicle*, 2 June
1899, p. 8. Montefiore himself wrote an open letter explaining his involvement. 'For my part I cannot bear that a single life should be lost to Judaism
… If these people will come to a service on Sunday, let them have a
service on Sunday; if they will come to one on Wednesday, let them have
one on Wednesday.' He could not avoid the temptation to point out that
'according to the newer view of Judaism and of the Bible, there is no divine
seventh day at all'. *Jewish Chronicle*, 30 June 1899, pp. 8–9.
67. Simon held his services in the Cavendish Rooms, Oxford Street, London.
The parallels to a Christian service were not lost on the *Jewish Chronicle*
which noted that the first service featured a hymn by Wesley, a prayer for
the Queen of England, a sermon, mixed seating, musical accompaniment
and a ladies' choir. It also commented that of the 80 people attending, 'a
good sprinkling were Gentiles', and noted that the service ended with a
collection plate held at the door 'to complete the Gentile analogy'. That
Montefiore was away in Bristol at the time was duly noted (despite a
letter from Montefiore signalling his continued support for the 'lofty aims
and the pure Jewish idealism' of the scheme). 'The meagreness of Mr
Simon's following is at once laid bare', the report concluded, 'and the
absurdity of those who clamoured that his efforts were directed to satisfy
a wide-spread yearning in the community is strikingly demonstrated'. *Jewish Chronicle*, 3 November 1902, pp. 8, 18.
68. At a special meeting of the West London Synagogue council in April 1896,
Sir Philip Magnus was unable to defeat an attempt by Montefiore to
reduce the majority needed to adopt the Revision of Ritual (based on the

recommendations of the Report of the Ritual Revision Committee sub-
mitted in March and April the previous year). In the event, Montefiore
achieved only a two-vote majority (not the one-fifth majority he needed)
when the vote was taken in May, despite arguing against the claims that
Hebrew was a necessary part of Judaism and that the adoption of the
changes would encourage 'American Judaism'. *Jewish Chronicle*, 24 April
1896, p. 7 and 22 May 1896, p. 10.

69. The council vote supporting the introduction of English prayers ('the
prayer for the congregation') into the Reform Synagogue ritual failed with
only 21 voting for and 16 against, again despite Montefiore's contribution
to the debate. *Jewish Chronicle*, 1 April 1898, p. 13.

70. L. Montagu, 'Spiritual Possibilities of Judaism Today', *Jewish Quarterly
Review*, XI (1898–99), pp. 216–18.

71. Reform congregations were established in West London (1840), Manchester
(1856), Bradford (1873). Reform services were also held in Hull in the 1850s
and in Clapham from 1875 to 1877.

72. C.G. Montefiore, 'Liberal Judaism in England: Its Difficulties and Its
Duties', *Jewish Quarterly Review*, XII (1899–1900), p. 627.

73. F. Temple *et al.*, *Essays and Reviews* (1860) was a collection of essays by seven
authors which represented the most sensational theological development
in nineteenth-century England after Darwin's *The Origin of Species* (1859).
The works were shocking not so much because they considered the
'historical question' and therefore questioned biblical authority and inspiration – Strauss' *Life of Jesus* (1835–36) had already done this – but because
they were derived almost entirely from Oxford educators and thus represented an attack from within, not a threat from without, such as German
rationalism had. Popularly, it introduced theological issues to the educated
public and made for a more liberal attitude towards religious differences.

74. G. Smith, 'Can Jews be Patriots?', *Nineteenth Century*, III (May 1878),
p. 875–87.

75. Ibid., p. 876.

76. 'Jews and Judaism: A Rejoiner', *Nineteenth Century* (July 1878); and 'Recent
Phases of Judaeophobia', *Nineteenth Century* (December 1881).

77. H. Adler, 'Jews and Judaism: A Rejoiner', *Nineteenth Century* (July 1878),
p. 139–40.

78. M. Joseph, 'The God of Israel: A History', in *Jewish Ideals and Other Essays*
(1896), originally published in *Nineteenth Century*, September 1879.

79. C.G. Montefiore, 'Is Judaism a Tribal Religion?', *Contemporary Review*
(September 1882).

80. *Jewish Chronicle*, 1 September 1882, p. 11. The article was reviewed by the
Jewish press with a mixture of respect and anxiety. 'Here we have for the
first time in English Judaism a consistent and systematic theory of Judaism.
We believe that theory to be utterly false and impracticable, but all the more
do we recognise that it is a theory that can be plausibly adopted as explain-
ing the nature of contemporary Judaism … He puts forth a new view of
Judaism (at least new in England, though sufficiently stale in Germany and
America).' Ibid.

81. There were at least two distinct reactions against the Evangelical doctrine
of the Atonement: Incarnationalists such as Westcott, Gore and Temple
emphasised Christ's role as bringing about the revitalisation of mankind,
the perfecting of humanity. Exemplorists such as Jowett and Rashdall
emphasised Christ's ethical example. For both, the humanity of Christ was
central.

82. D. Feldman, *Englishmen and Jews: Social Relations and Political Culture 1840–1914* (1994), p. 84.

83. C.G. Montefiore, 'The Jewish Religious Union: Its Principles and Future', *P.F.J.P.*, XXI (1918).

84. I. Mattuck, 'Why the Jews have no Missionaries', *Liberal Jewish Monthly* (October 1932), reproduced in C.G. Montefiore and I. Mattuck, 'Jewish Views on Jewish Missions', *P.F.J.P.*, XXXI (1933).

85. 'There has developed a kind of reluctance to accept proselytes. It is very strong in Orthodox Judaism.' Ibid., p. 46.

86. Ibid., pp. 17, 42.

87. K. Heasman, *Evangelicals in Action: An Appraisal of their Social Work in the Victorian Era* (1962), pp. 13–14.

88. D. Englander, 'Anglicised but not Anglican', in G. Parsons, ed., *Religion in Victorian Britain*, 4 vols (1988), I, p. 244.

89. Lady Battersea, one of the founders of the Association, even attributed its origins as due to Christian influences. She tells the story of becoming involved in Jewish social work after a Christian social worker came to her after having been approached by two needy Jewish girls, having failed to discover a 'Jewish Home or shelter'. 'Mrs Herbert [the social worker] expressed in no measured terms her astonishment that the Community owned no harbour of refuge for those of our own Faith.' Shamed, the 'Jewish Ladies' Society for Preventative and Rescue Work' was established, later to become the 'Jewish Association for the Protection of Girls and Women'. Constance Battersea, *Reminiscences* (London: Macmillan, 1922), pp. 419–21.

90. Henriques had come under Montefiore's influence in 1910, although he preferred to call himself Reform rather than Liberal. (L. Cohen, *Some Recollections of Claude Goldsmid-Montefiore 1858–1938* (1940), p. 137.) Toynbee Hall and Oxford House were university settlements established in the East End so that graduates from Oxford and Cambridge might live among, educate and encourage the poor of East London. St George's Settlement Synagogue was co-founded in 1925 by the Liberal Jewish and the West London synagogues. Its services were composed of a combination of Reform and Liberal liturgies together with a strong admixture of the thoughts and prayers of Henriques himself. A. Kershen and J. Romain, *Tradition and Change: A History of Reform Judaism in Britain 1840–1995* (1995), p. 96; also M. Leigh, 'Reform Judaism in Great Britain', in D. Marmur, ed., *Reform Judaism: Essays on Reform Judaism in Britain* (1973), p. 36.

91. Montefiore attacked Christian missionary activities many times. One example, originally printed in *The Times* read, 'It is a remarkable thing that the proselytising activities of the various conversionist societies seem to limit the sphere of their operations to the poorer and less cultivated class of Jews. Is it that only such persons are susceptible to the teas and treats and "medical missions" with which our East End workers are so familiar? People in my class of life receive once a year a silly little tract, but otherwise we are left severely alone ...' *Jewish Chronicle*, 2 May 1902, p. 11. In 1916 he resigned as patron from the Committee of Russian Jews Relief Fund in Edinburgh as soon as he discovered that it was 'closely associated with missionary work among the Jews'. *Jewish Chronicle*, 4 February 1916, p. 8.

92. Ibid., p. 32.

93. C.G. Montefiore, 'The Place of Judaism in the Religions of the World', *P.F.J.P.*, XII (1916), p. 16.

94. M.G. Bowler, *Claude Montefiore and Christianity* (1988), pp. 45–6.

95. Ibid., p. 42.

96. C.G. Montefiore, 'The Old Testament and Its Ethical Teaching', *P.F.J.P.*, XV (1917), p. 6.

97. C.G. Montefiore, *Liberal Judaism and Hellenism and Other Essays* (1918), p. 106.

98. C.G. Montefiore, *Judaism and St. Paul: Two Essays* (1914), p. 138.

99. 'It is pathetic to find Jewish students … still toiling at Maimonides and at medieval philosophy as if what was good and adequate for the needs of the 12th and 13th centuries was also good and adequate for the 19th and 20th!' C.G. Montefiore, *Liberal Judaism and Hellenism and Other Essays* (1918), p. 190.

100. Montefiore deplored what he saw as Jewish prostration to 'the fashionable Zionist Baal'. C.G. Montefiore, 'A Die-Hard's Confession', paper read at the L.S.S.R. (1935).

101. This explicit accusation was made by Solomon Schechter, for example, as cited in R. Apple, *The Hampstead Synagogue* (1967), p. 38.

102. L. Cohen, *Some Recollections of Claude Goldsmid-Montefiore 1858–1938* (1940), p. 133.

103. M.G. Bowler, *Claude Montefiore and Christianity* (1988), p. 33.

104. 'Their hands outstretched in yearning for the other shore' (Virgil, *Aeneid*, VI, 314) or 'Now the labourer's task is o'er; / Now the battle-day is past; / Now upon the further shore / Lands the voyager at last.' (Hymn by John Ellerton, 1826–93). My thanks to Rev. John Davies for suggesting these other possible solutions.

105. J.H. Newman, *Apologia Pro Vita Sua* (1904), p. 63, cited in M.G. Bowler, *Claude Montefiore and Christianity* (1988), p. 38.

106. C.G. Montefiore, 'Is There a Middle Way?', *P.F.J.P.*, XXIII (1920).

107. Ibid., pp. 14–15.

108. Montefiore came to view Marks' understanding of the contribution of Greece as 'naive', however. C.G. Montefiore, *Liberal Judaism and Hellenism and Other Essays* (1918), p. 184.

109. Ancient history had been added to the syllabus in 1830, well before Montefiore started in 1878. R. Jenkyns, *The Victorians and Ancient Greece* (1980), p. 63.

110. F.M. Turner, *The Greek Heritage in Victorian Britain* (1981), pp. 5–6.

111. Cited in R. Jenkyns, *The Victorians and Ancient Greece* (1980), p. 65.

112. F.C. Burkitt, ed., *Speculum Religionis* (1929), pp. 4–5.

113. Ibid., pp. 8–9.

114. T.K. Cheyne, *Psalter*, p. 295, cited in C.G. Montefiore, *The Hibbert Lectures: On the Origin and Growth of Religion as Illustrated by the Religion of the Ancient Hebrews* (1893), p. 378.

115. Cited in R. Jenkyns, *The Victorians and Ancient Greece* (1980), p. 71.

116. R. Jenkyns, *The Victorians and Ancient Greece* (1980), p. 65.

117. Cited in F.M. Turner, *The Greek Heritage in Victorian Britain* (1981), p. 418.

118. C.G. Montefiore, *Liberal Judaism and Hellenism and Other Essays* (1918), p. 183.

119. Ibid., p. 232.

120. Ibid., p. 222.

121. Ibid., p. 206.

122. Ibid., p. 230.

123. Ibid., p. 201.

124. 'The Hellenistic environment suggested or stimulated the impulse to expansion and universalism.' C.G. Montefiore, *The Hibbert Lectures: On the*

Origin and Growth of Religion as Illustrated by the Religion of the Ancient Hebrews (1893), p. 378.
125. C.G. Montefiore, 'The Old Testament and Its Ethical Teaching', *P.F.J.P.*, XV (1917), p. 243.
126. C.G. Montefiore, *Liberal Judaism and Hellenism and Other Essays* (1918), p. 190.
127. Ibid.
128. Ibid., p. 204.
129. Ibid., p. 209.
130. Ibid., pp. 219–20.
131. Ibid., p. 213.
132. Ibid., p. 217.
133. C.G. Montefiore, 'The Old Testament and Its Ethical Teaching', *P.F.J.P.*, XV (1917), p. 248.
134. F.M. Turner, *The Greek Heritage in Victorian Britain* (1981), p. 420.
135. Ibid., p. 432.
136. C.G. Montefiore, *Liberal Judaism and Hellenism and Other Essays* (1918), p. 236.
137. Ibid., p. 188.
138. Ibid., p. 220.
139. Ibid., p. 234.
140. B. Jowett, *Essays and Reviews* (1860), cited in C.G. Montefiore, 'The Religious Teaching of Jowett', *Jewish Quarterly Review*, XII (1899–1900), p. 314.
141. B. Jowett, *Dialogues of Plato*, III, xxxvii, cited in C.G. Montefiore, 'The Religious Teaching of Jowett', *Jewish Quarterly Review*, XII (1899–1900), p. 3.
142. G. Parsons, 'Biblical Criticism in Victorian Britain', in G. Parsons, ed., *Religion in Victorian Britain*, 4 vols (1988), II, pp. 244, 249.
143. Emanuel Deutsch was a Silician Jewish Semitic scholar and Hebraist at the British Museum. He published a lengthy article in *The Quarterly Review* that argued that rabbinic religion was a 'faith of the heart' in contrast to the Old Testament 'law'. E. Deutsch, 'The Talmud', *The Quarterly Review* (October 1867), pp. 417–64, 438.
144. Abraham Benisch, *Jewish Chronicle*, 16 September 1864, p. 2.
145. C.G. Montefiore, 'Some Notes on the Effects of Biblical Criticism upon the Jewish Religion', *Jewish Quarterly Review*, IV (1891–92), p. 294.
146. The German-Jewish philosopher Moses Mendelssohn (1729–86) had maintained that 'Judaism is not revealed religion, but revealed legislation'. Only their ceremonial laws were peculiar to the people of Israel and were unchangeable; doctrines and historical truths were not the product of Divine revelation and were therefore available to the rest of mankind. What was important, he believed, was that which was designed to preserve the Jewish ethnic group. Isadore Epstein, *Judaism* (London: Penguin, 1959), p. 288; also H.J. Schoeps, *The Jewish–Christian Argument* (1963), p. 104.
147. C.G. Montefiore, 'Some Notes on the Effects of Biblical Criticism upon the Jewish Religion', *Jewish Quarterly Review*, IV (1891–92), pp. 297–8.
148. Ibid., p. 305.
149. Letter from Benjamin Jowett to Humphrey Ward, 1892, cited in C.G. Montefiore, 'The Religious Teaching of Jowett', *Jewish Quarterly Review*, XII (1899–1900), p. 313.
150. Upon Marks' death, Montefiore wrote, '[To Marks] Jew and Hottentot were equally God's children. He did not care for the first more than for the second … If I may flatter myself that I am a devotee of toleration,

I owe it to Professor Marks. And much of the simple theism which pretty well sums up and constitutes my present faith, really goes back to him ... "[T]he Church, the Chapel, and the Mosque", how pleasantly we used to welcome the repetition of these familiar words.' *Jewish Chronicle*, 7 May 1909, p. 20.

151. C.G. Montefiore, 'The Religious Teaching of Jowett', *Jewish Quarterly Review*, XII (1899–1900), p. 329.
152. Ibid., p. 301.
153. Ibid., p. 374.
154. Letter from C.G. Montefiore to Lily Montagu, 12 April 1899, marked 'strictly private and confidential' and 'This letter for your eyes only'. Microfilm No. 2718, Correspondence of Lily H. Montagu, A.J.A.C.
155. C.G. Montefiore, 'Religious Differences and Religious Agreements', in *Truth in Religion and other Sermons* (1906), pp. 273–86. He wrote of four concentric circles of religious belief with whom he urged the liberal Jew to identify: those who accepted the Hebrew prophets' concept that religion and morality welded together; Jews, Unitarians and Theists; the Jewish community as a whole 'united by a common and striking past'; and liberal or progressive Jews.
156. B. Jowett, *College Sermons*, cited in C.G. Montefiore, 'The Religious Teaching of Jowett', *Jewish Quarterly Review*, XII (1899–1900), p. 332.
157. Ibid., p. 332.
158. F.C. Burkitt, ed., *Speculum Religionis* (1929), p. 14.
159. B. Jowett, *St. Paul* (1859), cited in C.G. Montefiore, 'The Religious Teaching of Jowett', *Jewish Quarterly Review*, XII (1899–1900), p. 304.
160. C.G. Montefiore, 'Some Notes on the Effects of Biblical Criticism upon the Jewish Religion', *Jewish Quarterly Review*, IV (1891–92), p. 296.
161. C.G. Montefiore, 'The Place of Judaism in the Religions of the World', *P.F.J.P.*, XII (1916), pp. 33–4.
162. Letter from Benjamin Jowett to Sir R. Mosier, undated, cited in C.G. Montefiore, 'The Religious Teaching of Jowett', *Jewish Quarterly Review*, XII (1899–1900), p. 333.
163. Montefiore's hegelianism can be traced to T.H. Green's Idealism and, perhaps, back to Jowett himself. For although Jowett always maintained that he was not Hegelian, he was firmly committed to the concepts of the evolution of the human mind and of particular Ideas over time. F.M. Turner, *The Greek Heritage in Victorian Britain* (1981), p. 418.
164. C.G. Montefiore, 'The Place of Judaism in the Religions of the World', *P.F.J.P.*, XII (1916), p. 8.

11

Montefiore and Christian Biblical Scholarship

It has been argued that Montefiore's religious world-view was profoundly influenced by the surrounding Victorian Christian environment. A case can also be made for the direct influence of Christian scholarship upon his thought. As a biblical critic, Montefiore contributed both to Old Testament and New Testament studies, and Christian research formed the backbone of much of his own work. His theological perspective determined the use he made of Christian scholarship, however, and he was not afraid to denounce the misportrayal of Judaism in contemporary nineteenth-century biblical studies. It is therefore especially important when focusing upon his biblical critical work to avoid the mistake of separating Montefiore the biblical critic from Montefiore the Liberal Jewish theologian.

BIBLICAL CRITICISM AND NINETEENTH-CENTURY THEOLOGICAL TRENDS

Errors in nineteenth-century theological thought have often been attributed to the over-influence of prevailing philosophical trends. It is certainly true that discredited systems of thought formed the background to the opinions maintained by many leading scholars of the day. For example, two influential biblical critics whose work was used extensively by Montefiore included the Idealist Julius Wellhausen and the Rationalist Abraham Kuenen. There is, however, no evidence that the rise of biblical criticism itself came about as a result of such contemporary philosophical presuppositions. The methods of criticism and its major conclusions were agreed upon by scholars of widely differing philosophical, religious and cultural backgrounds. Their underlying conviction was that an objective truth in biblical matters was attainable through scientific endeavour.[165]

It is not a coincidence that biblical criticism developed at a time of great interest in historical studies and techniques. Methods that had been applied to the history of Greece and Rome with resounding success were now used upon the history of Israel. The common assumption was that a foundation of historical fact could be attained by the use of the appropriate methods of study, and light shed upon the true nature of biblical beliefs. Initially, at least, the primary aim of Old Testament scholars was the historical reconstruction of the religion of Israel. From the 1870s onwards, there was a growing diversification of disciplines that investigated Israel's political, social and cultural history and, to some extent, nineteenth-century scholarship lost sight of its original goal. A deep concern with the origins of mankind's spiritual history had produced historical-critical methodology, but as time went on, this had become an end in itself. It became enough to know when the literature had been written and what its sources were; less interest was shown in using the information to better understand the life and religion of the people of Israel. Scholars like Wellhausen believed that historical truth was of a purer and nobler kind than theological truth. It is not surprising, then, that the historical conclusions reached by historical enquiry did not solve many important theological questions. Of course, the theological perspective was not altogether absent; many biblical scholars had become interested in critical research out of a deep religious attachment. But many of them, especially the liberals, concluded that it was simply not possible to extract a body of timeless Old Testament doctrines from their historical context. It became possible, and even the norm, to study the Bible without theological interest.

Montefiore felt that he had arrived on the scene when the assault on the Hebrew Bible had been under way for some time and the consequences for the New Testament were just beginning to filter through. For him, criticism was a means to an end: it provided a historical foundation upon which it was possible to build a theological system of thought. He was certainly concerned to promote historical truth and was firmly committed to the historical approach, but his central concern was always the development of a Liberal Jewish theology that could evaluate the historically conditioned biblical beliefs in an everyday religious context. Most of the Christian scholars who influenced Montefiore belonged to a liberal grouping of one form or another, and this new critical scholarship had a definite view of Judaism. Wellhausen, for example, understood it to have devolved from the high spiritual achievements of the Jewish pre-exilic religion to one of the law, increasingly dominated by the legalistic Pharisees. The Pharisees' and Rabbis' attempts to codify earlier moral and ethical insights were deemed to contradict the Prophets' teaching regarding man's freedom and responsibility. This was a central premise in Wellhausen's influential *Prolegomena* (1883),[166] and this contributed substantially to a common negative attitude regarding the development of Judaism amongst biblical (especially Protestant) scholars.

Understandably, some scholars have wondered whether the new methods of study were motivated by anti-Jewish presuppositions. There certainly seem to be cases for which this was true.[167] What is more, biblical criticism on the Hebrew Bible was generally accepted far more readily than on the New Testament, as Montefiore observed.

> The so-called higher criticism of the Old Testament is becoming more and more acknowledged and accepted by Christian theologians of every school ... We do not find among Christian theologians of England an equal readiness to assimilate and accept the higher criticism of the New Testament.[168]

While many Christians were prepared to accept what Montefiore described as the 'disintegration' of the Hebrew Bible, very few were happy to treat the New Testament critically, for a variety of reasons. This pro-Christian bias, the fact that they could more cheerfully accept criticism about the early Jewish religion than about the early Christian religion, could, arguably, be viewed as a form of anti-Judaism which reinforced the image of Judaism as a religion superseded by Christianity. Certainly, Montefiore and a small number of other Jewish scholars involved in critical research were greatly frustrated by what they saw as the ignorance and hypocrisy of Christian scholars on this subject. Even if it was not actually motivated by antisemitism, Montefiore believed that biblical criticism was often instrumental in reinforcing negative views of Judaism.

OLD TESTAMENT RESEARCH

The *Hibbert Lectures* (1893) was one of the more academic works that Montefiore produced; the series of lectures on which it was based were for scholars rather than for laymen. Montefiore had been invited to give the lectures by Jowett, who had explained: 'We want you to make the Hebrew religion more intelligible, more connected to us, to contain more of the principles in which a good man lives; to make it less of a source of religious enmity among mankind.'[169] It represented, in the words of the renowned biblical scholar F.C. Burkitt, an 'excellent survey of Old Testament history and its literature from Moses to Nehemiah. It is very nearly up-to-date now [1929] after the lapse of a whole generation, and in 1892 it must have seemed almost alarmingly up-to-date.'[170] Montefiore was fluent in German and having only recently returned from studies there, was familiar with contemporary German biblical research. In the preface, he mentions scholars 'on the results of whose labours my own small work is chiefly based and to whom I owe the most for direct information and for suggestive stimulation'. Apart from Solomon Schechter they were all Protestant Christians and included the Germans Bernhard Stade (1848–1906) and Julius Wellhausen (1844–1918), the Dutchman Abraham Kuenen (1828–91), and the Englishman Thomas K. Cheyne (1841–1915). Cheyne is best remembered for his furtherance of the more advanced conclusions of continental biblical criticism. Stade had produced the highly historical-critical *History of the People of Israel* (1887–88) while Kuenen had written the rationalist *The Religion of Israel* (1874–75). Montefiore's series of lectures, 'On the Origin and Growth of Religion as Illustrated by the Religion of the Ancient Hebrews', given in 1892, can be seen to continue in this tradition.

In terms of Montefiore's liberal Jewish theology, the influence of the German Bernhard Duhm (1847–1928) was especially important. In *Die Theologie der Propheten* (1875) Duhm had held that the foremost achievement of the Prophets lay in their theological ideas – especially their rejection or criticism of the cultic practices with which Israel had grown up and which they replaced with moral or 'ethical idealism'. This idea (which was Wellhausen's, too) viewed the historic context as the insignificant clothing for the lasting message. All this had obvious appeal to

Montefiore whose Liberal Judaism, he believed, was the true spiritual successor to the Prophets.[171]

In his cosmopolitan learning Montefiore was somewhat exceptional, for it was a time of academic parochialism and continental biblical research was not easily available in England. Ahead of many of his generation, Montefiore had fully accepted the Graf–Wellhausen position; the premise that the Prophets were written before the Law was central to his historical account of the development of the Israelites' religion.[172] As Burkitt commented, to his contemporaries Montefiore would have appeared 'as one of the new band of Modernists, taught by the new light from Germany to put the Old Testament into its proper perspective'.[173] But Montefiore never abandoned an essentially religious world-view as a result of his historical-critical studies. Even in the *Hibbert Lectures*, he showed a sensitive awareness of the limitations of biblical criticism. Writing on the origin of the Israelite religion, he commented,

> criticism speaks with no certain voice. In the main, its verdict is chiefly negative: it has shown the inadequacy of the traditional views, but replaced them with no unquestionable construction of its own.[174]

The influence of Jowett, who had been deeply disappointed with the often irreligious results of criticism, is obvious. While committed to academic integrity, something more than that which the biblical critics offered was needed. A taste for religious truths beyond the reach of historical research came to characterise Montefiore's thought, as it had Jowett's.

NEW TESTAMENT RESEARCH

It was in the field of New Testament studies that Montefiore made his most important contributions. He was greatly indebted to the Religio-Historical school of biblical study[175] and often referred to one of its founder members, the German Wilhelm Bousset (1865–1920). Bousset's *Kyrios Christos* (1913), together with his earlier *The Religion of the Jews in the New Testament (Later Hellenistic) Era* (1903) had put forward the thesis that there had been a fatal influx of Hellenistic thought-forms into the pure, early Christian religion. Jesus had became Lord (*kyrios*) only when Christianity left Palestine and entered the Hellenistic environment. Bousset believed that the new Christians had little interest in the historical details of the life of Jesus, but absorbed the drama of his death and resurrection into their mystery rituals and ecstatic hopes. For Montefiore, as for many others, Christianity was thus assigned a place in the natural evolution of man's beliefs, a view that settled comfortably in nineteenth-century evolutionary thought.

Montefiore can also be understood in the context of a later line of enquiry within New Testament scholarship, that is, an approach by which the background to the New Testament could be understood in terms outside those of Hellenistic-Jewish and Hellenistic-pagan religion. The Strack-Billerbeck Commentary and the writings of Gerhard Kittel are examples of (Christian) scholars seeking to show by comparison of early Rabbinic Judaism and early Christianity both the close similarities and the essential differences. W.G. Kümmel sees Montefiore belonging to the same movement.

> The use of rabbinical matter contributes both to the understanding of the New Testament text and to its differentiation from contemporary Judaism. Consequently it is a matter of no surprise, and even signifies a new and beneficial line of investigation, that modern historically orientated Jewish theology turned to the question of how we are to judge the distinctiveness of the New Testament and of Jesus in particular and their relation to Rabbinic Judaism.[176]

For this reason, Kümmel concentrates upon Montefiore's *Rabbinic Literature and Gospel Teachings* (1930) which considers whether and in what ways Jesus' teachings are to be judged unique. Since most of Montefiore's work was produced at a time when religion both for Judaism and for Protestant Christianity, in the shadow of Harnack's *What is Christianity?* (1901),[177] had been largely reduced to ethics, Montefiore concerned himself with Jesus' practical moral and ethical teachings. For a rarefied minority of Christians, mostly members of the Broad Church who inhabited the somewhat exclusive world of Oxford Anglicanism, religion was essentially ethical. It was with these Christians that Montefiore felt most at home. Their religion was cultured, sophisticated and, significantly, tolerant of religions other than their own.

Jowett is the obvious example of an Oxford Anglican who was primarily concerned with ethical religion and whose liberalism allowed him to accept the validity of another's faith. His influence can be seen particularly clearly with regard to Montefiore's views on Jesus. To the Master of Balliol, Christ was the ideal exemplar, a human embodiment of perfect morality and perfect religion. Montefiore observed,

> It was this half-historic, half-ideal way of regarding Christ which made the Master's teaching more sympathetic to Jews. He seemed to indicate that it was rather a question of circumstance or education whether you regarded the ideal in this personal way or not ... It was an ideal of morality and religion which everybody, Jew and Christian, would be in practical agreement.[178]

With such a view, it was possible for Jew and Christian to share a common attitude towards Christ. It is not at all surprising that such sympathy was possible when one considers Jowett's liberal (and platonic) musings. He once wrote,

> Is it possible to feel a personal attachment to Christ such as prescribed by Thomas á Kempis? I think that it is impossible and contrary to human nature that we should be able to concentrate our thoughts on a person scarcely known to us, who lived 1800 years ago. But there might be such a passionate longing and yearning for goodness and truth. The personal Christ might become the idea of goodness.[179]

Montefiore revealed just how much in tune with this kind of liberal Christian thinking he was in a letter to the Anglican moral philosopher and theologian, Hastings Rashdall (1858–1924). As he put it,

> I am in fuller sympathy with your religious and moral views, with your way of looking at things, with your view of the universe, than with those of any other living Christian theologian that I have read.[180]

While one was a leading Jew and the other a leading Christian, neither one's theological views would have much offended the other. Rashdall's Bampton lectures in 1915 had been on 'The Idea of the Atonement in Christian Theology' in which he upheld the Abelardian (or Exemplarist) theory of Atonement. This suited Montefiore's point of view, as he had learned it from Jowett. Another similarity was Rashdall's supreme confidence in the capacity of human reason, when rightly employed, to arrive at final truths of religion. This was central to Montefiore's approach to Liberal Jewish theology; the conscience (which was to be an instructed conscience) was the tool by which he collated religious truth. Such rationalism, which viewed the human mind as the supreme judge of Truth, was very much a view of the time. More particularly, what they shared in common was an ethical doctrine; in a treatise on moral philosophy, *The Theory of Good and Evil* (1907), Rashdall called it Ideal Unitarianism. As an advanced liberal, Rashdall, in turn, appreciated many of Montefiore's works and refers to him repeatedly in his famous *Conscience and Christ* (1916).[181] He once wrote to Montefiore: 'Your book [*The Synoptic Gospels*], if I may say so, shows much more real appreciation of Jesus than the work of a good many professedly Christian – some of them fairly Orthodox – theologians.'[182]

There were non-Anglicans with whom Montefiore shared a liberal outlook with regard to scripture. Alfred Loisy (1857–1940), a French priest, is generally credited as the founder of Modernism, a movement within the Roman Catholic Church which aimed at revising its dogmas to reflect the advances in science and philosophy. Loisy proposed a greater freedom of biblical interpretation in the development of religious doctrine. He came to regard Christianity as a system of humanist ethics rather than as a historical verification of divine revelation. The close affinity of aspects of Modernism to Montefiore's own thought explains his favoured status in Montefiore's writings.

The same could be said of Montefiore's friend Joseph Estlin Carpenter (1844–1927), who proof-read several of his manuscripts[183] and whose *The First Three Gospels* (1890) was well regarded by Montefiore. An eminent figure in modern Unitarianism, Carpenter was respected for his extensive knowledge in comparative religion and Semitic literature. Montefiore obviously shared similar interests; he also felt a great affinity with the position of the Unitarians. In an article in 1891, he described the liberal Jew as 'the man who stands to orthodox Judaism in something of the same relation as the modern Christian Unitarian stands to orthodox Christianity'.[184]

What exactly explains Montefiore's closeness to such Christian thinkers? The answer has to do with the three presuppositions that lie behind all his writings on the New Testament, presuppositions that he inherited from Jowett and shared in common with many of his contemporary Christian thinkers. These were: nineteenth-century rationalism, nineteenth-century idealism, and an over-arching concern for religious truth and the freedom to express it.

Being a rationalist, Montefiore did not consider the possibility of there being a historical foundation for the miraculous events described in the New Testament. Since orthodox Christianity has at the basis of its existence the belief in a historical incarnation and resurrection, this explains to some degree what W.R. Matthews has identified as Montefiore's lack of interest in and 'imperfect comprehension of the central doctrine of Christianity [the Incarnation]'.[185] Similarly, Montefiore would have viewed miraculous healing suspiciously, explaining it psychologically, and granting it little or no religious significance. Ever concerned with facts and historical truth, Montefiore greatly appreciated Bultmann's later attempts to demythologise the Gospels and was one of the first Englishmen to praise his *Geschichte der synoptischen Tradition* (1921).[186]

As regards idealism, Jowett's huge influence was obvious. It gave Montefiore his great sympathy with the world-view of men like Rashdall and thoroughly permeated his writings. One of the earlier Idealist Protestant theologians, the German Heinrich Holtzmann (1832–1910), featured repeatedly in Montefiore's work. Greatly influenced by nineteenth-century German Idealism, Holtzmann saw the Kingdom of God as an inner/spiritual change within the hearts of men, a kingdom of reason, intelligence, goodwill. The gospel had been reduced to what such scholars believed possible: Jesus was de-mystified and held up as an ethical prophet, and the Kingdom of God was reduced to an inward personal state. Montefiore was quite comfortable with such a view; the concern for an inner, rationalist religion characterised his own Liberal Jewish theology.

Montefiore's over-arching concern, however, was for religious truth as it could be applied in everyday life, just as it had been for his mentor Jowett. For him, the primary value in all religious teaching was Righteousness. He believed deeply in the supremacy of the moral law and in his treatment of the Gospels the first priority was alw ays to discover and estimate Jesus' ethics. It was this 'preoccupation with righteousness and ethical teaching' that has led to criticisms of his understanding of the Gospels since, from the Christian point of view, they were very much more than simply treatises on ethics.[187]

By the 1920s and 1930s there was considerable approximation to one another of Jewish and Christian biblical scholars in a way that, perhaps, there had not been before, and this was in the field of academic engagement with the subject. Montefiore was one of a number of Jewish scholars who worked in or around the New Testament field.[188] He was, however, especially highly regarded and often a source of great curiosity to Christian scholars. One reason for this was that whereas in the past Jews had tended to say that what was true in the Gospels was not new and what was new was not true, Montefiore was prepared to write that much of the Gospel material was both new and true. Another reason was that, even when explaining very real differences in Christian and Jewish interpretations of New Testament teaching, he was able to do so using Christian theological language that could be readily understood. Not only did he use a Christian vocabulary (as did Schechter and Abrahams, for example), but he also adopted a Christian agenda in terms of subject matter, even if the substance of his work was to present alternative Jewish understandings.[189] This made it easy for many to differentiate between the relative positions of the two faiths, in both their Traditionalist and Modernist forms. A third reason why he was so acceptable to liberal scholars was that, as far as his academic presuppositions and world-view was concerned, he could be regarded as one of their own. He came in on their level, so to speak, and was completely familiar with the contemporary issues of New Testament debate.

Montefiore's mastery of New Testament scholarship has been questioned by Walter Jacob, who criticises him generally for his 'insular' studies that almost never mentioned the work of other Jews (referring to earlier giants such as Maimonides and Mendelssohn) either to agree or disagree with them, and who complained that 'most of the contemporary Christian scholarship was also ignored'.[190] The failure to refer to Schweitzer's works on Jesus or Paul is cited as particularly negligent.[191] But even a brief reading of his works shows Montefiore to have been light-years ahead of any of his Jewish contemporaries in terms of familiarity with the findings of New Testament research, especially with regard to German scholarship. *The Four Gospels; A Study of Origins* was a summary of the recent results of New Testament studies by the British scholar Burnett H. Streeter (1874–1937) published in 1924.[192] In this survey, Streeter had reviewed the work of the previous 60 years of intensive research since the days of Holtzmann, and Montefiore, along with many others, held the book in high regard. But while the well-regarded Streeter never mentioned Form-criticism and the work of Dibelius, Schmidt or Bultmann, Montefiore had fully acquainted himself with their ideas, and made frequent reference to them in his own writings. Over all, then, he showed an excellent grasp of the real issues of New Testament studies, and, with very few exceptions, he followed and expanded upon the leading scholarship of his day.

As regards his work on the Gospels, Montefiore should be placed alongside those scholars who were caught up in 'the Quest for the Historical Jesus'.[193] This was an important movement in spite of its long-term failures, not least because it established a rational basis for the life of Jesus about which both Jewish and Christian scholars could debate. One result of emphasising the purely rational, historical approach was that these scholars tended to accept the two (or three) document hypothesis for the Synoptics but ignored John's Gospel as a theological, non-historical, Hellenistic treatise; Montefiore himself agreed with the Unitarian minister Joseph Carpenter who described John as 'an interpretation of the person and work of Jesus rather than a record of his deeds'.[194] Later studies on John have demonstrated that the Gospel can significantly contribute to a historical reconstruction of Jesus' ministry, and particularly with regard to Jewish aspects. But Montefiore's *Synoptic Gospels* reflected contemporary historical concerns and his own anti-mystical tendency, and his view was in keeping with the predominating critical views of the time.[195]

In his earlier Gospel writings, Montefiore quoted most often from Loisy, Wellhausen and Johannes Weiss. As time went on, Weiss and Wellhausen fell from favour in Montefiore's eyes. They had featured prominently in the first edition of the *Synoptic Gospels*, but Montefiore increasingly came to see them as championing 'an older, less critical and more orthodox point of view'.[196] The German theologian Weiss (1863–1914) is remembered for his eschatological interpretations of the Gospel (articulated as early as 1892) and for setting forth the principles of 'Form-criticism' in 1912.[197] While Montefiore greatly appreciated the form-critical approach, he was not in the least interested in christological questions. By the time of the second edition of the *Synoptic Gospels* (1927), he was referring instead to the works of Streeter, Burkitt and Lake. As has already been noted, he was also impressed with the newcomer, Bultmann.

Montefiore was certainly familiar with the results of Form-criticism through the writings of Bultmann, Schmidt and Martin Dibelius (1883–1947). These men pioneered the scientific study of the history of the literary forms in which the various traditions about Jesus have come down to us. Dibelius' major work, *Die Formgeschichte des Evangeliums* (1919),[198] was not translated until 1934 but this did not affect Montefiore, whose 1927 edition of the *Synoptic Gospels* made frequent reference to it. Dibelius presented an analysis of the Gospels in terms of oral traditions; working on the foundations of Weiss, he laid great emphasis on preaching as the medium for the transmission of Jesus' words. Also, throughout his writings Dibelius pursued the origins of ethical statements found in the New Testament and other early Christian writings. All this had great appeal for Montefiore whose own interest was primarily in the ethical teachings of Jesus.

This interest in ethics helps to explain why Montefiore tended to steer clear of certain Christian scholars, including Schweitzer (as Walter Jacob claimed). Montefiore avoided the Christ-centred questions that had come to dominate European New Testament studies through the writings of Harnack and Loisy.[199] From this point of view, a substantial proportion of the contemporary scholarship would have been irrelevant to him. An example of this would be the work of Francis Crawford Burkitt (1864–1935). Montefiore used his *Gospel History and its Transmission* (1920), in which the problems of Mark and its composition were discussed, in his introduction to the *Synoptic Gospels*. He was easily persuaded by Burkitt's suggestion that the important thing was not whether a parable or saying actually originated with Jesus, or when and where it was first uttered, but that 'one must realise that this is the kind of teaching which the Evangelist thought worthy to put in his Lord's mouth, and which the Church accepted as worthy'.[200] Such a stance well suited Montefiore's general approach of treating the 'overall spirit' of the Gospels, rather than worrying about precisely where teachings originated. On the other hand, the fact that Burkitt followed Weiss in rejecting the views of Liberal Protestantism and making an eschatological interpretation for Jesus' teachings meant little to Montefiore. He simply did not concern himself with questions that sought to elucidate the nature of Christ.

Schweitzer's (1875–1965) *The Quest of the Historical Jesus* (1906)[201] was a summary of a survey of all the critical research on the life of Christ carried out in Germany (and a few places elsewhere). It is difficult to believe that Montefiore had not seen the book, certainly by the time of the 1927 edition of the *Synoptic Gospels*, yet he makes no mention of it. In an article in 1931, Montefiore hinted at how it had been possible for him to have overlooked Schweitzer's contribution.[202] He admitted that the liberal view of Jesus had been 'somewhat shaken' by the emergence of the 'Apocalyptic' school of critics. Nevertheless, he reasoned, if Jesus had expected some sort of catastrophe, he would have attributed it to God, acting in the interests of humanity at large and not exclusively for the Jews. Thus he felt that 'the older, more peaceable [Liberal] view of Jesus has been able, with more or less success, to absorb the apocalyptic view, and still to continue its assertion of the non-national and non-political character of the teaching and the life of the Gospel hero'.[203] The fact that Schweitzer also took up Weiss' view that Jesus' preaching of the Kingdom had followed the general lines of contemporary apocalyptic meant that he was arguing along lines which, as noted previously, Montefiore was uninterested in; such an understanding of Jesus as Schweitzer proposed contradicted Montefiore's vision of Jesus as a prophetic moralist, a sort of proto-liberal. Another reason stems from the fact that, whilst simultaneously viewing the historical Jesus as a product of the remote and obscure first-century apocalyptic, Schweitzer had argued that the personality of Jesus was something from which modern man could learn of God – the implication being that it was no longer possible to separate the teaching of Jesus from Jesus himself, or view him as a 'modern' ethical teacher. Montefiore would not have been able to agree with any of this. Nor would he have agreed with

Schweitzer's eventual conclusion that no 'Life of Jesus' was possible since the material needed to produce something approaching a modern biography was unavailable.[204] Montefiore by no means rejected out-of-hand the possibility that there had been an eschatological strand to Jesus' teaching. In practice, however, he tended to overlook it in favour of what he regarded as the essentially ethical dimension.[205]

Of far greater interest to Montefiore was the direction in which other liberal Christian scholars, such as Kirsopp Lake (1872–1946), were headed. Lake was regarded as somewhat unorthodox by his contemporaries for *The Historical Evidences for the Resurrection of Jesus Christ* (1907) in which he argues that the resurrection could not have occurred in the way recorded in the New Testament. The story of the empty tomb was not, he felt, convincing evidence and so the resurrection must have happened in another way or in another sense. While Montefiore tended away from this highly controversial area himself, he would have sympathised with and been greatly encouraged by such Christian rationalism; he certainly felt comfortable enough to contribute a section to *The Beginnings of Christianity* (5 vols, 1920–33) which had been co-edited by Lake and Foakes Jackson.

While many Christian readers found Montefiore's work on the New Testament likewise outside the pale, Jews were suspicious of his apparent role as an apologist for Christianity.[206] *The Synoptic Gospels*, for example, was viewed as the thin end of a (conversionist) wedge by the Jewish Press, at the same time as being recognised as 'the most important and the most interesting [book] ever yet written by a Jew on the New Testament'.[207] In the company of like-minded liberals, however, he was better received. James Parkes later remarked upon 'the spirit of serene objectivity, humility and courtesy ... [of] his commentary on the synoptic gospels'.[208] And in his highly complimentary appraisal of Montefiore in *Speculum Religionis* (1929), F.C. Burkitt viewed their theological differences not so much as a barrier but as an opportunity; he emphasised the special contribution that Montefiore, as a non-Christian, had made to the field of New Testament studies. As he put it,

> Well, then, we Christians will not make the mistake of trying to praise Dr. Montefiore's works on the Gospels and their hero for the wrong thing, for their being very

nearly Christian. Their interest lies exactly in this, that they are not Christian.[209]

Many other liberal Christians also appreciated his outsider viewpoint.[210] By illuminating the Gospels with reference to Jewish sources in *Rabbinic Literature and Gospel Teaching* (1930), in particular, Montefiore reinforced the work of Jewish scholars such as Schechter in placing the roots of Christianity well and truly in the soil of first-century Judaism. He presented a fairer view of the Pharisees and of the higher ethical teachings of the rabbis (which included the Fatherhood of God and the need for repentance and forgiveness) for Christian theologians to digest. Such aspects of his work are of lasting value.

BIBLICAL CRITICISM AND JEWISH LEARNING

One important characteristic of Montefiore's writings on biblical criticism was his opposition to the contemporary misportrayals of both biblical and Rabbinic Judaism. This was certainly one of the reasons why the Jewish Press continued in their support of him, despite his radical views on other matters.[211] Biblical critical works, heavily influenced by the German Protestant view, tended to equate a religion of ordinances with a religion of slavery (Wellhausen's theories on the Hebrew Bible, for example, and the associated view of the Gospels not as a product of Pharisaic Judaism but as a successful protest against it). As a result, many Reform Jews were stung into exploring the first-century period in order to combat Christian claims of supersessionism.[212] As Montefiore himself once put it, 'my German masters ... led me to defend the Rabbis'.[213] He cited examples of such views in the writings of Schultz and Schürer in his *Hibbert Lectures* (1893),[214] views which were later taken up by Bousset and Harnack. Bousset's *The Religion of Judaism at the Time of the New Testament* (1903) had presented Judaism as a religion of external observance lacking sincerity; and while Harnack's *The Essence of Christianity* (1900) had acknowledged that Jesus had taught nothing new to Judaism, he argued that it had been taught in a new way: whereas Judaism had smothered its religious spirituality, Jesus' teachings were concentrated and untarnished by Pharisaism.

Codified ordinances have been central to Judaism from the time of Nehemiah onwards, and many scholars including Schultz felt that since the main bulk of the Law was ceremonial, then it could only have been observed out of fear of punishment or hope of reward. Montefiore denied that this was necessarily so. He argued that Jewish legalism 'is not precisely the legalism which the non-Jewish community supposes it to be'. While admitting that it had 'some of the characteristics of the conventional legalism', he insisted that the Hebrew Bible was also responsible for producing 'the excellencies of Jewish legalism … which made it, as it were, include the corrections to its own weaknesses'.[215] Likewise, in reminding his Christian readers that 'Torah is not quite rightly translated by Law'[216] he highlighted the misconceptions that gave rise to the negative attitude towards the Law.

Montefiore reacted against the fact that 'frequently, in Christian books, is Old Testament contrasted with New Testament: the one crude, elementary, imperfect; the other complete, perfect, incomparable'.[217] He found this to be especially true with regard to ethics, and in 1917 he wrote an article, 'The Old Testament and Its Ethical Teaching', which attempted to redress the balance. He was concerned to refute the idea that concepts of morality in the Hebrew Bible had been transcended, that the modern world had got beyond these altogether and that the highest moral conceptions always originated from sources other than the Old Testament.[218] He felt that the teachings of the Hebrew Bible were devalued in two ways. Firstly, too much emphasis was laid upon its most primitive, least ethical elements, which were regarded as characteristic of the whole; what he described as the 'best things in it' were either attributed to outside influences or simply ignored. Such 'excellencies of the Old Testament' should, he explained, be regarded as essential characteristics of the whole. They were not casual, disconnected or occasional. Rather, they were

> organically connected with the entire development, bone of its bone, spirit of its spirit. The ethical monotheism of the Prophets is reproduced in the Law and the Psalter and the Wisdom Literature. The virtues of justice and compassion are the keynotes of the growing morality.[219]

He felt that the three Old Testament virtues of justice, compassion and loving-kindness were the moving forces of the best of the Old Testament morality and made up the very essence of the whole. Secondly, on the other hand, the 'cruelties and the imprecations' which, he felt, were focused upon by Christian critics could be thought of as the primitive residue which the Israelite religion was working to overcome. He recognised the defects in many Old Testament 'doctrines' and, as a liberal, denounced the 'narrowness and particularism' which 'disfigured' it. But he denied that doctrines of retribution and 'tit-for-tat', for example, were evil as such, arguing that they were the results of an exaggerated and perverted desire for justice.[220] Likewise, the idea of loving one's neighbour and hating one's enemy was not, in Montefiore's opinion, a characteristic teaching of the Hebrew Bible, as Christian critics claimed. These 'painfully anxious' attempts to show up the limitations of the Old Testament were, he suspected, motivated by their need to leave more space for the originality of Jesus.[221]

Montefiore was well placed to see the limitations of Christian scholarship. As Burkitt observed, 'It needed someone who was independent of the masterful thought of St. Paul to do justice to the religion of the Law.'[222] But it was not just their concept of biblical Judaism that needed re-thinking. Montefiore made an even more important contribution by arguing with Christian scholars that the rabbinic religion was, contrary to their beliefs, in many respects higher than the teachings of the Old Testament. An example of this (one that, perhaps, only Montefiore could have suggested), was the rabbis' non-literal approach to the Hebrew Bible. As he put it,

> It is rather anachronistic to regard the Rabbis as a sort of early example of Progressive and Liberal Jews, but, nevertheless, they did a great work for Judaism. They saved us from becoming a book religion in the sense that every word of the book must be accepted in its most literal sense, as perfect and unimprovable. Their 'readings in', their developments, their additions, maintained a certain flow, a certain unrigidity. They prevented the slaughter of the spirit by the letter ... In a pre-critical age the Rabbinic interpretations and developments were, in a sense, the pre-cursor ... of Modernist freedom. The old Rabbinic development paved the way for the new liberal developments.[223]

While there were other Jews with similar agendas, including Solomon Schechter and Israel Abrahams in England,[224] few Christians were sympathetic or prepared to revise their misconceptions. One exception was the American biblical scholar George Foot Moore (1851–1931) whose own research followed similar lines, and of whom Montefiore was very impressed; in 1897 Montefiore referred to 'a great book on Judaism ... by that amazing creature G.F. Moore'.[225] Later, in his *Judaism in the First Centuries of the Christian Era* (3 vols, 1927–30), and in a long article 'Christian Writers on Judaism',[226] Moore attempted to show that the Jewish belief that it was necessary to keep the Torah was not intended to earn membership within the people of God, but was an expression of it.[227] He also pointed out that the Jews did not despair when they failed; they could repent and had the sacrificial system to deal with sins committed under the Law. In addition, Moore did not accept that apocalyptic interests lay within the main current of Jewish thought and was therefore prepared to accept the rabbinic sources as the best representation of mainstream Judaism.

Yet it seemed to Montefiore (who was by no means looking upon the world with traditional Jewish eyes), as though he and his fellow champions of Jewish learning were hitting their heads against a solid wall of Christian resistance. In an article entitled 'Jewish Scholarship and Christian Silence' (1903), he expressed his frustration at 'the absolute neglect of everything which is said upon the other side', something which in other fields of scholarship, he protested, was unusual or unknown.[228] Targeting especially the German Protestant scholars with whom he was so familiar, he charged the biblical critical Christian fraternity with almost entirely ignoring what the Jewish scholars had to say. The German Protestant scholars occupied a 'peculiar position', he observed dryly.

> To them by no means every statement contained in the New Testament is accurate, but at least every statement against the 'Pharisees' and the Rabbinic religion is accurate.[229]

Protesting against this one sided, traditionally biased approach, he asked of men as well-known as Holtzmann, Harnack and Schürer,

> Is it possible that what the Jewish scholars have to say is so silly, so contemptibly prejudiced, so utterly erroneous, that it is really too much to expect that any Christian scholar can notice it?[230]

The situation was in Montefiore's eyes ridiculous since, with a very few exceptions such as Dalman and Delitzsch,[231] no Christian was familiar with the subject on a first-hand basis. 'Who writes a page on the subject without reference to the inevitable Weber?' he complained, referring to a German Protestant attempt to outline a systematic Talmudic theology.[232] He suggested that Jewish scholars carried part of the blame in failing to provide better alternatives and for failing to provide their own translations of the Midrash. Jewish scholars, he felt, had done little to make their historic theology available for non-Jewish scholars. This could be explained in terms of their isolationism and ghetto-ised intellectualism.

> They have not lived enough in Christian society, been sufficiently in touch with Christian life, or adequately versed in Christian literature, to know what was the sort of thing which wanted saying, or the kind of defence which was required.[233]

Such a background was, of course, precisely the kind that Montefiore himself had enjoyed, and it enabled him to contribute as much as he did. *A Rabbinic Anthology* (1938), written in association with Herbert Loewe, is perhaps the best example of how he himself went about answering the need as he had seen it in 1903; this classic work, although undeniably dated in its presentation and format, remains a useful collection of rabbinic materials. At the time of 'Jewish Scholarship and Christian Silence', however, Montefiore drew attention to the work of his friend and tutor Solomon Schechter, who had recently published a series of articles on rabbinic theology in the *Jewish Quarterly Review*. As he pointedly observed, 'If Schechter is right, [then] the ordinary commonplaces of Christian theologians about Rabbinic Judaism are wrong.' To his bewilderment, the articles of 'one of the greatest Rabbinical scholars of the world' had gone unnoticed.[234]

The answer to the overwhelming Christian silence, Montefiore concluded, lay in their reluctance to face the consequences of accepting Jewish scholarship. After all, rabbinic theology had some relation to the history of Christianity, especially with regard to Paul, and it certainly made a difference whether the rabbinic religion was to be regarded as good or bad. If, as the Jews insisted, it had been good, there would follow a re-assessment of much of the New Testament teaching. 'Is that the real reason why the Christian scholars refuse to listen?' he asked.[235]

In recent times, E.P. Sanders and others have exposed the way in which German scholars (particularly Weber, Schürer, Bousset, Billerbeck and Bultmann) had expounded Judaism in terms borrowed (anachronistically) from Reformation polemic.[236] Sanders saw no parallel between Paul's argument with the Judaism of his day and Luther's condemnations of the legalism of the Church of Rome, and he denied that Paul could be thought of as a sort of proto-Protestant. He was very critical of the way in which these men had created through their massive scholarly output an aura of apparent objectivity around a false position. Susannah Heschel has shown that Wellhausen, Schürer, Bousset and the others do not say anything original, that their anti-Judaism is not new but simply repeats older motifs.[237] This is all the more damning since it cannot be excused by ignorance. By the last quarter of the nineteenth-century, Christian scholars were clearly no longer writing in an environment closed off from Jewish thought, but rather in an intellectual atmosphere in which Jewish writers like Montefiore were championing their own case.[238] For whatever reasons, scholars were better prepared to listen to Sanders after the Second World War than they had been to acknowledge Montefiore, Abrahams, Schechter, Moore and others before.

Conclusion

This section began by asking the question 'What were the specifically Christian factors which made for Montefiore's special relationship with Christianity?' In answering it, the nature of the Jewish reforming movements was re-examined and the extent of the effect of the Christian critique upon them was assessed. The influences of various Christian models including Tractarianism, Evangelical conversionism, and Anglican liberalism were then considered, together with the influences of the ancient Greek thought and the social fixation upon Progress which combined so powerfully in England towards the end of the century. The overall impression is that many of the factors that contributed to Montefiore's peculiar view can be largely explained in terms of various *Christian* influences. Of course there was much more to it than that, and the Jewish influences should not be understated. But there can be no doubt that a number of identifiable strands of Christian thought were absorbed by Montefiore to a profound effect, and integrated and expressed in his understanding of Judaism.

This section has also attempted to assess the undoubted impact of Christian scholarship, especially Liberal Protestant scholarship, upon Montefiore's own biblical studies. Yet he had his own way of going about it, determined by his intense desire to teach religious truth, as he saw it. He approached both the Hebrew Bible and the New Testament in a very similar fashion to the way in which he had approached the rabbinic and Hellenistic literatures. For much of the time he seemed to work with the New Testament as a collection of documents to be analysed with reference to other scholars. The rest of the time he worked with what he perceived as its overall spirit for what might be regarded as devotional purposes, and seemed little interested in the conclusions of critical scholarship. Even while taking into account the widespread influences of nineteenth-century rationalism and idealism, it will have to be admitted that there is a grain of truth to Schechter's claim that 'What the whole thing means, is not Liberal Judaism, but Liberal Christianity.'[239] Montefiore himself violently disputed this, but his over-arching concern for Righteousness and religious truth, from wherever it might be found, and the resulting eclectic nature of Liberal Jewish theology, has left him vulnerable to the charge.

NOTES

165. R.E. Clements, *100 Years of Old Testament Interpretation* (1976), p. 3.
166. The English translation, *The History of Israel*, was published in 1885.
167. A notorious example, Gerhard Kittel (1888–1948), the German editor of the *Theological Dictionary of the New Testament* (begun in 1931, finished in 1976) has been condemned for his 'solid and impenitent Nazi sympathies' (S. Neill and T. Wright, *The Interpretation of the New Testament 1861–1986* (1989), p. 374, n.1).
168. C.G. Montefiore, 'Some Notes on the Effects of Biblical Criticism upon the Jewish Religion', *Jewish Quarterly Review*, IV (1891–92), p. 293.
169. Letter from Benjamin Jowett, 16 October 1891. L. Cohen, *Some Recollections of Claude Goldsmid-Montefiore 1858–1938* (1940), p. 54.
170. F.C. Burkitt, ed., *Speculum Religionis* (1929), p. 2.
171. One aim of Liberal Judaism was to be 'the realisation of justice and compassion; the accomplishment of the prophets' dream'. C.G. Montefiore, *Outlines of Liberal Judaism* (1923), p. 277.
172. Montefiore diverged significantly from Wellhausen only with respect to Wellhausen's (negative) estimation of the Jewish Law, to which we shall return later.
173. F.C. Burkitt, ed., *Speculum Religionis* (1929), p. 2.
174. C.G. Montefiore, *The Hibbert Lectures: On the Origin and Growth of Religion as Illustrated by the Religion of the Ancient Hebrews* (1893), p. 4.
175. Pfleiderer (1836–1900) has been called the father of religio-historical study in Germany. In any case, the *Religionsgeschichtelichte* sought to interpret Jesus and early Christianity by reference to the beliefs and practices of late Hellenism; it saw the New Testament as part of the religious processes at work in the Levant in the period before and after Christianity. For the Religio-Historical school as for the Ritschlians, Christianity was not to be understood to be either historically or phenomenologically unique. Instead, it was a complex 'syncretistic religion', a product of Late Judaism (whose apocalypticism, according to Bousset, involved a strain of Persian influence), Oriental eschatology, Greek mysteries, Gnosticism and Stoicism. Christianity was thus a synthesisation of Western and Oriental ideas at a time when they were converging.
176. W.G. Kümmel, *The New Testament: The History of the Investigations of its Problems* (1973), pp. 346–9.
177. The German original, *Das Wesen des Christenthums* was published in 1900.
178. C.G. Montefiore, 'The Religious Teaching of Jowett', *Jewish Quarterly Review*, XII (1899–1900), p. 314.
179. B. Jowett, *Life* (1879), II, 85, cited in C.G. Montefiore, 'The Religious Teaching of Jowett', *Jewish Quarterly Review*, XII (1899–1900), p. 312.

180. Letter from C.G. Montefiore to Hastings Rashdall, June 1916. MS Eng. Lett. c348, fol. 100–11, Bodleian.

181. In a letter to Rashdall (26 December 1919) Montefiore thanked him for his consistently favourable reviews. 'I am very obliged for your kind references to my little books, and am proud that you found them any good.' MS Eng. Lett. c349, fol. 202–5, Bodleian.

182. Letter from Hastings Rashdall to C.G. Montefiore, 31 December 1913, cited in H. Handley, 'Claude Montefiore', *The Modern Churchman*, p. 415, ACC/3529/4/9, L.M.A.

183. Including C.G. Montefiore's *The Synoptic Gospels* (1909).

184. C.G. Montefiore, 'Some Notes on the Effects of Biblical Criticism upon the Jewish Religion', *Jewish Quarterly Review*, IV (1891–92), p. 297.

185. W.R. Matthews, 'Claude Montefiore: The Man and his Thought', 1st Claude Montefiore Lecture, Southampton (1956), p. 13.

186. Writing in the mid-1920s, he observed, 'The detailed and elaborate work of Bultmann in this connection seems little known or appreciated so far in England ... Though his conclusions, as regards the authenticity and "historicity" of many stories and sayings, is much overdone, it is (as it seems to me) very improbable that his work will leave things as they were and remain without influence or effect.' C.G. Montefiore, *The Synoptic Gospels*, 2nd edn, 2 vols (1927), I, pp. lvi–lvii. It should be noted that Bultmann's programme of demythologising was only explicitly set out in an essay published in 1941, after Montefiore's death.

187. Matthews calls this a 'hard saying' since Montefiore's 'zeal for righteousness was one of his most salient and most loveable characteristics'. W.R. Matthews, 'Claude Montefiore: The Man and his Thought', 1st Claude Montefiore Lecture, Southampton (1956), p. 14.

188. For example, Joseph Klausner, Hebrew University in Jerusalem, who wrote *Jesus of Nazareth* (1929), and Israel Abrahams who wrote *Studies in Pharisaism and the Gospels* (1917–24).

189. Thus, for example, Montefiore's *Outlines of Liberal Judaism* (1912) considered *inter alia* the problem of evil, the development of the idea of God, the idea of miracles, of the individual, of immortality, and the differences between Christianity and Judaism; it appropriated a modern Christian agenda. While Schechter's *Some Aspects of Rabbinic Theology* (1909) used a similar vocabulary, it focused mainly on Torah, the place of Israel, and sin and repentance; in comparison, it was more concerned with defending Judaism on certain subject areas of Christian interest than in utilising these areas to define Judaism itself.

190. W. Jacob, 'Claude G. Montefiore's Reappraisal of Christianity', *Judaism*, IXX (Summer 1970), p. 342.

191. W. Jacob, *Christianity Through Jewish Eyes: The Quest for Common Ground* (1974), p. 109.

192. In the introduction of the *Synoptic Gospels* Montefiore viewed favourably Streeter's famous 'four document hypothesis' and expressed his admiration for Streeter's originality and comprehension of the 'Synoptic Problem'.

193. The first edition of *The Synoptic Gospels* (1909) was written before Schweitzer's *The Quest of the Historical Jesus* (the German original *Von Reimarus zu Wrede* was published in 1906). The second edition (1927) also makes no mention of Schweitzer's works.

194. Joseph Carpenter, *First Three Gospels* (1890), p. 9, cited in C.G. Montefiore, *The Synoptic Gospels*, 2nd edn, 2 vols (1927), I, p. xxi. An eminent figure in

modern Unitarianism, Carpenter was respected for his extensive knowledge in comparative religion and Semitic literature. He wrote *The First Three Gospels* (1890) and *The Johannine Writings* (1927). He was a good friend of Montefiore and proof-read many of his works.

195. Montefiore's anti-mystical tendency might be the main reason for his general dismissal of John's Gospel; his close colleague Israel Abrahams is cited (without a reference) as commenting, 'to us Jews the Fourth Gospel is the most Jewish of the four', in S. Neill and T. Wright, *The Interpretation of the New Testament 1861–1986* (1989), p. 338, n.2.

196. C.G. Montefiore, *The Synoptic Gospels*, 2nd edn, 2 vols (1927), I, p. x.

197. That is the analysis of biblical passages through examination of their structured form (*formgeschichte*).

198. That is, 'Form-criticism of the Gospels'; English translation *From Tradition to Gospel* (1934).

199. In *What is Christianity?* (English translation 1901), Harnack had suggested that the authentic teachings of Jesus (a sort of individualist piety) had been lost amongst a historical build-up of dogma. Loisy, in *The Gospel and the Church* (English translation 1903), had argued that Jesus had preached a supernatural kingdom that, far from being lost in historic developments, had found its ultimate expression in the Church. Montefiore was not the least bit interested in such matters.

200. F.C. Burkitt, *Gospel History and its Transmission*, 4th edition (1920), p. 206, cited in C.G. Montefiore, *The Synoptic Gospels*, 2nd edn, 2 vols (1927), I, pp. lxxxi–lxxxii.

201. The German original, *Von Reimarus zu Wrede*, was published in 1906; the first English translation appeared in 1910.

202. C.G. Montefiore, 'Dr. Robert Eisler on the Beginnings of Christianity', *Hibbert Journal*, XXX (1931–32), pp. 304–5.

203. Ibid.

204. Of course, Schweitzer nevertheless offered his own sketch of the 'historical Jesus' (as did Bultmann).

205. For instance, discussing the end-of-times passage in Mark 13, Montefiore explained that although it was by no means inconceivable that Jesus had thought in such terms, nevertheless such material 'has very slight interest for us today and little or no religious value'. C.G. Montefiore, *The Synoptic Gospels*, 2nd edn, 2 vols (1927), I, p. 296.

206. The Jewish scholar, Adolph Büchler, who himself praised *The Synoptic Gospels*, warned in a letter to Montefiore (1927), 'It is a fine piece of work and of literary presentation, which, in spite of its usual objectivity and moderation, will only be accepted after a prolonged struggle and with heart-burning.' ACC/3529/4/4, L.M.A. Leonard Montefiore, Claude's son, collected together some of the letters which his father had received regarding *The Synoptic Gospels* for the Liberal Jewish Archives. In a covering letter (27 August 1956) he makes the point that despite its positive reception by Christian scholars, Claude's position was by no means mistaken at the time as a Christian one. 'Conceivably the future historian of the L.J.S. [Liberal Jewish Synagogue] might use some of them to refute any suggestions that the Wharncliffe Rooms, Hill St, St. John's Wood Rd [that is, some of the J.R.U. and Liberal Jewish places of worship] were stations on the way to conversion – or apostasy.' ACC/3529/4/4, L.M.A.

207. *Jewish Chronicle*, 17 December 1909, p. 26.

208. J. Parkes, 'Theology of Toleration', 10th Claude Montefiore Lecture (1966).

209. F.C. Burkitt, ed., *Speculum Religionis* (1929), p. 7.

210. Several of the letters Montefiore received in response to the second edition of *The Synoptic Gospels* (1927) have survived. Thus T.K. Cheyne regarded it 'as an important contribution to the reconciliation of two great kindred religions'. A.C. Clark wrote that the work 'appears to me both novel and fascinating … I have been talking about the book to a colleague of mine, B.H. Streeter, who is wrapt up in The Synoptic Problem, and I am going to lend it to him'. H. Handley commented, 'I believe your book to be a classic. Our noble friend Rashdall, so competent, I have heard speak of it [the 1909 edition] in the highest terms and say that he frequently used it.' And A.S. Peake observed, 'I have always thought that the fullness with which you reported and often quoted at length the views of foreign scholars made the first edition very valuable to students … It is gratifying to see that the more recent literature has been rendered accessible in the same way.' ACC/3259/4/4, L.M.A.

211. From the time of his Hibbert Lectures (1892), the *Jewish Chronicle* argued that Montefiore's advanced viewpoint was counterbalanced by his work in correcting Christian misconceptions of Judaism. 'Far from being antagonistic to Judaism, Mr Montefiore has performed a signal service to it; and this opinion may be held without conceding that Mr Montefiore has found the truth.' The value of the lectures lay in their function as 'a defence of Rabbinism. We should not be going too far if we described them as a glowing glorification of it, in some of its aspects, at least.' *Jewish Chronicle*, 10 June 1892, p. 11.

212. M. Hilton, *The Christian Effect on Jewish Life* (1994), p. 130.

213. C.G. Montefiore, 'Liberal Judaism and the Law', cited in E. Kessler, 'Claude Montefiore', *Jewish–Christian Relations*, XXI (Winter 1988), p. 10.

214. This is significant because Emil Schürer's later *History of the Jewish People in the Time of Jesus* (3 vols, 1886–90; English translation 5 vols, 1890–91), although dated, remains a standard work on the subject. Montefiore regards Schürer's attitude to be too negative towards the spirit of Judaism.

215. C.G. Montefiore, 'The Old Testament and Judaism', in W. Robinson, ed., *Record and Revelation*, (1938), p. 436.

216. Ibid., p. 435.

217. Ibid., p. 451.

218. C.G. Montefiore, 'The Old Testament and Its Ethical Teaching', *P.F.J.P.*, XV (1917), p. 234.

219. Ibid., p. 236.

220. Ibid., pp. 237, 239, 243.

221. Ibid., p. 244.

222. F.C. Burkitt, ed., *Speculum Religionis* (1929), p. 6.

223. C.G. Montefiore, 'The Old Testament and Judaism', in W. Robinson, ed., *Record and Revelation*, (1938), pp. 428–9.

224. For example, in an article in 1899, Abrahams condemned Schürer for failing to have taken Montefiore's criticisms into account in the third edition of his *History of the Jewish People in the Time of Jesus*. He wrote, 'Is this to go on? Is the Law to be searched for no other purpose than to find justifications for Paul? Are the Rabbinical sayings to be examined simply as foils to the Gospels? … Why is it that a man like Mr. Montefiore has been moved to such unwonted heat when dealing with Schürer's charges against the Law?' I. Abrahams, 'Prof. Schürer on Life Under Jewish Law', *Jewish Quarterly Review*, XI (1899), p. 640–1.

225. Letter from C.G. Montefiore to Lucy Cohen, 9 April 1897. L. Cohen, *Some Recollections of Claude Goldsmid-Montefiore 1858–1938* (1940), p. 171.

226. G.F. Moore, 'Christian Writers on Judaism', *Harvard Theological Review*, XIV (1921), pp. 197–254.
227. 'Covenantal Nomism', as E.P. Sanders later called it.
228. C.G. Montefiore, 'Jewish Scholarship and Christian Silence', *Hibbert Journal*, I (1903), p. 336.
229. C.G. Montefiore, 'Jewish Scholarship and Christian Silence', *Hibbert Journal*, I (1903), p. 339.
230. Ibid., p. 336.
231. Montefiore cited Gustaf Dalman (1855–1941), who was a biblical scholar with an intense interest in the archaeology of the Holy Land. He produced important studies on the language, ideas and customs of the first-century Palestine. As Montefiore pointed out, he was one of the highly exceptional Christian scholars who were at home in the rabbinical literature. Another was Franz Delitzsch, a Lutheran Old Testament scholar of Jewish descent, who wrote extensively on rabbinic subjects.
232. Ferdinand Weber, *System of Palestinian Theology in the Early Synagogues* (1880). The second edition was entitled *Jewish Theology Exhibited on the Basis of the Talmud and Allied Writings* (1897). Montefiore was not impressed with Weber.
233. C.G. Montefiore, 'Jewish Scholarship and Christian Silence', *Hibbert Journal*, I (1903), pp. 335–46, 337.
234. Ibid., p. 338.
235. Elsewhere Montefiore wrote on a similar vein that German critics 'freely use the language of mocking irreverence … [I]n Wellhausen, who is responsible for this ugly fashion, brilliance and even genius cover the gravity and the descent from the language of Ewald. But in the hands of ordinary clever and industrious German professors, this laborious humour is quite unendurable, and the anti-Semitic prejudice, which is presumably at the bottom of it all is only too easily and clumsily revealed.' C.G. Montefiore, 'Biblical Criticism and the Pulpit', *Jewish Quarterly Review*, XVIII (1906), p. 310, cited in E. Kessler, 'Claude Montefiore: Defender of Rabbinic Judaism?', *Jewish Historical Studies: Transactions of the Jewish Historical Society of England*, XXXV (1996–98).
236. For example, E.P. Sanders, *Paul and Palestinian Judaism* (1977).
237. S. Heschel, 'The Image of Judaism in Nineteenth-Century New Testament Scholarship in Germany', in M. Perry and F.M. Schweitzer, eds, *Jewish–Christian Encounters over the Centuries* (1994), pp. 231–2.
238. Ibid., p. 232.
239. Cited in R. Apple, *The Hampstead Synagogue* (1967), p. 38.

PART THREE

MONTEFIORE AND JEWISH
APPROACHES TO JESUS AND PAUL

12

Montefiore and Jesus

INTRODUCTION

Montefiore was a Jewish pioneer in Gospel research, and the study of Jesus and his teachings took up a considerable amount of his time and energy. The central figure of the Christian religion was important to him both psychologically and theologically. For Montefiore, Jesus belonged well and truly within the realm of discourse within the Jewish tradition,[1] and he was convinced that once Christendom had rid itself of antisemitism, Jews would be willing to think more positively about the founders and the sacred books of Christianity.[2] An understanding of Montefiore's peculiar appreciation of Jesus therefore throws much light upon his own distinctive thought and upon his hopes for absorbing many aspects of Christian teaching into Liberal Judaism.

Montefiore stands out from other Jewish authors for his uncommon fascination with Jesus, his voluminous writings on the subject, and his contribution to mainstream New Testament studies. He is also remarkable for the way in which he anticipated later Jewish approaches. His studies of Jesus abandoned the concerns of previous Jewish writers (who had focused on issues such as Jewish guilt regarding Jesus' death) and emphasised instead Jesus' ethical teachings. He led the way in actually combining the critical techniques of mainstream New Testament studies with the insights gained from a knowledge of the rabbinic literature.[3] Many of the assumptions he made concerning the Gospel evidence in his reclamation of Jesus as a Jew characterise those of subsequent Jewish scholarship. And, to a lesser extent, he was followed by later Jewish writers in the way in which he approached Jesus with a view to enriching his own understanding of Judaism, and in his avoidance of any unnecessary antagonism of Christian sensitivities. As Donald Hagner put it in 1984, 'When one is familiar with [Montefiore's] writings, one finds little that is really new in the burgeoning Jewish literature of our day.'[4]

In response to Jewish criticism, Montefiore admitted to a certain reliance upon Christian scholarship but he always reserved the right to disagree with them and to correct them when he felt it necessary.[5] He produced two works in particular in which he demonstrated his understanding of contemporary Gospel research and his perception of where the gaps in knowledge lay. *The Synoptic Gospels* (1909), an introduction, translation and commentary on the first three Gospels, was exceptional among Jewish studies both in terms of its familiarity with Christian scholarship and in terms of the relatively greater attention it received from Christian scholars.[6] A few years after the second edition was published in 1927, it was supplemented by *Rabbinic Literature and Gospel Teachings* (1930).[7] With this book, Montefiore attempted to demonstrate the proximity of rabbinic thought to Jesus' own, and to correct some of the distortions contained in the influential Christian *Kommentar* by Strack and Billerbeck.[8] As always with Montefiore, who himself recognised that he 'looked at both the Gospel and the Rabbinic material through the spectacles of Liberal Judaism',[9] there was a tension between approaching the material from a purely historically critical perspective, and allocating a value-judgement to it. Scholarship was only a tool and, even in these books which are amongst his most technical and specialist works, it was of secondary importance. He was more concerned with the implications of the texts for later Jewish and Christian thought and the relevance of the material for his own day.[10]

JEWISH VIEWS ON THE ORIGINALITY OF JESUS' TEACHING

The vast majority of Jews drawn to the study of Jesus have been Reform or Liberal, and there are doubtless many reasons for this. The tendency among reform minded Jews to move away from the idea of Judaism as a nation, and to view it rather as a religious fellowship, was very much related to the new emphasis on ethics as central to their religious message. In this context, Jesus and his ethical teaching appeared interesting and relevant. Also, for those who were critical of Orthodox Jewish ritual, Jesus represented the struggle of free spirituality against ceremonialism in an earlier era. Yet Jewish reclamations of Jesus were driven by more than simply the intellectual concern to recover an earlier Jewish ethical tradition, or the satisfaction of discovering an ancient champion of an ethically centred Judaism. Since Luzatto, Salvador, Graetz and Geiger, a stock argument among Jewish writers had been that Jesus' ethical teaching had been wholly Jewish, of one sort or another, and had included nothing new or original. Such treatments provided a platform from which to launch attacks on Christianity, in that they stressed the Jewishness and therefore the humanity of Jesus in contradiction to the traditional christological view of Jesus. In England, Gerald Friedlander's *The Jewish Sources of the Sermon on the Mount* (1911) was a polemical work that emphasised the Jewishness of much of Jesus' teaching. Despite the fact that it was 'of little practical value for everyday life', Friedlander was quick to point out that 'all the teaching in the Sermon [on the Mount] … is in harmony with the spirit of Judaism'.[11] In his anti-Christian apology, *Wesen des Judentums* (1905), Baeck claimed that a full appreciation of the greatness of Jesus was only possible for a Jew, since 'a man like him could have grown only in the soil of Judaism, only there and nowhere else'.[12] This way of confronting Christian claims (regarding Jesus and Judaism) by describing him as essentially Jewish, rather than essentially alien and heretical, was new. It can be at least partially explained by the reaction to Christian critique and the underlying psychological need to justify Judaism in the eyes of the Western (Christian) world. If, as the Orthodox Paul Goodman put it, Jesus had 'added no important original element to the religious and moral assets which had been accumulated by the Jewish prophets and sages',[13] then what justification had Christians for condemning Jewish teaching as inferior to Jesus' teaching? Maintaining Jesus' Jewishness had become a way of justifying Judaism to Christians. Such a view is supported by Schwartz's observation that no non-western Jew has written extensively on Jesus, since the concern to justify Judaism was of no importance, relatively speaking, to Jews outside the West.[14]

Nevertheless, for Jews interested in studying Jesus – even for those who wanted to use Jesus in this particular way – it was difficult to ignore those aspects of his teaching and behaviour which had traditionally been regarded as 'un-Jewish'. There was therefore something of a tension between the desire to hold up Jesus to justify Judaism to a surrounding Christian world, and the often acutely felt obligation to distance Judaism from certain elements of his thought.[15] For example, almost in spite of himself, Goodman had picked up on the idea of non-resistance as something that had no obvious parallel to 'the teaching of the Jewish schools'.[16] Israel Abrahams had been keen to draw attention to the similarities between Jesus' style of teaching and that of the Pharisees, including the use of parables and style of prayer,[17] yet he was also sensitive to certain nuanced differences, such as the greater inclination of Jesus to seek out sinners and the idea of forgiveness as presented in the Lord's Prayer.[18] And, even today, the differences noted by Vermes, while also differences of emphasis rather than of content, included Jesus' tendency to overemphasise the ethical as compared to the ritual and to underestimate those needs of society that are met by organised religion.[19] The tension was exacerbated by the very real risk of being perceived as overly sympathetic towards 'that man' and thereby provoking a backlash from traditionalists who regarded anyone who was even faintly interested in Jesus as traitors to Judaism, be they Liberal or Orthodox. It comes as no surprise to discover that Montefiore's positive assessment of Jesus was denounced for demonstrating 'an anti-Jewish tendency'[20] and led to accusations implying his being a crypto-Christian.[21] But other less positive works were also regarded as betrayals of Judaism. The Zionist Orthodox Jew and disciple of Ahad Ha-Am, Joseph Klausner, saw his *Jesus of Nazareth* (1929) attacked as 'a trucking and kow-towing to the Christian religion, and an assertion of great affection for the foggy figure of its founder, a denial of the healthy sense of our saintly forefathers'.[22]

In distancing themselves from Jesus' distinctive thought, Jewish writers rarely, if ever, contemplated the idea that Jesus' distinctive or allegedly non-Jewish teachings might be beneficial contributions. Rather, they were viewed as mistakes that could be used as foils to demonstrate the superiority of the writer's own view of Judaism. In this sense, it is true to say, as Jacob Agus does, that for many Jewish scholars, Jesus was made to stand for whatever it was that the particular scholar repudiated and excoriated.[23] Very few Jews have focused upon those elements of Jesus and his teachings which distinguished him from his contemporaries unless, for polemical reasons, they intended to criticise him and thus, by association, Christianity. Klausner, whose *Jesus of Nazareth* (1929) illustrates the background dynamics well, provides an interesting example. He certainly wrote admiringly of Jesus and, from a cursory reading, appeared to hold Jesus' originality in high regard, in sharp contrast to the majority of Jewish writers.

> In [Jesus'] ethical code there is a sublimity, a distinctiveness and originality in form unparalleled in any other Hebrew ethical code; neither is there any parallel to the remarkable art of his parables. The shrewdness and sharpness of his proverbs and his forceful epigrams serve, in an exceptional degree, to make ethical ideas a popular possession. If ever the day should come and this ethical code be stripped of its wrappings of miracles and mysticism, the Book of the Ethics of Jesus will be one of the choicest treasures in the literature of Israel for all time.[24]

Nevertheless, Klausner's response to Jesus' originality was more complex than this vague eulogy indicates, and must be weighed against his belief that although Jesus had obviously not been a Christian during his lifetime, he had become one (or should be regarded as one), for his history and his teaching had severed him from Judaism.[25] When it came to concrete examples of Jesus' distinctive teaching, Klausner could not help viewing them as ultimately impractical. Thus Jesus' instruction to 'Give unto Caesar that which is Caesar's and unto God that which is God's' effectively undermined the authority of the civil authorities; his commands to 'resist not evil', to 'swear not at all' and to share all one's possessions with the poor, were simply not practical in society; by forbidding divorce he did not solve family difficulties; and in his recommendation to be like 'the lilies of the field which toil not' he revealed his lack of interest in economic and political achievements.[26] Klausner went on to explain Jesus' failure in the eyes of Judaism in terms of his being *too* Jewish. But more to the point, he criticised the teachings as 'un-Jewish' in the light of his own Zionist, nationalistic view of Judaism.

> In all this Jesus is the most Jewish of Jews, more Jewish than Simeon ben Shetah, more Jewish even than Hillel. Yet nothing is more dangerous to national Judaism than this *exaggerated* Judaism; it is the ruin of national culture, the national state, and national life … This teaching Jesus had imbibed from

the breast of Prophetic and, to a certain extent, Pharisaic Judaism; yet it became, on one hand, the negation of every-thing that had vitalised Judaism; and, on the other hand, it brought Judaism to such an extreme that it became, in a sense, *non-Judaism*.[27]

In other words, Klausner's criticism of Jesus' distinctive teachings was rooted in his own deeply felt, essentially nationalistic view of Judaism. While for other writers, especially reform minded Jews, the nationalistic element was not as important, their criticisms, too, were shaped by their own particular views of Judaism.

To summarise: since the time of Salvador, it had not been uncommon for Jews (mainly among Reform and Liberal circles) to point to Jesus as exemplifying many of the best aspects of an ideal Judaism, so as to demonstrate that so-called Christian virtues were not foreign to modern Judaism. At the same time, while Jesus' alleged differences with Judaism ceased to be as fiercely condemned as they had been in more ancient treatments, such differences continued to be used as foils by which to demonstrate the superiority of the writer's own view of Judaism. One result of the enormous pressure upon Jewish writers to find the teachings of Jesus inferior to those of Judaism was that all too often, even when they agreed with Jesus' teaching, the discussion degenerated into an apologetic argument of mere chronological priority (the implication being that whoever said it first was superior). Sandmel warned that the question of originality was all too often a 'misguided one' for this very reason.[28]

MONTEFIORE'S VIEWS ON THE ORIGINALITY OF JESUS' TEACHING

Montefiore, too, pointed to those teachings that Jesus shared with Judaism as illustrative of its high development and sophistication. And he also recognised the need to correct Christian triumphalism. His *Rabbinic Literature and Gospel Teaching* (1930) was firmly focused upon challenging the Christian over-emphasis of Jesus' originality with respect to the rabbis. Assisted by the rabbinic scholarship of Herbert Loewe, he demonstrated that despite Jesus' apparent criticism of rabbinic legalism, Jesus actually stood closer to the Pharisees/rabbis than Christian scholars were generally prepared to admit. Regarding their conceptions of salvation, for example, while Montefiore did not think that Jesus would have agreed with 'the legalism of the Rabbis', yet 'so far as God's grace and human effort and freedom of will and human weakness and human repentance and God's forgiveness are concerned, the Rabbis and Jesus were by no means poles apart'.[29] Similarly, concerning their respective views of non-Israelites, the differences had been over-emphasised in the past since the rabbis were not *wholly* particularistic and Jesus was not *entirely* universal.[30] Montefiore also reiterated that in the light of the development of their respective theologies, Jesus' teaching could make no claim to religious superiority over the rabbis'. Thus Jesus' attack on the Pharisees as presented in Matthew 23 was, in large measure, unwarranted and unfair.[31]

In the context of an inter-Jewish debate, however, and with regard to the question of Jesus' priority, Montefiore was ready to admit that in many instances Jesus' teachings had chronological priority over those of the rabbis. The issue was largely irrelevant, though, as he explained in 'The Originality of Jesus' (1929),

> For if the later rabbinic parallels are native developments ... then the originality of Jesus, though not to be neglected, is yet, to my mind, a secondary, and comparatively unimportant, originality. A good deal, moreover, depends upon the question whether a doctrine is central and essential for Jesus, but unusual or exceptional for the Rabbis or in the Old Testament. If the latter, then a high degree of originality belongs to Jesus, even though one or two good parallels can be adduced.[32]

It was this higher kind of difference between Jesus' teaching and that of Jewish tradition which most interested him. In contrast to most of his fellow Jewish scholars, who used Jesus' perceived differences as foils for their own ideas of Judaism, Montefiore approached these very same differences in an extremely innovative way and with a distinct set of assumptions. He was not only prepared to accept the originality of some of Jesus' thought but often praised it and even suggested that Judaism could learn from it. In this context, it is important to understand that 'originality' meant more to him than merely 'fresh expression of universal truths' (that is, *Jewish* universal truths) as some have suggested.[33] In 'The Originality of Jesus' (1929), Montefiore defined his use of the term 'original' as *relative*, that is, original in comparison with the ideals and the teaching of Jesus' Jewish contemporaries. He readily admitted that he did not mean absolute originality,[34] and he also denied that by 'originality' he automatically implied excellence.[35] Even so, Jesus' teachings were often, for Montefiore, 'off the main Jewish line of development'. Pursuing, as he was, a radical reform of Judaism, he could not help but hold Jesus in high regard when he saw many of his own anti-Orthodox concerns paralleled in the Gospel narratives. Almost unconsciously, he used Jesus – and Jesus' 'un-Jewish' idiosyncrasies – as a vehicle for expressing his own vision of Judaism. This was possible for Montefiore in a way that it did not seem to be for other Jewish thinkers, even other reformers, primarily because of his particular background which had freed him of the traditional anti-Christian bias and the related fear of betraying Judaism by studying Jesus.[36] As will become clear, Montefiore used Jesus not only to defend Judaism against Christianity but also as a means by which to set out and distance his own vision of Judaism from either Reform or Orthodoxy.

MONTEFIORE'S LIBERAL JUDAISM AND JESUS

Liberal Judaism had sought to address the question of how modern Judaism related to Christianity (or, at least, to various aspects of Christian thought). Montefiore used his studies of Jesus as opportunities to explore this relationship. In particular, he was concerned to have Christians take Jewish thought seriously. To encourage this, he made a special effort to project an aura of objectivity around his own work, including the way he approached Jesus' teachings. In 'The Synoptic Gospels and the Jewish Consciousness' (1905), for example, he outlined some common Jewish criticisms of Gospel teaching. Much of the teaching, he explained to his Christian readers, was regarded by Jews as 'impractical and overstrained' and the ideals espoused as too high and incapable of realisation. The Gospels tended to make a man 'take a too selfish interest in the saving of his own soul' and to emphasise too ascetic a morality. The general Jewish view of Jesus' teaching, he observed, was that it was 'not fully suited to a society which expects to continue'.[37] However, in sharp contrast to 'ordinary and average Judaism', Montefiore was careful to make it clear that *he* started with the hypothesis that the Synoptic Gospels contained teaching that was original, new and true.[38] This very deliberate distancing of himself from negative Jewish opinion came to characterise the preambles of many of his Gospel studies and reflected his concern to avoid needlessly antagonising his Christian readers. He was also quick to point out that none of the 'original excellencies of the Synoptics', by which he meant those teachings of lasting religious value, were inconsistent with 'prophetic and liberal Judaism'.[39]

At the same time as demonstrating his detachment from Jewish bias, Montefiore wanted to challenge the mind-set of those who sought to prove the superiority of Christianity over Judaism. Studies on Jesus, it seemed, represented especially appropriate opportunities. In a lecture he gave to an audience in Manchester composed of the Students' Christian Union and the Jewish Students' Union, entitled 'The Religious Teaching of the Synoptic Gospels in its Relation to Judaism' (1922), he described the negative idea of Judaism in the mind of the 'average Christian' as 'a rather disagreeable sort of religion, chiefly made up of antitheses and contradictions to the religious teachings of Jesus'.[40] Having indicated how simplistic a view this was, he went on to contrast Christian claims of a higher teaching in the Gospels with the pragmatism of the rabbinical literature, observing,

> The ethical teaching of the Synoptic Gospels is eager, para-doxical, high-strung; the ethical teaching of the Rabbis is pure and good, but, on the whole, more pedestrian, and, in some respects, more suited to ordinary folk and every day.[41]

Such arguments, by which he hoped to redress the damage done by Christian ignorance, are common in his articles about Jesus, and by no means reflect an unusual point of view for a Reform or Liberal Jew. What is more interesting is that such articles were counter-balanced by much more substantial writings which approached the Gospels for a quite different reason, that is, for what the teachings of Jesus had to offer Judaism.

The Synoptic Gospels (1909) set the tone for Montefiore's approach to Jesus. While seeking to reconcile the views of Jewish and Christian scholars (the former tended to regard all New Testament material as tainted by a sectarian agenda while the latter felt exactly the same about the rabbinic literature), it was aimed primarily at a Jewish audience. Montefiore's guiding principle was to focus attention upon those Gospel passages that he believed had religious value or interest for modern Jews.[42] In practice, he explained, this interest lay in the teachings ascribed to Jesus, rather than in the personality or the life, despite the fact that the Gospels had been produced for entirely the reverse reasons.[43] He therefore ignored Christian theological issues, such as the meaning of the resurrection or the divinity of Jesus, in favour of his own Liberal Jewish concerns, such as Jesus' view of the Law or of Jewish nationalist hopes.[44] This had certain consequences for his methodology.

Whether estimating the religious value of 'Hellenistic thought', or defending 'Rabbinic thought' against Christian criticism, Montefiore had always tended to treat a tradition in its entirety, preferring to speak of its underlying spirit than to focus upon distracting details. He followed a similar approach with regard to Jesus' teachings. While his analysis of Gospel text was by no means uncritical or unsophisticated, his *use* of it was pastoral. The very reason he had approached it in the first place was because he saw it as a repository of ethical teachings. One consequence of this approach was that he consciously treated the texts as wholes. In *Some Elements in the Religious Teaching of Jesus* (1910), he explained,

> The greatness of the teachings do not depend so much upon the details of the particular things said as upon the manner in which they are said, and still more upon their effects as a whole . . . The beauty, the distinction, in a word, the genius of the form, must surely be taken into account as well as the excellence of the matter.[45]

With regard to the nature of God and his relations to mankind, Jesus' original contribution was 'not only to be found in its separate sentences and teachings, but in its general character, its spirit, its atmosphere'.[46] For the rabbis, for example, the idea of 'fatherhood' had been largely applied to God's relationship to Israel, but for Jesus, God was his father and the father of all those around him, in virtue of a common humanity in which 'the element of race and nationality seemed to fade away'. Montefiore felt that the intensity of the feeling in Jesus' everyday usage was of a different order. While it was not an entirely new doctrine, its apparent freshness stemmed from the high degree of purity, warmth and concentration with which it was presented.[47] Similarly, while he suspected that there was nothing novel or original about Jesus' philosophical understanding of God, Montefiore accepted that Jesus seemed to have felt God's nearness 'with a vivid intensity unsurpassed by any man'.[48] Central to understanding his interest in Jesus was Montefiore's admiration of the tone and quality of the 'spirit' of Jesus' thought. It was precisely this atmosphere of intense, all embracing, individualised religion that Montefiore believed lay at the heart of Judaism and which he wished to inculcate among his followers. Jesus' teaching was one more 'devotional aid' which could be used to inspire the Liberal Jewish movement, and which, he hoped, would eventually work its way through to revitalise Judaism as a whole.

In emphasising Jesus' uniqueness, Montefiore felt that part of 'the distinction and the original greatness of the teacher of Nazareth' had been his active desire to redeem and convert marginalised groups in society, including women and 'sinners'.[49] Jesus had been not only 'a collective prophet' but also 'the individualist prophet – the seeker of souls'. This seeking out of the sinner with Jesus' methods and intensity was, in Montefiore's opinion, something new in the religious history of Israel, especially when it was connected to the idea of redemption.[50] One of the reasons why he was attracted to this aspect of Jesus' ministry was that it echoed his own strong desire to reach out and rescue the Jewish masses disenchanted by traditional Judaism – one of the driving forces behind the establishment of the Liberal Jewish movement. It also paralleled his own social concerns, as reflected in the types of charitable work with which he was associated, including the Jewish Association for the Protection of Women and Children and Basil Henriques' social-educational programme for Jewish boys in the East End of London.

In line with the Liberal trend to 'spiritualise' Judaism, Montefiore had worked hard to distance Judaism from the ritualised, legalistic religion of Christian critique. Unconcerned about questions of priority, he identified with those aspects of Jesus' teaching which helped to accomplish this. With regard to

God's grace and the concept of His rewards as gifts, he was inclined to view Jesus' attitude that man has no claim upon God as 'comparatively new and original', in spite of the parallels that existed in the rabbinic literature.[51] Similarly, although teachings on self-denial had not been unknown before Jesus' time, Montefiore felt that the vivid expression of the ideal in the Gospels, together with its teaching regarding the renunciation and abandonment of the earthly for the heavenly, of this world for the next, were 'surely new and original contributions to the history of religion and morality'.[52] Regarding what he described as 'the heroic element in the paradoxes of the sermon on the mount', Montefiore freely admitted that they could never be the laws of a state. Nevertheless, they remained 'the principles of the hero, which heroes every now and then can put in practice, and which, as ideals and as spirit, are still fresh and valid and true'.[53] It was exactly this sort of romantic, idealist comment that provoked men like Ahad Ha-Am to question the authenticity of Montefiore's Jewishness. And in fact, Montefiore's championing of such stoic ideals as renouncement and self-denial had been due more to the influence of nineteenth-century hellenised or anglicanised Christianity than they had been due to the influence of Jewish thought or even that of the first-century Gospel texts.[54] Moreover, it was his adoption of apparently non-Jewish value-judgements and attitudes that explains his readiness (in contrast to many of his co-religionists) to attribute such teachings to Jesus as 'new and original' and to regard them as worthy of emulation rather than of disparagement.

Overall, it is not difficult to see what drew Montefiore to Jesus. Walter Jacob was not too far off the mark when he suggested that the Jesus portrayed in *The Synoptic Gospels* and in *Some Elements in the Religious Teaching of Jesus* was 'an idealised Montefiore in miniature'.[55] For Montefiore, as for many of the other Jewish writers, most of Jesus' teaching appeared to be rooted well within the confines of first-century Jewish thought.[56] But when Jesus' teachings appeared to stray outside these perimeters, Montefiore was often sympathetic, openly expressing his support, because he felt a sort of kinship and like-mindedness. It was easy for him to eulogise the 'heroic element', the 'largeness of views' and the 'grand simplicity' which he felt characterised Jesus' ministry,[57] because, not to put too fine a point upon it, he saw these very same attributes as characteristic of his own

Liberal Jewish struggle. Somewhat paradoxically, praising Jesus' allegedly 'un-Jewish' teachings thus gave him the opportunity to justify similar actions and beliefs of his own to his Jewish critics. Understanding this use of Jesus also helps explain Montefiore's differences with regard to his particular categorisation of Jesus, his view of Jesus' nationalism, and his understanding of Jesus' relationship to the Law.

JEWISH CATEGORISATIONS OF JESUS

For Montefiore, Jesus was primarily a Prophet. In *Some Elements in the Religious Teaching of Jesus* (1910), he argued that Jesus' preaching had been prophetic in its denouncing of sin and oppression, and also in its self-assurance of his own divine inspiration.[58] Jesus' speeches had echoed the prophets in the clarity of his vision and the intensity of his feeling, and were also notable for their power and hyperbolic exaggeration. Moreover, 'The inwardness of Jesus, the intense spirituality of his teaching show his connection and kinship with the Prophets.'[59] Most of all, however, it was Jesus' emphasis upon ethics which demonstrated to Montefiore his prophetic credentials. This is not to say that he regarded Jesus as *merely* a prophet. In 'The Originality of Jesus' (1929), Montefiore suggested that one of the most interesting things about Jesus had to do with the *sort* of prophet he had been. He regarded it as a remarkable and unique achievement for Jesus to have been 'a prophet of the eighth-century BC type' in the first-century CE, that is, at a time when the Law and the sacred canon of scripture were well established.[60] After all, Montefiore himself appreciated the difficulties of emphasising spirit over law in a tradition-bound context, and he marvelled that 'the conception of the Law and of scripture, to which the attitude of Jesus points forward, was not theoretically reached until modern times'.[61]

In the second chapter of *The Old Testament and After* (1923), Montefiore focused upon 'advances' and 'un-Jewish' developments in Jesus thought. He skimmed over questions about Jesus' faith and his trust in God (which he considered essentially Jewish),[62] and concentrated instead upon what he described as 'the most contentious portion of the teaching', his ethics. There were four characteristics of the teaching which, he felt, distinguished it from that of the contemporary religious authorities. Firstly, it was heroic and idealistic in what it demanded of a man. Secondly, it was pro-active, in that a man was not merely to wait on circumstances. Thirdly, it was paradoxically both altruistic (because one was to put the other first) and self-regarding (because of the reward of everlasting life). And fourthly, it contained the germ of a double ethic, in that there seemed to be a lower demand for some and a higher demand for others. Montefiore argued that while the fourth characteristic was admittedly 'somewhat off the line of Jewish development', the first three, or at least their beginnings, could be traced back to the Prophets.[63] He also felt that Jesus' belief in 'the approaching end' had produced the ascetic element in his teaching, his bias against wealth, and the sharp distinction between the service of God and the service of mammon. These, too, were reminiscent of the prophetic teaching, and he wondered if this aspect of Jesus' thought explained some of the differences between the New Testament and the rabbinic literature.[64]

Despite the fact that he was primarily interested in Jesus for his ethical teachings, Montefiore did not ignore the question of Jesus' self-perception. Jesus' emphasis on the Kingdom had led Montefiore to his conclusion that 'The relation in which Jesus believed that he stood, or would stand, to the Kingdom was that of its Chief or head. The Chief of a kingdom is its king. And the king of the Kingdom of God was the Messiah.'[65] Yet there was, in Montefiore's opinion, nothing so very unworthy of Jesus even if he did believe that he was destined to be the theocratic ruler and lord of the Jews in that messianic kingdom so soon to be ushered in by God, especially since he had played down the political aspects of what it meant to be the messiah, and had emphasised the servitude of the office.[66] He wrote that, like the Prophets before him, Jesus' teaching and bearing had suggested that to disbelieve his message was to disbelieve in God, but that Jesus had gone beyond even the Prophets' self-assurance when he had asked for renunciation or sacrifice 'for my sake'.[67] This was, for Montefiore, a new motive for action and sacrifice that has been of tremendous power and effect in the religious history of the world.[68] It was this 'touch of personal authority' in Jesus' teachings, a sense in which there seemed to be 'nothing between him and God', which set him apart.[69] It goes without saying that despite his consideration of the self-identity of Jesus and despite his readiness to recognise its uncommon qualities, Montefiore consistently rejected Christian claims of Jesus' unique nature. Regarding Mark's Gospel, which he viewed as the most historically reliable, he wrote,

> With the best will in the world, trying hard to peer through the mist and see the facts as they were, trying hard not to be prejudiced and prepossessed, I cannot see in the life of Jesus as recorded in Mark i–xiii anything about which to be lost in marvelling admiration or adoration. The character revealed, as far as *it is* revealed, appears undoubtedly strong and sweet, firm and tender, ardent and compassionate; but the evidence in Mark i–xiii for regarding Jesus as the most wonderful and perfect character which ever existed seems to me to be lacking.[70]

Almost without exception, Jewish writers have recognised a prophetic side to Jesus, and some have also regarded it as the key to understanding Jesus. Michael Friedländer believed, like Montefiore, that Jesus had perfected the Prophet's universalist teachings by spiritualising the people's 'national limitations and political hopes', under the influence of Hellenistic thought.[71] And Hyam Maccoby argued that as Jesus 'became a Prophet', his teachings developed a 'much more political, activist aspect' which ultimately led to his death as a rebel against Rome.[72] Even so, in their attempts to categorise Jesus in terms of the Judaism of his day, Jewish writers have tended to emphasise other, non-prophetic aspects of his life and teaching.

The idea of Jesus as a kind of Pharisaic rabbi has been the most popular view. While Joseph Jacobs compared Jesus favourably to the Prophets,[73] he focused more upon the similarity of Jesus' teachings to Hillel's, and consequentially regarded him as a rabbi.[74] Geiger described Jesus simply as a Pharisee 'with Galilean colouring',[75] and Buber took Jesus' Pharisaism quite for granted.[76] Ben-Chorin suggested that only the *am ha-aretz* or common-folk had thought of 'rabbi' Jesus as a prophet,[77] and Flusser also viewed Jesus as a sort of proto-rabbi, commenting, 'Although not really a Pharisee himself, [Jesus] was closest to the Pharisees of the school of Hillel.'[78] Maccoby argued forcibly that Jesus' teachings showed an unmistakable affinity to Pharisaism, and especially to the teachings of Hillel,[79] as did Paul Winter who insisted that 'in historical reality, Jesus was a Pharisee'.[80] Lapide's article 'Two Famous Rabbis' (1976) is one of the most recent assessments of Jesus as, essentially, a rabbinic teacher.[81]

There have been alternatives to 'Jesus the Prophet' and 'Jesus the Pharisee-Rabbi'. Salvador argued that Jesus should not be regarded as a Pharisee in spite of the fact that many of his teachings could be found in the contemporary literature, since he had over-emphasised the future life and had rejected the hedge around the Law, in contrast to the Pharisees who had concentrated upon the regulation of all aspects of this earthly life (moral, social and ceremonial) in order to preserve Israel. For Salvador, the key to understanding Jesus lay in his self-belief that he was the messiah and in his eschatological preaching.[82] Graetz considered Jesus' teaching reminiscent of Rabbi Hillel's, but saw far greater parallels with the Essenes' renunciation of this world and categorised Jesus accordingly.[83] Klausner did not consider Jesus a prophet since he had not shared the 'wide political perspective of the Prophets, nor their gift of divine consolation to the nation'.[84] And although Jesus' teachings had been entirely rabbinic in tone, he had set himself apart from the Pharisees by emphasising *aggadah* to the exclusion of *halakhah* and by investing himself with an authority that they would dare not have claimed for themselves.[85] Thus, for Klausner, Jesus was one of the 'many varieties of the mystic, visionary type – "quietistic Pharisees", Essenes and the like'.[86] Similarly, while noting the closeness of Jesus' teaching to that of the Pharisees, Vermes maintained that 'It would be a gross over-statement to portray him as a Pharisee himself.'[87] Nor was he satisfied with Montefiore's idea of prophethood, even though he found Jesus' preaching of *teshuvah* or repentance reminiscent of 'holy men' or prophets of earlier times. Vermes' conclusion was that the best description of Jesus was as a Galilean *hasid* or holy man.[88] For others, the problem of categorising Jesus was impossible. Buber's high regard for the originality of Jesus convinced him that 'a large place in the faith history of Israel belongs to him, [but] that this place can be described by none of the customary categories'.[89] And Sandmel agreed, although for a different reason. 'I simply do not know enough about him to have an opinion', he explained, 'and I simply do not have enough to set him, as it were, in some one single category.'[90]

So what was it about Montefiore that caused him to focus almost exclusively upon the prophetic side of Jesus? As noted previously, one of the ways by which Montefiore had distinguished his own Liberal Judaism from Orthodox Judaism had been to contrast the former's prophecy-orientated position with the latter's Law-orientated one. To his mind, the writings of the Hebrew prophets lay at the root of true Judaism as the revealers of ethical-monotheism, and he was keen to foster the impression that Liberal Jews were simply following in their footsteps. Since Liberal Judaism derived so much from the prophets, he argued, it should come as no surprise that it could find much to admire and use in Jesus, the ethical teacher.[91] Studying the Gospels thus gave him a useful opportunity for propounding the Liberal Jewish cause, albeit indirectly.

JEWISH VIEWS OF JESUS AND NATIONALISM

Another example of what might be viewed as a manipulative use of Jesus can be seen in the way Montefiore promoted his anti-nationalist view of Judaism. Generally speaking, Jewish writers did not attach universalist sentiments to Jesus to anywhere near the same extent as they did for, say, the apostle Paul. And when they did consider the issue, there was no consensus of opinion. Joseph Jacobs wrote that Jesus had indicated his lack of care for Jewish nationalist hopes by treating his listeners 'not as Jews but as men'.[92] Klausner had also recognised a lack of political-national interest in Jesus, although he did not share the positive value-judgement of it. Despite the fact that Klausner regarded Jesus as 'undoubtedly a "nationalist" Jew by instinct',[93] as we have seen, he differentiated Jesus from the Prophets for his lack of political perception, and from the Pharisees for undermining their efforts to strengthen the national existence.[94] As a fervent Zionist himself, Klausner went on to criticise Jesus for the way in which he 'came and thrust aside all the requirements of the national life ... [and] ignored them completely'.[95] Yet there were Jewish scholars who took a quite opposite view. Schoeps, for example, regarded Jesus in essentially nationalistic terms.[96] He argued that, among other things, Jesus had preached almost exclusively to Jews, that even when he had dealt with individual Gentiles he had emphasised his mission to the House of Israel, and that he had always remained within the borders of Palestine.[97] Vermes, too, was sensitive to Jesus' 'share of the notorious Galilean chauvinism' evident in various 'xenophobic' statements attributed to him.[98] But Vermes, like the majority of Jewish writers, did not tend to define Jesus in such terms.

Montefiore, on the other hand, *did* define Jesus in terms of nationalism (or rather, anti-nationalism). Vehement anti-nationalism was one of the most important characteristics of Montefiore's thought in general, and it can be regarded as an important factor in understanding his attraction to Jesus (and, even more, to the apostle Paul). In *Some Elements in the Religious Teaching of Jesus* (1910) he reacted strongly to those who claimed for Jesus a nationalistic understanding of Judaism, describing the idea of Jesus as a purely political messiah as nothing less than 'a caricature'. He argued that such a view over-emphasised the Jewish hopes for outward prosperity, the World Empire, the warrior-king, and the vassalage of the nations, at the expense of the equally Jewish hopes for the righteous ruler, the righteous judge, peace, goodness, the knowledge of God, and the conversion of the heathen to the true religion. 'It is an unattractive picture', he wrote, 'and can be shown to have been alien to the character and convictions of Jesus.'[99] As a successor of the Prophets, Jesus had never considered race as a protection against sin but had been 'against this false and irreligious confidence, which could so easily lead to careless living and odious sins, far more than against any theoretic particularism'.[100] Furthermore, there was good evidence to suggest that, like the prophets before him, Jesus had imagined that Gentile believers in the Kingdom would take up the places of sinful Jews.[101] Montefiore was even prepared to suggest that Jesus' universalism had been his most important legacy to the world. In 'The Significance of Jesus for his Own Age' (1912), he addressed himself to the question of what factors lay behind the 'gigantic results' of Christianity. These included the manner and occasion of Jesus' death, the widespread belief in his resurrection, the life and teaching of Paul, and the influence of non-Jewish doctrines and cravings.[102] Yet these four causes did not adequately explain the world-wide phenomenon of Christianity for Montefiore. Something else was required, and this something else was best understood as the success of Jesus in bringing about the diffusion and universalism of some of the fundamental tenets of Judaism.[103] (Once again Montefiore was concerned to demonstrate his objectivity by describing this as an 'unusual' statement for a Jew to make, since it was commonly understood that Jesus' teachings had been anti-Jewish.)[104] This 'diffusion of Judaism' into the Gentile world was, self-evidently, of far greater significance for those outside Judaism than for those within, but this did not make it any less Jewish a phenomenon. As Montefiore saw it, a Judaism which had re-appropriated this fundamentally Jewish teaching could only prosper; it was an important element of the Liberal Jewish agenda. Reinforced by the Liberal Anglican universalist view of Jesus with which he had become so familiar, Montefiore thus used Jesus to forward his own universalist message.

JEWISH VIEWS OF JESUS AND THE LAW

A final example of Montefiore's utilisation of Jesus can be found in his treatment of Jesus' attitude towards the Law. Despite the complexity and ambiguity of the Gospel evidence on this issue, one of the most constant features of Jewish studies of Jesus has been the assertion of his faithfulness to Torah. This was, of course, one way of using Jesus to nullify Christian critique against Judaism. Geiger's argument that Jesus had basically affirmed the eternal validity of the Law although he had not always been entirely consistent, was specifically aimed at demonstrating that Jesus had had nothing to do with the rise of Christianity (which was understood at the time to have emerged as a result of the abrogation of the Law).[105] Klausner was emphatic that Jesus had never dreamed of annulling the Law or of setting up a new Law of his own.[106] Sandmel had viewed Jesus' controversies as differences with his fellow Jews rather than with his inherited Judaism,[107] and Vermes had similarly argued that Jesus had never set himself in opposition to the Torah in principle, nor even in any important particular.[108] (Both Sandmel and Vermes admitted a possible exception with regard to the food laws.) Even when it was recognised that Jesus' interests had veered towards *aggadah* rather than *halakhah* and that he had emphasised the ethical rather than the legal aspects of life, modern Jewish thinkers like Flusser have steadfastly maintained his fundamental orthopraxy. Some writers went even further, suggesting that Jesus had been *too* rigorous in his support of the Law. Solomon

Zeitlin complained that 'Jesus, an ethical teacher, was so concerned to reach a Utopian society that, disregarding man's frailty, he could not tolerate a person's ever transgressing God's laws.'[109] And Sandmel pointed out that, in the context of divorce in particular, Jesus had been more rigorous than Moses.[110]

To a certain extent, Montefiore toed the Jewish line with respect to Jesus and his attitude to the Law. For example, he voiced his doubts whether, except in cases of stress and conflict, Jesus had ever intended to put his own teaching in direct contrast with, or substitution for, either 'the teachings of those around him, or the teaching of the Law'.[111] And, in common with other Jewish writers, Montefiore used his study of Jesus' view of the Law to discredit Christian criticisms of Jewish legalism. 'All that I beg of you to remember', Montefiore wrote in a chapter dedicated to the subject, 'is that you can have (and still do have in many Jewish circles) a combination of the purest and most saintly piety with the most careful and minute observance of every detail of the ceremonial law.'[112] While he was quite prepared to admit that the traditional Jewish emphasis upon legalism had, on occasion, led to abuses of the system, he was also quick to decry the picture of the Pharisees in the Gospels as 'a *ludicrous* caricature of the average Pharisee, a *monstrous* caricature of the Pharisaic ideal'.[113]

Where Montefiore was prepared to go further than other Jewish writers was to accept that Jesus' disgust with certain individuals and with those results of the system which struck him as wrong and improper, had led him to a half-unconscious attack, or implied attack, upon the system itself.[114] This view has been criticised. In his 'Prolegomenon' to the 1968 reprint of *The Synoptic Gospels*, Lou Silberman attacked Montefiore for not being able to make up his mind regarding Jesus' approach to the Law. He had difficulty in reconciling Montefiore's statement concerning the dietary laws: 'It may indeed be argued that ... Jesus virtually abrogates Pentateuchal Law', with what he had written a little later: 'It cannot be assumed offhand that Jesus himself transgressed the laws.'[115] Montefiore's idea that '[Jesus'] practice may not have squared with his theory' was, in Silberman's opinion, 'a way of having it both ways at once'.[116] So Montefiore is criticised for suggesting that Jesus' view of the Law was inconsistent. But the idea that Jesus had abrogated the Law in principle without intending to do so was later championed by

Klausner who argued that while Jesus had not actually set aside the ceremonial laws, he had nevertheless so devalued them that it was later possible for Paul, the originator of Christianity, to break away from Judaism. Sensitive to nuance, he wrote,

> *Ex nihilo nihil fit*: had not Jesus' teaching contained a kernel of opposition to Judaism, Paul could never *in the name of Jesus* have set aside the ceremonial laws, and broken through the barriers of national Judaism. There can be no doubt that in Jesus Paul found justifying support.[117]

Where Montefiore differed from Klausner was that, firstly, he could not help projecting onto Jesus some of his own Liberal musings and thus a sense of principle and intention. And secondly, that he regarded this development as a good thing. As he went on to elucidate in *Some Elements in the Religious Teaching of Jesus* (1910), while Jesus had never disputed theoretically the belief that the Law was 'divine', there had been for the teacher of Nazareth 'something still more divine – the inspiration of his thoughts and words as, in the stress and strain of the moment, the Divine Spirit seemed to suggest them to his mind'.[118] He found evidence for this in several of Jesus' confrontations with the Pharisees. For example, on the question of rabbinical regulations regarding the washing of hands Montefiore understood Jesus to have argued that 'things' could not defile 'persons' and that one's spiritual personality could only be spiritually defiled. 'Logically and consistently, the right was on the side of the Rabbis', he admitted, '[but] universally, ultimately, and religiously, the right was on the side of Jesus.'[119] It goes without saying that such an assessment was not common among Jewish writers. Montefiore took a similarly idealist approach to Jesus' teaching on divorce.

> From one point of view the Rabbis were right and Jesus was wrong, but ... *from another and higher point of view Jesus was more right* ... the Mosaic law of divorce was really a limitation, if not a concession ... the Law was in considerable portions of it, a sort of compromise with old, popular customs of heathen origin.[120] (Italics mine)

With regard to the Sabbath controversies, Jesus appeared to Montefiore to be fighting for a principle which he could not quite formulate – a principle which Montefiore, the Liberal Jew, found no difficulty in expressing: Jesus had meant either that ritual enactments should never be performed at the cost of putting aside deeds of love, or, perhaps, that the Sabbath rest must be interpreted by its spirit and by the higher law of righteousness and compassion.[121] In language strikingly similar to that with which he himself attacked the literalism of Orthodox Judaism, Montefiore maintained,

> Jesus would have upheld, or rather would not have touched, the validity of the *written* Pentateuchal law; what he would have attacked was the interpretation put upon the Law of God by human commentators and casuists.[122]

Significantly, Montefiore justified Jesus' somewhat strained relationship with the Law by claiming that it was a result of his having preached the Prophets' message under conditions which had not existed in earlier times. 'In the face of the Law which makes no clear distinction between morality and ceremonialism, but demands them both with equal insistence and equal authority', he asked, 'how could a new teacher enunciate afresh the doctrines of the Prophets, in direct application to the conditions and life of his time, without coming at least near to a conflict with the letter of the Law?'[123] This was revealing because it echoed the argument which he had used to justify the need for a Liberal Jewish movement: that the changing circumstances of the modern, progressive world necessitated new expressions of the old ethical, monotheistic teachings. Once again, Montefiore's presentation of his own Liberal Jewish views was facilitated by his analysis of what he regarded as Jesus' improvements upon the Judaic system. Inevitably, by appearing to side with Jesus against the rabbis in this way, Montefiore left himself open to charges of betraying Judaism.

CONCLUSION

Commenting on the *Synoptic Gospels*, Klausner accused Montefiore of having attempted to demonstrate 'that the Gospels are generally superior to the Talmud and are Hebrew works which should be acceptable to Jews'.[124] While this was, as Sandmel put it, a twisted summary of Montefiore,[125] it has very often been the common view among Jewish critics. There was also puzzlement among Christians as to why he had not converted. 'What a Jew Thinks About Jesus' (1935), written three years before his death, was Montefiore's last formal attempt to re-clarify and defend his own Liberal Jewish position regarding Jesus and to distance it from the opinions of Christian orthodoxy and Unitarianism. He began by demonstrating the divergence of opinion among those who held 'high views' of Jesus. Traditional Christianity, he argued, had not drawn much of a contrast between the Old and New Testaments with the result that less stress had been placed upon the perfection of Christ. The main emphases had been on Jesus' atoning death, his miraculous resurrection and his work of abiding redemption.[126] In contrast, as he understood them, modern Unitarians and Liberals claimed that while all men were created in the image of God, yet in Jesus God was so perfectly and fully revealed that he was to be regarded as unique; as Montefiore put it, 'In him a difference in quality or degree becomes a difference in kind, and so in him we may see God incarnate.'[127] He concluded that,

> The less strictly orthodox Christians seem to be, the less the sheer divinity of Jesus seems to be stressed, the more the emphasis seems to be laid upon the perfection of the life, the character and the teaching.[128]

Montefiore then went on to explain why he, as a Jew, rejected such 'high views' of Jesus. Firstly, Judaism was not obsolete but a legitimate and fully functioning religion which did not, by implication, need or require a morally perfect Jesus. Secondly, from the Gospel evidence it was quite possible to question the superlative greatness and originality of Jesus' teaching. Thirdly, it was also possible to question the unique perfection and beauty of his character and life.[129] With these three rebuttals, Montefiore firmly reiterated his position once again. Years of delicately phrased, well honed analyses had coalesced into two distinct lines of argument. From a historical perspective, he insisted,

> I infer a fine, a very fine, character, unlike the teachers of his own age, a sort of eighth-century prophet born out of season, a combination of Amos and Hosea. Jesus is for me

> *one* of the greatest and most original of our Jewish prophets
> and teachers, but I should hesitate to say that he was *more*
> original than any of them.[130]

From a philosophical perspective, and even more to the point,
Montefiore maintained that he could not follow those liberal
Christians for whom 'the real life and ideal life [of Jesus] had
become fused into one'. This idealisation which included within
it all perfection was no more possible for Jesus, he wrote, than it
was for Moses or Jeremiah or Rabbi Akiba.[131]

Somewhat naïvely and in spite of the criticism he had
received over the years for harvesting the ethical teachings of
Jesus for the benefit of Judaism, Montefiore had always hoped
and argued that his high regard for Jesus should not be mis-
interpreted as making him any less a Jew (or any more a
Christian). But those of his writings which were generally aimed
at a Christian audience and which were concerned to justify
(Liberal) Jewish thought, by no means counter-balanced the
unsettling effect of those of his writings which tended to be
written primarily for a Jewish audience and in which he had
consistently argued the reasonableness of utilising aspects of
New Testament teaching. This interest in and dependence upon
Jesus was out of all proportion in Jewish eyes. Even if, looking
back with hindsight, one agrees with Sandmel who wrote, 'I see
clearly that, where he admired a Christian matter more than a
Jewish, this is in no way a conflict with his unflagging Jewish
loyalty',[132] the question remains: Why did the leader of Anglo-
Liberal Judaism choose to use his studies of *Jesus*, of all people,
to express his own religious views? What was it about his
understanding of Judaism that allowed him to see the central
figure of the Gospel narratives as an exemplar?

For those Jewish writers such as Klausner who can be
regarded as part of the modern trend to collect and treasure the
spiritual creations of Jewry (such as Hasidism), the study of
Jesus was a rescue attempt from the hands of Christendom of a
figure whom Jews can claim to be, historically and humanly,
their own.[133] For reform minded Jews, Jesus' teachings could be
used as support against Christian critique. For those (in more
recent times) interested in Jewish–Christian dialogue, the study
of Jesus encouraged amenable understanding. These motives are
undoubtedly applicable to Montefiore. But Jesus was more

immediately relevant to Montefiore in that he offered an opportunity to represent and express the teachings of Liberal Judaism;
it is only a slight exaggeration to claim that he regarded Jesus as
a member of the Liberal wing of the Jewish tradition.[134] In contrast
to those who had simply stressed Jesus' Jewishness whilst decrying the traditional Christian view of Christ, Montefiore had been
drawn to Jesus for his *differences* with the Judaism of his day and
because he had seen so much of himself in the hero of the
Gospels: a Prophet in the Age of Law and a reformer who had
striven to free Judaism from the constraints of orthodoxy.[135]

Schechter's claim that Montefiore's teaching, in general, was
not so much Liberal Judaism as Liberal Christianity[136] is applicable to his treatment of Jesus, in particular. As noted previously,
his brand of Liberal Judaism can, from a certain point of view, be
regarded as the Jewish counterpart of Liberal Christianity, having
appropriated many of its value-judgements and interests. What
was still missing was a paragon of all that was good – or, rather,
all that was good *in Liberal Judaism*. A case can be made that
Montefiore's treatment of Jesus is best explained in terms of this
perceived lack, and that his use of Jesus should be understood as
an unconscious appropriation of a Liberal Christian ideal. In his
grand view of religion, Montefiore's interpretation of Jesus as an
exemplar of true Judaism and Jewish ethics made Jesus a legitimate
source of inspiration for the Jewish people. And this way of using
the Gospels, which is apparently unique to Montefiore, is also
apparent in his approach to the apostle Paul.

NOTES

1. Montefiore's motive, as always, was to enhance the religious value of
   Liberal Judaism. He asked, 'Why should we not make our religion as rich
   as we can? – Jesus and Paul can help us as well as Hillel and Akiba. Let them
   do so. What is good in them came also from God.' C.G. Montefiore, *The Old
   Testament and After* (1923), p. 291.
2. C.G. Montefiore, 'Liberal Judaism in England: Its Difficulties and Its Duties',
   Jewish Quarterly Review, XII (1899–1900), p. 628.
3. In his well regarded survey of New Testament research, Kümmel singled
   out Montefiore as the one scholar who more than any other 'raised the
   decisive question' of how to assess the similarities and differences between
   Jesus and Rabbinic Judaism. His 'extremely objective investigation' also
   addressed the essential question of the 'actual meaning of the text and one's
   personal attitude towards its message'. W.G. Kümmel, *The New Testament:
   The History of the Investigations of its Problems* (1973), pp. 346, 347.

4. D.A. Hagner, *The Jewish Reclamation of Jesus: An Analysis and Critique of the Modern Jewish Study of Jesus* (1984), p. 38. Hagner is, of course, referring to Klausner, Sandmel, Flusser, Lapide and Vermes in particular.
5. C.G. Montefiore, *The Synoptic Gospels*, 2nd edn, 2 vols (1927), I, p. xxii.
6. Montefiore's familiarity with scholarship concerned with the 'Quest for the Historical Jesus' did not result in his following Schweitzer down the 'apocalyptic' path, however.
7. Reprinted in 1970 by KTAV, New York.
8. Strack-Billerbeck, *Kommentar zum Neuen Testament aus Talmud und Midrasch*, vol. 1, Matthais (1922) and vol. 2, Markus, Lucas, etc. (1924). The commentary, which has never been fully translated into English, was an attempt to sort out the date and provenance of those quotations from the rabbinic literature that could be regarded as relevant for the study of the New Testament. While in the *Synoptic Gospels* Montefiore had concentrated upon Mark primarily, followed by Matthew and Luke, in *Rabbinic Literature and Gospel Teachings* the longest treatment was reserved for Matthew. Montefiore held Mark to be more historical than Matthew and Luke, and Matthew to be more akin to the Talmudic literature.
9. C.G. Montefiore, *Rabbinic Literature and Gospel Teachings* (1930), p. xix.
10. As he explained in the case of *Rabbinic Literature and Gospel Teachings* (1930), 'I take the Rabbinic literature as a whole, and I ask: What was its ethical and religious product?' Ibid., pp. xvi–xvii.
11. G. Friedlander, *The Jewish Sources of the Sermon on the Mount* (1911), pp. 262–3. Friedlander believed that practically all the genuine teaching of Jesus had been apocalyptic in character. Despite the fact that it must have been *Jewish* apocalypticism, he maintained that it was opposed to the best of Jewish thought and sentiment. Ibid., p. 3.
12. L. Baeck, *Wesen des Judentums* (1905, English translation, *The Essence of Judaism*, 1936) cited in A. Cohen, *The Natural and the Supernatural Jew: An Historical and Theological Introduction* (1962), p. 200; also S. Ben-Chorin, 'The Image of Jesus in Modern Judaism', *Journal of Ecumenical Studies*, XI (Summer 1974), p. 408.
13. P. Goodman, *The Synagogue and the Church* (1908), p. 233.
14. G.D. Schwartz, 'Explorations and Responses: Is There a Jewish Reclamation of Jesus?', *Journal of Ecumenical Studies*, XXIV (Winter 1987), p. 107. Of course, antisemitism in the East was an important factor and also helps explain the relative silence.
15. Jacob Agus has observed, 'Jewish historians are generally torn between the desire to prove the Jewishness of Jesus and the opposing wish to "justify" the rejection of his person and message.' J. Agus, 'Claude Montefiore and Liberal Judaism', *Conservative Judaism*, XIII (Winter 1959), p. 21.
16. P. Goodman, *The Synagogue and the Church* (1908), pp. 271–2.
17. I. Abrahams, *Studies in Pharisaism and the Gospels*, 2nd edn, 2 vols (1923), pp. 91, 90, 97.
18. Ibid., pp. 58–9, 97–8.
19. G. Vermes, 'Jesus the Jew', in J.H. Charlesworth, ed., *Jesus' Jewishness: Exploring the Place of Jesus in Early Judaism* (1991), p. 118.
20. M. Friedländer, 'Notes in Reply to My Critic', *Jewish Quarterly Review*, III (1892), p. 437.
21. In his critique of Montefiore's *Synoptic Gospels* (1909), Ahad Ha-Am had detected 'a subservience of the Jewish thinker [Montefiore] to the Christian doctrine'. Ahad Ha-Am, 'Judaism and the Gospels', reprinted in

American Hebrew Journal, LXXXVII, no. 21 (23 September 1910), from *The Jewish Review*, I (3 September 1910), p. 203.

22. Aaron Kaminka in *Ha-Toren* (New York) May 1922, cited in H. Danby, *The Jew and Christianity: Some Phases, Ancient and Modern, of the Jewish Attitude Towards Christianity* (1927), pp. 102–3. The fact that Klausner was a fervent Zionist and a disciple of Ahad Ha-Am made no difference to those who condemned him.

23. J. Agus, 'Claude Montefiore and Liberal Judaism', *Conservative Judaism*, XIII (Winter 1959), p. 7. Agus is too simplistic in his analysis of the Jewish treatment of Jesus, however, when he writes, 'As it was the tendency of Christian historians and philosophers to see in Jesus an ideal representation of their own ideals, so it became the practice among Jewish scholars to represent Jesus as the protagonist of the forces that they opposed.' He neglects to take into account the Jewish desire to justify Judaism in the face of Christian criticism and the utilisation of Jesus for that purpose.

24. J. Klausner, *Jesus of Nazareth: His Life, Times, and Teaching* (1929), p. 414.

25. Cited in S. Sandmel, *We Jews and Jesus* (1965), p. 91. Such a view, of course, helps explain Klausner's popularity with Christian scholars, for his criticism effectively acknowledged the usual Christian interpretation of Jesus' life and teachings. As Montefiore pointed out, this was in contrast to scholars such as Eisler, whose view of Jesus as a political rebel directly disputed the facts as Christians saw them. C.G. Montefiore, 'Dr. Robert Eisler on the Beginnings of Christianity', *Hibbert Journal*, XXX (1931–32), p. 300.

26. J. Klausner, *Jesus of Nazareth: His Life, Times, and Teaching* (1929), pp. 373–4.

27. Ibid., pp. 374, 376.

28. S. Sandmel, *We Jews and Jesus* (1965), p. 109.

29. C.G. Montefiore, *Rabbinic Literature and Gospel Teachings* (1930), p. 195.

30. Ibid., p. 207.

31. Ibid., pp. 322–3.

32. C.G. Montefiore, 'The Originality of Jesus', *Hibbert Journal*, XXVIII (1929), p. 99.

33. E. Kessler, *An English Jew: The Life and Writings of Claude Montefiore* (1989), p. 167.

34. C.G. Montefiore, 'The Originality of Jesus', *Hibbert Journal*, XXVIII (1929), pp. 98–9.

35. Once again distancing himself from 'current Jewish criticism', he nevertheless recognised 'a degree of originality … [and] of excellence' in the paradoxes of the Sermon on the Mount. Ibid., p. 107.

36. Buber's *Two Types of Faith* (English translation, 1951) presented Jesus' faith as the highest and most classic expression of Jewish *emunah*. Thus, Buber, too, used Jesus as a vehicle to express his own vision of Judaism. The essential difference was that Montefiore utilised various elements in Jesus' teaching that he readily admitted were original or non-Jewish.

37. C.G. Montefiore, 'The Synoptic Gospels and the Jewish Consciousness', *Hibbert Journal*, III (1904–05), p. 656.

38. Ibid., p. 657.

39. Ibid., p. 667. Even in the context of distancing himself from non-liberal Jews, he was prepared to defend Rabbinic Judaism (to a degree). He suggested that it was unreasonable to connect formalism and hypocrisy with a legal religion, since 'it is possible to follow the letter of the Law in the spirit of the Gospel'. Ibid.

40. C.G. Montefiore, 'The Religious Teaching of the Synoptic Gospels in its Relation to Judaism', *Hibbert Journal*, XX (1921–22), p. 435.

41. Ibid., p. 441.

42. C.G. Montefiore, *The Synoptic Gospels*, 2nd edn, 2 vols (1927), I, pp. 1–2.

43. Ibid., p.xxiv. As he put it, the Gospels had been produced not on the basis of teachings, but 'of a great historic figure and genius'.

44. Sandmel saw no contradiction in Montefiore's approach. 'While Montefiore always made it clear that he wrote from the bias of liberal Judaism, his works are as near an approach to objective scholarship as can be envisioned.' S. Sandmel, *We Jews and Jesus* (1965), p. 89.

45. C.G. Montefiore, *Some Elements in the Religious Teaching of Jesus* (1910), pp. 110, 111.

46. Ibid., p. 85.

47. Ibid., pp. 92–3; also C.G. Montefiore, 'The Originality of Jesus', *Hibbert Journal*, XXVIII (1929), p. 104.

48. C.G. Montefiore, *Some Elements in the Religious Teaching of Jesus* (1910), pp. 88–90.

49. Ibid., pp. 38, 44.

50. Ibid., pp. 55, 57–8. This had also been one of Abrahams' observations.

51. Ibid., pp. 97–8.

52. Ibid., pp. 105, 107.

53. Ibid., p. 105.

54. Jesus' declaration that true rule is true service was, in Montefiore's mind, the most original feature of his conception of the messiah, and yet this idea of kingship echoed Platonic rather than Jewish thought. Ibid., pp. 131, 136. 'His [Jesus'] idea of kingship was that of Plato; he only is the king whose life is given for his people. Kingship is service.' Ibid., pp. 106–7.

55. W. Jacob, *Christianity Through Jewish Eyes: The Quest for Common Ground* (1974), p. 103.

56. For example, Montefiore agreed with many other Jewish writers that the concept of the Kingdom and the coming Judgement, while central to Jesus' world-view and emphasised in his teachings, was essentially a Jewish doctrine. He held that it was not created by Jesus or even considerably changed by him. C.G. Montefiore, *Some Elements in the Religious Teaching of Jesus* (1910), p. 60.

57. C.G. Montefiore, *Liberal Judaism and Hellenism and Other Essays* (1918), p. 103.

58. C.G. Montefiore, *Some Elements in the Religious Teaching of Jesus* (1910), p. 21.

59. Ibid., pp. 19, 20.

60. A view he felt was supported by Christian scholarship generally. He quoted the ex-Catholic scholar, Loisy: 'In his age Jesus incarnated and renewed the spirit of the Prophets, the best of Judaism.' C.G. Montefiore, 'The Originality of Jesus', *Hibbert Journal*, XXVIII (1929), p. 102.

61. Ibid., p. 103. He added, 'One could hardly expect the rabbis to be 1900 years before their time, and if the suggestion were right, the high originality of Jesus and of his glorious inconsistency would, perhaps, even be diminished.'

62. Jesus' faith 'runs along more Jewish lines … Through faith man puts himself into the right attitude for receiving that which God can give him.' C.G. Montefiore, *The Old Testament and After* (1923), p. 225.

63. Ibid., pp. 241, 265.

64. Ibid., p. 266.

65. C.G. Montefiore, *Some Elements in the Religious Teaching of Jesus* (1910), p. 125.

66. Ibid., pp. 122, 131.

67. Ibid., p. 21.
68. As Montefiore points out, however, the immense power of 'for my sake' has been historically due to Jesus' death, rather than his life. C.G. Montefiore, *Some Elements in the Religious Teaching of Jesus* (1910), pp. 132–3.
69. Ibid., pp. 113–15, 119.
70. C.G. Montefiore, *The Synoptic Gospels*, 2nd edn, 2 vols (1927), I, p. 306.
71. M. Friedländer, *Die religiösen Bewegungen innerhalb des Judentums in Zeitalter Jesu*, cited in J. Klausner, *Jesus of Nazareth: His Life, Times, and Teaching* (1929), p. 117.
72. Maccoby understood the role of prophet as one of political leadership, and likened Jesus to John the Baptist as a 'figure of strong political significance'. H. Maccoby, *Revolution in Judaea: Jesus and the Jewish Resistance* (1973), pp. 143, 147.
73. While Jesus was one of those who 'spoke the oracles of God as if they were using the very words of the Lord', he also lacked patriotic feelings. J. Jacobs, *As Others Saw Him: A Retrospect, A.D. 54* (1895), p. 85.
74. Jesus did, however, differ from the 'other rabbis, who kept themselves apart from all other transgressors against the Law till they had repented and done penance'. Ibid., p. 11.
75. Cited in S. Sandmel, *We Jews and Jesus* (1965), p. 64.
76. M. Buber, *Two Types of Faith* (1950), pp. 137, 159–60.
77. S. Ben-Chorin, *Bruder Jesus* (1967), cited in D.A. Hagner, *The Jewish Reclamation of Jesus: An Analysis and Critique of the Modern Jewish Study of Jesus* (1984), p. 232.
78. D. Flusser, 'Jesus, His Ancestry, and the Commandment of Love', in J.H. Charlesworth, ed., *Jesus' Jewishness: Exploring the Place of Jesus in Early Judaism* (1991), p. 173. Flusser believed that although Jesus had probably not been 'an approved scribe', the term 'Rabbi' was applicable since it was in common use in the first century to describe scholars and teachers of Torah. Ibid., p. 161.
79. H. Maccoby, *Revolution in Judaea: Jesus and the Jewish Resistance* (1973), p. 140.
80. P. Winter, *On the Trial of Jesus*, 2nd edn (1974), cited in D.A. Hagner, *The Jewish Reclamation of Jesus: An Analysis and Critique of the Modern Jewish Study of Jesus* (1984), pp. 231–2.
81. Cited in D.A. Hagner, *The Jewish Reclamation of Jesus: An Analysis and Critique of the Modern Jewish Study of Jesus* (1984), p. 232.
82. Cited in J. Klausner, *Jesus of Nazareth: His Life, Times, and Teaching* (1929), pp. 106–8. According to Salvador, Jesus' differences with the Pharisees and his apparent lack of interest in the protection of Israel, lay behind the ultimate rejection of his teachings by the Jews.
83. In addition, Essene influence on Jesus' teachings was apparent in his 'love of poverty, community of goods; dislike of oaths, power to heal those possessed with demons …' H. Graetz, *History of the Jews: From the Earliest Times to the Present Day*, II (1901), p. 305.
84. J. Klausner, *Jesus of Nazareth: His Life, Times, and Teaching* (1929), p. 410.
85. Ibid., p. 91. Also, Jesus had not apprehended the positive side of their work nor exerted himself as they had to strengthen the national existence. Ibid., p. 414.
86. Ibid., p. 173. Klausner also pointed out that there would not have been Pharisees or Sadducees in Galilee, only Zealots and what he described as 'the meek of the earth' who had abandoned interest in temporal things to dream of a future life based on the messianic idea. Ibid.

87. G. Vermes, *Jesus the Jew: A Historian's Reading of the Gospels* (1973), p. 35. Like Klausner, Vermes picked up on Jesus' geographical background, suggesting that Jesus, along with Galileans in general, would not have shown much interest or expertise in matters halakhic.

88. Vermes suggests the choice need not be between prophet or holy man, since the terms 'to heal', 'to expel demons' and to 'forgive sins' were interchangeable synonyms. G. Vermes, *Jesus the Jew: A Historian's Reading of the Gospels* (1973), J.H. Charlesworth, ed., *Jesus' Jewishness: Exploring the Place of Jesus in Early Judaism* (1991), pp. 117, 118.

89. M. Buber, *Two Types of Faith*, cited in S. Ben-Chorin, 'The Image of Jesus in Modern Judaism', *Journal of Ecumenical Studies*, XI (Summer 1974), p. 413.

90. S. Sandmel, *We Jews and Jesus* (1965), p. 108.

91. C.G. Montefiore, *The Old Testament and After* (1923), p. 229.

92. J. Jacobs, *As Others Saw Him: A Retrospect, A.D. 54* (1895), p. 210.

93. Klausner cites Jesus' treatment of the Canaanite woman and his use of derogatory language such as 'the heathen and the publican'. J. Klausner, *Jesus of Nazareth: His Life, Times, and Teaching* (1929), p. 413. Klausner felt that Jesus revealed 'the same national pride and aloofness (Thou hast chosen us) for which many Christians now and in the Middle Ages have blamed the Jews'. Ibid., p. 363.

94. J. Klausner, *Jesus of Nazareth: His Life, Times, and Teaching* (1929), p. 92.

95. Ibid., p. 390.

96. Schoeps, a student of Leo Baeck and a conscious anti-Zionist, had rejected the national renaissance of the Jewish people as a historical sidetrack. C. Roth, ed., *Encyclopaedia Judaica* (1971), p. 991.

97. Cited in S. Ben-Chorin, 'The Image of Jesus in Modern Judaism', *Journal of Ecumenical Studies*, XI (Summer 1974), pp. 410–11.

98. G. Vermes, 'Jesus the Jew', in J.H. Charlesworth, ed., *Jesus' Jewishness: Exploring the Place of Jesus in Early Judaism* (1991), p. 118.

99. C.G. Montefiore, *Some Elements in the Religious Teaching of Jesus* (1910), pp. 129, 130.

100. Ibid., p. 67.

101. Ibid., pp. 70–1.

102. C.G. Montefiore, 'The Significance of Jesus for his Own Age', in *Hibbert Journal*, X (1911–12), p. 766.

103. Ibid., p. 767.

104. Ibid., p. 768.

105. D.A. Hagner, *The Jewish Reclamation of Jesus: An Analysis and Critique of the Modern Jewish Study of Jesus* (1984), p. 63.

106. Klausner quoted Luke 11:42, 'Woe to you Pharisees! For you tithe mint and rue and every herb, and pass over judgement and the love of God: but these ought ye to have done, and not to leave the other undone.' This verse, he believed, proved 'in the strongest possible fashion' that Jesus never rejected Torah, or even the ceremonial laws. J. Klausner, *Jesus of Nazareth: His Life, Times, and Teaching* (1929), p. 367.

107. He even questioned the historical authenticity of the Gospel accounts of Jesus' controversies with his contemporaries. S. Sandmel, *We Jews and Jesus* (1965), p. 137.

108. Thus Vermes argues that there was not any evidence for a Pharisaic conspiracy for Jesus' death. G. Vermes, *Jesus the Jew: A Historian's Reading of the Gospels* (1973), p. 36.

109. S. Zeitlin, 'Jesus and the Pharisees', in T. Weiss-Rosmarin, ed., *Jewish Expressions on Jesus: An Anthology* (1977), p. 150.

110. Although Jesus had not contravened Moses. S. Sandmel, *We Jews and Jesus* (1965), p. 137.
111. C.G. Montefiore, *Some Elements in the Religious Teaching of Jesus* (1910), p. 80.
112. Ibid., p. 37.
113. Ibid.
114. Ibid., p. 40.
115. C.G. Montefiore, *The Synoptic Gospels*, 2nd edn, 2 vols (1927), I, pp. 146, 147.
116. L.H. Silberman, 'Prolegomenon', in the 1968 edition of C.G. Montefiore, *The Synoptic Gospels*, p. 13.
117. J. Klausner, *Jesus of Nazareth: His Life, Times, and Teaching* (1929), p. 369. E.P. Sanders points out that this theory did not explain why James and Peter had failed to reach the same conclusions when looking at Jesus' words and deeds. E.P. Sanders, *Jesus and Judaism* (1985), p. 53.
118. C.G. Montefiore, *Some Elements in the Religious Teaching of Jesus* (1910), pp. 46–7.
119. Ibid., pp. 49–50.
120. Ibid., pp. 45–6.
121. Ibid., pp. 42–3.
122. Ibid., p. 43.
123. Ibid., p. 41.
124. J. Klausner, *Jesus of Nazareth: His Life, Times, and Teaching* (1929), p. 114.
125. S. Sandmel, *We Jews and Jesus* (1965), p. 93.
126. C.G. Montefiore, 'What a Jew Thinks About Jesus', *Hibbert Journal*, XXXIII (1935), p. 513.
127. Ibid., p. 514.
128. Ibid., p. 515.
129. Ibid., p. 516.
130. Ibid.
131. Ibid., p. 520.
132. S. Sandmel, *We Jews and Jesus* (1965), p. 90.
133. H. Danby, *The Jew and Christianity: Some Phases, Ancient and Modern, of the Jewish Attitude Towards Christianity* (1927), p. 101.
134. As Walter Jacobs does in 'Dialogue in the Twentieth Century: The Jewish Response', in L. Klenicki, ed., *Towards a Theological Encounter: Jewish Understandings of Christianity* (1991), p. 72.
135. For example, while it was difficult to establish precisely what Jesus had meant by 'No man pours new wine into old wineskins' (Mark 2:22), it comes as no surprise to see that Montefiore accepted the obvious, anti-legal and revolutionary interpretation. C.G. Montefiore, *Some Elements in the Religious Teaching of Jesus* (1910), p. 157.
136. 'What the whole thing means, is not Liberal Judaism, but Liberal Christianity.' Cited in R. Apple, *The Hampstead Synagogue* (1967), p. 38.

13

Montefiore and Paul

Traditionally, Jews have regarded Paul's attacks upon the Law as entirely unjustified and not a little puzzling. Traditionally, Christians have defended their champion resolutely and regarded Judaism as a legalistic religion. It was largely as an attempt to correct this perceived injustice that some Jews entered into New Testament studies. Montefiore, however, was interested in Paul primarily because he was fascinated by the question of how to explain Paul's view of Judaism if one was to start from the assumption that Paul was sincere and that the apostle's criticisms accurately reflected the Judaism with which he was familiar. Montefiore was also drawn to the study of Paul because his Liberal Jewish philosophy primed him to attempt to salvage what he could from any religious writing, and especially from those writings whose author he had described on record as a religious genius. Significantly, neither of these concerns could be described as characteristic of any previous Jewish approach.

Montefiore produced two extended articles on Paul, both published in the *Jewish Quarterly Review*. 'First Impressions of St. Paul' (1894) concentrated upon what he regarded as distinctly Pauline, such as his christology and his conception of sin and the Law; it also discussed the merits of his ethics. 'Rabbinic Judaism and the Epistles of St. Paul' (1901) returned to the difficulties in Paul's doctrines regarding the Law and sin, and also contrasted how Paul, the rabbis and Jesus respectively treated common motifs in their thinking. *Judaism and St. Paul* (1914), Montefiore's only book on the subject, was written in essay format; references to sources were almost non-existent and although he took into account the works of contemporary and authoritative Christian writers such as Loisy and Harnack, he seldom referred to Jewish writers.[137] The first part represented Montefiore's contribution to Pauline scholarship; it covered most of his earlier treatment before systematically attacking the idea that Paul was a rabbinic Jew and offering an alternative theory concerning the nature of Paul's pre-Christian religion. In the process, Montefiore addressed certain topics that he had not fully developed elsewhere, including Paul's mysticism and his new universalism. The second part characteristically picked up on those aspects of the epistles which might be salvaged for the benefit of Liberal Judaism, such as Paul's rejection of religious particularism, his attitude towards suffering and against giving needless offence, and even elements of his mysticism. Montefiore's attitude can be gauged from the comment: 'What is positive [in Paul's theology] is so much more pleasant and useful than what is negative.'[138]

THE SILENCE OF JEWS WITH REGARD TO PAUL

Until relatively recent times Jews have very rarely written about Paul. There are a few possible exceptions in the rabbinic literature. The Christian scholar Kittel suggested that it was Paul who was described in Avot 3:12 as one who

> profanes the Hallowed Things and despises the set feasts and puts his fellow to shame publicly and makes void the covenant of Abraham our father, and discloses meanings in the Law which are not according to the Halakhah.[139]

Later Klausner argued that it was Paul who was referred to in Shabbath 30b, which speaks of a pupil of Gamaliel who 'went wrong' and who 'interpreted the Torah in a perverse manner'.[140] And Baeck accepted the alleged reference to Paul in Ruth Rabba, Petikha 3: 'This man ... made himself strange to the circumcision and the commandments.'[141] But even allowing for these few tenuous possibilities, the silence of ancient Jewish writers on this subject is striking. In an essay entitled 'Paul in Modern Jewish Thought' (1980),[142] Donald Hagner has argued that there were two main reasons for this. Firstly, Paul's missionary success made him a dangerous opponent for the rabbis; while his theology was patently wrong, they felt that the best way to deal with his threat was to ignore him and give him as little publicity as possible. Secondly, and more importantly, Jews had lived within Christendom from the fourth century until the nineteenth-century Emancipation, under oppression; their silence was simply a reflection of their awareness of the political danger of engaging with Jesus, Paul or Christianity. For Hagner, 'the new climate of freedom produced by the gradual acceptance of Jews into European society' brought to an end the centuries of silence.[143]

Of course Hagner is right in his observation that more Jews have written about Paul and engaged with his teachings since Emancipation than before, and that a very important factor in this was the diminished threat of recrimination from their Christian neighbours. With the general increase in their familiarity with the surrounding Christian world, the fear of contamination from the heretical Apostle would also have diminished, and a greater number of Jews would have read his writings. For those who were coming to regard Jesus as faithful to Judaism, attention might also have been expected to shift towards the man increasingly held responsible for the movement of early Christianity away from its Jewish roots. It seems logical to conclude that with the dissolution of the two main concerns, the silence would be broken. One might also have expected that for those who were coming to regard Jesus as faithful to Judaism, Paul would have drawn increasing attention as being the man responsible for beginning the movement of early Christianity away from its Jewish roots. However, one is struck by the very small number of Jewish writers who have produced a dedicated study on Paul, in comparison with those who have written about Jesus.[144] When the fact that several of the authors produced essays rather than full-length works when writing on Paul is taken into account, the implication that the tide has turned and the claim that in modern times Jewish scholars have 'no small fascination for Saul of Tarsus' seems less convincing.[145] It appears that, for the vast majority of them, the Apostle to the Gentiles was of little or no interest.

Why was, and is, this the case? It is not a satisfactory answer to say that Jewish writers simply regarded Paul as less relevant than Jesus or the Church for Judaism and that their relatively small written output reflected their lack of interest. Pauline thought and Christian interpretations of it have significantly shaped the Church, especially the Protestant Church, with which Judaism has struggled. An understanding of Paul is thus essential in understanding Christianity and one would expect a good deal more Jewish study of Paul, especially from those concerned with

Jewish–Christian relations. One possible reason for the Jewish silence was that, as far as the vast majority were concerned, the Jewish position regarding the apostate Paul was quite clear – what need was there for a re-examination? For centuries the Jewish understanding of Paul had been hindered by the same clumsy reading of the apostle of which Christians were similarly guilty, a reading which over-emphasised his apparent anti-Jewishness and his contrast of faith versus works. To a certain extent this traditional presupposition underlies the works of several of the Jewish writers, notably Buber and Kohler.[146] Another reason for the continued silence was the Christo-centricism of the apostle's writings. Unlike Jesus whose teachings could, in the main, be easily reconciled with Judaism, Paul's fixation upon a super-natural messiah could not easily be overlooked in favour of his more 'Jewish' teachings.[147] As a consequence, there was very little reason to try to reclaim Paul in the way that modern Jews had attempted to reclaim Jesus. As will become clear, even Montefiore struggled to salvage much from Paul's writings. Overall then, there was no incentive for Jews to study Paul, other than to refute Christian views of Judaism derived from Paul's misrepresentation of the Jewish Law.

A LIBERAL JEWISH APPROACH TO PAULINE SCHOLARSHIP

At the turn of the century, the scholarly debate concerning the Apostle Paul and how he was perceived to have related to Judaism was very much dominated by Christian tradition. The general consensus among both Christian and Jewish theologians was that, even though many particulars of his thought were rooted in Judaism, Paul was basically antithetical to it; a good example of this was H. St John Thackeray's *The Relation of St Paul to Contemporary Jewish Thought* (1900). Pauline scholars did not reach this position by simply reading the epistles at face value, but rather believed that studies made of rabbinic texts confirmed it. Thus Thackeray, who admitted that his knowledge of Rabbinic Judaism was entirely derivative, made constant use of Weber's systematic theology of Rabbinic Judaism which presented Judaism as a form of righteousness by works.[148]

Increasingly, however, questions began to be raised by those Jewish and Christian thinkers who were more knowledgeable about Rabbinic Judaism, and who had difficulties in relating Paul's criticisms to Judaism as they knew it. Montefiore was one of the first Jews to take this issue into the realm of mainstream Pauline scholarship. He thought that by abandoning the well trodden paths of religious polemicism, he had found for himself a better place from which to judge the Apostle to the Gentiles: both the short-comings, which had been the traditional diet of Jewish apologists down through the ages, and the achievements, which he preferred to dwell upon. He explained, 'I hate seeming to belittle or cavil at any of the world's heroes (e.g. Paul). It seems so irrelevant.'[149] As a Jew with an unusually positive regard for Christianity and Christian scholarship, and with what one Jewish observer described as a 'cross-bench mind',[150] he was able to criticise Paul in a non-confrontational, non-polemical manner.

Since the time of Schweitzer, Pauline studies have focused upon four areas of investigation: the history-of-religions approach, theology, exegesis and hermeneutics.[151] Montefiore's contributions were most original with regard to the first and last of these categories. Greatly influenced by the *Religionsgeschichte* school of thought, he was the first to attempt to define Hellenistic Judaism as part of his approach to Paul.[152] While his suggestion that the apostle's criticisms of Judaism were actually targeted at Diaspora Judaism has attracted limited support, the questions he raised have had a considerable impact upon New Testament scholarship. This is reflected in the fact that two of the most important post-war works on Pauline thought, by W.D. Davies and E.P. Sanders, have considered Montefiore's contributions at length.[153] Regarding Pauline theology and exegesis, Montefiore had little to offer which was original or radical; he generally followed the traditional reading of Paul. When it came to hermeneutics, however, and considering in what ways Paul could be appropriated for the modern world (and especially the modern Liberal Jewish world), Montefiore's positive approach was unique among Jewish thinkers. The importance of religious truth for him, wherever it was found, was paramount. If Paul's letters contained universal truths, then as far as the founder of Anglo-Liberal Judaism was concerned, these fragments were worth incorporating into its teachings, albeit in a modified form.[154] Montefiore's main concern with Paul was to present these truths in such a way as to be intelligible and even desirable to Jews. He felt this was quite possible, especially if, as he wrote elsewhere, 'so far as we can learn from Jesus and even from Paul, we learn from Jews, and not from aliens'.[155]

Montefiore was well aware of the importance of Paul's theology for Christianity and therefore for Jewish–Christian understanding, and it made up much of the background to his own voluminous writings more generally. His greater interest, however, lay in the Gospel teachings and their rich ethical content, which he hoped to harness for the benefit of Liberal Judaism. The doctrines and dogma of Paul's epistles appeared less profitable in this respect and thus appealed less to him, and so fewer works were devoted to the subject. Even so, Montefiore did approach Paul positively and so distinguished himself from the majority of Jewish Pauline scholars whose goal was either to legitimise the traditionally hostile stance taken against Paul, or to simply reconstruct Paul historically without making value-judgements.

MONTEFIORE'S UNDERSTANDING OF PAUL

The Question of Identifying Paul as a Rabbinic Jew
Montefiore had a sophisticated grasp of the dynamics of Paul's background and thought. In 'Rabbinic Judaism and the Epistles of St. Paul' (1901), he identified four possible 'strands' or factors which had contributed towards Pauline theology.[156] Firstly, the apostle's own religious genius. Secondly, Christianity, which he defined as 'whatever came to Paul by revelation, tradition, or any means, concerning the life, death and resurrection of Christ'. Thirdly, Hellenism, both 'the direct contact of St. Paul's mind with the Hellenism of his day' (the extent of which he admitted was difficult to ascertain), and 'the influence of Hellenism refracted through a Jewish medium'.[157] And, fourthly, Rabbinic or Palestinian Judaism, which he differentiated elsewhere from Apocalyptic and Hellenistic Judaisms.

Montefiore began the essay with a warning about directly comparing Paul's writings with those of the rabbis. He was keen to avoid the practices of traditional Jewish and Christian apologists who had highlighted the best of their respective systems whilst denigrating those of their opponents. But his rationale for viewing such a contrast as 'unfair' was, for a Jew, unusual to say the least:

St. Paul was a religious genius of the first order, who writes in the flush of fresh enthusiasm. The Midrash is a confused jumble of sermons, parables, sayings, and anecdotes without system or plan. There are indeed occasional flashes of genius, but most of it is of very second and third-rate order of literary merit.[158]

While recognising the 'contradictions and antinomies' in Paul's theology, he felt that there was still an overall coherence which made Paul far more systematic than the rabbis, making it unfair to compare the two.[159] Classically educated and concerned to present religious truth as effectively as possible, Montefiore admired this quality of Paul's teaching. If, however, Paul was more systematic in his theology than the rabbis, he could also be 'transitory, unmystic, hard, irreligious, immoral'.[160] One of the consequences of this, Montefiore argued, was Paul's dogmatic attitude towards the Law, which was far more 'juridic' than that of the rabbis'. Today, a student of Paul is warned against the dangers of treating Paul as a systematic theologian, or of approaching the epistles as anything other than specific responses to actual situations and dilemmas facing various churches in Asia Minor.[161] Montefiore would not have disputed this. His point was simply that Paul's epistles, written by a Hellenistically influenced individual, were more systematic in nature and presentation than was the more eclectic collection of writings contained within the vast rabbinic literature.

In the early articles, Montefiore was not prepared to address directly the question of 'how far Paul's Judaism was rather modelled upon the Hellenistic Judaism of Philo than on the Rabbinic Judaism of Hillel, Gamaliel or Akiba'.[162] And he was content to leave it to other scholars to determine whether the Judaism of 50 was the same as that of 500. He suggested it was enough that

> The main elements of the Rabbinic religion underwent little change from 50 to 500 AD. Above all, the central position of the Law was not shaken or altered.[163]

This was an important assumption, for the sources of his understanding of the 'Rabbinic Judaism of the time' were of uncertain relevance: Apocalyptic literature, which he observed could only be used with great care and caution (and which in practice he ignored), and the rabbinic literature itself, composed of Talmud and Midrash, which had been written several centuries after the apostle's death. He was well aware that he was on shaky ground in describing the Judaism of 50 CE as 'Rabbinic Judaism' and, in fact, subsequent scholarship has shown it to have been an over-simplification.[164] Modern research relies to a far greater extent upon the works of Josephus and Philo, the Dead Sea scrolls together with other early Jewish writings, and archaeological discoveries for its understanding of first-century Judaism(s); it is less reliant upon the rabbinic texts in these matters. It would, of course, be unfair to condemn Montefiore for the limited resources available to him – the Dead Sea scrolls, for example, were only discovered in 1947 – but his failure to give due weight to the writings of Philo or Josephus, with which he was quite familiar, cannot simply be put down to the contemporary lack of interest amongst scholars; it is all the more surprising when one considers that Montefiore was quick to see the relevance of Philo for studies of other Christian writings.[165] Despite this, the central pin to his argument that the centrality of the Law was common to both first- and fifth-century Judaism remains an acceptable hypothesis today.[166]

By the time of *Judaism and St. Paul* (1914), Montefiore was prepared to posit more definitely that there was no great difference between the Judaism practised in the first century and that practised in the fourth, fifth or sixth centuries. In his opinion, Judaism in 500 was certainly not legalistic works-righteousness.[167] As far as he was concerned, there was no reason to think that the Judaism of 50 CE was grossly inferior. While he admitted that he was by no means an authority on first-century Judaism, it seemed that there was only one major difference, a 'weakness' of first-century Judaism in despising the 'sinners' and outcasts; but this was the background to Jesus' teachings, he argued, and had nothing to do with Paul's.[168]

At first, Montefiore had been at a loss as to how to explain the apostle's apparent misrepresentation of Judaism. Paul's description of Judaism was quite unrecognisable to him. As he put it,

> St. Paul beats the air with words, which, magnificent as they are, seem out of relation to the actual Jewish religion ... [Paul's arguments] leave the impression: either this man

was never a Rabbinic Jew at all, or he has quite forgotten what Rabbinic Judaism was and is.[169]

Later, however, and in contrast to the traditional Jewish view that regarded Paul as intentionally misrepresenting Judaism due to a Christian bias, Montefiore accepted Paul's criticisms as actually representing the Judaism with which he had been familiar. *Judaism and St. Paul* was his attempt to demonstrate that the Judaism with which Paul had been familiar had not been Rabbinic Judaism but another kind. Significantly, then, Montefiore did not attempt a defence of Judaism against Pauline criticism but rather sought to move Rabbinic Judaism out of the line of fire.

Montefiore went about this by examining various aspects or characteristics of Pauline thought and contrasting them with contemporary Rabbinic Judaism. He dealt first with the traditional Jewish complaints: if Paul had been a Pharisaic Jew, could he have evolved a concept of the messiah that was so alien to rabbinic Jews? And could he have become so interested in non-Jews? He concluded that there was little or no evidence that Paul's thinking was outside the pale of the Judaism of his time. Although the christology of, say, Romans and Corinthians might be unacceptable to a modern rabbinic Jew, he suggested that during the first half of the first century, there was no such difficulty or impossibility in accepting a messiah who was 'a regular divine being',[170] an observation supported by the later work of W.D. Davies and others.[171] An important theme in Davies' work was that the idea of the messiahship of Jesus was actually a vital element of Paul's thought (that is, not a peripheral element) and that the Apostle to the Gentiles retained a distinctly Jewish idea at the centre of his thought.[172] However, in common with the vast majority of Protestant scholars at that time who generally explained Paul's concept of Christ in Hellenistic terms, Montefiore would not have agreed to such an emphasis in Paul's thought with the result that this important indicator of Paul's Jewishness was not given due weight.[173] With regard to Jewish interest in Gentile proselytes, Montefiore argued that it had not been uncommon in the first century; there had even been cases of rabbis advising proselytes that only baptism was required for conversion and that circumcision was not essential.[174] Montefiore did conclude, however, that any ideas Paul had had about breaking down the wall of distinction between Gentile and Jew had probably been suggested from a non-Jewish environment.[175]

There were other questions which Montefiore felt were more pertinent in demonstrating that Paul had never experienced Rabbinic Judaism. For instance, how could his theological pessimism ever have evolved from there? In comparison with the rabbis' optimistic world-view, Paul was strikingly pessimistic.

> [Paul] was obsessed by a sense of human frailty and sinfulness: he had discovered no remedy strong enough to cope with the Yetzer ha-Ra, the evil inclination, the wicked promptings of the heart. God was not near and loving enough for him as he was to the Rabbinic Jew; repentance and the Day of Atonement did not enter so deeply into the very make and texture of his being; the good impulse (the Yetzer ha-Tob), the right promptings of the heart were less real to him ... He had always the horrid feeling of the unconquered evil inclination gnawing within his soul.[176]

He felt that Paul was too pessimistic about the power of the sin or the evil impulse, and about the need for a supernatural deliverer. As he put it elsewhere, 'The cry, "Who shall deliver me from the body of this death?" is, on the whole, an un-Rabbinic cry.'[177] A saying from the Tanchuma, 'Whatever the Righteous do, they do through the Holy Spirit', better illustrated for Montefiore the beliefs of the rabbis of the period. The absence of this 'current dogma of Paul's time' in the Epistles, that is, the absence of the pre-Christian working of the Holy Spirit and of the good impulse, was one of the many puzzles which his writings posed for Montefiore.[178] Montefiore's conclusion was that it would never have been possible for someone from a background of Rabbinic Judaism to have developed such a pessimistic world-view. In this, he was followed by other Jewish thinkers including Kohler,[179] Klausner,[180] Buber and Maccoby.[181] Buber even went so far as to describe the pessimistic world-view of the epistles as 'Paulinism'.[182]

Likewise, Montefiore felt that Paul's apparent attraction towards Hellenistic mysticism was difficult to explain if his background had been Rabbinic Judaism. Montefiore did not emphasise Paul's Christ-mysticism (that is, being 'in Christ') to anywhere near the same degree as, for example, Schweitzer would do.[183] Nevertheless, he pointed to the parallels between Paul's theology and Hellenistic ideas such as rebirth through rites of initiation, dying to live again, endowment of supernatural vigour, conquest over sin, and the belief in the indwelling god as the source of the cult followers' new and higher life. Montefiore's powers of empathy led him to suggest that deep down, Paul ached for

> that new heart and new spirit which the Prophets had declared was to be the gift of God to Israel in the Messianic Age. And that new spirit was to be God's spirit. The new personality would, in a sense, be divine. No longer need one sin, no longer need one be told in many enactments what to do and from what to refrain; the divine spirit, the new heart, would assuredly impel towards the right.[184]

Although accepting the existence of mysticism (that is, the desire to achieve union with the Divine) within historical Judaism, Montefiore felt that it was not characteristic of the religion. Rabbinic Judaism did not, he maintained, readily produce 'a mystic temper or soul', and 'its saint does not naturally speak of being in God, or of God being in him'.[185] Thus he saw Paul's mystic leanings as further evidence of his independence from Rabbinic Judaism. In this, Montefiore was not unanimously followed by later Jewish writers. While Kohler[186] and Maccoby[187] agreed with Montefiore and dismissed Paul's mysticism as 'un-Jewish', Sandmel[188] and Klausner[189] were able to reconcile the mystical tendencies with Paul's Jewishness, and both Wise[190] and Segal[191] actually defined Paul in terms of Jewish mysticism.

Later Pauline scholarship suggests that Montefiore's definition of Judaism was too narrow and exclusive and that his *Religionsgeschichte* approach, in which the mystical element in Paul's thought was explained in terms of Hellenistic syncretism, was of limited use. W.D. Davies, for example, has argued that it is unnecessary to go outside Rabbinic Judaism to account for Paul's pessimism,[192] and, following the work of G. Scholem, it has become generally accepted that the mystic experience is a legitimate expression and has been a common occurrence within Judaism down through the centuries.[193] Even before Montefiore wrote his book in 1914, Schweitzer had written *Paul and his Interpreters*, published in English in 1912, in which Paul was presented as an eschatologically minded apocalyptic Jew (that is, that Paul's thought was essentially Jewish). The fact that Montefiore failed to address Schweitzer's claim does not reflect well on Montefiore's scholarship.[194] Montefiore's description of Pauline pessimism and mysticism as 'un-Rabbinic' had mixed support from Jewish scholars. Furthermore, his analysis can be shown in the light of later mainstream New Testament scholarship to have been overly simplistic.

It was Paul's concept of the Law, however, which most puzzled Montefiore and which was treated at length in 'First Impressions of St. Paul'. This was not simply the common Jewish complaint that Paul's 'violent antithesis between works and faith' would have been incomprehensible to the rabbis who had harmonised the two quite unconsciously. It was more to do with Paul's idea regarding the purpose of the Law. The idea that 'Through the Law comes the knowledge of sin' (Rom. 3:20) led Montefiore to agree with his old tutor Benjamin Jowett that, for Paul, sin was 'regarded as the consciousness of sin' and was therefore inextricably linked to the Law, a position he could at least understand. But Paul's idea that 'the giving of the Law was to make things worse, to increase the quality and accentuate the sharpness of sin' was another matter.[195] This position was, to Montefiore, in total opposition to the Jewish conception of the Law and could not be explained by reference to Hellenism – it could only be put down to the radical originality of its author.[196] Montefiore went on to examine various aspects of Paul's teaching on the Law, one by one. He concluded his survey by contrasting Paul's beliefs with the traditional ones.

> We have seen that while [the Law was] given apparently for eternity, its real purpose [according to Paul] was only temporary. Its seeming object was to make men better, and to qualify them for the kingdom of God; its true object was to create the knowledge and lust of sin. At its best, its intended result was to stimulate a desire for redemption through the medium of a spiritual despair; at its worst it led almost inevitably to self-delusion, hypocrisy and pride. It claims fulfilment, but no man can fulfil it; it demands obedience, but none can obey. It threatens the transgressor with a curse, but was only given that transgression might abound; it promises the doer of it reward, but the reward is

beyond man's power to attain. It assumes that its commands may be obeyed, but the assumption of obedience is more fatal than the consciousness of transgression. Its only end is death: death for him who tries and knows that he has failed, death to him who tries and thinks that he has accomplished ... Truly an awful gift of God; a marvellous issue of evil from that which in itself was 'holy and righteous and good'. Surely the disproportion of effect to cause is itself enough to prove the error of the argument.[197]

Taken as a whole, he felt that Paul's attitude towards the Law was lamentable and complained that the apostle made no distinction between moral and ceremonial ordinances and that his opinion alternated between 'good and divine' one minute, and 'the cause of sin and a curse' the next.[198] However, Montefiore did not want to overstate his case, adding, 'One must not ... suppose that Paul was really full of passionate hatred of the Law as such. He only got irritated when people tried to introduce the Law among Gentile converts.'[199] But he came down firmly that the apostle's view of the Law was nonetheless alien to Rabbinic Judaism. In this, as one might expect, Montefiore was followed by the majority of Jewish scholars. The traditional view was maintained by those like Hertz[200] and Graetz[201] who saw Paul as an opportunist for Gentile converts. Loewe[202] and Klausner[203] argued that his anti-Law teachings demonstrated a mistaken understanding of Judaism, while Kohler[204] and Buber[205] explicitly argued that Paul's skewed view of the Law had been over-influenced by Gnosticism. Sandmel[206] and Maccoby[207] explained Paul's position as the result of his own failure to observe the Law and the need to find an alternative. Thus, with the exception of Baeck[208] and Schoeps,[209] who felt that Paul understood the Gospel to transcend the Law, there has been almost unanimous agreement among Jewish writers with Montefiore's view of Paul as an abrogator of the Law.

On the related subject of repentance, Montefiore was emphatic in his condemnation of Paul. The apostle had believed that since the Law could not save men from the power of sin, Christ had come to end the Law and, among other things, grant them forgiveness. Montefiore simply could not reconcile this need for forgiveness with the concept of repentance, which he considered to be an integral element of Rabbinic Judaism. God might be angry, he reasoned, but he was also compassionate and 'delights in the exercise of forgiveness far more than the exercise of punishment'.[210] There was thus no need for Paul's despair.

> In no other respect do the Epistles of St Paul more clearly show their curious lack of relation to the actual religion of his contemporaries. And yet it is just here where the very hinge of his whole theology is fixed. I am at a loss to explain the puzzle.[211]

While he was aware that the idea of vicarious atonement was not unknown to the rabbis, Montefiore argued that such passages as referred to 'the merits of the Fathers' or 'the merits of the Righteous' were but a drop in the ocean compared to the overwhelming mass of passages about repentance and forgiveness. If anything, he protested, the rabbis erred on the side of compassion and were perhaps a little too inclined to think that God would inevitably pardon their transgressions.[212]

Once again, Montefiore's approach can be criticised in the light of subsequent New Testament scholarship. It is likely that Paul's view of the Law was not as unique amongst first-century Jews as Montefiore and his contemporaries had believed. In the Apocalypse of Ezra, for example, the Law is regarded as a special divine gift to Israel, which nevertheless cannot redeem the sinner; and W.D. Davies has stressed that 'in their attitude to the Law, despite their recognition of its impotence, both Paul and the author of 4 Ezra are typically rabbinic'.[213] More significantly still, many Pauline scholars (following E.P. Sanders) understand Paul's attitude towards the Law as a consequence of his discovery that Jesus was the messiah who had inaugurated the messianic age. That is, Paul is understood to have begun with the solution that God had saved his people through Christ, before finding fault with the Law; to Paul's mind, Christ had come to save, and hence the Law could never have been intended to do so.[214] In this context, repentance for breaking the commandments was neither here nor there – the important thing for Paul was that salvation could only have come through Christ. In line with the Protestant scholarship of his day, and concentrating almost exclusively on Romans and Galatians, Montefiore viewed Paul's theological journey as beginning with doubts about the Law and ending with his discovery of the solution in Christ. Reinforcing this view was Montefiore's own anti-halakhic convictions, which lay behind the founding of Anglo-Liberal Judaism. Since a liberation-from-tradition stance had been the justification for his own reformation and an integral element of his own self-identity, Montefiore could hardly have helped perceiving Paul's criticisms of the Law as anything other than central to the apostle's message.[215] In any case, his confidence in describing Paul's treatment of the Law as 'un-Rabbinic' now appears less certain, as does the idea (shared by many Christians and Jews) that Paul's criticism of Torah was central to his thought.

In summary, Montefiore felt that it was quite possible to imagine a hypothetical rabbinic Jew who had become a Christian and believed that Jesus was the messiah; who attacked the various abuses within the system; whose mysticism freed him from the shackles of sin; and who even taught that the Law was not binding on Gentiles (since the messianic era was at hand). What he had difficulty in accepting was that such a rabbinic Jew could have produced the theory of the Law found in Romans, have emphasised mysticism and pessimism to such a degree, or have ignored the rabbinic teachings on repentance and God's forgiveness. As he put it,

> From the Rabbinic Judaism of 500 as basis, many of the salient doctrines of the great Epistles could never have evolved. They would have been so very unnecessary, and, because unnecessary, they could not have been thought out.[216]

His argument was two-fold. Firstly, Paul's criticisms of Judaism rang hollow in the light of the evidence of rabbinic texts. Secondly, Paul could not have ignored key elements of Rabbinic Judaism if he had known them. The implication was that the apostle had not been familiar with Rabbinic Judaism. Thus he found himself 'disposed to look with suspicion' upon the idea that Paul was a disciple of Gamaliel, and maintained that 'Paul was no Rabbinic Jew'.[217] As regards the first charge, subsequent scholarship has shown Montefiore's conception of first-century Judaism to have been too limited in scope, that many of those aspects of Paul's thought which he identified as 'un-Rabbinic' could indeed be found in the rabbinic literature, and that his understanding of the apostle had been warped by the contemporary over-emphasis upon the critique of Judaism and of the teaching on justification by faith found in a restricted selection of the epistles. Nevertheless, Montefiore's second point, the question of why Paul seemingly ignored essential aspects of Judaism, has proved to have been of lasting influence. It has led scholars (following Sanders) to re-prioritise justification by faith in Paul's thought as a subsidiary, though not unimportant, element introduced for polemical purposes.[218]

Paul's 'Pre-Christian Religion'
The Jewish dilemma regarding Paul's background as Jewish or non-Jewish was clearly articulated by Solomon Schechter in 1909.

> Either the theology of the Rabbis must be wrong, its conception of God debasing, its leading motives materialistic and coarse, and its teachings lacking in enthusiasm and spirituality, or the Apostle to the Gentiles is quite unintelligible.[219]

As far as Schechter was concerned, one could not have it both ways. Either Paul had been familiar with the Judaism of his day and his criticisms had been justified; or, as Jews had protested down through the centuries, Paul had not been familiar with Judaism, his views had quite misrepresented the Jewish position and he had, in fact, attacked a Judaism which had never existed. (Schechter himself was at a loss to explain such a view.)

It was not until 1914 and *Judaism and St. Paul* that Montefiore was prepared to address the question of the nature of Paul's 'pre-Christian religion' directly.[220] In contrast to those Jews who had written before him, including Graetz,[221] Wise[222] and Kohler,[223] but in common with the majority of Protestant New Testament scholars, Montefiore had accepted Paul's criticisms as accurately representing the Judaism with which the apostle was familiar. (The idea that Paul might have exaggerated or misrepresented Judaism as a result of the heated polemicism had apparently not occurred to them.) He had therefore come to believe that the only fair and reasonable explanation of Paul's apparent ignorance of Rabbinic Judaism was that (i) Paul had come from a Judaism other than Rabbinic, and (ii) that he had been influenced by religious conceptions and practices that were non-Jewish. As he put it, 'The religion of Paul antecedent to his conversion must have been different from the typical and average Rabbinic Judaism of 300 or 500.'[224] By piecing together what Paul had to say about his pre-conversion religion, Montefiore concluded that the apostle's experience had been of a poorer, inferior kind of Judaism. In his opinion, it had been

> more systematic, and perhaps a little more philosophic and less child-like, but possibly for those very reasons it was less intimate, warm, joyous and comforting. Its God was more distant and less loving ... The early religion of Paul was more sombre and gloomy than Rabbinic Judaism; the world was a more miserable and God-forsaken place; there were fewer simple joys and happinesses ... The outlook was darker: man could be, and was, less good ... God was not constantly helping and forgiving.[225]

Another feature of this 'poorer religion' which helped to explain Paul's later theology was its more developed, less 'human' conception of the messiah.[226] Montefiore evaded Schechter's dilemma that Paul's writings had to be either essentially accurate in their analysis of Judaism, or totally misrepresentative and incomprehensible, by arguing that the pseudo-Judaism described by Paul was best understood as a transcendental, philosophic form of Judaism brought about from exposure to Hellenism.

Montefiore was by no means alone in viewing Hellenistic Judaism as 'transcendental'. G.F. Moore had written, 'How innocent were the Palestinian masters of an abstract or transcendent or any other sort of philosophical idea of God?'[227] and Abelson had considered the Hellenistic conception of God, as presented by Philo, as 'too impersonal. He is too much of a metaphysical entity.'[228] But others, including Abrahams and Bentwich, had argued contrary,[229] and Davies has pointed out that Jewish apocalypticism could have easily supplied the element of transcendentalism in place of Hellenistic philosophy.[230] Montefiore's neglect of certain Jewish eschatological writings had led him to describe Paul's attitude towards the Law as 'un-Rabbinic'; this is another case of where his general avoidance of the eschatological aspects of Paul's thought had flawed his understanding of the apostle. Schweitzer had been the first to criticise those writers who regarded eschatology as an aspect of Paul's thought which could be isolated, when in fact it had conditioned his theology throughout.[231] Similarly, Davies later argued that any treatment of Paul was, in a wider sense, a treatment of Jewish eschatology.[232] As far as Montefiore was concerned, however, Paul's expectation of the end of the world had been an unfortunate mistake, and one on which he would not dwell. Thus, as Bultmann would later do,[233] he marginalised the apostle's apocalyptic roots, and contextualised him instead in the world of Hellenistic-Jewish syncretism.[234]

Montefiore had redefined Paul's pre-conversion religion in terms of a first-century Judaism whilst simultaneously placing much of his thinking outside that of the rabbinic stream of thought. In this he was followed by James Parkes who interpreted Paul's criticisms to be against Diaspora Judaism[235] and by G.F. Moore who also agreed that the apostle's polemic was incomprehensible if directed against rabbinic Jews.[236] Even so, the idea that Paul should be understood primarily on the basis of Hellenistic Judaism rather than Rabbinic (or Palestinian) Judaism has not substantially influenced subsequent Pauline scholarship.[237] Nor has it found support among Jewish scholars who, with the exceptions of Baeck and Sandmel,[238] have approached Paul's background as either essentially Jewish[239] or essentially Hellenistic (non-Jewish).[240] Much of what Montefiore suggested was inadequate, not least his neat compartmentalisation of Hellenistic and Rabbinic Judaism, and the fact that several of the motifs which he regarded as derived from Hellenistic Judaism (such as Paul's pessimism, mysticism and transcendentalism) could, in fact, be found within the rabbinic literature. As Schoeps observed, it was almost inevitable that Montefiore's attempt to replace one unknown quantity, the theology of Saul, by another unknown quantity, the theology of the Pharisaic Diaspora, would have failed.[241] Even so, the eminent New Testament scholar E.P. Sanders, recognising the value of Montefiore's contribution in exploring the identity of Paul's pre-Christian religion, has criticised early twentieth-century scholars for failing to have taken up Montefiore's point that there must have been some reasonable explanation for why essential aspects of Rabbinic Judaism were missing from Paul.[242]

MONTEFIORE'S APPROPRIATION OF PAUL

In seeking to introduce Paul to a Jewish audience, Montefiore had been well aware of the obstacles in his path, not least the challenge of impartiality. He wrote,

> It may be that the Jew is both too near Paul and too far from him to do him justice or even adequately to understand him. The ashes of old controversies still glow within the Jew's mind and heart. Just as it is very hard for the modern Christian ... to understand and appreciate the Rabbinic religion, so it may also be very hard for the modern ... Jew to appreciate and understand Paul.[243]

Nevertheless, his characteristic optimism led him to argue that if there were spiritual benefits to be gained from reading Paul – and he was convinced there were – then it would be in the interests of modern Jews to approach the epistles with a more open mind. This attitude did not, however, prevent him from condemning those aspects of the apostle's thought which he felt were erroneous, as demonstrated in his treatment of Paul's view of Christ, and of his ethical and universalist teachings.

Paul and Christ

Montefiore based his assessment of Paul upon a limited number of letters.[244] One effect of this was to reject as Pauline the more developed christology of other epistles. He fully recognised the central importance of Christ in Paul's message; for the apostle, 'Christianity is not the Law plus Christ. It is Jesus Christ alone.'[245] But he imagined Paul's authentic view to have been that Christ, although pre-existent before his human birth, had originally been created by God, and suggested that the apostle had not sought to 'imply the co-eternity or co-equality of Christ with God'.[246] Obviously, since he was seeking to introduce the apostle to a Jewish audience in as positive a light as possible, it was in Montefiore's interest to play down Paul's conception of the divinity of Christ where he could. Nevertheless, this was a remarkable statement and set Montefiore apart from his Jewish contemporaries. Rightly or wrongly he had attempted to rescue Paul, to reinterpret the traditional reading of him, when all other Jews had been content to reject him *in toto*. Both as a Jew and as a Liberal, Montefiore had opposed any claim of divinity for Jesus. The superimposition of one's beliefs onto Jesus has by no means been an uncommon occurrence among either Christians or Jews who wished to enrol Jesus as a supporter of their ideas. What was remarkable was that Montefiore, as a Jew, should have chosen to treat the Great Apostate in such a way.

Of course, there were many aspects of Paul's teachings that Montefiore could not salvage or reinterpret. When this occurred, he made his unconditional rejection of Paul's teaching clear. An obvious example can be seen in their differing appreciations of Christ's significance. Montefiore pointed out that the epistles rarely alluded to Jesus' recorded teachings, and suggested that Paul's relationship to Christ was that of disciple to master only as far as the messiahship, crucifixion and resurrection were concerned.[247] He could not sympathise with Paul's conception of the nature of Christ's work for man:

> First and foremost, it is not the work which Christ himself essayed to do in the narratives of the Synoptics. It is not the work of a great teacher. For Paul the significance of Christ's work lies almost exclusively in his crucifixion and resurrection. His work is essentially miraculous and super-natural. It is conditioned by his nature.[248]

To Montefiore, whose rationalistic world-view excluded the miraculous, and who so admired the ethical sermons of Jesus, this was a very unfortunate misrepresentation of the Jewish teacher. That the apostle seemingly placed Christ's ethical work in a secondary position – 'ethical not only in the creation of human faith with all its issues, but also because it was, in itself, an exhibition of goodness and love'[249] – was to be regretted.

Another example was a difference in the reasoning behind Jesus' and Paul's disagreements with Judaism. In 'Rabbinic Judaism and the Epistles of St. Paul', Montefiore argued that the apostle did not attack Judaism for the 'real evils and defects which Jesus found and censored in the religion of his time' but for theological and theoretical differences with Christianity.[250] While Jesus attacked the replacement of morality with legal ritual, Montefiore could find no similar charge made in the epistles; he argued that for Paul the Law was sin, 'not in virtue of its containing a number of purely ritual enactments, but because it is law and all that law implies'.[251] Again, Montefiore pointed out that while Paul censored 'boastings', these were not 'the practical and everyday evils which are so nobly castigated by Jesus', that is, the self-righteousness and spiritual pride of the super-religious. And finally, while Montefiore could understand Jesus' attacks on the weaknesses of the 'ill-directed intellectualism' which he felt had hampered first-century Judaism, he found no parallel in Paul's rejection of wisdom and knowledge which 'springs from different roots and has different implications'.[252] He argued,

> It is the theological opposition between human merit and divine grace which is the dominating subject before the writer's [Paul's] mind, not an actual society of men.[253]

In contrasting Jesus' internal criticism with Paul's external, metaphysical concerns, Montefiore had found a way by which he hoped to validate, and then incorporate, Jesus' Jewish teachings, whilst remaining free to reject what he regarded as Paul's non-Jewish doctrines. To Jews, the two had been linked together for a long time and Montefiore wanted the differences to be clear: Paul came from outside the fold and was influenced by Hellenistic concepts, while Jesus was a reformer, concerned with correcting certain specific abuses within Judaism. In particular, Paul's christology had emphasised the saving work of Christ at the expense of the teachings of Christ, and therefore could not easily be appropriated.

Paul's Ethics and Universalism
Due to his somewhat distorted perception of Paul, Montefiore regarded the apostle's ethical teaching as peripheral, that is, constituting only a small part of his teachings as a whole. His fixation upon Paul's critique of Judaism and championship of justification of faith over works (as emphasised in Romans and Galatians) had blinded him to the centrality of the theme of being 'in Christ' – and thus to the closely related issue of social behaviour. What is now regarded as an essential area of study within Pauline scholarship[254] was, for Montefiore, essentially only a passing reference to the debt Paul owed Judaism. Nonetheless, he felt that Paul's ethical teachings were

comprehensive and wrote admiringly of the wealth of ethical language.[255] The apostle's exhortations did not exceed the best moral teachings of the Old Testament and rabbinic literature since, as he reminded his Jewish readers, it had originated from these sources (a view supported by Sanders).[256] Yet he could not help but admire their 'spirit and sureness of touch, a vigour and connectedness essentially their own'.[257] There was a unity in Paul's ethics; his beliefs, in contrast to the rabbis' writings were,

> deducible from certain principles, so that they become something more than isolated and heterogeneous maxims. They may fairly be said to flow from the one central principle of Love.[258]

Ever concerned with what practical use he could make of religious teachings, Montefiore pointed out several other advantages which he felt Paul's ethical writings possessed over the rabbis': they were easily available, were conveniently contained within a single volume, and were 'nobly expressed and redolent of enthusiasm and genius'.[259]

Montefiore found Paul's ethical writings deeply inspirational. He suggested that the apostle's religious and moral enthusiasm was the secret to his 'perennial power over the hearts of men' and he found in his hatred of sin a continual challenge.[260] Also, he recognised and admired Paul's attempt to base his religion upon the love of God, that is, on the love of God to man and on the love of man towards God, and was keen to commend this to his Jewish audience.[261] It was this inspirational aspect of Paul's ethical teachings that he most wanted to appropriate for the modern day.

A more significant departure from Rabbinic Judaism, Montefiore noted, had been Paul's universalist teachings. As a Liberal Jew, Montefiore considered the particularism of Rabbinic Judaism to have been its 'great outstanding fault'.[262] He regretted the fact that, historically, the Jew of 500 (just like the Christian of 500) expected his 'enemy' to receive damnation. At the same time, Montefiore wanted to emphasise that

> this indifference, dislike, contempt, particularism, – this ready and not unwilling consignment of the non-believer

and the non-Jew to perdition and gloom, – was quite consistent with the most passionate religious faith and with the most exquisite and delicate charity.[263]

It was not that he failed to understand how the situation had arisen, but that he felt that the conditions that had determined the exclusion of Gentiles within Judaism no longer applied in the modern day. This was an integral part of the teaching of Montefiore's own Liberal Judaism. It does not come as a surprise, then, to find him praising those aspects of Paul's teaching which were concerned with 'breaking down the wall of distinction between Jew and Gentile'.[264] He himself had come to the same conclusion as Paul, namely that 'Judaism could not become a universal religion together with its inviolate Law'.[265] He believed that Paul's knowledge of the Hellenistic mystery cults had influenced his pre-Christian thinking and made him ready and eager to discover a universal method of salvation, suited and predestined for all mankind. But while he commended Paul for preaching universalism and solving the 'puzzle of the universal God and the national cult',[266] he could not accept the new form of religious particularism which Paul had forged. Neither could he credit Paul for originating the idea. He felt that, keeping in mind Old Testament universalist passages such as those found in Jonah, Isaiah 51 and several Psalms, 'one has to acknowledge that Paul has only smoothed more completely, more definitely, what these others had begun to smooth before him'.[267]

In this, of course, Montefiore was reiterating a common contemporary Jewish claim that God had always intended Judaism to have been a universal religion, transcending national and racial boundaries. As Montefiore was well aware, however, Paul had taught that only those 'in Christ' could be 'saved', something quite different from the Liberal aspirations for a non-racial, non-religious Judaism. Thus Montefiore's appropriation of the apostle's universalist teachings was necessarily limited.

CONCLUSION

Looking back over Paul's theology as a whole, Montefiore could not avoid regarding it as fatally flawed. The vast mass of Paul's theology had to be rejected, he explained, because

> If all men are 'saved' *whether they believe in Christ or reject him*, whether they are idolaters or monotheists, [then] the basis of Pauline theology collapses. The whole scheme and fabric tumble like a pack of cards to the ground. [Italics mine][268]

Significantly, Paul failed not so much because Montefiore was a Jew but because he was a Liberal. In the light of his Liberal beliefs, and in spite of his original plan (to preserve as much religious truth in Paul's teachings as possible), Montefiore could not help but regard the majority of Paul's teaching as redundant. 'Is, then, anything left over?' he wondered.

> What a mass we have rejected! Paul's pessimism, his Christology, much in his conception of sin, his conception of the Law, his conception of God's wrath, his demonology, his view of human past and human future, have all gone by the board.[269]

Nor could Paul be of much use with regard to the Holy Spirit, or the character of God. This was because Paul's doctrine concerning these had to be pruned and curtailed before any use could be made of it, and even what remained did not significantly go beyond what had been taught in the Old Testament, the Apocrypha and in the rabbinical literature.[270]

Even so, there were fragments of the apostle which it suited Montefiore's purposes to concentrate upon, and which he felt might well be profitable for Liberal Judaism to appropriate. At the top of this list was, of course, Paul's introduction of a practical (although imperfect) universalism. Again, he admired the apostle's teaching in not giving needless offence for the benefit of those who were 'weaker' in faith. This was a policy which he attempted to practice in the context of the Anglo-Jewish response to his own Liberal teachings, especially with regard to the lax Liberal observation of the dietary laws.[271] Similarly, Montefiore felt that the controversial use of the vernacular in synagogue services could be justified along the lines of argument that Paul had offered so many centuries before.[272] There was even one element of Paul's objection to justification by works that was worth salvaging. According to Montefiore, the apostle had taught that one failed to win righteousness by fulfilling the Law

because one could never fulfil it; worse still, one failed to win
righteousness even if one did fulfil the Law. In spite of his recognition that 'no Jew ever looked at the Law from this point of view',
Montefiore admitted that he felt there was, indeed, a danger that
'works righteousness' could lead to self-righteousness and self-
delusion.[273] Interestingly, he also admired Paul's mysticism, 'its
solemnity, its power and its beauty' even as a 'double outsider
... that is, a Jew who is not a mystic'.[274] He especially appreciated
Paul's teaching regarding the reproduction of the death and the
risen life of the messiah in the experience of each individual
believer, seeing in it a parallel to the rabbinic teaching that a
proselyte, brought to the knowledge of the One God, was made
new and recreated.[275] Paul's attitude towards suffering could
also be learned from. He observed,

> Paul not only rises superior to his sufferings, but he rejoices
> in them. And perhaps in this exultation and rejoicing lies
> the most peculiar and instructive feature of his career, the
> feature, moreover, in which he was, though perhaps un-
> consciously, in fullest accordance with the teaching of his
> Master and Lord.[276]

Far more than any of his Jewish contemporaries, Montefiore
had approached Paul as a source of inspiration and religious
insight, someone whom modern Jews would do well to study.
With his hope for a future religion that would encompass the
best of both Judaism and Christianity, he was able to credit Paul
for his contributions to religious evolution. Essentially, however,
his appropriation of Paul was limited to what he regarded as
fresh expressions of Jewish teaching. Montefiore has been criticised for having over-emphasised 'the purely ethical side of the
Apostle's teaching' and for having 'destroyed much of the "real"
Paul and substituted a new individual'.[277] Certainly, his understanding of Paul's thought had been biased by the traditional
Protestant and Jewish view of an intensely anti-nomian and
anti-Jewish Apostle to the Gentiles. But in terms of the Pauline
scholarship of his day, Montefiore's views were understandable.
The criticism is true, however, in the context of his hermeneutical
treatment of Paul; if one were to recreate Paul according to the
aspects that Montefiore regarded as 'positive' in his teaching, he
would be unrecognisable. In this sense, Montefiore's Paul, even

more so than Montefiore's Jesus, is incompatible with Christian tradition. But it is so precisely because his primary concern was to interpret Paul to the Jews for whom the traditional image was repulsive; thus, in sharp contrast to previous Jewish practice, he openly praised what he felt the epistles had to offer Judaism and quietly rejected all that he believed was unserviceable.

NOTES

137. It is no coincidence that it is liberal theologians (Alfred Loisy, a French Catholic modernist, and Adolf Harnack, a German Protestant liberal) who were so greatly favoured by Montefiore and are referred to repeatedly. Other Christian theologians mentioned in Montefiore's writings on Paul include Dieterich, Reitzenstein, Pfleiderer and Weizacker, Kirsop Lake and van Manen, Bousset, Vernon Bartlet. Montefiore seems to refer to Jews (Isaac Abrahams, Büchler, Bacher and Solomon Schechter) only with respect to the character of early Rabbinic Judaism.
138. C.G. Montefiore, *Judaism and St. Paul: Two Essays* (1914), p. 142.
139. G. Kittel, 'Paulus im Talmud', in *Rabbinica, Arbeiten zur Religionsgeschichte des Urchristentums* 1, 3 (Leipzig, 1920), cited in D. Hagner, 'Paul in Modern Thought', in D.A. Hagner and M.J. Harris, eds, *Pauline Studies: Essays Presented to F.F. Bruce* (1980), p. 160.
140. J. Klausner, *From Jesus to Paul* (1943), pp. 310–11.
141. A commentary on Proverbs 21:8, which refers to the 'man' whose 'way is forward and strange'. L. Baeck, 'The Faith of Paul', *Journal of Jewish Studies*, III (1952), p. 109.
142. D. Hagner, 'Paul in Modern Thought', in D.A. Hagner and M.J. Harris, eds, *Pauline Studies: Essays Presented to F.F. Bruce* (1980).
143. Ibid., p. 144.
144. Hagner's list includes Heinrich Graetz, C.G. Montefiore, Kaufmann Kohler, Joseph Klausner, Martin Buber, Leo Baeck, Samuel Sandmel, Hans Joachim Schoeps, Schalom Ben-Chorin and Richard L. Rubinstein. Ibid., pp. 144, 145. Other treatments include Isaac M. Wise, Hugh Schonfield, David Flusser, Pinchas Lapide, Hyam Maccoby, Nancy Fuchs-Kreimer, Alan Segal and Daniel Boyarin.
145. Ibid., p. 144.
146. M. Buber, *Two Types of Faith* (1951) and K. Kohler, 'Saul of Tarsus', in I. Singer, ed., *Jewish Encyclopaedia*, XI (1905), pp. 79–87.
147. Leo Baeck expresses this well. 'The first thing we see is that there is a centre about which everything turns. The point on which everything depends, round which everything revolved in Paul's life, and the point at which his faith became his life was the vision which overpowered him when one day he saw the Messiah and heard his voice. This vision immediately became, and remained, the central fact of Paul's life ... One must start from it in order to understand Paul, his personality and his confession.' L. Baeck, 'The Faith of Paul', *Journal of Jewish Studies*, III (1952), p. 94.
148. E.P. Sanders, *Paul and Palestinian Judaism* (1977), pp. 2–3. However, while Thackeray might not have been familiar with the rabbinic writings, he

did translate Josephus and was thus more familiar with first-century Judaism(s) than perhaps he realised; more recent scholarship certainly places greater emphasis upon Josephus' writings than upon the rabbis' in reconstructing first-century Judaism(s).

149. Letter from C.G. Montefiore to Lucy Cohen, date uncertain. L. Cohen, *Some Recollections of Claude Goldsmid-Montefiore 1858–1938* (1940), p. 85.

150. The comment was made in the context of Montefiore's appreciation of both St Paul and the rabbis. *Jewish Chronicle*, 8 February 1901, p. 27.

151. S. Neill and T. Wright, *The Interpretation of the New Testament 1861–1986* (1989), pp. 408–9. The meaning of 'hermeneutics' adopted here is that of 'the reinterpretation of past tradition to make sense of present realities'.

152. The *Religionsgeschichteliche* (Religio-historical school) sought to interpret Jesus and early Christianity by reference to the beliefs and practices of late Hellenism; it saw the New Testament as part of the religious processes at work in the Levant in the period before and after Christianity.

153. In particular, E.P. Sanders, *Paul and Palestinian Judaism* (1977) has dominated Pauline studies over the past two decades. His understanding of Judaism in terms of 'covenantal nominism' came about largely as a response to the critique of Montefiore (and others) of the Lutheran-Protestant view of Judaism, as he explains in his introduction. It is worth noting that Sanders' new perspective, namely, that the rabbinic discussions *presupposed* the covenant and were largely directed toward the question of how to fulfil the covenantal obligations rather than how to ensure salvation, is not disputed by even his fiercest critic, Jacob Neusner (who takes exception only to his methodology).

154. As he put it, 'There may be a good deal [of Paul's teaching] to adapt, although comparably little to adopt.' C.G. Montefiore, *Judaism and St. Paul: Two Essays* (1914), p. 142.

155. C.G. Montefiore, *The Old Testament and After* (1923), p. 590.

156. C.G. Montefiore, 'Rabbinic Judaism and the Epistles of St. Paul', *Jewish Quarterly Review*, XIII (1901), pp. 165–7.

157. In this context Montefiore quoted the Hellenistic Jew Philo, whom he described as 'a contemporary of St Paul … a strictly observant Jew', whose advice he felt might well have applied to Paul: 'There are some who, when they have discovered the spiritual meaning of the Law, think that they are free from the letter, and need no longer observe the ordinances.' Ibid., p. 166.

158. C.G. Montefiore, 'Rabbinic Judaism and the Epistles of St. Paul', *Jewish Quarterly Review*, XIII (1901), p. 170.

159. Ibid.

160. Ibid., p. 172.

161. Sanders has suggested that on certain subjects (including the Law and the salvation of Israel) Paul got himself into muddles from which scholars should not try to extricate him. While deeply concerned with theological problems, Paul was not systematic, that is, he did not attempt to reconcile his responses to varying Church difficulties. S. Neill and T. Wright, *The Interpretation of the New Testament 1861–1986* (1989), p. 424; E.P. Sanders, *Paul and Palestinian Judaism* (1977), p. 128.

162. C.G. Montefiore, 'Rabbinic Judaism and the Epistles of St. Paul', *Jewish Quarterly Review*, XIII (1901), p. 162.

163. Ibid., p. 164.

164. Montefiore was not the only Pauline scholar to have treated the rabbis too uniformly. W.D. Davies' seminal work *Paul and Rabbinic Judaism* (1948)

has been similarly criticised, as has E.P. Sanders. The fine-tuning of the rabbinic texts by scholars such as Jacob Neusner for chronological and other distinctions is a relatively recent phenomenon.

165. For example, he referred extensively to Philo in 'Notes on the Religious Value of the Fourth Gospel' (1895).
166. Torah-centricity does not, of course, rule out different understandings of the Torah, as was certainly the case in the first century when many Jewish religious systems co-existed side by side.
167. Elsewhere he wrote that the 'Rabbinic Religion' knew nothing of any opposition between faith and works. C.G. Montefiore, *The Old Testament and After* (1923), p. 384.
168. C.G. Montefiore, *Judaism and St. Paul: Two Essays* (1914), p. 89.
169. C.G. Montefiore, 'Rabbinic Judaism and the Epistles of St. Paul', *Jewish Quarterly Review*, XIII (1901), pp. 205–6.
170. C.G. Montefiore, *Judaism and St. Paul: Two Essays* (1914), pp. 61–2.
171. For example, Davies argued that the figures of the (supernatural) Son of Man and that of the messiah had been merged in Jewish literature before the Christian era. W.D. Davies, *Paul and Rabbinic Judaism* (1955), pp. 279, 280.
172. Ibid., p. 352.
173. It has been suggested that the full weight of Davies' case has yet to be taken on-board by mainstream New Testament scholars. S. Neill and T. Wright, *The Interpretation of the New Testament 1861–1986* (1989), pp. 412–13.
174. No sources are given for this example. That there was 'in the first century, strong interest in proselytes and proselytism' was taken as read: 'The facts are well-known and reported in detail in the text-books.' C.G. Montefiore, *Judaism and St. Paul: Two Essays* (1914), pp. 62–3.
175. Ibid., p. 64.
176. Ibid., pp. 114–15.
177. C.G. Montefiore, *The Old Testament and After* (1923), p. 385.
178. C.G. Montefiore, 'Rabbinic Judaism and the Epistles of St. Paul', *Jewish Quarterly Review*, XIII (1901), p. 187.
179. Paul had 'robbed human life of its healthy impulses, the human soul of its faith in its own regenerating powers … and in its inherent tendencies to do good'. K. Kohler, 'Saul of Tarsus', in I. Singer, ed., *Jewish Encyclopaedia*, XI (1905), p. 87.
180. Referring to the Talmudic categorisation of seven types of Pharisee (which condemned both 'the Pharisee "out of fear"' and the one who asked 'What is my duty that I may perform it?'), Klausner suggested that on the evidence of Romans 7 alone, the pre-conversion Paul would have been counted among the condemned. J. Klausner, *From Jesus to Paul* (1943), p. 499.
181. Maccoby felt that such a world-view was central to the apostle's psychology, insisting 'The importance of the conception of an evil power or the Devil in Paul's thought, or rather mythology, cannot be overestimated.' H. Maccoby, *The Mythmaker: Paul and the Invention of Christianity* (1986), p. 186.
182. 'Paulinism' could characterise both Christian and Jewish thought, although for Buber, of course, the tendency was less pronounced in Judaism with its emphasis upon, and hope inherent in, *emunah* faith, in contrast to Pauline Christian *pistis* faith. M. Buber, *Two Types of Faith* (1951), p. 169.
183. A. Schweitzer, *Paul and his Interpreters* (English translation, 1912) was

translated from the German original *Geschichte der Paulinischen Forschung* (1912), and *The Mysticism of Paul the Apostle* (English translation, 1931) was translated from the German original *Die Mystik der Apostels Paulus* (1930).

184. C.G. Montefiore, *Judaism and St. Paul: Two Essays* (1914), pp. 116–17.

185. Ibid., p. 50.

186. Paul's condemnation of 'human wisdom, reason and common sense' and his appeal to 'faith and vision' had opened wide the door for 'all kinds of mysticism and superstition'. K. Kohler, 'Saul of Tarsus', in I. Singer, ed., *Jewish Encyclopaedia*, XI (1905), p. 87.

187. Maccoby denounced Paul's idea of 'being in Christ' (which he, Maccoby, understood as 'a kind of unity with, or sinking of the individual into the divine personality of Jesus'), as having no parallel in Jewish literature, and as a teaching that 'involves a relationship to the Divine that is alien to Judaism'. H. Maccoby, *The Mythmaker: Paul and the Invention of Christianity* (1986), p. 63.

188. Paul's mystical experience had resulted in 'new and heightened insights within his inherited and precious Judaism' reminiscent of the Old Testament prophets. Mysticism and prophecy were interwoven in Sandmel's mind. S. Sandmel, *The Genius of Paul: A Study in History* (1958), pp. 75, 92, 89.

189. Klausner did not admire mysticism, but he wrote, 'There is nothing in the teaching of Paul – not even the mystical elements in it – that did not come to him from authentic Judaism.' J. Klausner, *From Jesus to Paul* (1943), p. 466.

190. For Wise, mysticism was the key to understanding Paul, whom he identified with the Talmudic figure, Acher. 'That passage [II Cor. 12] gave rise to the story of Jesus appearing in person to Paul, just as the rabbinical mystics claimed to have had frequent intercourse with the prophet Elijah, who had been transported alive to heaven.' I. Wise, 'Paul and the Mystics', in I.M. Wise, *Three Lectures on the Origin of Christianity* (1883), pp. 58–9.

191. Segal went even further in suggesting that Paul was the only early Jewish mystic whose personal, confessional writing had come down to us; central to the formation of his theology, *Merkabah* mysticism accounted for the great emphasis the apostle placed upon the transformation of the believer 'in Christ'. A.F. Segal, *Paul the Convert: The Apostolate and Apostasy of Saul the Pharisee* (1992), p. 34.

192. W.D. Davies, *Paul and Rabbinic Judaism* (1955), p. 13.

193. For example, G.G. Scholem, *Major Trends in Jewish Mysticism*, 3rd edn (1955).

194. Schweitzer's *The Mysticism of Paul the Apostle* (German original 1930, English translation 1931) developed several central themes of his earlier work, including the importance of Christ-mysticism (being 'in Christ') in the thought of the apostle over and above his teaching regarding justification by faith. This reversal of the traditional understanding had no effect on Montefiore.

195. C.G. Montefiore, 'First Impressions of St. Paul', *Jewish Quarterly Review*, VI (1894), p. 437.

196. Ibid., p. 438.

197. Ibid., pp. 447–8.

198. Ibid., p. 446.

199. Ibid., p. 438.

200. J.H. Hertz, *Affirmations of Judaism* (1927), p. 154n.

201. H. Graetz, *History of the Jews: From the Earliest Times to the Present Day*, II (1901), pp. 226, 228, 321.

202. C.G. Montefiore and Herbert Loewe, eds, *A Rabbinic Anthology* (1938), p. 669.

203. J. Klausner, *From Jesus to Paul* (1943), pp. 415, 603.

204. K. Kohler, 'Saul of Tarsus', in I. Singer, ed., *Jewish Encyclopaedia*, XI (1905), pp. 84–5.

205. M. Buber, *Two Types of Faith* (1951), pp. 80, 82–3.

206. S. Sandmel, *The Genius of Paul: A Study in History* (1958), pp. 28–32.

207. H. Maccoby, *The Mythmaker: Paul and the Invention of Christianity* (1986), pp. 95, 131, 188-9.

208. L. Baeck, 'The Faith of Paul', *Journal of Jewish Studies*, III (1952), pp. 106–7.

209. H.J. Schoeps, *Paul: The Apostle in the Light of Jewish Religious History* (1961), pp. 173, 213.

210. C.G. Montefiore, *Judaism and St. Paul: Two Essays* (1914), p. 42.

211. C.G. Montefiore, 'Rabbinic Judaism and the Epistles of St. Paul', *Jewish Quarterly Review*, XIII (1901), p. 199.

212. Ibid., pp. 201, 203.

213. W.D. Davies, *Paul and Rabbinic Judaism* (1955), p. 11.

214. E.P. Sanders, *Paul and Palestinian Judaism* (1977), p. 100.

215. Montefiore was not the only one. Chief Rabbi Hertz also saw a connection and described the Liberal Jewish attitude towards the Law as 'an echo of Paul'. J.H. Hertz, *Sermons, Addresses and Studies*, 3 vols (1938), p. 157.

216. C.G. Montefiore, *Judaism and St. Paul: Two Essays* (1914), p. 82.

217. Ibid., p. 91.

218. Before Sanders, this position was championed by Schweitzer and W.D. Davies. S. Neill and T. Wright, *The Interpretation of the New Testament 1861–1986* (1989), p. 414n.

219. S. Schechter, *Some Aspects of Rabbinic Theology* (1909), p. 18.

220. The phrase 'Paul's pre-Christian religion' and even the idea of 'Paul the Christian' are arguably simplistic. Such concerns were typical of late nineteenth-century New Testament scholarship.

221. H. Graetz, *History of the Jews: From the Earliest Times to the Present Day*, II (1901).

222. I. Wise, 'Paul and the Mystics', in I.M. Wise, *Three Lectures on the Origin of Christianity* (1883).

223. K. Kohler, 'Saul of Tarsus', in I. Singer, ed., *Jewish Encyclopaedia*, XI (1905).

224. C.G. Montefiore, *Judaism and St. Paul: Two Essays* (1914), p. 81.

225. Ibid., pp. 81–2.

226. Ibid., p. 126.

227. G.F. Moore, *Judaism in the First Centuries of the Christian Era: The Age of the Tannaim*, 7th impression, 3 vols (1954), II, p. 28f.

228. J. Abelson, *The Immanence of God in Rabbinical Literature* (1912), p. 72.

229. Abrahams protested, 'Does not Philo again and again compare God to a Father? Philo is full of warmth.' (J. Abelson, *The Immanence of God in Rabbinical Literature* (1912), p. 72n.) Bentwich agreed, observing, 'Before his God he [Philo] retains the child-like simplicity of the most un-Hellenic rabbi, and the perfect humility of the Hasid.' (N. Bentwich, *Philo-Judaeus of Alexandria*, 139.) Cited in W.D. Davies, *Paul and Rabbinic Judaism*, 11.

230. W.D. Davies, *Paul and Rabbinic Judaism* (1955), p. 12.

231. A. Schweitzer, *Paul and his Interpreters* (1912), p. 53.

232. W.D. Davies, *Paul and Rabbinic Judaism* (1955), p. 285. Eschatology is the study of the End Times.

233. Bultmann differed in that he reacted by translating Paul's thought into other categories, specifically existentialist ones. S. Neill and T. Wright, *The Interpretation of the New Testament 1861–1986* (1989), p. 411.
234. The world of the aforementioned *Religionsgeschichtliche Schule*, represented by men such as Bousset, Dieterich and Reitzenstein, which had been shunned by Schweitzer. C.G. Montefiore, *Judaism and St. Paul: Two Essays* (1914), pp. 112–29.
235. J. Parkes, *Jesus, Paul and the Jews* (1936), p. 124.
236. It should be noted that while Moore agreed that Paul was wrong about matters that were essential to Rabbinic Judaism, he disagreed with Montefiore's solution (that is, he disagreed that Paul was addressing Hellenistic Jews). He suggested that Paul's attacks were comprehensible if, instead, he had been writing to Gentiles, trying to persuade them that only Christ saves, and not Judaism – whether by works or forgiveness. In this case, it would be of no consequence which elements of Judaism he had emphasised or neglected. G.F. Moore, *Judaism in the First Centuries of the Christian Era: The Age of the Tannaim*, 7th impression, 3 vols (1954), III, p. 151.
237. Montefiore's arguments are considered at length by both W.D. Davies and E.P. Sanders, although ultimately rejected. Within Jewish studies the theory has been described by Walter Jacob as 'original and tempting'. W. Jacob, 'Claude G. Montefiore's Reappraisal of Christianity', *Judaism*, IXX (Summer 1970), p. 341.
238. Both Baeck and Sandmel understood Paul as an authentic Diaspora or Hellenistic Jew. Following Montefiore, each accepted that, ultimately, Paul could only be explained in terms of both Jewish and non-Jewish influences.
239. In discussing Paul's background, he has been defined alternatively as a Pharisaic Jew (Graetz and Schoeps), a Talmudic Rabbi (Wise) and a mystic-Pharisee (Segal).
240. In emphasising Paul's non-Jewish background, he has been defined as primarily Hellenistic by Kohler, Klausner, Buber and Maccoby.
241. H.J. Schoeps, *Paul: The Apostle in the Light of Jewish Religious History* (1961), p. 26.
242. E.P. Sanders, *Paul and Palestinian Judaism* (1977), p. 10.
243. C.G. Montefiore, *Judaism and St. Paul: Two Essays* (1914), pp. 133–4.
244. These were I Thessalonians, Galatians, I and II Corinthians, Romans and Philippians. C.G. Montefiore, 'First Impressions of St. Paul', *Jewish Quarterly Review*, VI (1894), p. 428.
245. C.G. Montefiore, *Judaism and St. Paul: Two Essays* (1914), p. 129.
246. C.G. Montefiore, 'First Impressions of St. Paul', *Jewish Quarterly Review*, VI (1894), p. 430.
247. Ibid., p. 429.
248. Ibid., p. 450.
249. Ibid.
250. C.G. Montefiore, 'Rabbinic Judaism and the Epistles of St. Paul', *Jewish Quarterly Review*, XIII (1901), p. 168.
251. Ibid.
252. Ibid., pp. 168–9.
253. Ibid., p. 169.
254. As Sanders puts it, the Pauline epistles represent early attempts to offer a code of behaviour which is founded upon the Jewish principle of 'love thy neighbour' together with the apostle's new principle of 'union with Christ'. E.P. Sanders, *Paul and Palestinian Judaism* (1977), p. 116.

255. C.G. Montefiore, 'First Impressions of St. Paul', *Jewish Quarterly Review*, VI (1894), p. 468.
256. Sanders writes of Paul, 'When forced to think, he was a creative theologian; but on ethical issues he was seldom forced to think, and simply sought to impose Jewish behaviour on his Gentile converts.' E.P. Sanders, *Paul and Palestinian Judaism* (1977), p. 116.
257. C.G. Montefiore, 'First Impressions of St. Paul', *Jewish Quarterly Review*, VI (1894), p. 466.
258. Ibid., pp. 466–7. This view of Pauline theology as somehow fixed and complete would now be regarded as rather dated. Today, the majority of New Testament scholars tend towards a view of Paul as struggling to harmonise his thinking and certainly do not find him quite so systematic.
259. C.G. Montefiore, *Judaism and St. Paul: Two Essays* (1914), pp. 208–9.
260. C.G. Montefiore, 'First Impressions of St. Paul', *Jewish Quarterly Review*, VI (1894), p. 472.
261. 'Nor can we forget that the great Apostle of Faith has yet placed Faith below Love'. Ibid., p. 473.
262. C.G. Montefiore, *Judaism and St. Paul: Two Essays* (1914), p. 53.
263. Ibid., p.56.
264. Letter from Benjamin Jowett to C.G. Montefiore, 14 September 1884. L. Cohen, *Some Recollections of Claude Goldsmid-Montefiore 1858–1938* (1940), p. 35.
265. C.G. Montefiore, *Judaism and St. Paul: Two Essays* (1914), p. 145.
266. C.G. Montefiore, *Liberal Judaism and Hellenism and Other Essays* (1918), p. 119.
267. C.G. Montefiore, *The Old Testament and After* (1923), p. 287.
268. C.G. Montefiore, *Judaism and St. Paul: Two Essays* (1914), p. 137.
269. Ibid., p. 141.
270. C.G. Montefiore, *The Old Testament and After* (1923), p. 208.
271. C.G. Montefiore, *Judaism and St. Paul: Two Essays* (1914), p. 183.
272. He quoted Paul's comments, 'If I know not the meaning of the language, the speaker is unintelligible to me' and 'How shall the unlearned say Amen to your thanksgiving, if he does not understand what you say?' Ibid., pp. 192–4.
273. C.G. Montefiore, 'First Impressions of St. Paul', *Jewish Quarterly Review*, VI (1894), pp. 443–4.
274. C.G. Montefiore, *Judaism and St. Paul: Two Essays* (1914), p. 194. In a letter to Lucy Cohen, he remarked, 'I am no good at mysticism, only respectful.' L. Cohen, *Some Recollections of Claude Goldsmid-Montefiore 1858–1938* (1940), p. 113.
275. C.G. Montefiore, *Judaism and St. Paul: Two Essays* (1914), pp. 193–4, 200.
276. Ibid., p. 201.
277. W. Jacob, 'Claude G. Montefiore's Reappraisal of Christianity', *Judaism*, IXX (Summer 1970), p. 339.

Conclusion

As has happened to me before I shall probably be attacked by both Jews and Christians. To the second I shall not go nearly far enough; to the first, a great deal too far. I can, however, only set down what seems to me the facts and the truth. (Claude Montefiore)[1]

My originality is my queer mixture, half Jew and half Christian, as Zangwill once said of me. (Claude Montefiore)[2]

As a British intellectual Jew living in the late nineteenth and early twentieth centuries, the challenges facing Claude Montefiore and his conception of 'the Englishman of the Jewish persuasion' included, firstly, the general threat of modernity and the consequent challenge of religious apathy. Secondly, the related conflict between nationalist and non-nationalist conceptions of Jewishness. Thirdly, the question of how to reconcile loyalty to Judaism with admiration of the cultural, intellectual and even theological achievements of the surrounding Christian environment. Fourthly, and lastly, the need to correct anti-Jewish biblical scholarship. It has been argued that the formation of Anglo-Liberal Judaism and the development of its distinctive theological views came about essentially as the result of one man's highly individualised response to these historically conditioned dilemmas.

This book began with an analysis of Montefiore's immediate religious background, Anglo-Reform Judaism. It went on to trace the development of his controversial Liberal Judaism as an alternative to both Reform and Orthodoxy in Britain, and demonstrated its independence from similar movements in Germany and America. Montefiore's position regarding various issues hotly debated among western Jewish intelligentsia in his day was then explored, including the relevance of Rabbinic Judaism and nationality, and also the unfamiliar ways in which he expressed his Jewishness in terms of its essence and theology. The result was the distinct impression that a non-Jewish influence had profoundly shaped his thought, the identity of which was hinted at in his conviction that Jewish and Christian teaching ideally complemented one another.

In Part Two, the precise ways in which the surrounding Christian culture had affected Anglo-Jewry in general and Montefiore in particular were outlined. This involved re-examining some of the material treated earlier from a different angle, including the nature of both Reform and Liberal Judaism and the impact of Christian critique upon each, which was substantial. Among the most significant factors influencing Montefiore's conception of Judaism were the nineteenth-century belief in religious progress and the phenomenon of 'assimilated Hellenism'. These also profoundly coloured his religious studies, as can been seen from any consideration of his contribution to, and ultimate dependence upon, Christian biblical scholarship.

Part Three considered Montefiore's comprehensive engagement with mainstream critical scholarship in contrast to other Jewish writers interested in the Gospels. Regarding his Liberal Jewish agenda, Montefiore's utilisation of Jesus was treated in terms of his originality, his prophetic office, and his views on the Law and nationalism. Similarly, Montefiore's writings on Paul were placed in the context of Jewish approaches and his important and lasting contributions to Pauline studies were considered in the light of his stated intention to convince his fellow Jews that the Epistles could be approached as a source of inspiration and religious insight.

This book has sought to demonstrate that Montefiore's own personal conception of Liberal Judaism should be regarded as more than simply a progressive Jewish denomination, and rather as an attempt to re-mould Reform Judaism in terms of, or with special reference to, contemporary liberal Christianity; he himself explicitly wrote of translating liberal Christian thought into a Jewish context.[3] For Montefiore, Christian and Jewish teachings were complementary, at least in their liberal formulations, and while he steadfastly rejected much of its theology, nevertheless he was convinced that Liberal Jews could benefit from a number of specific Christian ideas and forms of expression. Even his vision of the future of religion was one of an amalgamation of the best teachings of each; religious truth, wherever it came from, was the important thing for Montefiore. Negatively, his closeness to Christian thought and sympathies meant that he was sensitive to Christian criticism of Judaism. He therefore condemned what he perceived among religious Jews to be an over-dependence upon tradition and authority and an absence of both internalised faith and clear-cut theology. The profound impact of Christian influences (personal, educational, institutional, intellectual) is all the more striking when his writings are analysed in the context of nineteenth- and twentieth-century Jewish thought. Most remarkable was his use of New Testament study as an opportunity to set out and propound his Liberal Jewish agenda. Certainly, the extent to which he was interested in and incorporated the teachings of Jesus and Paul into his own ethical and theological musings makes him unique among Jewish reformers.

With his writings on the Gospels and Epistles, Montefiore aimed to give his Jewish readers what he perceived to be a relatively objective presentation of Jesus and Paul, an alternative to the accounts offered by overly sympathetic Christians and overly antagonistic Jews. Familiar with the complex scholarship, he believed he could produce an analysis free from traditional bias. At the same time, from his vantage point as a Liberal Jew, Montefiore was interested in what these ancient Jews had to say about God for the modern world. He was drawn to Jesus as someone who had struggled with the orthodoxy of his own day and as a Prophet in the Age of Law. The spirit of Jesus' teachings seemed to represent for Montefiore the essence of true Jewish religion. Similarly, he argued that the writings of the Apostle to the Gentiles could serve as a kind of devotional aid for modern Jews, especially with regard to his Universalist teachings. Thus, in contrast to other Jewish commentators, Montefiore engaged the teachings of Jesus and Paul (as recorded in the New Testament) in a sympathetic, constructive manner, rather than as an opportunity for voicing anti-Christian grievances. Furthermore, he argued passionately that modern Jews should reclaim rather than disown two of Israel's most influential sons, despite their failings. In so doing, he brought down upon himself the wrath of those who believed that he had betrayed Judaism.

Montefiore's solutions to the dilemmas he faced have not found widespread support among world Jewry. Even in his own day, many of his writings represented less the consensual views of his fellow Liberal Jews and more the hopes and opinion of a much beloved spiritual leader whose eccentricities regarding Christianity and a theologised Judaism were, in the main, tolerated. He himself inhabited a world of ideas in which a spiritualised conception of Liberal Judaism was entirely satisfactory, but for others his liberalism was too abstract and removed too much in terms of tradition and ceremony. With the events of the Second World War encouraging internalisation and a determination to preserve the particularist elements of Judaism, Montefiore's efforts to liberalise and to unite eastern and western Jews in a theologically expressed, rationalistic religion soon fell out of favour. Likewise, his Universalist hopes for Judaism were swept away by the development and eventual triumph of Zionism and the birth of the State of Israel. Nor can there be any doubt that, in the light of post-modern religious thought, his Enlightenment-influenced confidence in human progress meant that he placed too much emphasis upon Reason. Certainly, later reform-orientated Jews have not accepted his diametrical opposition of authority and (intellectual) freedom, nor have they sought to systematically theologise Jewish religious teachings, as he did.

In terms of his scholarship, Montefiore is best remembered as a pioneer. He was one of the first British Jews to whole-heartedly accept and apply the findings of historical- and literary-critical analysis to the Hebrew Bible. His early contribution to Gospel research in correcting misconceptions and offering an alternative, highly distinctive point of view makes him one of the best known of the Jewish commentators. His attempt to systemise rabbinic thought and to utilise it in the study of the New Testament was one of the factors that led to his anthology of rabbinic literature, still regarded by many as a fine modern language selection. Criticism can be made, however, of the way in which he was inclined to compare rabbinic and Gospel thought as wholes. Similarly, his contribution to Pauline studies is significant not only as an exceptionally sympathetic Jewish treatment but, in terms of his critique of Christian research, for the seriousness with which it has been taken by later mainstream Pauline scholars. Once again, the main criticism must be his tendency to over-compartmentalise, in this case, Hellenistic and Palestinian Judaisms. In no way, however, do the limitations of his scholarship detract from his achievement of approaching the religious writings of both Christianity and traditional Judaism with remarkable sympathy. As he once wrote, 'For their beloved Law occupies to Orthodox Jews something of the same position as Jesus Christ occupies to Christians, and though I myself stand in different ways outside both sanctuaries, I have lived so much among those who are within both that I can appreciate their feelings.'[4]

Montefiore belongs to that important group of learned laymen who have sought to revolutionise Judaism. He was an innovative religious thinker, a passionate spokesman for an advanced liberal Jewish theology, an influential leader in both communal representation and Jewish education, a moral crusader and an outspoken British patriot. Despite the limitations of his nineteenth-century world-view and scholarship, Montefiore remains worthy of study as an important figure in Anglo-Jewish history whose complex identity reflects the difficulty and confusion inherent in attempting to make Judaism genuinely relevant to the modern world. In his dealings with Christians and Christian thought, he can also be regarded as a forerunner to those who would later fully partake in Jewish–Christian dialogue, even though his conception of Christianity was idealised and he expressed his understanding of, and hopes for, Judaism in unfamiliar ways.

NOTES

1 C.G. Montefiore, *The Old Testament and After* (1923), p. 201.
2 Letter from Montefiore to Lucy Cohen (5 August 1931). L. Cohen, *Some Recollections of Claude Goldsmid-Montefiore 1858–1938* (1940), p. 189.
3 'The main tenor of [Jowett's] teaching was in harmony and agreement with a progressive and enlightened Judaism. It can be translated, and it needs to be translated, into Jewish. Very imperfectly and stumblingly I have sought to do this from time to time.' C.G. Montefiore, 'The Religious Teaching of Jowett', *Jewish Quarterly Review*, XII (1899–1900), p. 374.
4 C.G. Montefiore, *Some Elements in the Religious Teaching of Jesus* (1910), p. 116.

Chronology

1802 Solomon Hirschell becomes Chief Rabbi.
1815 Establishment of Reform Judaism in Berlin.
1818 Establishment of Reform Judaism in Hamburg.
1836 Petition for reform made to the governing board of the Orthodox Synagogue, Bevis Marks, London.
1840 Establishment of West London Reform Synagogue with David Marks as first minister.
1842 *Herem* (or ban) pronounced upon West London Reform Synagogue by Chief Rabbi.
1845 Nathan Adler becomes Chief Rabbi.
1849 *Herem* on West London Reform Synagogue lifted by Chief Rabbi.
1854 Oxford University opens its doors to Jewish students.
1855 Establishment of Jews' College, London.
1856 Licence to register marriages granted to West London Reform Synagogue. Establishment of Manchester Reform Synagogue.
1858 Montefiore born. Full civil equality granted to British Jews.
1860 *Essays and Reviews* published, with a contribution by Benjamin Jowett.
1866 Philip Magnus becomes a minister at West London Reform Synagogue.
1870 Act of Parliament constituting the United Synagogue.
1871 Oxford University abolishes religious tests for entry. The Anglo-Jewish Association is established.
1873 Establishment of Bradford Reform Synagogue.
1878 Montefiore studies 'Greats' at Oxford.
1879 Montefiore's brother, Leonard, dies in America.
1881 Montefiore graduates from Oxford. He and Oswald Simon initiate synagogue Sunday school classes.
1882 Montefiore studies at the *Hochschule* in Berlin. He joins the board of the Fröbel Institute upon his return to England.

1883 Montefiore's father, Nathaniel, dies. He assumes the additional surname Goldsmid by letters patent.
1884 Montefiore's sister, Charlotte, marries a Gentile.
1885 Montefiore's great-uncle, Moses Montefiore, dies.
1886 Montefiore marries Thérèse Schorstein.
1888 Montefiore and Abrahams establish the *Jewish Quarterly Review*. Montefiore elected onto the London School Board.
1889 Montefiore's only child, Leonard, is born. His wife, Thérèse, dies.
1890 Schechter becomes lecturer in rabbinics at Cambridge.
1891 Hermann Adler becomes Chief Rabbi.
1892 Montefiore delivers the Hibbert Lectures.
1893 Morris Joseph becomes minister of West London Reform Synagogue.
1895 Montefiore becomes President of the Anglo-Jewish Association.
1899 Montefiore becomes President of the Jewish Historical Society of England. Oswald Simon establishes the Sunday Movement.
1902 Montefiore's mother, Emma, dies. He marries Florence Ward. Together with Montagu he establishes the Jewish Religious Union for the Advancement of Liberal Judaism. Schechter leaves for America to found Conservative Judaism. Abrahams becomes lecturer in rabbinics at Cambridge.
1904 Establishment of the London Society for the Study of Religion.
1908 Montefiore becomes vice-president of University College, Southampton.
1909 Montefiore resigns from the Jewish Religious Education Board. The decision is taken to form a new congregation and a Liberal Jewish manifesto is published.
1910 Establishment of the Liberal Jewish Synagogue. Montefiore becomes the first president of the Liberal Jewish Synagogue. He delivers the Benjamin Jowett Lectures. He meets Basil Henriques. He tours Reform synagogues in America.
1912 Israel Mattuck becomes minister of Liberal Jewish Synagogue.
1913 Joseph Hertz becomes Chief Rabbi. Schechter establishes the United Synagogue of America.
1915 Montefiore becomes president of University College, Southampton.

1917 Establishment of the League of British Jews. Montefiore publicly supports *The Times'* anti-Zionist manifesto. He helps advise government regarding Balfour Declaration.
1918 Women allowed to preach in Liberal Jewish Synagogue.
1919 Loewe becomes lecturer in rabbinic Hebrew at Oxford. Establishment of the *Jewish Guardian*.
1920 Women allowed to read prayers from the pulpit of the Liberal Jewish Synagogue.
1921 Montefiore awarded honorary degrees from University of Manchester and the Jewish Institute of Religion, New York. Montefiore resigns from the Anglo-Jewish Association.
1924 Establishment of the London Society of Christians and Jews. Montefiore awarded an honorary degree from Hebrew Union College, Cincinnati.
1925 Liberal Jewish Synagogue opens in St John's Wood Road.
1926 Montefiore becomes the first president of the World Union for Progressive Judaism.
1927 Montefiore awarded an honorary degree from Oxford University.
1930 Montefiore awarded the British Academy medal for biblical studies.
1931 Loewe becomes lecturer in rabbinics at Cambridge.
1938 Montefiore dies. Montefiore's wife, Florence, dies.

Archival Sources

THE AMERICAN JEWISH ARCHIVES, CINCINNATI, OHIO, USA

MS 2/36/1   Henry Hurwitz/Menorah Assoc. Memorial Collection
Correspondence with Claude Montefiore

MS 5 A-19/12   Hebrew Union College Papers
Correspondence between J. Morgenstein and Claude Montefiore

MS 15/3/5   Wolsey Papers
Correspondence with Claude Montefiore

MS 16/2/13   Authority Committee
Paper by Claude Montefiore

MS 16/12/4   World Union for Progressive Judaism Papers
Obituaries for Montefiore by J.J. Kaplan and S. Wise

MS 19/27/7   Jewish Institute of Religion Papers
Correspondence with Claude Montefiore

MS 25/1/23   Henry Berkowitz Papers
Correspondence with Claude Montefiore

MS 33/4/12   Max Heller Collection
Correspondence with Claude Montefiore

MS 35   David Philipson Papers
Correspondence with Montefiore

MS 41   William Rosenau Correspondence
Correspondence with Claude Montefiore

MS 42/1/4   Isadore Singer Papers
Correspondence with Claude Montefiore

MS 123/3/2   Gotthard Deutsch Papers
Correspondence with Claude Montefiore

MS 165/1/12   Sheldon and Amy Blank Papers
Correspondence with Claude Montefiore

MS 187   Ephraim Frisch Papers
Correspondence with Claude Montefiore

MS 282/3/7   Lily H. Montagu Papers
               Sermons and Addresses
SC 5278   Henry Hurwitz Papers: Personal Correspondence
               Correspondence with Sheldon Blank
Microfilm No. 2718 Lily H. Montagu Correspondence
               Correspondence with Claude Montefiore

THE BODLEIAN LIBRARY, OXFORD

MSS Fisher 58, 59, 60, 61, 65, 70, 71, 72, 74
               Correspondence with Claude Montefiore (21)
MSS Milner dep. 25, 27, 30, 54, 55, 186, 200, 206, 215, 216, 217,
               218, 605, 676
               Correspondence with Claude Montefiore
MSS Gilbert Murray 537
               Correspondence between Lady Murray and
               Claude Montefiore
MS Eng. Lett. c348, c349, d362, c351
               Correspondence between Hastings Rashdall and
               Claude Montefiore
MS Eng. misc. d124
               Correspondence between William Sanday and
               Claude Montefiore
MS Eng. Hist. c708
               Correspondence between Violet Milner and
               Claude Montefiore

BALLIOL COLLEGE, OXFORD

MS 64   A.L. Smith Collection
               Correspondence with Claude Montefiore
MS 123   Papers of Benjamin Jowett
               Correspondence with Claude Montefiore
MS 395   Catalogue of Manuscripts of Balliol College
               Oxford (19)
               Correspondence between Claude Montefiore
               (1877–93) and Mark Pattison, Arnold Toynbee,
               Matthew Arnold, Leonard Montefiore, Thomas
               Hill Green, Benjamin Jowett

THE CENTRAL ZIONIST ARCHIVES, JERUSALEM, ISRAEL

MS A36/133   Files of the Jewish Territorial Organisation
              Correspondence between Israel Zangwill and
              Claude Montefiore
MS A77/3/13   Files of the Jewish Territorial Organisation
              Correspondence between Herbert Samuel and
              Claude Montefiore
MS A120/454   Files of the Jewish Territorial Organisation
              Correspondence between Israel Zangwill and
              Claude Montefiore

HEBREW UNIVERSITY NATIONAL LIBRARY, JERUSALEM, ISRAEL

MS 169   Claude J.G. Montefiore
              Correspondence with unknown receiver (1)

THE LONDON METROPOLITAN ARCHIVES, LONDON
(HOLDING THE LIBERAL JEWISH SYNAGOGUE ARCHIVES)

ACC/3529/4/1 Claude G. Montefiore: Letters to Rabbi Mattuck
ACC/3529/4/2 Claude G. Montefiore: Letters
ACC/3529/4/4 Claude G. Montefiore: Reviews
ACC/3529/4/7 Claude G. Montefiore: Miscellaneous Papers
ACC/3529/4/9 Claude G. Montefiore: Newspaper clippings

UNIVERSITY OF SOUTHAMPTON SPECIAL COLLECTIONS,
SOUTHAMPTON

MS 60   Papers of Rev. James William Parkes
              Articles and Lectures
MS 108   Papers of C.J. Goldsmid-Montefiore
              Administrative papers
MS 175   Papers of Chief Rabbi J.H. Hertz
              Correspondence with Claude Montefiore

THE JOHN RYLANDS LIBRARY, MANCHESTER

(No MS ref.)   Samuel Alexander Papers
                   Correspondence with Claude Montefiore (21)

Bibliography

NOTE ON THE SYSTEM OF REFERENCE

Full details of the partial references given in the text can be found in the bibliography, which is divided into Reference Works; Books; Pamphlets, Papers and Sermons; Articles in Journals; and Unpublished Papers and Theses.

REFERENCE WORKS

Dictionary of Jewish Biography, ed. by Geoffrey Wigoder (New York: Simon and Schuster, 1991).

Dictionary of National Biography, ed. by L.G. Wickham Legg (London: Oxford University Press, 1950).

Encyclopaedia Judaica, ed. by Cecil Roth (Jerusalem: Keter Publishing, 1971).

Jewish Encyclopaedia, ed. by Isadore Singer (New York: Funk and Wagnalls Company, 1901–16).

Jewish Encyclopaedia, ed. by A.M. Hyamson and A.M. Silberman (London: Shapiro, Vallentine, 1938).

New International Dictionary of the Christian Church, ed. by J.D. Douglas (Exeter: Paternoster Press, 1974).

Oxford Dictionary of the Christian Church, ed. by F.L. Cross, 2nd edn (London: Oxford University Press, 1974).

BOOKS

Israel Abrahams, *Studies in Pharisaism and the Gospels*, 2nd edn, 2 vols (Cambridge: Cambridge University Press, 1923).

J. Abelson, *The Immanence of God in Rabbinical Literature* (London: Macmillan, 1912).

Geoffrey Alderman, *Modern British Jewry* (Cambridge: Clarendon Press, 1992).

R. Apple, *The Hampstead Synagogue* (London: Vallentine Mitchell, 1967).

Leo Baeck, *The Essence of Judaism*, trans. from German original (1905) by Victor Grubwieser and Leonard Pearl (London: Macmillan, 1936).

Leo Baeck, *Judaism and Christianity* (Philadelphia: The Jewish Publication Society of America, 1958).

Constance Battersea, *Reminiscences* (London: Macmillan, 1922).

Norman Bentwich, *Solomon Schechter: A Biography* (Cambridge: Cambridge University Press, 1938).

Chaim Bermant, *The Cousinhood: The Anglo-Jewish Gentry* (London: Eyre & Spottiswoode, 1971).

Eugene C. Black, *The Social Politics of Anglo-Jewry: 1880–1920* (Oxford: Blackwell, 1988).

Maurice G. Bowler, *Claude Montefiore and Christianity* (Atlanta, GA: Scholars Press, 1988).

Michael Brenner, Rainer Liedtke and David Rechter, eds, *Two Nations: British and German Jews in Comparative Perspective* (Tübingen: Mohr Siebeck, 1999).

Martin Buber, *Two Types of Faith*, trans. from German original (1950) by N.P. Goldhawk (London: Routledge, 1951).

Martin Buber, *I and Thou*, trans. from German original (1923) by W. Kaufmann (Edinburgh: T. & T. Clark, 1970).

F.C. Burkitt, ed., *Speculum Religionis* (Oxford: Clarendon Press, 1929).

David Cesarani, ed., *The Making of Modern Anglo-Jewry* (London: Blackwell, 1990).

David Cesarani, *The Jewish Chronicle and Anglo-Jewry 1841–1991* (Cambridge: Cambridge University Press, 1994).

James H. Charlesworth, ed., *Jesus' Jewishness: Exploring the Place of Jesus in Early Judaism* (New York: Crossroad Publishing, 1991).

Bruce Chilton and Jacob Neusner, *Judaism in the New Testament: Practices and Beliefs* (London: Routledge, 1995).

Ronald E. Clements, *100 Years of Old Testament Interpretation* (Philadelphia: The Westminster Press, 1976).

Arthur Cohen, *The Natural and the Supernatural Jew: An Historical and Theological Introduction* (New York: Pantheon Books, 1962).

Lucy Cohen, *Some Recollections of Claude Goldsmid-Montefiore 1858–1938* (London: Faber & Faber, 1940).

Stuart A. Cohen, *English Zionists and British Jews: The Communal Politics of Anglo-Jewry, 1895–1920* (Princeton: Princeton University Press, 1982).

Dan Cohn-Sherbok, *Fifty Key Jewish Thinkers* (London: Routledge, 1997).

Herbert Danby, *The Jew and Christianity: Some Phases, Ancient and Modern, of the Jewish Attitude Towards Christianity* (London: Sheldon Press, 1927).

W.D. Davies, *Paul and Rabbinic Judaism* (London: S.P.C.K., 1955).

Todd M. Endelman, ed., *Jewish Apostasy in the Modern World* (New York: Holmes and Meier, 1987).

Todd M. Endelman, *Radical Assimilation in English Jewish History, 1656–1945* (Bloomington, IN: Indiana University Press, 1990).

Isadore Epstein, *Judaism: A Historical Presentation* (London: Penguin, 1968).

David Feldman, *Englishmen and Jews: Social Relations and Political Culture 1840–1914* (New Haven & London: Yale University Press, 1994).

Gerald Friedlander, *The Jewish Sources of the Sermon on the Mount* (London: Routledge, 1911).

Nancy Fuchs-Kreimer, *The 'Essential Heresy': Paul's View of the Law According to Jewish Writers, 1886–1896* (Ann Arbor, MI: University of Michigan Press, 1991).

Abraham Gerger, *Das Judentum und seine Geschichte: in vierunddreissig Vorlesungen* (Breslav: W. Jacobsohn, 1910).

W.T. Gidney, *History of the London Society for Promoting Christianity amongst the Jews* (London: London Society for Promoting Christianity amongst the Jews, 1908).

W.T. Gidney, *Missions to the Jews: A Handbook of Reason, Facts and Figures* (London: London Society for Promoting Christianity amongst the Jews, 1912).

Morris Goldstein, *Jesus Within the Jewish Tradition* (New York: Macmillan, 1950).

Paul Goodman, *The Synagogue and the Church* (New York: Routledge, 1908).

Heinrich Graetz, *History of the Jews: From the Earliest Times to the Present Day*, ed. by and trans. from German original (1853–70) by Bella Lowy, II (London: Jewish Chronicle, 1901).

Donald A. Hagner and M.J. Harris, eds, *Pauline Studies: Essays Presented to F.F. Bruce* (Exeter: Paternoster Press, 1980).

Donald A. Hagner, *The Jewish Reclamation of Jesus: An Analysis and Critique of the Modern Jewish Study of Jesus* (Grand Rapids, MI: Zondervan, 1984).

Adolf von Harnack, *What is Christianity? Sixteen lectures delivered in the University of Berlin during the winter-term 1899–1900*, translated by Thomas Bailey Saunders (London: Williams and Norgate; New York: Putnam, 1901) (*Das Wesen des Christentums: sechzehn Vorlesungen vor Studierenden aller Facultaten im Wintersemester 1899/1900 an der Universitat Berlin gehalten* (Leipzig: J.C. Hinrichs, 1900)).

Kathleen Heasman, *Evangelicals in Action: An Appraisal of their Social Work in the Victorian Era* (London: Geoffry Bles, 1962).

Basil Henriques, *The Indiscretions of a Warden* (London: Methuen, 1937).

Joseph H. Hertz, *Affirmations of Judaism* (London: Oxford University Press, 1927).

Joseph H. Hertz, *Sermons, Addresses and Studies*, 3 vols (London: Soncino Press, 1938).

Susannah Heschel, *Abraham Geiger and the Jewish Jesus* (Chicago and London: University of Chicago Press, 1998).

Michael Hilton, *The Christian Effect on Jewish Life* (London: S.C.M. Press, 1994).

Walter Jacob, *Christianity Through Jewish Eyes: The Quest for Common Ground* (Cincinnati: Hebrew Union College Press, 1974).

Joseph Jacobs, *As Others Saw Him: A Retrospect, A.D. 54* (London: Heinemann, 1895).

Louis Jacobs, *The Jewish Religion: A Companion* (Oxford: Oxford University Press, 1995).

Richard Jenkyns, *The Victorians and Ancient Greece* (Oxford: Basil Blackwell, 1980).

Morris Joseph, *Jewish Ideals and Other Essays* (London: Macmillan, 1896).

Jacob Katz, ed., *Toward Modernity* (US: Transaction Books, 1987).

Anne Kershen and Jonathan Romain, *Tradition and Change: A History of Reform Judaism in Britain 1840–1995* (London: Vallentine Mitchell, 1995).

Edward Kessler, *An English Jew: The Life and Writings of Claude Montefiore* (London: Vallentine Mitchell, 1989).

Joseph Klausner, *Jesus of Nazareth: His Life, Times, and Teaching* (New York: Macmillan, 1929).

Joseph Klausner, *From Jesus to Paul*, trans. from Hebrew original (1939) by W.F. Stinespring (London: Allen & Unwin, 1943).

Leon Klenicki, ed., *Towards a Theological Encounter: Jewish Understandings of Christianity* (New York: Paulist Press, 1991).

K. Kohler, *Jewish Theology: Systematically and Historically Considered* (New York: Macmillan, 1918).

Werner G. Kümmel, *The New Testament; The History of the Investigations of its Problems* (London: S.C.M. Press, E.T. 1973).

Pinchas Lapide and Peter Stuhlmacher, *Paul: Rabbi and Apostle*, trans. from the German original (1981) by Larence W. Denef (Minneapolis, MN: Augsburg Publishing, 1984).

Herbert Loewe, *Israel Abrahams* (A. Davis Memorial Trust, 1944).

Louis Loewe, *Diaries of Sir Moses & Lady Montefiore*, 2 vols (London: Griffith, Farran, 1890).

Hyam Maccoby, *Revolution in Judaea: Jesus and the Jewish Resistance* (London: Ocean Books, 1973).

Hyam Maccoby, *The Mythmaker: Paul and the Invention of Christianity* (London: Weidenfeld & Nicolson, 1986).

David Marks, ed., *Forms of Prayer used in the West London Synagogue of British Jews*, with an English translation (London: J. Wertheimer, 1840–41).

David Marks, *Sermons Preached on Various Occasions* (London: Groombridge, 1851).

David Marks, *The Law is Light: A Course of Four Lectures on the Sufficiency of the Law of Moses as the Guide of Israel* (London: S. Joel, 1854).

Don Marmur, ed., *Reform Judaism: Essays on Reform Judaism in Britain* (Oxford: Alden Press, 1973).

Alexander McCaul, *Sketches of Judaism and the Jews* (London: Wertheim, 1838).

Alexander McCaul, *The Old Paths: or A Comparison of the Principles and Doctrines of Modern Judaism with the Religion of Moses and the Prophets*, 2nd edn (London: British Society for the Jews, 1846).

Michael A. Meyer, *Response to Modernity: A History of the Reform Movement in Judaism* (New York: Oxford University Press, 1988).

C.G. Montefiore, *The Hibbert Lectures: On the Origin and Growth of Religion as Illustrated by the Religion of the Ancient Hebrews* (London: Williams & Norgate, 1893).

C.G. Montefiore, *The Bible for Home Reading* (London: Macmillan, 1899).

C.G. Montefiore, *Liberal Judaism: An Essay* (London: Macmillan, 1903).

C.G. Montefiore, *Truth in Religion and Other Sermons* (London: Macmillan, 1906).

C.G. Montefiore, *Some Elements in the Religious Teaching of Jesus* (London: Macmillan, 1910).

C.G. Montefiore, *Outlines of Liberal Judaism* (London: Macmillan, 1912).

C.G. Montefiore, *Judaism and St. Paul: Two Essays* (London: Max Goschen, 1914).

C.G. Montefiore, *Liberal Judaism and Hellenism and Other Essays* (London: Macmillan, 1918).

C.G. Montefiore, *The Old Testament and After* (London: Macmillan, 1923).

C.G. Montefiore, *The Synoptic Gospels*, 2nd edn, 2 vols (London: Macmillan, 1927).

C.G. Montefiore, *Studies in Memory of Israel Abrahams* (New York: Jewish Institute of Religion, 1927).

C.G. Montefiore, *Rabbinic Literature and Gospel Teachings* (London: Macmillan, 1930).

C.G. Montefiore, *The Synoptic Gospels* (New York: K.T.A.V. Publishing, 1968), with 'Prolegomenon' by Lou H. Silberman.

C.G. Montefiore and Israel Abrahams, *Aspects of Judaism*, 2nd edn (London: Macmillan, 1895).

C.G. Montefiore and Herbert Loewe, eds, *A Rabbinic Anthology* (London: Macmillan, 1938).

George Foot Moore, *Judaism in the First Centuries of the Christian Era: The Age of the Tannaim*, 7th impression, 3 vols (Cambridge: Cambridge University Press, 1954).

Alfred Myers, *The Jew*, 6th edn (London: London Society for the Promotion of Christianity amongst the Jews, 1874).

F. Jackson and K. Lake, eds, *The Beginnings of Christianity*, 5 vols (London: Macmillan, 1920–33).

Morris Joseph, *Judaism as Creed and Life*, 2nd edn (London: Routledge, 1909).

Stephen Neill and Tom Wright, *The Interpretation of the New Testament 1861–1986* (Oxford: Oxford University Press, 1989).

Simon Noveck, ed., *Contemporary Jewish Thought: A Reader* (London: Vision Press, 1964).

Gerald Parsons, *Religion in Victorian Britain*, 4 vols (Manchester: Manchester University Press, 1988).

James Parkes, *Jesus, Paul and the Jews* (London: S.C.M. Press, 1936).

M. Perry and F.M. Schweitzer, eds, *Jewish–Christian Encounters over the Centuries* (New York: Peter Lang, 1994).

David Philipson, *The Reform Movement in Judaism*, 2nd edn (New York: Macmillan, 1931).

W. Robinson, ed., *Record and Revelation* (Oxford: Clarendon Press, 1938).

Franz Rosenzweig, *The Star of Redemption*, trans. from German 2nd edn (1930) by William Hallo (London: University of Notre Dame, 1985).

Cecil Roth, *The Record of European Jewry* (London: Frederick Muller, 1950).

Fritz A. Rothschild, ed., *Jewish Perspectives on Christianity* (New York: Crossroad, 1990).

Jonathan Sacks, *One People: Tradition, Modernity, and Jewish Unity* (London: Littman Library of Jewish Civilization, 1993).

E.P. Sanders, *Paul and Palestinian Judaism* (London: S.C.M. Press, 1977).

E.P. Sanders, *Jesus and Judaism* (London: S.C.M. Press, 1985).

Samuel Sandmel, *The Genius of Paul: A Study in History* (New York: Farrar, Straus & Cudahy, 1958).

Samuel Sandmel, *We Jews and Jesus* (New York: Oxford University Press, 1965).

Solomon Schechter, *Studies in Judaism*, 3 vols (London: A. & C. Black, 1896–1924).

Solomon Schechter, *Some Aspects of Rabbinic Theology* (London: A. & C. Black, 1909).

Solomon Schechter, *Documents of Jewish Sectaries*, 2 vols (Cambridge: Cambridge University Press, 1910).

Hans Joachim Schoeps, *Paul: The Apostle in the Light of Jewish Religious History*, trans. from German original (1959) by Harold Knight (Philadelphia, PA: Westminster, 1961).

Hans Joachim Schoeps, *The Jewish–Christian Argument* (London: Faber & Faber, 1963).

G.G. Scholem, *Major Trends in Jewish Mysticism*, 3rd edn (London: Thames & Hudson, 1955).

Emil Schürer, *History of the Jewish People in the Time of Jesus*, 5 vols (Edinburgh: T. & T. Clark, 1890–91) (*Geschichte des jüdischen Volkes im Zeitalter Jesu Christi*, 3 vols (Leipzig: J.C. Hinrichs, 1856–90).

Albert Schweitzer, *Paul and his Interpreters* (London: A. & C. Black, 1912).

Albert Schweitzer, *The Mysticism of Paul the Apostle*, 2nd edn (London: A. & C. Black, 1956).

Albert Schweitzer, *The Quest of the Historical Jesus*, 3rd edn (London: A. & C. Black, 1954).

Alan F. Segal, *Paul the Convert: The Apostolate and Apostasy of Saul the Pharisee* (New Haven and London: Yale University Press, 1992).

Leon Simon, ed., *Ahad Ha-Am: Essays, Letters, Memoirs* (Oxford, East and West Library: Phaidon Press, 1946).

Leon Simon, ed., *Selected Essays of Ahad Ha-Am* (New York: Meridian Books, 1962).

Joshua B. Stein, *Lieber Freund: The Letters of Claude Goldsmid Montefiore to Solomon Schechter 1885–1902* (Washington: University Press of America, 1988).

F. Temple, R. Williams, B. Powell, H.B. Wilson, C.W. Godwin, M. Pattison and B. Jowett, *Essays and Reviews*, 9th edn (London: Longman, 1861).

Henry St John Thackeray, *The Relation of St Paul to Contemporary Jewish Thought* (London: Macmillan, 1900).

Frank M. Turner, *The Greek Heritage in Victorian Britain* (London: Yale University Press, 1981).

Ellen Umansky, *Lily Montagu and the Advancement of Liberal Judaism* (New York: The Edwin Mellen Press, 1983).

Geza Vermes, *Jesus the Jew: A Historian's Reading of the Gospels* (London: Collins, 1973).

Thomas Walker, *Jewish Views of Jesus* (London: Allen & Unwin, 1931).

Ferdinand Weber, *System der altsynagogalen palästinischen Theologie* (Leipzig: Dürffling & Franke, 1880).

Ferdinand Weber, *Jüdische Theologie auf Grund des Talmud und verwandter Schriften, gemeinfasslich dargestellt* (Leipzig: Dürffling & Franke, 1897).

Trude Weiss-Rosmarin, ed., *Jewish Expressions on Jesus: An Anthology* (New York: KTAV, 1977).

Bill Williams, *The Making of Manchester Jewry 1740–1875* (Manchester: Manchester University Press, 1976).

Isaac Meyer Wise, *Three Lectures on the Origin of Christianity* (Cincinnati, OH: Bloch, 1883).

Yosef H. Yerushalmi, *Zakhor: Jewish History and Jewish Memory* (New York: Schocken Books, 1989).

PAMPHLETS, PAPERS AND SERMONS

Nathan Adler, 'Solomon's Judgement: A Picture of Israel' (London: Wertheimer, 1854).

James Barr, 'Judaism – Its Continuity with the Bible', 7th Claude Montefiore Lecture, Southampton (1968).

Norman Bentwich, 'Claude Montefiore and his Tutor in Rabbinics: Founders of Liberal and Conservative Judaism', 6th Montefiore Memorial Lecture, Southampton (1966).

Leslie Edgar, 'Claude Montefiore's Thought and the Present Religious Situation' (London: Liberal Jewish Synagogue, 1966).

Basil Henriques and C.G. Montefiore, 'The English Jew and his Religion' (Liberal Jewish Synagogue, 1918).

Louis Jacobs, 'Montefiore and Loewe on the Rabbis' (London: Liberal Jewish Synagogue, Claude Montefiore Lecture, 1962).

Nicholas de Lange, 'Covenant', unpublished CCJ conference, 24 June 1996.

W.R. Matthews, 'Claude Montefiore: The Man and his Thought', 1st Claude Montefiore Lecture, Southampton (1956).

Israel Mattuck, 'Our Debt to Claude G. Montefiore' (Liberal Jewish Synagogue, 1938).

Lily Montagu, 'The Jewish Religious Union and Its Beginning', *P.F.J.P.*, XXVII (1927).

Lily Montagu, 'Notes on the Life and Work of Claude G. Montefiore' (Liberal Jewish Synagogue, 1938).

Lily Montagu, 'Claude Montefiore as Man and Prophet' (Liberal Jewish Synagogue, June 1958).

C.G. Montefiore, 'Enlarge the Place of Thy Tent' (Jewish Religious Union, January 1906).

C.G. Montefiore, 'Biblical Criticism and the Pulpit', *Jewish Quarterly Review*, XVIII (1906).

C.G. Montefiore, 'The Jewish Religious Union and Its Cause', unpublished address (1908).

C.G. Montefiore, 'The Place of Judaism Among the Religions of the World', *P.F.J.P.*, XII (1916).

C.G. Montefiore, 'The Old Testament and Its Ethical Teaching', *P.F.J.P.*, XV (1917).

C.G. Montefiore, 'Judaism and Democracy', *P.F.J.P.*, XVI (1917).

C.G. Montefiore, 'The Dangers of Zionism', *P.F.J.P.*, XX (1918).

C.G. Montefiore, 'The Jewish Religious Union: Its Principles and Future', *P.F.J.P.*, XXI (1918).

C.G. Montefiore, 'The Justification of Liberal Judaism', *P.F.J.P.*, XXII (1919).

C.G. Montefiore, 'Is There a Middle Way?', *P.F.J.P.*, XXIII (1920).

C.G. Montefiore, 'Do Liberal Jews Teach Christianity?', *P.F.J.P.*, XXV (1924).

C.G. Montefiore and Israel Mattuck, 'Jewish Views on Jewish Missions', *P.F.J.P.*, XXXI (1933).

C.G. Montefiore, 'A Die-Hard's Confession', paper read at the London Society for the Study of Religion (1935).

Hugh W. Montefiore, 'Sir Moses Montefiore and his Great Nephew: A Study in Contrasts', 11th Montefiore Lecture, Southampton (1979).

James Parkes, 'Theology of Toleration', 10th Claude Montefiore Lecture (1966).

S. Schwartzchild, 'Franz Rosenzweig (1886–1929): Guide of Reversioners' (London: Hillel Foundation, no date).

ARTICLES IN JOURNALS

Israel Abrahams, 'Prof. Schürer on Life Under Jewish Law', *Jewish Quarterly Review*, XI (1899).

Phyllis Abrahams, 'Claude Goldsmid-Montefiore', *Synagogue Review* (January 1962).

Hermann, Adler, 'Jews and Judaism: A Rejoiner', *Nineteenth Century*, IV (July 1878).

Hermann, Adler, 'Recent Phases of Judaeophobia', *Nineteenth Century*, X (December 1881).

Jacob Agus, 'Claude Montefiore and Liberal Judaism', *Conservative Judaism*, XIII (Winter 1959).

Ahad Ha-Am, 'Judaism and the Gospels', reprinted in *American Hebrew Journal*, LXXXVII, no. 21 (23 September 1910), from *The Jewish Review*, I (3 September 1910).

Leo Baeck, 'The Faith of Paul', *Journal of Jewish Studies*, III (1952).

Lawrence Barmann, 'Confronting Secularization: Origins of the London Society for the Study of Religion', *Church History*, LXII, no. 1 (March 1993).

Steven Bayme, 'Claude Montefiore, Lily Montagu and the Origins of the Jewish Religious Union', *Transactions of the Jewish*

Historical Society of England, XXVII (1982).

Schalom Ben-Chorin, 'The Image of Jesus in Modern Judaism', *Journal of Ecumenical Studies*, XI (Summer 1974).

Maurice G. Bowler, 'C.G. Montefiore and his Quest', *Judaism*, XXX (Autumn 1981).

Maurice G. Bowler, 'Montefiore's Three Mentors', *Jewish Chronicle* (14 May 1982).

Maurice G. Bowler, 'Zion – Neither Here nor There?', *Judaism*, XXXIII (1984).

Bernard Drachman, 'An Answer to Mr. Claude G. Montefiore', *American Hebrew Journal*, LXII, no. 24 (8 April 1898).

M. Friedländer, 'Notes in Reply to My Critic', *Jewish Quarterly Review*, III (1892).

A.T. Hanson, 'A Modern Philo', *The Modern Churchman*, XX (1977).

Bernard Jackson, 'Legalism', *Journal of Jewish Studies*, III (1979).

Joseph Jacobs, 'The Gospel According to Claude Montefiore', *American Hebrew*, LXXXVII (17 June 1910).

Walter Jacob, 'Claude G. Montefiore's Reappraisal of Christianity' in *Judaism*, IXX (Summer 1970).

Edward Kessler, 'Claude Montefiore', *Jewish–Christian Relations*, XXI (Winter 1988).

Edward Kessler, 'Claude Montefiore: Defender of Rabbinic Judaism?', *Jewish Historical Studies: Transactions of the Jewish Historical Society of England*, XXXV (1996–98).

Robert Liberles, 'The Origins of the Jewish Reform Movement in England', *AJS Review*, I (1976).

Jonathan Magonet, 'The Liberal and the Lady: Ester Revisited', *Judaism*, XXIX (Spring 1980).

Lily Montagu, 'The Spiritual Possibilities of Judaism Today', *Jewish Quarterly Review*, XI (1899), pp. 216–38.

C.G. Montefiore, 'Is Judaism a Tribal Religion?', *Contemporary Review* (September 1882).

C.G. Montefiore, 'A Justification of Judaism', *Unitarian Review* (Boston: August–September 1885).

C.G. Montefiore, 'Dr. Ritter's Text-Book of Reformed Judaism', *Jewish Quarterly Review*, I (1889), pp. 271–8.

C.G. Montefiore, 'Dr Friedländer on the Jewish Religion', *Jewish Quarterly Review*, IV (1891).

C.G. Montefiore, 'Some Notes on the Effects of Biblical Criticism upon the Jewish Religion', *Jewish Quarterly Review*, IV (1891–92).

C.G. Montefiore, 'First Impressions of St. Paul', *Jewish Quarterly Review*, VI (1894).

C.G. Montefiore, 'Notes on the Religious Value of the Fourth Gospel', *Jewish Quarterly Review*, VII (1895).

C.G. Montefiore, 'Some Misconceptions of Judaism and Christianity by Each Other', *Jewish Quarterly Review*, VIII (1896).

C.G. Montefiore, 'Unitarianism and Judaism in their Relations to Each Other', *Jewish Quarterly Review*, IX (1896).

C.G. Montefiore, 'The Religious Teaching of Jowett', *Jewish Quarterly Review*, XII (1899–1900).

C.G. Montefiore, 'Liberal Judaism in England: Its Difficulties and Its Duties', *Jewish Quarterly Review*, XII (1899–1900).

C.G. Montefiore, 'Rabbinic Judaism and the Epistles of St. Paul', *Jewish Quarterly Review*, XIII (1901).

C.G. Montefiore, 'Jewish Scholarship and Christian Silence', *Hibbert Journal*, I (1903).

C.G. Montefiore, 'The Synoptic Gospels and the Jewish Consciousness', *Hibbert Journal*, III (1904–5).

C.G. Montefiore, 'Should Biblical Criticism be Spoken of in Jewish Pulpits?', *Jewish Quarterly Review*, XVIII (1906), pp. 302–16.

C.G. Montefiore, 'The Significance of Jesus for his Own Age', *Hibbert Journal*, X (1911–12).

C.G. Montefiore, 'The Old Testament and Its Ethical Teaching', *Hibbert Journal*, XVI (1917–18).

C.G. Montefiore, 'Anti-Semitism in England', *Hibbert Journal*, IXX (1921).

C.G. Montefiore, 'The Religious Teaching of the Synoptic Gospels in its Relation to Judaism', *Hibbert Journal*, XX (1921–22).

C.G. Montefiore, 'IA: 1858–1925', *Transactions of the Jewish Historical Society of England*, XI (1924–27).

C.G. Montefiore, 'The Originality of Jesus', *Hibbert Journal*, XXVIII (1929).

C.G. Montefiore, 'Dr. Robert Eisler on the Beginnings of Christianity', *Hibbert Journal*, XXX (1931–32).

C.G. Montefiore, 'What a Jew Thinks About Jesus', *Hibbert Journal*, XXXIII (1934–35).

George Foot Moore, 'Christian Writers on Judaism', *Harvard Theological Review*, XIV (1921).

John Rayner, 'C.G. Montefiore: His Religious Teaching', *The Synagogue Review*, XXXII (June 1958).

Victor E. Reichert, 'The Contribution of Claude G. Montefiore to the Advancement of Judaism', *Central Conference of American Rabbis Yearbook*, XXXVIII (1928).

Frederick C. Schwartz, 'Claude Montefiore on Law and Tradition', *Jewish Quarterly Review*, LV (1964).

G. David Schwartz, 'Explorations and Responses: Is There a Jewish Reclamation of Jesus?', *Journal of Ecumenical Studies*, XXIV (Winter 1987).

S. Sharot, 'Reform and Liberal Judaism in London: 1840-1940', *Jewish Social Studies*, XLI (1979).

Steven Singer, 'Jewish Religious Observance in Early Victorian London, 1840–1860', *Jewish Journal of Sociology*, XXVIII (December 1986).

Vivian G. Simmons, 'Claude Goldsmid Montefiore', in *Transactions of the Jewish Historical Society of England*, XIV (1935–39).

Goldwin Smith, 'Can Jews be Patriots?', *Nineteenth Century*, III (May 1878).

R.M. Smith, 'The London Jews' Society and Patterns of Jewish Conversion in England, 1801–1859', *Jewish Social Studies*, XLIII (1981).

Arnold J. Wolf, 'The Dilemma of Claude Montefiore', *Conservative Judaism*, XIII (Winter 1959).

UNPUBLISHED PAPERS AND THESES

Frederick C. Schwartz, 'Anglo-Jewish Theology at the Turn of the Twentieth Century', Doctor of Hebrew Literature dissertation, Hebrew Union College, Cincinnati (1959).

Index

biblical literalism, 58
biblical studies: by Montefiore, 5;
  historiography, 44–6; Jewish learning
  and, 235–40; New Testament
  research, 225–35; Old Testament
  research, 224–5; theological trends,
  nineteenth century, 221–3
bibliocentricism, 59
Black, Eugene, 38, 177
Board of Deputies, 14, 57, 58, 178
Bousset, Wilhelm, 225, 235
Bowler, Maurice, 28, 31–2, 33, 100, 192,
  194
Bradford Reform Movement, 65, 76, 186
Bradley, Andrew Cecil (tutor of
  Montefiore), 5
Breslau Reform Seminary, 87
Britain: Anglo-Jewry reform, 56–67;
  patriotism of Montefiore towards, 9,
  111
Broad Church, 226
Brown Judaic Studies series, 31
Buber, Martin: and Christianity, 162–3,
  165; and essence of Judaism, 134,
  135, 136, 138, 141; and
  historiography, 29, 40; and Jesus
  Christ, 263
Bultmann (writer), 229, 232
Burkitt, Francis Crawford: and biblical
  scholarship, 224, 225, 232, 233, 237;
  Hellenism, 197; historiography, 44;
  and religious progress, 209–10

Cambridge lectureship in Rabbinic
  Studies, 13
Carpenter, Joseph Estlin, 159, 228, 231
Catholicism, 180, 192–3, 228
Cheyne, Thomas Kelly, 6, 224
Chief Rabbinate, 58, 65
Chilton, B., 125
Chosen People, 152, 185, 187
Christ *see* Jesus Christ
Christian Effect on Jewish Life (Michael
  Hilton, 1994), 125, 147, 184
Christian–Jewish relations *see*
  Jewish–Christian relations
Christianity: apathy, religious, 75; and
  assimilation, 174–6; attitudes of
  Montefiore, 4–5, 6, 31, 83, 315;
  biblical scholarship, 221–48;
  conversionist efforts, 83; defined,
  125–6; Hellenism, 195–203; Judaism
  and, 61, 63, 147, 156–66; Liberal
  Judaism and, 30, 36, 82, 185–91; New
  Testament research, 225–35;
  progress, religious, 203–11;

Protestant dominance of, 31; Rabbi
  Mattuck's antagonism to, 90–1; and
  Reform movement, 176–9; reforms
  in, 187; theological interest of
  Montefiore, 39–40; Tractarianism,
  192–5; Victorian culture, 174–220;
  writings of Montefiore, 18; *see also*
  Jesus Christ; Judaism; Paul,
  Apostle
Christianity Through Jewish Eyes (Walter
  Jacob, 1974), 40
Church of England, 184, 193
Church of Rome, 180, 240
circumcision, 83
Claude Montefiore and Christianity
  (Maurice Bowler, 1988), 28, 31–2, 33,
  100, 192
'C.M.'s Night Club', 17
Cohen, Arthur, 67, 110
Cohen, Hermann, 86, 132–3
Cohen, Lucy (cousin of Claude
  Montefiore): biographical study by,
  28–9, 34; correspondence with
  Claude, 194; description of Claude,
  3, 7, 9, 10; memoirs, 36; on Prophets,
  126; on Zionism, 111
Cohen, Stuart, 37–8
Cohn-Sherbok, Dan, 40
colleges *see* educational institutions;
  religious education institutions
communal responsibilities/
  committees, 7, 11
Conjoint Foreign Committee, 14, 115
Continental Reform Movement, 61
controversy, inter-denominational,
  82–5
Cousinhood (Chaim Bermant, 1971), 3,
  34, 37, 65, 66, 67
criticism, historical, Liberal Judaism,
  72–5

Daily Chronicle, 129
Danby, Herbert, 43
Darwin, Charles, 44
Davies, W.D., 45, 46, 284, 288, 290, 293
Day of Atonement, 133
Dead Sea scrolls, 287
decorum, 184
degrees, honorary, 10
de Rothschild, Baron, 114
Deutsch, Emanuel, 205
dialogue, inter-denominational, 162–4
Diaspora Jews, 116
Dibelius, Martin, 232
Die Formgeschichte des Evangeliums
  (Martin Dibelius, 1919), 232